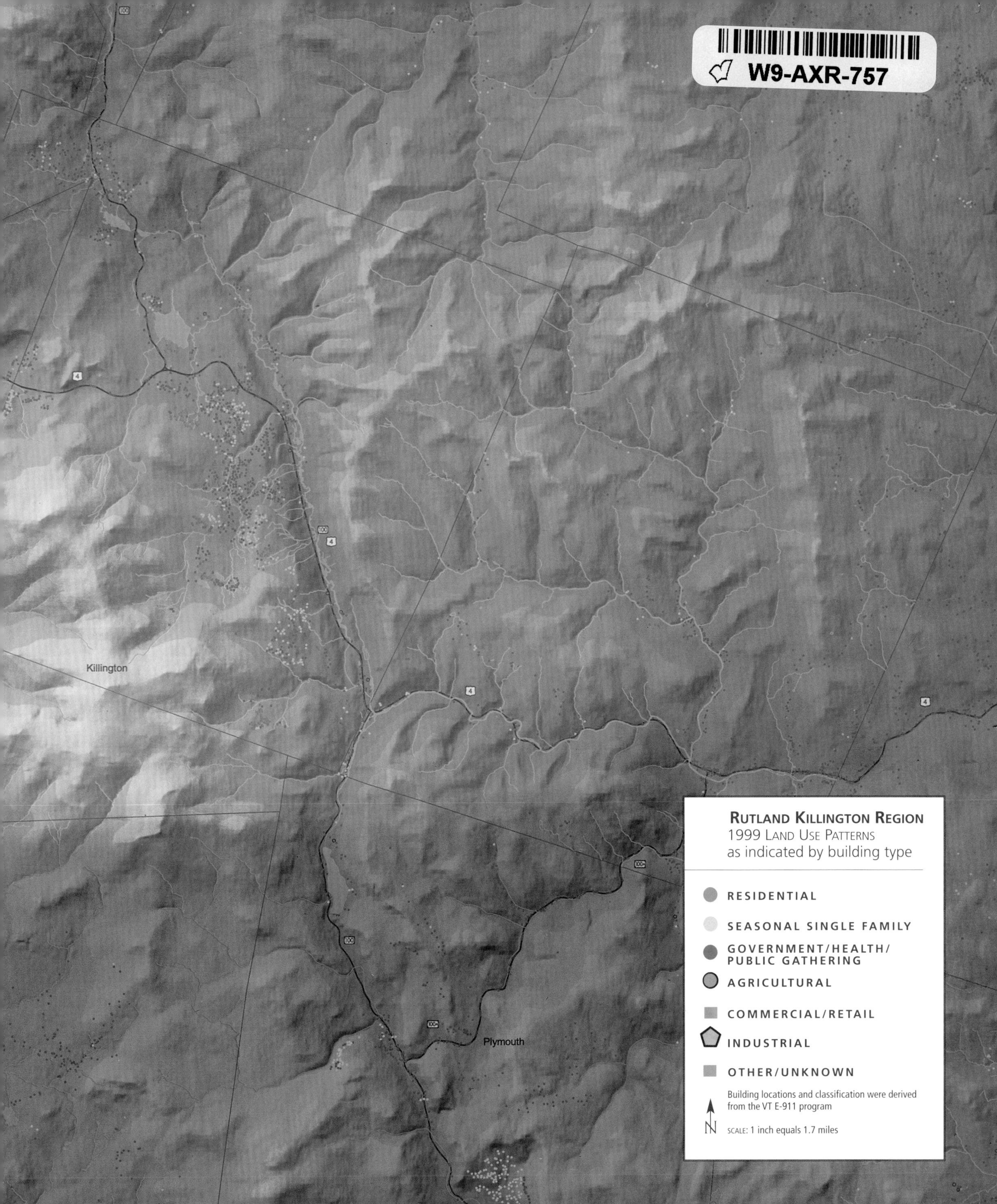

W9-AXR-757
Killington
Plymouth
RUTLAND KILLINGTON REGION
1999 LAND USE PATTERNS
as indicated by building type
RESIDENTIAL
SEASONAL SINGLE FAMILY
GOVERNMENT/HEALTH/
PUBLIC GATHERING
AGRICULTURAL
COMMERCIAL/RETAIL
INDUSTRIAL
OTHER/UNKNOWN
Building locations and classification were derived from the VT E-911 program
N
SCALE: 1 inch equals 1.7 miles

# HANDS ON THE LAND

## A HISTORY OF THE VERMONT LANDSCAPE

# HANDS ON THE LAND

## A HISTORY OF THE VERMONT LANDSCAPE

JAN ALBERS

PUBLISHED FOR

The Orton Family Foundation

Rutland, Vermont

BY

The MIT Press

Cambridge, Massachusetts

London, England

Published by The MIT Press for The Orton Family Foundation

The MIT Press
Cambridge, Massachusetts
London, England



Designed by Leslie Morris Noyes
Printed in the United States by The Stinehour Press, Lunenburg, Vermont

First Edition



Library of Congress Cataloging-in-Publication Data

Albers, Jan.
Hands on the land : a history of the Vermont landscape / Jan Albers.
p. cm.
Includes bibliographical references (p. ) and index.
ISBN 0-262-01175-1 (hc : alk. paper)
1. Vermont—History. 2. Landscape—Vermont—History. 3. Human geography—Vermont. I. Title.
F49.A63 1999 98-31767
974.3—dc21 CIP

Printed in the United States of America

Peacham, Vermont: Alan Jakubek

HANDS ON THE LAND

# CONTENTS

# FOREWORD

Over the last 300 years, the bedrock of Vermont's mountains and valleys has endured, unchanging, while the landscape upon it has been in constant and fascinating flux. With the turning of the centuries, hillsides have gone from thickly forested, to open and cleared, and back again to forested. Generation by generation, there have been the additions—and subtractions—of roads and bridges and dams, homes and churches and factories, farms and villages and cities. As this book demonstrates, these powerful movements on and over our state are largely the result of Vermonters' own *Hands on the Land.*

The conclusion is clear: change the patterns of land use and you change Vermont. The landscape made by previous generations is their legacy to us; the way we turn our hands to the land will be our legacy to those who follow us in the 21st century. It's a challenging concept: the things we create on the land today, and the patterns in which we create them, will have an impact for centuries to come. The cumulative effects of what we do and the choices we make will be far greater than we can possibly anticipate.

We have an advantage over our ancestors: by studying history (such as that presented in this book), we are able to recognize the long-term effects our decisions create. As a young boy in the late 1940s, I found my summertime world darkened by my mother's warning to stay out of the river, which served as the sewage disposal system for our village. Doubtless, the urgency of "economic progress" at one time justified such an arrangement. But 50 years later clean air and water top every poll of what Vermonters consider important to their quality of life; running sewers into rivers would be unthinkable today.

Nevertheless, economic progress—the principal rationale driving our land-use decisions—remains as important for us as it was for our forebears. At the same time, our choices are infinitely more numerous and complex. The Orton Family Foundation has undertaken the preparation and publication of *Hands on the Land* with the belief that history provides useful perspectives for looking at what is happening today, enabling us to discern both working solutions, and warning signs. We are looking for a delicate balance. At times, in the past, Vermonters have found it, and it would behoove us to discover how.

Our Foundation believes that long-term growth, community vitality, and a rural way of life can be combined for the benefit of all. It is therefore our mission to help citizens of rural America define the future, shape the growth, and preserve the heritage of their communities. We emphasize citizens because that is where the most fundamental decisions need to be considered and made. How each individual thinks about his or her own property, neighborhood, town, and state lies at the root of what happens to the land.

We also emphasize communities because it is by the actions of groups of citizens that things happen. Information is key. The more broadly disseminated information is among a citizenry, the better decisions the community is likely to make. Our goal is to develop tools that bring clear and complete information to all citizens. Then it's up to them to decide, as a community, on what actions to take.

In reading this book I hope you take away some lessons about what determines land use, and what economic, social, cultural, and environmental consequences land-use choices may have. I hope you seek ways to become involved in your community's efforts to define its future, while realizing that the future's scenarios are written by today's actions.

Lyman Orton, *Chairman*
THE ORTON FAMILY FOUNDATION

---

THE ORTON FAMILY FOUNDATION
*Headquarters/Northeast Region:* Rutland, Vermont *Rocky Mountain Region:* Steamboat Springs, Colorado
www.orton.org

# INTRODUCTION

The perfect Vermont village seems frozen in time. Here, caught in a long shot, the village of Tunbridge sits in photographic silence, basking in the rays of its 238th summer sun. All the elements of a classic village are there to see—a line of pretty houses, a close-cropped green, a white church steeple sheltered by the rising green hills. The village seems to have sprung whole from its environment, the foundations built of this stone, the walls hewn from these trees. It has an air of being unchanged, the perennial repository of the stalwart values of simpler times.

But photographs do not always tell the real story of a landscape. The white-painted perfection of the Tunbridge we see did not all spring up at an early moment in the past, creating a static shell within which generations of people have lived their lives. Its current beauties belie a more complex past. Tunbridge village has had many identities, reflected in a string of names and nicknames. The village we see here has been called Tunbridge Center, Tunbridge Market, or just "The Market," denoting an early commercial importance. Another Tunbridge lived on this spot in an unhappier incarnation, bearing the nickname "Poortown." In the face of tough times, a tradition of local humor here is reflected in the name of the once raucous "Tunbridge World's Fair," held every September. The village was once even dubbed "Jiggertown," after a local institution called the Jigger Central Electric Railroad, actually a horse-and-coach that picked up its passengers at the Chelsea train and brought them on to Tunbridge.

Paul O. Boisvert

Each of these Tunbridges had a different shape and left a different mark on the land. Some buildings remained through it all, others were razed or changed beyond recognition. Landscapes do not just spring, fully formed, from the earth. At any moment, they represent the accumulated total of the decisions made by hundreds and thousands of men and women over time. Houses, trees, roads, churches, lawns, hills: all have their histories. The people of Tunbridge have made a lot of good landscape choices lately.

What is a landscape? The word originally came from the seventeenth-century Dutch, "landschap," which meant "a place on the land where a community had formed." The Dutch talent for painting beautiful scenes of their snug, flat farms under big skies soon attached the word to painting, so that it came to describe a picture of a scene, rather than the scene itself. By the eighteenth century, landscape paintings had so successfully trained people to think of certain types of places as beautiful that landscape gardeners, especially in England, started trying to change the land itself to make it look more like paintings. In our own world, the word "landscape" has come full circle, to describe again a real place on the land rather than only a picture of a place.

Landscapes have a history, just as people do, and much of their history is the history of what people do. Think about what you need from the land—food, shelter, clothing—or what you might want from a place—a flower garden, a paved driveway, a forest, a shopping mall. Now try to understand what is possible in a given place, including the limitations imposed by climate, topography, and the availability of natural resources. Your culture and your own attitudes will also put constraints on the form your changes to the land might take. Use whatever technology is available to put your ideas into physical form on the earth, and you will have created a small piece of landscape. Your predecessors have done the same before you, piling landscape upon landscape on the land.

Europeans and Americans have long had different ideas about landscapes. In Europe, the word almost always implies a working landscape, where people have made their mark. This is not surprising, when you think that in England, for example, the average landscape has been cleared and planted for 150 generations. In New England, Native Americans farmed, but intensive European-style agriculture goes back fewer than a dozen generations. Perhaps because of this relative newness, Americans have tended to prefer the idea of "natural" landscapes, where wilderness is untainted by man. Traditionally, American nature writers from Thoreau to John Muir to contemporary environmentalists have idealized the wilderness at the expense of the created environment we see around us every day. As Americans destroyed the vast North American wilderness in our great march west, we compensated by creating a spiritual wilderness inside ourselves. We have been worshipping it ever since. The most frequently quoted line in American nature writing may well be Thoreau's injunction that "In Wildness is the preservation of the World."

But wilderness itself is a mirage, since we transform it into a working landscape, subject to human actions, the minute we enter it. It cannot be otherwise. We need to turn our attention to understanding how to preserve and promote human environments that provide beauty and community. We cannot do this effectively until we have accepted a crucial lesson of American history: people cannot live in a wilderness.

## TUNBRIDGE VILLAGE, 1760–1999

Landscapes show the accumulation of human decisions made over time, as illustrated by this photograph of the center of Tunbridge.

Paul O. Boisvert Thanks to Euclid Farnham, and Jean Wolfe of Tunbridge for the identifications.

Some cultures transform nature more fully, or more destructively, than others. But all people transform nature in order to live.

A history of the landscape is the story of how different cultures saw fit to alter the earth to meet their needs, express their beliefs, and satisfy their whims. While geography, biology, and climate will all be major characters, the heart of a landscape history is how human cultures take physical form on the land. Imagine a tree, for example. Because this is Vermont, make it a sugar maple. If you were an early Abenaki Indian, living in the future Vermont, you might look at the tree and believe that it has its own spirit. Because of this, you would not want to cut it down. But if you had to, you would tell the tree what you were doing, ask its forgiveness, and thank it for having given you sugar in the past. If you were an early Yankee settler in Vermont, you might see the sugar maple as an obstacle that was keeping you from farming your new stake of land. You would feel justified in cutting it down for what you believed to be the higher purpose of civilizing a wilderness. If you lived in the late nineteenth century, you might look at the tree and rhapsodize about its glories, eulogizing the many similar trees that had been destroyed to make America. Living in the present, you might fight to preserve this example of Vermont's great heritage of sugar maples so that visitors with full wallets would continue to come to the state to enjoy them. Or you might cut it down in order to clear a site for the Maple Tree Place mall. In each of these cases, beliefs about nature, society, economics, religion, and the whole stew of attitudes that make up a culture tell people how to act on the land.

At the heart of the history of Vermont's landscape is the creation and evolution of communities. "Community" is a changeable word, its meaning altering with culture and the times. In this history of the landscape it refers to groups of people and where they live: countryside, village, or urban center. But it also suggests their efforts to live together in ways that create a sense of common interest among those who have come to share a common ground. The struggle to reach a consensus over land use often serves to express a community's political, economic, and social forms, along with its most valued customs, rituals, and ideals. This book is largely the history of those struggles over how Vermonters have chosen to use the land.

Landscape historian John Brinckerhoff Jackson has complained that people keep writing about their perceptions of the landscape, and not about "the history of the landscape itself, how it was formed, how it has changed, and who it was who changed it, and...the nature of the American landscape." This book is an attempt to rectify that for one place, by looking at how the rolling-hilled, white-steepled, farm-quilted, wood-bordered state of Vermont came to be the beautiful place it is, and how its richness can be maintained in the face of forces that threaten to turn it into another mall-ridden American suburbia.

This is a landscape history of Vermont, but its broad principles could be applied anywhere. All people can learn to be historians of their home ground. One of the most exciting things about landscape history is that so much remains to us: houses, churches, bridges, roads, farmers' fields, village greens. We can drive or walk through the landscape and see signs of the past all around us, if we know what we are seeing. And knowing can help us make better decisions once we have our own hands on the land.

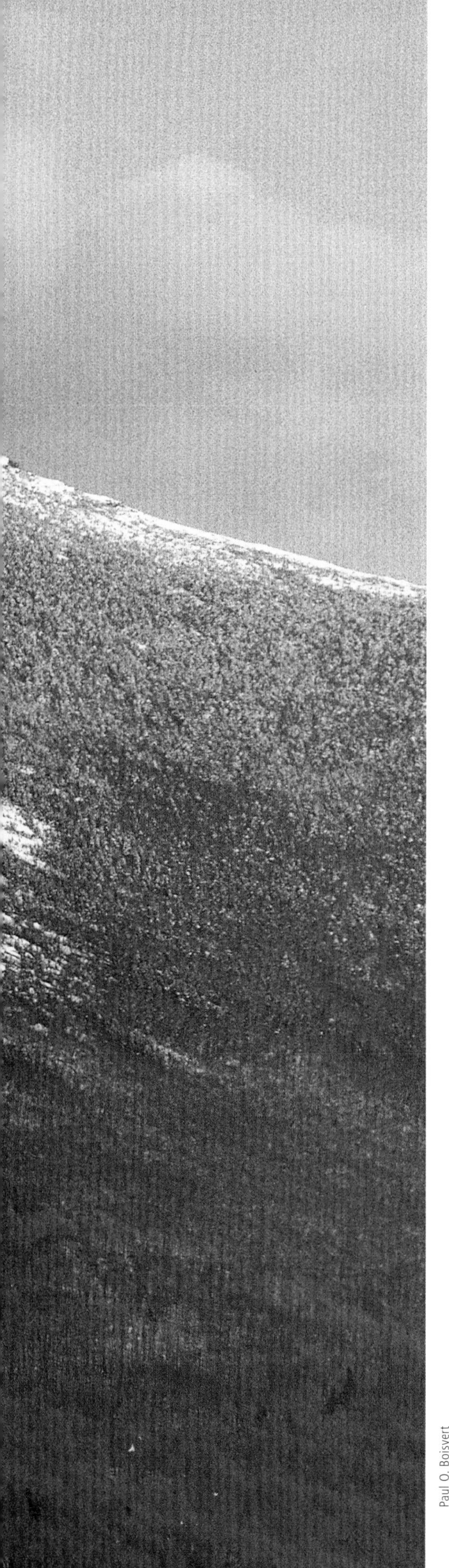

Mount Mansfield's "face" lies looking peacefully skyward. The top of its head faces south, with its forehead, nose, lips, and jutting chin (at its highest point) stretching north toward Canada.

Paul O. Boisvert

CHAPTER 1

# NATIVE VERMONT

*That man is, in fact, only a member of a biotic team is shown by an ecological interpretation of history. Many historical events, hitherto explained solely in terms of human enterprise, were actually biotic interactions between people and land. The characteristics of the land determined the facts quite as potently as the characteristics of the men who lived on it.*

—Aldo Leopold, *A Sand County Almanac*

Vermont's highest peak, Mount Mansfield, has a face. Native Americans noted it, and even today, it is not hard to make out its manly profile. Nearby, at Smugglers' Notch, a natural rock formation is called "The Hunter and His Dog." And all of New England is scattered with hills referred to as "The Sleeping Giant." Like the mythological Narcissus, who could not stop staring at himself in a pool of water, we look into the otherness of nature, and see ourselves.

These are reassuring metaphors; if we think of them as sleeping giants, the Green Mountains take on a comforting human quality, yet lie static and unchanging, a contentedly somnolent Gulliver, with us the tiny, even harmless Lilliputians scurrying around on his body.

But the earth is not asleep, much as we may like to think of it that way. As the great conservationist Aldo Leopold recognized, the land is acting on us at least as much as we are acting on the land. We are wrong to think that nature only changes when we do something to it. Nature was changing long before homo sapiens came on the scene. In our constant conversation with nature, it was nature that had the first word, and nature will probably have the last.

But while nature is ever-changing, it does not have the ability to make decisions and exercise options; that is the curse and blessing of humankind alone. There was never a "golden age" when people lived on the land without altering it. Different cultures have created landscapes with widely varying environmental impacts, but it is part of our human heritage that we need to alter our environment to survive. Paleoindians hunted some beasts to extinction; native people burned woods to make the forest more easily traversed; the early Abenaki brought significant agricultural changes to the northern forests. All this took place before the first Europeans ever hacked their anxious way through the trees of this strange New World.

Vermonters set great store by being "natives," but if you keep working back in the world there is always someone or something that preceded you. Before the coming of European settlers, the natural history of Vermont—geology, biology, climate, and wildlife—helped to set the boundaries of what was possible in this place. The original Native Vermonters related to the gifts and challenges of the Vermont environment in ways that are very different from our own.

The place we are observing is Vermont, but the same questions could be asked about every place. What is it that determines what people can do in a given spot? Is geology at the bottom of everything, constraining us as it doles out mountains, river courses, soil types? Are climate and biology the crucial elements, as the growing season limits the types of trees and plants that will mysteriously find their way to these hills and valleys? Or are we the masters of our fates, with most physical limitations just minor impediments to our own scientific and technological ingenuity? What are the ramifications of our cleverness? Can people ever live on the land without destroying it? What possible lives could be lived in Vermont?

## AN INITIAL DISCOVERY

One place to start our search for the answers to these questions is at the tiny Perkins Museum of Geology on the campus of the University of Vermont. There, a large oak-and-glass case contains the skeleton of a whale, its bones carefully wired together with meticulous knots tied by Victorian fingers, now skeletons themselves. It is a Vermont whale, given the name Charlotte because it was found in that town in 1849 by a crew digging the bed of the first railroad. How could they possibly have found a whale so far from the sea, in Vermont? A Vermont with salt-water beaches would have been a very different place from the one we know today.

To the left of the door is a slab containing the fossils of nautiloids, small-shelled sea creatures that have not lived on the earth for 460 million years. They could only make their homes in warm, tropical waters, yet these examples were found in a limestone quarry on Isle la Motte, in northwestern Vermont. So there was another Vermont with a climate at least as warm as present-day Florida. Another case contains rocks that have a shiny, polished surface and are scored with deep, straight lines. These marks were created by glaciers that covered the whole land with ice a mile deep. As hard as it is to imagine, there was a Vermont that was locked under the ice as surely as Antarctica is today.

The Perkins Museum is contained in one room, but its exhibits represent a number of different Vermonts. There is nothing we can take for granted. By reading the rocks, we find that the place that would become Vermont has had higher mountains and has been flattened to the flattest plains. It has been touched by salt water and fresh. The climate has run from the hottest tropics to the most frigid Arctic blasts. Geology completely changes our perspective on time: a million years are like a day, a billion years are like a year. In geological time the human era is such a tiny blip that we are forced to abandon our sense of superiority for a moment, to leave aside the hubris that traps us like the fossil shells of an ancient sea creature. Here, as Ralph Waldo Emerson said of a similar museum, "The limits of the possible are enlarged, and the real is stranger than the imaginary."

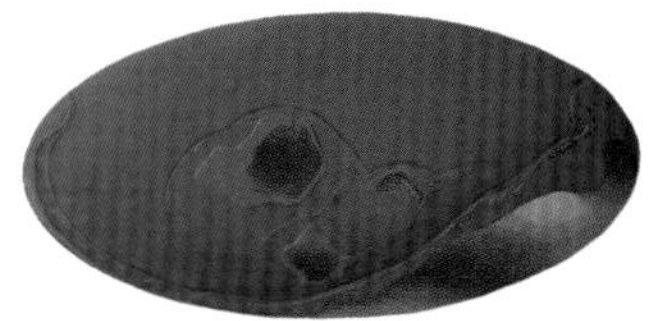

| ERA: **PRECAMBRIAN** | **PALEOZOIC** "OLD LIFE" | | |
|---|---|---|---|
| **4600** Million Years Ago | **570–510** CAMBRIAN | **510–439** ORDIVICIAN | **439–408** SILURIAN |
| Earth forms; oceans and continents appear | Future Vermont on a plate called Laurentia | Fish appear, the first vertebrates | Vermont mountains at their highest altitudes |
| Atmosphere develops | Laurentia sits on equator | Animals creeping onto land | Hinesburg and Champlain faults occur |
| Vermont's plate sits on the equator | Taconic orogeny forms early Green Mountains | Plants diversifying | Taconics pushed off the tops of the Green Mountains |
| Grenville orogeny creates mountain range, now oldest rocks in bedrock of Green Mountains | Sea animals with shells | Future fossils forming on shores of Lake Champlain | Winged insects appear |
| First simple fossils | | | |

Alternate Vermonts have left us signs on the land. The message they have to give us is that nature has never been passive. It has been transforming itself far more than people are capable of transforming it since the dawn of time. Men and women are constantly reinventing what we mean by nature and finding new ways to conceptualize our relationship with the physical environment. Nature is not doing the same amount of thinking about us. The natural world continues to reinvent itself in ways that far transcend our ability to transform it.

## VERMONT'S SIX REGIONAL ENVIRONMENTS

Nature exists outside us—streams flow, glaciers grind, the famed tree falls in the forest—but we can never really experience it on its own terms. People cannot help projecting their own beliefs and assumptions onto the land. Our culture seems to need to start its relationship with nature by drawing lines around parts of it. "Vermont" itself is an arbitrary political entity that people have imposed on a seamless expanse of nature. In some places, the borders of the state reflect genuine differences in land forms, while in others we are reminded that borders are human inventions, serving human purposes. If you compare the view of Vermont you get on a geological map with what you could see looking down from a plane, you are quickly reminded that borders do not show from the air. The southern Green Mountains run into the Berkshires, the Northeast Kingdom becomes the White Mountains, the great northern hardwood forest stretches from the Maritimes to Minnesota with few breaks. To an early Abenaki, these political boundaries would have been meaningless, replaced with designations like "Iroquois country" or "the sacred mountains." Yet other natural features, like the Connecticut

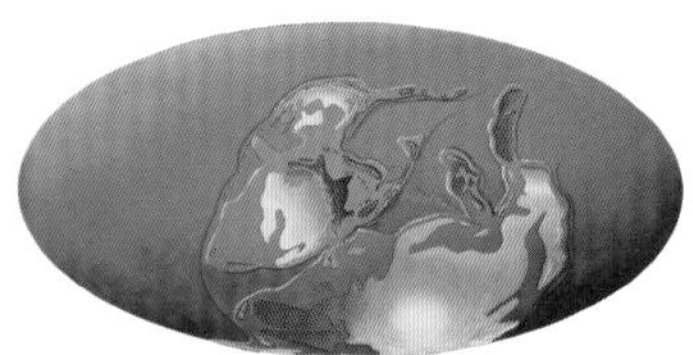

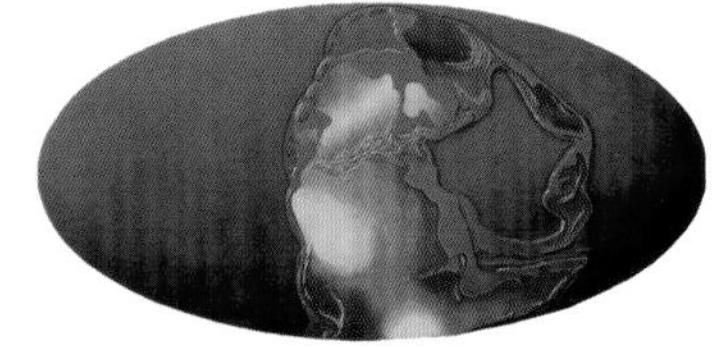

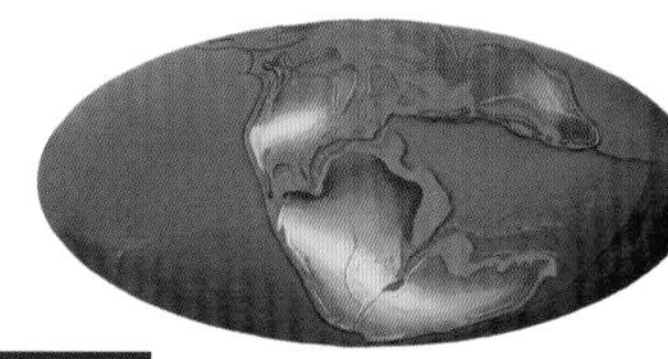

**MESOZOIC** "MIDDLE LIFE"

**408–362** DEVONIAN
Acadian orogeny begins, creating Green Mountains we see today
Mountain-building time
Greening of the earth

**362–290** CARBONIFEROUS
North Appalachians rising

**290–245** PERMIAN
Allegheny orogeny raises South Appalachians
Pangaea forms
First amphibians appear
Time of the Great Dying

**245–205** TRIASSIC
Pangaea drifting north
Africa pressed up to New England
Reptiles appear
Conifers develop

**205–146** JURASSIC
Pangaea rifts apart
Atlantic Ocean forms
Age of the dinosaurs
First birds
Mass extinctions caused by meteor

River or Lake Champlain, were boundaries for them as they are for us.

Geographers have traditionally divided Vermont into six distinct physiographic regions, each with its own geology, climate, and plant life. From a global perspective, these regions might seem to run the gamut from A to B; but on a local level, they represent micro-environments that offer people different challenges in the interplay of nature and culture. With the exception of the Northeast Highlands, all these areas follow the folds of the mountains, running in long, narrow bands from north to south. Taken together, their origins provide a brief overview of the geological inheritance given to those who would live in this place. In all parts of the future Vermont, the most important periods in the region's geological history were the times of mountain building and the Ice Ages.

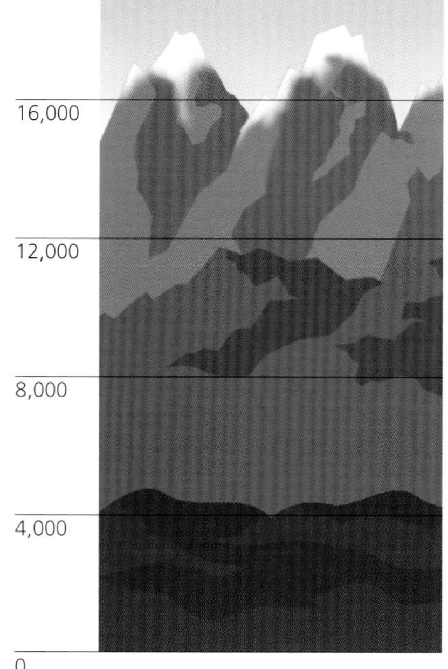


The Green Mountains were once as tall as the Himalayas, eroding to the height of the Rockies before reaching their present low and rounded contours. Here are relative sizes of these three mountain ranges today, illustrating how the once-mighty Greens have diminished through the inexorable power of erosion.

## GREEN MOUNTAINS

If anything is timeless in Vermont, surely it must be the mountains. Through all of oral and recorded history, the Green Mountains have been the most important physical feature in the region, stretching from north to south, part of the long Appalachian Mountain system that runs from the Gaspé Peninsula in eastern Canada to northern Alabama. Geologists have a theory called plate tectonics, which argues that the earth's crust is divided into about a dozen huge plates, and these plates are always slowly moving over a sea of semi-molten rock deep within the earth. According to this theory, the tectonic plate on which Vermont sits may have once pressed against the plate that forms the bedrock of modern Europe. Imaginatively squeeze the plates back together for a moment, and you will find that the Appalachians form a perfect line with the Caledonian Mountains in Scotland.

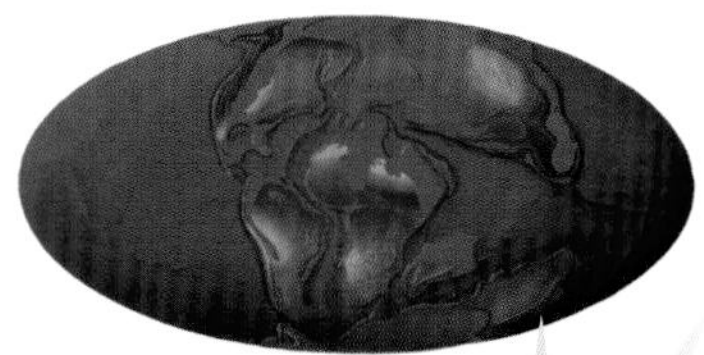

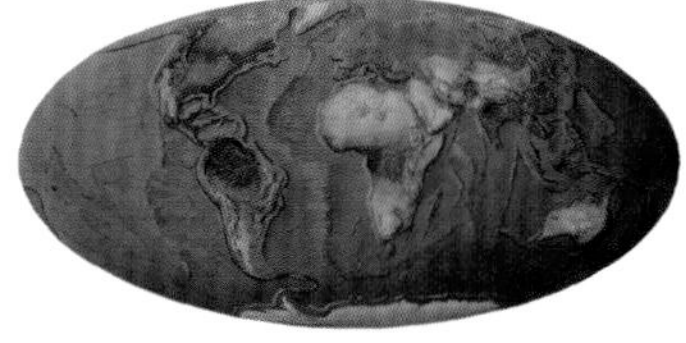

**146–66** CRETACEOUS

Flowers appear

First mammals

Extinction of dinosaurs

**CENOZOIC** "RECENT LIFE"

**66–1.6** TERTIARY

Vermont peneplain rising

Alps and Himalayas rising

Great age of mammals

**1.6** QUATERNARY

Four Ice Ages bring glaciers

Lake Vermont floods land

Champlain Sea goes salty

Humans appear

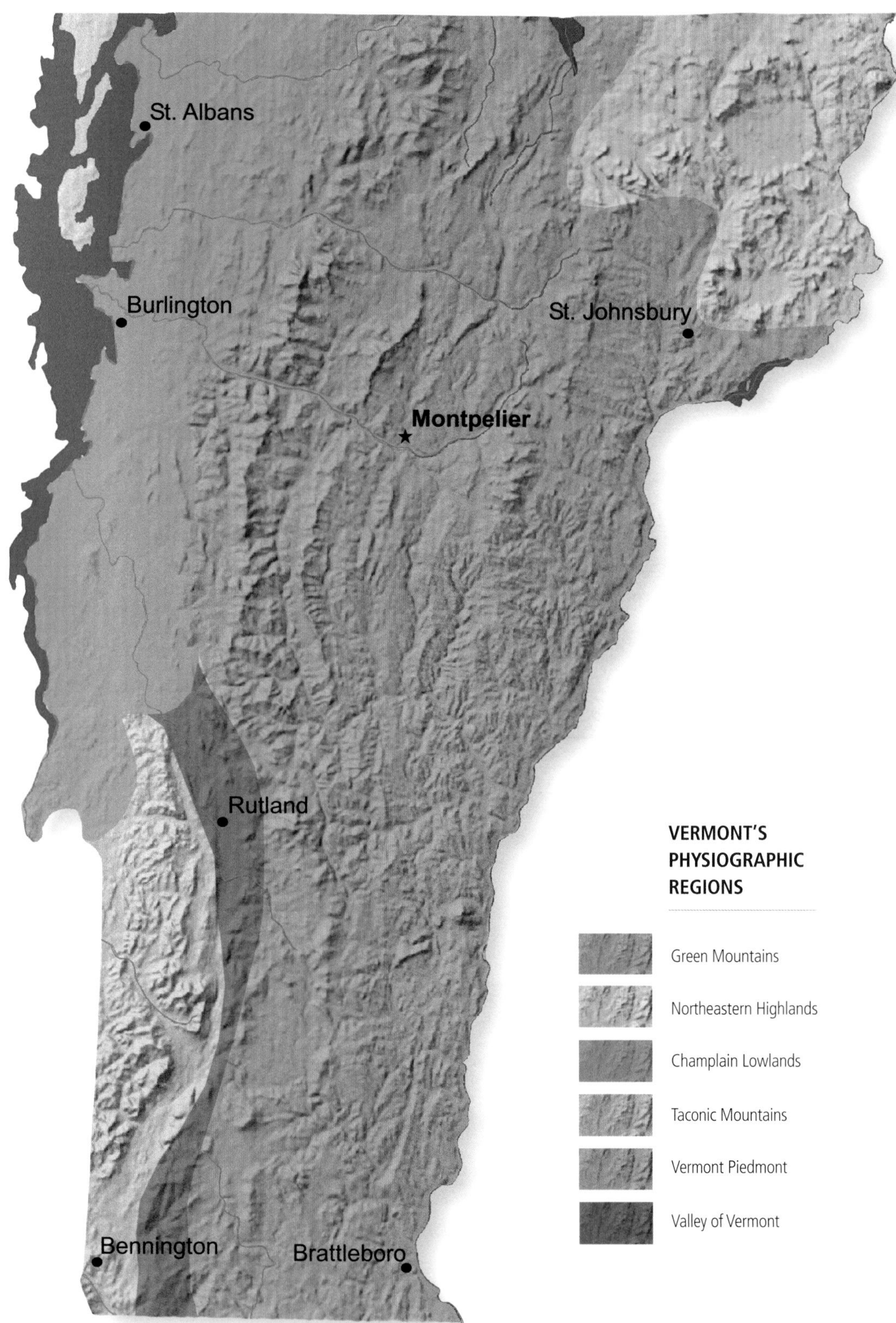


Adapted from Charles Johnson, The Nature of Vermont, 1980, p. 22, by Middlebury College Department of Geography

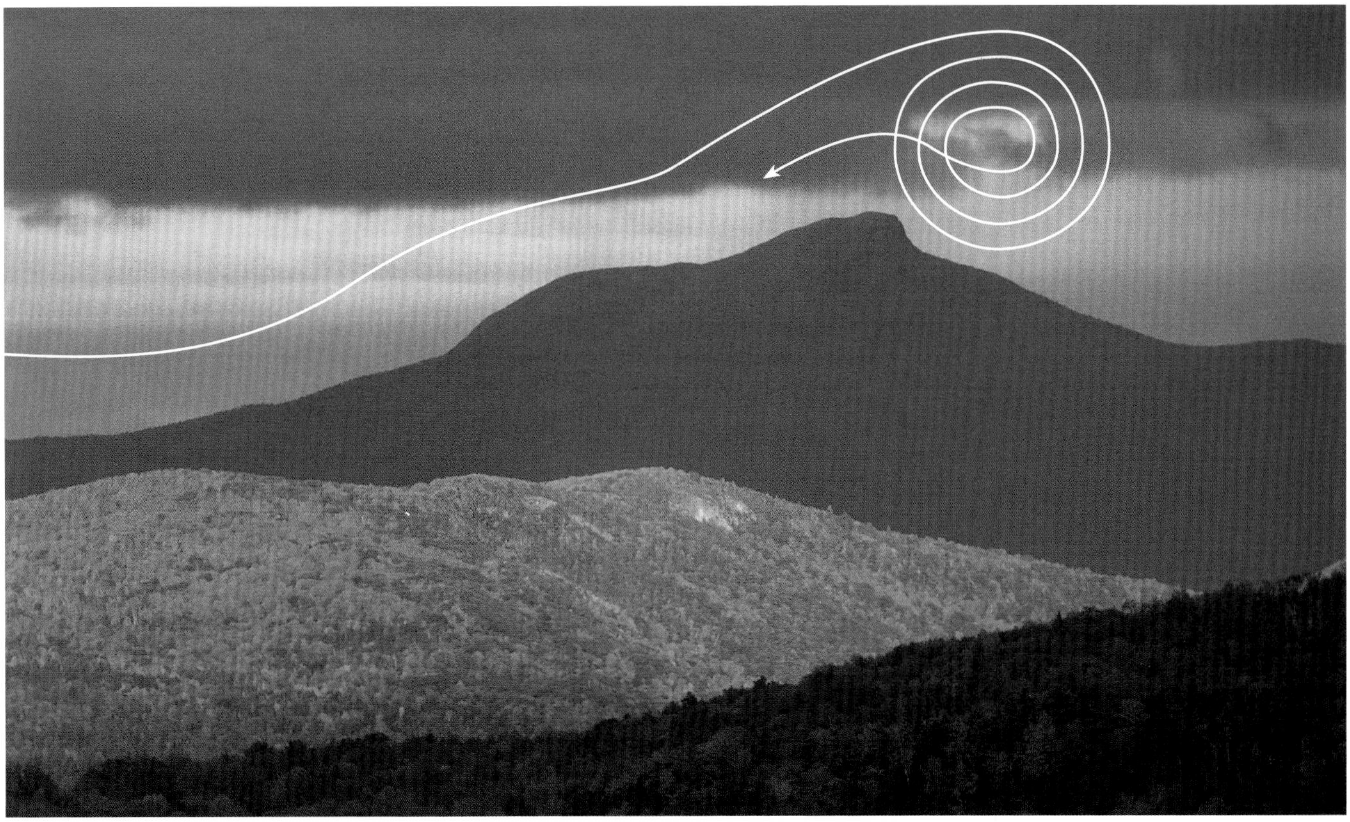

To the human eye, the Green Mountains seem to have been here forever and unchanging. But the screen of peaks we know was formed relatively recently in the long span of geological time. Great pressures under the earth have folded solid rock up into mountains three times in the place that would later become Vermont. These mountain-building periods are called orogenies. Each time the mountains reached their maximum altitudes, wind and rain began to wear them down. Erosion has none of the drama of mountain-building, but its dumb mission to reduce the earth to sea level is just as thorough and unrelenting.

The oldest rocks in Vermont, formed during the first mountain-building time about a billion years ago, can now be found exposed in a core of bedrock in the central and southern Green Mountain range. They eroded over millions of years, making the region as flat as Kansas. In this time, the Champlain Valley rocks were deposited, extending across the Green Mountains to where Route 100 lies today. The second mountain-building period raised snow-capped mountains in the future Vermont that towered as high as 15,000–20,000 feet. These Himalayan peaks attained their highest altitudes about 440 million years ago, towering three or four times higher than the present Green Mountains. The pressure that folded them upwards also

Glaciers smoothed the northern summits of the Green Mountains as they moved from north to south. The distinctive mountain profile of Camel's Hump (above, top) was created when glacial ice moved over the top and then quarried out the southern underside on its way south.

As seen at the edge of a modern glacier (above), considerable geological debris is left in the glacial wake.

created two long parallel north-south fault lines, now known as the Hinesburg fault on the east and the Champlain fault on the west. These ridges would one day furnish favored lookouts for prehistoric hunters.

If you want to date the Green Mountains of human history, they were pushed upwards in the third mountain-building period, a scant (in geological terms) 380 million years ago. These mountains were originally about twice as high as they are now and largely made up of a metamorphic rock called schist, which comes in different forms according to its origins deep in the earth.

One of the best examples of geological thrust faulting on earth—the pushing of a piece of bedrock over the top of a newer formation—can be found along the Champlain Fault at Lone Rock Point (above) on Lake Champlain just north of Burlington. Here, the light-colored Dunham dolomite was thrust right over the top of a younger, darker piece of Utica shale. It is a dramatic example of the sheer power of tectonic movements.

The soft folds of the Green Mountains (opposite) stretch for 160 miles, north to south, with an average width of about 30 miles.They lie atop some of the earth's oldest bedrock.

The great mountain-building periods gave the Green Mountains their height, but their shapes were largely determined by the glaciers that once covered New England in a continuous sheet from the North Pole to as far south as Long Island. No one is sure what causes the earth's climate to cool and glaciers to form. There may be tectonic explanations; glaciers seem to have developed more often when the tectonic plates containing the continents have drifted near the poles. In any case, we know the glaciers have advanced and retreated at least four times since the last mountain-building era, hitting their last period of maximum coverage in Vermont about 20,000 years ago. The final glacier did not melt until 10,000 years ago—again, the blink of an eye in geological time. When that last glacier was retreating, it has been estimated that there may have been 20 million people alive on the earth to see it.

The last glacier covered every inch of New England, at a depth that completely obscured the top of Mount Mansfield. The ice bulldozer eroded the pointed summits of the Green Mountains more quickly and thoroughly than wind and rain could have done.

Glacial erosion did not scour the earth equally. As a look at the summit of Camel's Hump shows, the glacier smoothed the north face as it moved down from Canada, gouging out the south face with loose bedrock and melt water. All over the Green Mountains, these differing north/south profiles can be seen in less pronounced forms on the mountains' summits.

The whole state shows glacial scratches on the bedrock where the glaciers passed through, their ice full of rubble and rocks. They also widened the valleys into sharp Vs or more pastoral Us. They made a passage through Smugglers' Notch and gouged lake beds for Lake Willoughby, Lake Groton, and others, especially in the north-central region. Nevertheless, Vermont was left with far fewer lakes than any other New England state. Lakes were often formed in glacial debris, and much of Vermont's debris was pushed further to the south.

Glacial ice is not pristine, for it carries all the rock and rubble it picks up on its journey. When the ice retreated to the north, this dirty glacio-trash was left behind. Glacial drift still covers some of Vermont to a great depth.

Paul O. Boisvert

Alan Jakubek

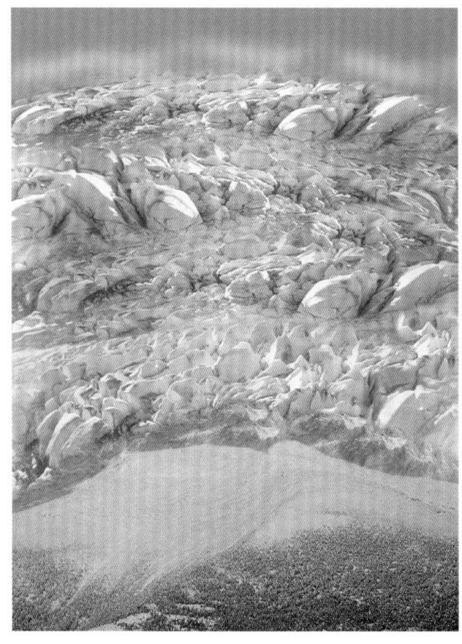

## 50,000 YEARS OF PACKED GRANULAR IN STOWE

If there had been skiing at Stowe 12,000 years ago, it would have to have been cross country because during the last Ice Age, the summit of Mount Mansfield lay beneath a flat sheet of ice stretching from present-day New York City all the way to the North Pole. The image above shows the ratio of glacial ice depth to the height of the present Mount Mansfield.

As this ice began to melt, the huge glacial Lake Stowe inundated the Stowe Valley to a depth of 12,000 feet. Billions of tons of sand and rock scraped off the mountains by the glaciers were deposited on the valley floor.

Once the ice receded from the Lamoille River basin, the melt water finally found a way out of the valley. Smugglers' Notch was left an eerie place, cut deep and steep by the glaciers, with loose rocks scattered precariously on its sides.

The bowl-like shape of the ski area on Mount Mansfield is probably a glacial cirque, formed by a small alpine glacier that remained on the mountainside after the ice cap had melted away from the valleys.

Photomontage: Alan Jakubek, from a photograph of Mount Mansfield by Paul O. Boisvert

The area has few of the well-known forms of glacial deposits—moraines, eskers, and kettle holes—more common in flatter places like Maine. But as they melted down, the retreating glaciers left millions of tons of debris over about three-quarters of Vermont's land area. Rocky till settled in moderate and higher elevations, where it would have great consequences for later human settlers. Below 400 feet or so, gravel, sand, and clay were deposited by the glacial Lake Vermont and the Champlain Sea.

The Green Mountains that remained into the time of human settlement have rounded tops because of erosion. Only a few of these peaks extend above the tree line. The highest peak in Vermont is Mount Mansfield (now listed at 4,395 feet, after being revised upwards by two feet in 1997) and five more are over 4,000 feet tall. Many are in the 3,000-foot range. Most of their younger rocks have been highly metamorphosed during the pressures of mountain building. They are high enough to have impeded human travel from east to west from earliest times. Some passes, like those surrounding Lincoln Gap and Smugglers' Notch, are still impossible to drive over in bad winter weather.

Deep inside the Green Mountains, minerals and rocks developed that would later intrigue—and often disappoint—human beings. Flecks of gold are tucked into the dirt from one end of the range to the other, but only in small quantities. Asbestos and talc deposits run along a line down the central part of the state. Many interesting rockhound minerals lie hidden here, their names romantic mouthfuls: magnetite, malachite, pyrite, vesuvianite, tourmaline.

The soil deposited on the Green Mountains is thin, sandy, and acidic, although deeper soils are often found in the valleys. According to Harold Meeks's analysis of the Soil Conservation Service inventories, about 80 percent of the soil in the state has been deemed "unsuitable for agriculture"; this is true of virtually all the land in the mountains. The boreal forests that covered the mountain tops were happy on this insubstantial ground, but the thin soil would prove disastrous for farming. Glacial deposits also left heavy rocks on the slopes of the mountains, which were later to convince more than one hill farmer to pack up and move to the rockless loam of the Midwest.

The climate of the mountains has also proved ill-suited to agriculture. Frosts come earlier at higher altitudes and last later into the spring. Most of the mountains have a short growing season of around 100–110 days. As Harold Meeks has explained, the effect of latitude on temperature is strongest in winter, when it combines with altitude to make the air colder (prolonging the ski season in the northern Green Mountains). Altitude also tends to cause precipitation, as air cools and releases its moisture when it rises over the mountains. This gives Mount Mansfield an average of 73 inches of

## HALF-A-BILLION SUMMERS AT YOUR CAMP ON LAKE CHAMPLAIN

Pretend, for a moment, that you were able to get a good deal on a camp on Lake Champlain during the Cambrian period, 500 million years ago. (You should have your pick of spots. There will not be another human being for over 499 million years.)

The weather is lovely and tropical, but the beach is barren because all of the plants still live in the water. Little shelled sea creatures cling to the limestone rocks, and in only a couple of million years the fishing will start to get good.

**Between 500,000,000 years ago and today:**

■ The mountains will rise up from the shore and be almost entirely eroded away three times.

■ You will be blessedly free of mosquitoes and cockroaches—but only for the first 100 million years.

■ The land will turn green with plants and animal life will diversify steadily.

■ Nearly half of all plant and animal species around you will be wiped out at least three times, probably due to clouds of thick dust created by huge meteors hitting the earth. The dust is so thick that it keeps light and most heat away from all life forms until it settles in a year or two. Not good summers for you, either.

■ Your tropical paradise gets steadily colder as the tectonic plate on which you ride drifts to the north.

■ Tectonic movements tilt the rocks on your beach.

■ Four Ice Ages occur, with glaciers up to two miles thick covering the site of your camp.

■ When the glaciers start to melt, your camp is flooded as the waters extend nearly to the base of the Green Mountains.

■ As the last glacier recedes, sea water rushes in from the North; you find yourself living on an arm of the Atlantic Ocean.

■ The present lull occurs between Ice Ages. Catch some sun before the glaciers come back...and keep up payments on your homeowner's insurance.

rain a year, more than twice that of Burlington. In winter, the mountains get far more snow, particularly in south-central Vermont, where they pick up moisture from the Atlantic. Readsboro, on the central Massachusetts border, once had 50 inches of snow in a single blizzard. Waitsfield and Killington have both had almost 200 inches in a season, making for fine skiing. High-altitude precipitation also makes the mountains the starting point for most of the major rivers in the state.

The coniferous forests that cover the higher elevations of the Green Mountains are not as rich in wildlife as the lower-altitude deciduous forests, but they add to the diversity of fauna in the region. Moose lumber through the evergreens; some naturalists believe that wildcats like the Canada lynx, or even the catamount (mountain lion), still sneak quietly through the trees.

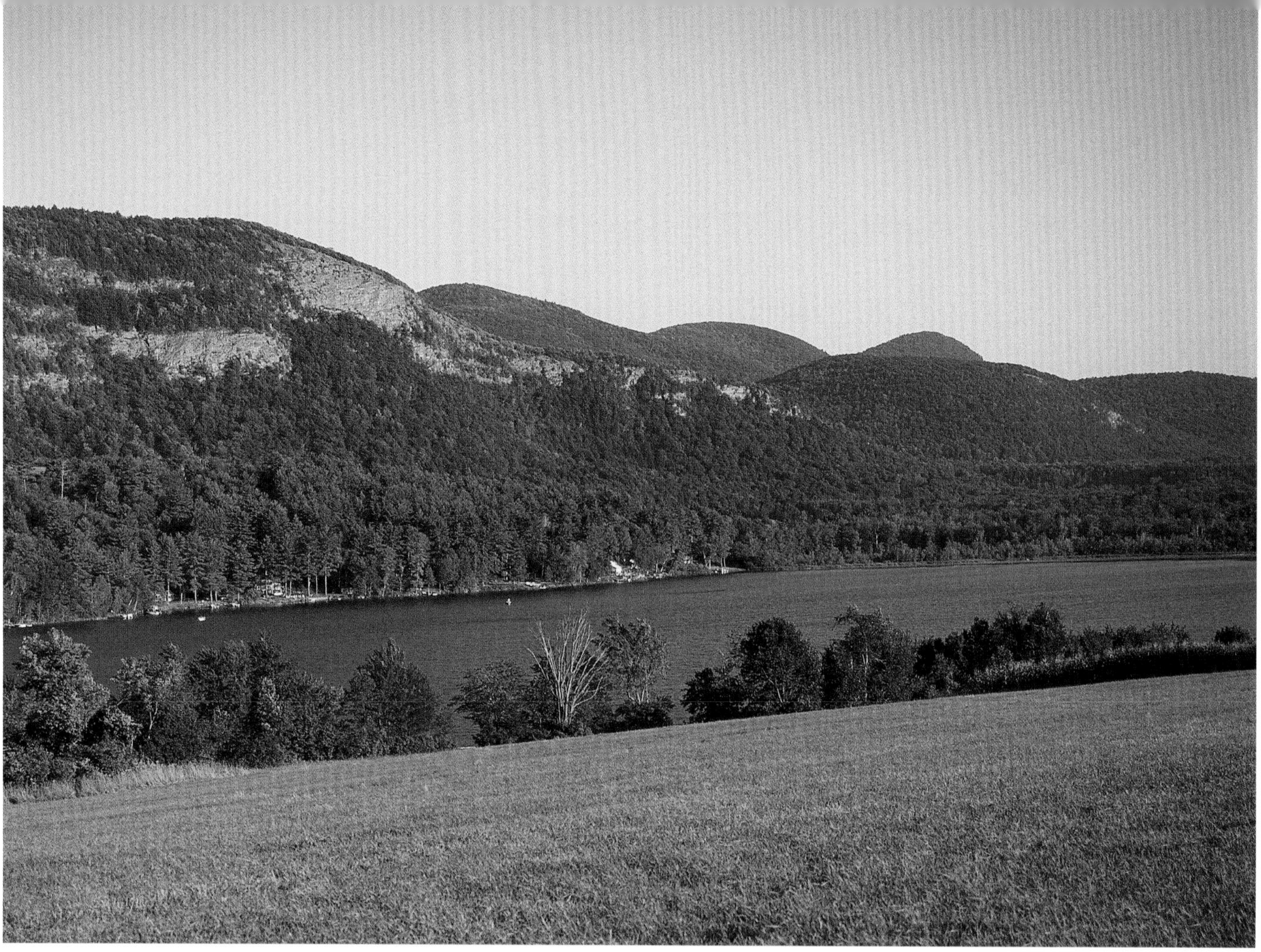

The Taconics face the Green Mountains across the narrowest of valleys; yet the two ranges have different geological origins. Some of the world's most beautiful white marbles and blue-green slates underlie the region. Here the rounded forms of the Taconics are seen behind Lake St. Catherine, in Wells.

Most of the other mammals are small—red squirrels, voles, mice, and snowshoe hares. Charles Johnson has described life here as a struggle, because evergreen forests provide a limited range of foods. As one descends from the pine-fragrant summits to the middle altitudes, usually around 2,400 feet, the deciduous trees of the northern hardwood forests light up the hillsides in autumn and provide for greater floral and faunal diversity year-round. A milder climate and more varied plants make for more wildlife. Deer and coyotes, bears and bobcats make their homes among the maples.

The Green Mountains form the spine—and perhaps the heart—of Vermont. They are cold, snowy, and harsh in winter and wet but comfortable in summer. The growing season is short and the land is uncooperative. The coniferous forests are appealing, but furnish little biological diversity to feed wildlife. For early people in the region, they often proved to be more beautiful to look at than to live in.

## THE TACONICS

The Taconic Mountains lie like a smaller sidekick to the Green Mountains, paralleling them on the west, with the Valley of Vermont running in-between. The range makes up most of the southwestern part of the state, running

south for 75 miles from Lake Bomoseen, near Rutland, to the Massachusetts border. The Taconics are lovely, low, rounded mountains, ground into soft knobs by millions of years of erosion.

The origins of the rocks in the Taconic Mountains, around 420 million years ago, furnish one of Vermont's greatest geological mysteries. The range is made up of rocks as old as the rocks of the Green Mountains, but they sit on top of younger limestone and dolomite. How did older rocks get to be above younger rocks? Geologists could not explain this inversion until plate tectonics showed them that large chunks of the earth's crust could break away and move. One popular theory held that the Taconics were pushed right off the tops of the Green Mountains and deposited whole on the other side of the valley, but recent work has tended to suggest otherwise.

The Taconics are rich in stone, including one of America's best deposits of high-quality slate. Since slate is metamorphosed from the sedimentary rock, shale, the Taconic rocks must once have been deposited at the bottom of an ocean. The dark-colored slates lie near the surface between Lakes Bomoseen and St. Catherine, tucked beneath what is now the town of Poultney.

Slate quarrying leaves a great scar on the land, as the remains of this quarry in Poultney show (top). Slate tends to be very impure, with 85 percent of stone taken from the ground ending up as waste. But slate that is usable is remarkably durable; on this barn roof (bottom), the slate has outlasted both the farmer and the stock that once sheltered here.

This is a wet region; the growing season is longer than in most parts of Vermont, averaging 140 days. A number of rivers flow from the Taconics, including great trout streams, like the Battenkill, the Waloomsac, the Hoosic. They supply the four percent of the state's water that drains into the Hudson River. The longest river in the state, Otter Creek, also has its head here, rising just outside Dorset and flowing north for 100 miles to empty into Lake Champlain. All this access to water does not help agriculture in this region very much, however, because the Taconic soil is as rough and stony as that of the Green Mountains. Small slate fragments are found all through the earth of this region. At best, the hills might be suitable for pastures, and they have usually been covered with northern hardwoods. With its valuable slate, the land offered more for extraction than production.

### THE VALLEY OF VERMONT

The narrow and intimate Valley of Vermont runs north-south for 85 miles from Brandon to the Massachusetts border. It is never more than five miles wide, its steep sides made up of the Green Mountains on the east and the Taconics on the west. The combination of its narrowness and the height of the surrounding mountains gives the light here an interesting, slightly eerie quality. The Valley forms a wind tunnel, and the occasional destructive winds whistling up its length were dubbed "shirkshires" by local settlers.

On its surface, the valley is made of limestone; below ground the pressures of a mountain-building orogeny metamorphosed this sedimentary rock

Viewed from Mt. Baker, in the Big Branch WIlderness Area, the thin line of the Valley of Vermont (right) snakes to the south between the Green Mountains and the Taconics. Its limestone base makes it rich in marble and underlies fertile dairying country.

In eastern Vermont (below), the "Piedmont," or foothills, roll softly to the shores of the Connecticut River. The Connecticut Valley is still home to dairy cows and apple orchards, but as the land rises away to the mountains, the stone walls of abandoned hill farms run through the woods.

Top: A. Blake Gardner; bottom: Paul O. Boisvert

into some of the whitest and most beautiful marble in the world. The marble gives the whole valley a classy foundation, but would prove to be most superb and plentiful near Proctor, just north of Rutland.

Limestone is also a good base for agriculture, and the Valley of Vermont is well-suited to farming. The soil is richer than most in the state, and the growing season is a moderate 120 days. The original forest cover was northern hardwoods. Now pretty farms hug the primary road running through the valley, their narrow fields squeezed between the eastern and western mountain ranges so closely that the region sometimes seems to have the shortest days in Vermont.

### THE VERMONT PIEDMONT

The strip of country running straight north on the eastern side of Vermont, often through the Connecticut River Valley, is known as the Piedmont. The Vermont Hills form the eastern foothills of the Green Mountains, rolling in soft waves to the narrow river valley. This beautiful countryside seems to produce more scenic calendar photographs than any other region of the state.

The Connecticut River forms a natural boundary between Vermont and New Hampshire. But this splendid valley falls just to the east of one of the most important plate tectonic boundaries in the United States. Everything west of a line that runs near the present Route 100 was always part of the continental plate that became North America. It formed the east coast of the continental shelf, giving Vermont a seashore. Some geologists believe that the land to the east of this line and into New Hampshire actually split off from another plate, possibly the one containing Africa. It was eventually crushed onto the North American continent around 420 million years ago. The plates were then sitting on the equator, and the climate was like that of much of modern sub-Saharan Africa: temperatures running in the 70s and 80s, with a definite rainy season. The plates eventually split apart again, with the Atlantic Ocean forming between them.

In southern New England, the Connecticut River Valley is known for having been home to many varieties of dinosaurs during the Jurassic period, 100 million years ago. If dinosaurs lived in Vermont—and it is likely that they did—they probably came into the state along this route.

The climatic changes that created the Ice Age began about 1.6 million years ago and continued into the recent geological past. In places, the ice eventually covered Vermont to a depth of over a mile. By 11,000 years ago, the repeated meltings of successive glaciers created huge, cold lakes in Vermont. One stretched for over 200 miles through the Connecticut River Valley. It is called Lake Hitchcock, after one of Vermont's first geologists, who identified it. It endured for about 2,400 years, until 8700 B.C., when it was able to create a channel to the south and drain into Long Island Sound. A smaller glacial lake—Lake Upton—succeeded it in the river valley between Springfield and St. Johnsbury. These glacial lakes helped to determine the shape of the valley known in human times. The Piedmont region sweeps up to the north-central part of the state, an area that today boasts more lakes than any other part of Vermont.

Rich deposits of copper lie beneath the ground on the sites of Vershire, Corinth, and Strafford, north of White River Junction. But the most important resource in the area is hidden beneath the land outside East Barre. There, one of the largest and most perfect deposits of granite in the world extends for hundreds of feet straight down from the surface; today it is mined as the Rock of Ages quarry.

The Rock of Ages Quarry, in Barre, is currently 350 feet deep, making it the largest granite quarry in the world. Granite is one of the most expensive rocks to mine, because its fine grain makes it exceptionally hard.

The soils in this region range from some of the best to some of the worst in Vermont, depending upon how close you are to the Connecticut River. The river valley has pockets of good farmland—sometimes heavy clay, sticky but rich. A wide band running between the Valley and the Green Mountains is fair-to-middling for farming, productive enough with hard work. Many of the upland soils in the central and eastern parts are too rocky and acidic to be used for agriculture.

The Green Mountains exert their influence over the climate here, sheltering the hills from the western blasts. They also cause the area to get a great deal of rain and snow, as the clouds that cool in their soft jump over the mountains release their moisture. Despite general moderation, isolated pockets in the region are subject to extremes. Most of Vermont's rainfall records come from the far southeast corner, in Windham County. Somerset once had 8.77 inches in 24 hours. This is because this region catches moisture from coastal storms, as well as those hitting the rest of Vermont. In the same area, the hottest place in Vermont is the town closest to Florida, Vernon, where the temperature has soared to 105 degrees. This garden spot also has the longest growing season in the state, at 166 days. Brattleboro and Putney are like a little Champlain Valley, home to many apple orchards. The region also has some cold pockets, where small valleys catch the winter and hold it, making growing seasons among the shortest in the state. Cavendish has one of only 112 days, and Woodstock's is not much longer at 116.

With the Connecticut River Valley, the many glacial lakes of the north-central part of the state, and the high rainfalls, the Piedmont is the most watery part of the state. It is crossed by numerous rivers, with 41 percent of the state's water—from the West and White Rivers and their tributaries—draining into the Connecticut. Most of the time the Piedmont is insulated from the strongest winds, its climate sheltered and moderate. The undulating hills are agriculturally marginal, but particularly picturesque.

Paul O. Boisvert

The Northeastern Highlands, frequently referred to as the Northeast Kingdom, are often perceived as the last unspoiled outpost of the old Vermont. Here is a wild-looking Lake Willoughby, with Mount Pisgah and Mount Hor rising over it.

### THE NORTHEASTERN HIGHLANDS

The Northeast Kingdom, as the Northeastern Highlands are usually called, is often thought to exemplify the spirit of Vermont in its purest form. In fact, geologically it is not Vermont at all, but an extension of the White Mountains of New Hampshire. There is an age difference between the Green Mountains, which are around 400 million years old, and the younger uplands in the Northeast Kingdom, which formed less than 200 million years ago. And while the Greens are made of metamorphic schists, the Whites are made of light-colored granite. Granite is an igneous rock, so the White Mountains that extend into the Northeastern Highlands were created from hot magma from the earth's core, rather than folding upwards under pressure like their Green Mountain neighbors. It is high country, and still remarkably remote in as much a psychological as a physical sense. The area is wild enough that some remote hills here are still unnamed.

The soil is among the poorest in the state, as generations were to discover while trying to wrest a living from it. The only thing that seems to grow here happily are boreal forests of fir and spruce, which give the Northeast

Paul O. Boisvert

Kingdom much of its distinctive atmosphere. The only stone with commercial potential here is granite. The climate is extremely harsh; the coldest day ever recorded in Vermont bottomed out at minus-50 degrees in Bloomfield, in the far northeast, a community with a growing season of only 113 days. Rain falls heavily on the rocky peaks, swelling the Passumpsic River system as it flows toward the Connecticut Valley. Remoteness imparts an attractive, time-warped quality to the region, but it has long been a hard place to make a living.

### THE CHAMPLAIN LOWLANDS

The long, low valley that runs along Lake Champlain in northwestern Vermont is known as the Champlain Lowlands. It is 109 miles long and up to 20 miles wide, edged by the Green Mountains on the east and the Lake and the Adirondacks on the west. If there is a "cradle of Vermont civilization," it is surely the Champlain Valley. It is likely that the majority of all the people who have ever lived in Vermont have lived in this place.

In this view from Shoreham, Lake Champlain and its valley stretch below the hulking shapes of New York's Adirondack Mountains. This fertile valley has been Vermont's most hospitable human environment from Paleoindian times right up to the present.

Five hundred million years ago, the ancestral Green Mountains lay at the edge of a continental plate, with a warm ocean lapping at their western shore. New life forms were appearing in this era and made their home in Vermont's waters. Little sea creatures—brachiopods, mollusks, trilobites—burrowed in the sand, floated on the currents, and searched for food. The fossilized remains of these 400-million-year-old ocean-dwellers are common in the Champlain Valley, especially in the shoreline rocks at the D.A.R. State Park in Addison and at scattered sites in the Champlain Islands.

Near the end of the last Ice Age, only 20,000 years ago, the glacial ice cover was over one mile deep, completely obliterating the highest peaks in the Green Mountains. An ice pack of these dimensions contains an enormous amount of water, and when it finally began to melt, it had to go somewhere. A glacial lake formed on the site of the present Lake Champlain, and it went through three distinct stages. First, the body of water known today as Lake Vermont began to grow when melting water was blocked to the north by the retreating glacier. The lake initially drained out

Shale ledges (opposite) meet the waters of Lake Champlain at D.A.R. State Park in Addison. On this beach, the limestones contain the fossils of some of the earth's oldest sea creatures—trilobites, brachiopods, and bryozoans.

to the south, near present-day Coveville, New York, emptying into the Hudson. This is known as the Coveville stage of Lake Vermont. It was a huge lake, extending eastward and completely swamping the sites of the future Burlington, St. Albans, Bristol, and Middlebury; its water level was 625 feet in Burlington and 400 feet in Brandon. Snake Mountain, in Addison, and Mount Philo, in Charlotte, were tall enough to rise as islands above this icy sea. In Burlington, only the top of the hill on which the University of Vermont now sits escaped the water. The lake eventually found a large new outlet to the south near Fort Ann, New York, lowering the lake level during its middle stage.

The North American glaciers were extremely heavy—solid ice as much as two miles thick. They were so weighty that they depressed the land below sea level. As the final glacier melted back to Canada around 10,000 B.C., the level of the land was low enough that the Atlantic Ocean backed up the St. Lawrence into Lake Vermont. Lake Vermont slowly filled with

## TROPICAL VERMONT: A FOSSIL TOUR OF D.A.R. STATE PARK

The beach at D.A.R. State Park in Addison looks like many others on Lake Champlain. Large chunks of tilted rock come down to the shore, ledges extend underfoot, and the water is always chilly before August.

If you had stood here half-a-billion years ago, however, a tropical sun would have beaten down on you, and the water would have felt blood-warm. The future Vermont sat astride the equator, and the lake teemed with tiny marine creatures.

We know they were here, because even a cursory glance at the beach rocks shows their fossils everywhere. Trilobites—tiny ancestors of crabs and lobsters—swam in great numbers, some sporting eyes on stalks to help them survey the scene. Brachiopods, looking like little bivalved seashells, clung to the rocks. (They divide into two poetically named classes, the *Articulata* and the *Inarticulata*.) Their inarticulate descendants still live in the tropics today. Large colonies of tiny bryozoa clung together in the warm and shallow waters.

The rich marine history of Lake Champlain can be read in the fossils so readily found along its shoreline. They include (top) maclurites, a snail that was very common in this area, and (bottom) girvanella, an algae nicknamed the "cocktail onion" because of its concentric layers.

They lived their lives on this spot before there were winged insects or amphibians or even plants on the earth. The age of the dinosaurs was still 300 million years in the future.

Their outlines remain clear in the limestones and shales at the lake's edge, where they were deposited and fossilized. The stones were later pushed to an angle by the mighty pressures of the Taconic upheaval. By then, the shells of our marine predecessors had hardened into the rocks.

IF YOU GO: Enjoy looking for fossils, but please remember that it is illegal to harvest them in the State Parks.

A. Blake Gardner

salt water, becoming the Champlain Sea. For 2,000 years, until about 8200 B.C., marine creatures burrowed into its banks, porpoises and seals sunned on its rocks, and whales spouted in Burlington Bay.

The valley's geological base is made up of sedimentary rocks that were deposited eons before the Ice Age. Underlying limestones have been metamorphosed in places into beautiful marbles; the whole town of Middlebury rests on this elegant base. Lime also sweetens the soil for agriculture, and the Champlain Valley has 80 percent of the best farmland in the state—flat, fertile, and relatively rock-free. Lake Vermont and the Champlain Sea left a legacy of fine particles that are now clay. The clay soils of the region are heavy and wet, but also tend to be rich and productive.

The Champlain Valley is one of the warmest regions of the state, although try telling that to the residents of the cold pocket of Shoreham on a January night. The protection of the mountains, low elevation, and proximity to the lake help to moderate the climate. The only weather records set in the region are for dryness, although seldom to the point of causing problems for agriculture. The Lowlands also have the least snow of any place in Vermont, with Burlington getting about 78 inches a year, compared to twice that on Mount Mansfield. But there is still a lot of water here, because so many rivers cross the Valley on their way to the lake and the St. Lawrence basin. From north to south, the Missisquoi, Lamoille, and Winooski Rivers, and the Otter Creek take this route from the mountains to the lake; 55 percent of the water in the state drains out by this route. Lake Champlain is too narrow to produce a lot of lake effect, so its shores are as hot as anywhere in Vermont in the summer. It has more of a moderating effect on temperatures in fall and winter, because the lake freezes late, usually not until the end of January. The growing season averages the longest in Vermont, lasting over 150 days. Conditions here are perfect for growing apples, because the clay soil keeps the trees from budding until the air is too warm to make frost, and the late autumn gives them time to ripen for harvest.

The Champlain Valley is the airiest region of Vermont, a land of expansive perspectives in contrast to the intimacy of more mountainous regions. There are many spectacular views of the Green Mountains and the Adirondacks, and the lowlands are often awash in the special, watery light you see in Dutch landscape paintings. The great wetland at Dead Creek attracts thousands of migratory birds in the fall, the snow geese flying in white formations against the dark side of Snake Mountain.

The regions of Vermont have had their own histories, but even they are only temporary. The retreat of the last glacier marked the most recent major reshaping of the region's geology. The process is, of course, continuing. We are lucky enough to be living in a glacial lull, but all of the evidence

## WHALE-WATCHING IN CHARLOTTE

Early nineteenth-century farmers in Addison County were often surprised to turn up the shells of salt-water creatures in their fields when plowing. They had no good explanation for how marine shells could be so far inland, and the issue stimulated speculation.

Casual chat quickly became shocked excitement in 1849, when a crew excavating the first railroad line in Charlotte dug up a strange skeleton. Vermont's foremost naturalist, Zadock Thompson of Burlington, was called in, and quickly identified it as the remains of a whale. The whale rested in a layer of blue clay that had been deposited within the last 12,000 years. Surrounding it were the shells of other recognizable cold-water animals, clams, and oysters. The leviathan was found to be a white beluga, closely related to similar mammals swimming in the cold oceans of our own day. Thompson took it back to the University and carefully wired it together with his own hands. It sits there now, in the Perkins Museum.

Whales? In Vermont? It was almost impossible to imagine how they could have come to be here. And yet this whale was the key to the discovery that Lake Champlain had, quite recently, been full of salt water—a Champlain Sea where early men and women may have held clambakes on the shore and listened to the songs of the whales.

suggests to geologists that a glacier will come to Vermont again. Geologists believe that the North American continent is slowly drifting toward Asia and away from Europe. Every year, a thin layer of dust erodes from the tops of the mountains, carried away by wind and water, while beneath us the great tectonic pot is boiling. From Himalayan heights to Iowan flats, tropical heat to glacial deep freeze, Vermont's geological history is a reminder that the earth's most salient characteristic is its dynamism. The bedrock beneath our feet is not in a state of eternal slumber. Even the massive rocky bulks of the mountains are shifting sand.

## THE GREENING OF THE GREEN MOUNTAINS

We tend to think that, before the coming of the Europeans, the great green forest had stood, unchanging, since the dawn of time. But vegetation is even more mutable than rock. When the place that was to become Vermont sat on the equator, it was tropical, its vegetation basking in the sun like giant hothouse plants. Later, when ice covered the land, everything green was frozen and scraped away from the surface of the earth. The history of Vermont vegetation as we know it begins with the retreat of the last glacier, somewhere around 10,000 B.C.

But how can we know what was growing here 12,000 years ago? Our best source lies at the bottom of some of the bogs that were created when the glaciers melted. Plants produce pollen as part of their reproductive cycles, and it blows over the surface of nearby bodies of water. Where the water is still, as in a bog, the pollen settles to the bottom, where layers and layers accumulate over the course of centuries. Botanists can take core samples from the beds of these bogs, identify the plant matter in each layer, and establish their ages with radiocarbon dating.

Vermont's post-glacial pollen record begins around 10,000 B.C. When the glaciers began to melt, they first created large areas of what is called an arctic-alpine landscape. This consists of tundra similar to what can be seen in northern Canada or on the tops of high mountains today. Tundra contains low and creeping plants that can handle extreme cold and rocky soil. You do not have to travel to the Arctic Circle to see tundra. Modern Vermont retains two small areas of this alpine habitat: about 250 acres on the top of Mount Mansfield and 10 acres on the peak of Camel's Hump.

As the climate warmed again, spruce and fir—the boreal forest—began to grow near the cold lakes that were pooling from the melting ice. These are trees that can survive in a frigid, moist climate like that of the late Ice Age. The retreat of the glaciers signaled a slow warming trend that led to the addition of pine and hemlock in these emergent forests. Maple was the first of the hardwoods to begin making its way back into the north, to be

Silhouetted here are contemporary engravings of the whale skeleton discovered in Charlotte in 1849, along with details of its bones. The whole skeleton can be seen at the Perkins Museum at the University of Vermont. Hovering above: a white beluga whale, the modern-day equivalent of the creature whose skeletal remains so amazed nineteenth-century Vermonters.

A dense second-growth forest has returned to the Lincoln Gap.

Alan Jakubek

followed by the other familiar northern hardwoods, like beech and birch. At one point, about 6,000 years ago, the climate had become even warmer and drier than it is today. We know this because oak and hickory, more typical of southern New England, began to appear. Only one major stand of this oak-hickory forest remains in Vermont, near Dead Creek in Addison County. Despite the dangers of global warming in the future, the botanical evidence suggests that the climate here has begun cooling again, favoring maple, birch, and spruce.

## THE HISTORIES OF TREES

North America did not have a single forest with a history that stretched back until some unquantifiable "dawn of time," but a succession of widely differing forests, alternating with periods in which no forest could live. The size, composition, and heartiness of a forest depend upon a complex interplay of biological factors interacting with such things as climate, soil type, and altitude. As these factors have changed, the forests have changed as well.

Early ecologists tended to look at plant life as going through predictable stages from meadow to scrubby trees to large, mature trees. This last stage was called the "climax"; all natural forces were taken to be moving in that direction. The model suggested that, without interference, the ultimate "natural vegetation" of any place on the earth would emerge, and then endlessly replicate itself in perpetuity. Anything that interfered with this march toward maturity—wind, fire, disease—was labeled "disturbance." And if ever there was anyone who had neglected to read the "Do Not Disturb" sign, it was mankind—the unwanted interloper in this sylvan Eden.

The problem with the climax theory was that it turns out that "disturbance" is also natural and, as with fire, sometimes beneficial. More recent forest ecologists and environmental historians are searching for models to describe both changes in the forest itself and the roles of human beings within it. It is a more holistic approach that looks at the complex relationships between different ecosystems. The emphasis is less on a notion of moving toward an inevitable climax state and more on looking at how elements of the landscape are interacting now. What has become clear is that the forest has always been changing in response to geology, climate, fire, transmission of seeds, and human intervention. No forest has ever lasted in perpetuity.

## THE PRESETTLEMENT FOREST IN VERMONT

Where can we find the forest primeval, that soaring canopy of megatrees, growing undisturbed through the eons, sheltering the Native Americans and providing an awe-inspiring greeting to the first Europeans? In our romantic imaginations, the ancient forest existed outside history—huge, dark, encompassing, and unchanging. How do we reconcile the timeless virgin stands in our mind's eye with what science has told us about the successive stages of the post-glacial forest?

When the Europeans first came to North America, it has been estimated that 45 percent of the North American continent was covered by forests, of which four-fifths lay to the east of the Great Plains. An environmental historian, Gordon Whitney, has recently studied large numbers of early European accounts of the North American forests, identifying prominent features of their descriptions. Many observers mentioned the great size and age of the trees, compared to those found in Europe. They also noticed that there tended to be quantities of dead wood on the forest floor—something that had not been common in the highly utilized forests of Northern Europe. There seemed to be more lichens and mosses on trees in the New World, and this was often commented upon. Finally, the ancient forests of North America were said to be particularly dense.

Aspen leaf

New research indicates that this picture needs some modification. While there were undoubtedly magnificent stands of huge and ancient trees in North America at the time of European settlement, the latest studies suggest that they have never been the norm. Individual forests have histories that usually involve the periodic occurrence of a variety of natural calamities. Vermont's prominent forest ecologist, Charles Cogbill, has extended a study of the Maine forest to Vermont, showing that trees on a given site would have burned down an average of once every 215 years and blown down once every 1,000 years, giving an average tree's disturbance rate as once every 244 years. A 244-year-old tree is a big, old tree, but these native trees of the Northeast are nowhere near the age or size of California's many-centuries-old sequoias, for example. Most Vermont tree varieties would never attain the age of a sequoia. Red spruce can live to about 400 years, for example, while other varieties seldom survive for more than 200.

Beech leaf

Vermont's primeval forests may have escaped some of the

calamities that befell those in Maine. Maine has mainly fir and spruce, which burn more readily than northern hardwoods (we have little information on how much of Vermont was covered in softwoods). It is also closer to the coast, and so more subject to blowdowns from hurricanes, although hurricanes and windstorms have done plenty of damage to Vermont's forests, too. Gordon Whitney has estimated that Vermont gets a devastating hurricane once every century. He also believes that spruce forests burn once every 100–200 years, while a stand of northern hardwoods can only be expected to burn down once every 800–1,400 years. But while large disasters were relatively infrequent, Vermont's forests could expect to have had repeated small disasters. Climatic changes squeezed out some species, insect pests attacked others, and individual trees were constantly losing the competition for light and root space. The primeval forest almost never consisted solely of large, old trees, but always contained a mix of trees of all ages.

Maple leaf

## WHAT TREES WERE THESE?

Vermonters know that their forests have varied in size, but tend to think they have been pretty much the same in composition. Today, the state is home to four main types of forests. The largest is the northern hardwoods—deciduous trees dominated by maple, beech, and birch. They live all over the state at elevations below 2,400 feet. Above that altitude and throughout the Northeast Kingdom there are the more cold-tolerant evergreens, mainly spruce and fir. Higher yet are the fragile alpine areas discussed before, clinging to the exposed rocks over 4,000 feet. Young forests often go through a stage of being mainly light-trunked aspen and birch. You can get some idea of how long a forest has been regenerating by looking at the proportion of white birch trunks among the darker ones. In transitional zones, most of these trees can be found mixed together in various combinations.

How can we know what kind of trees were growing in Vermont centuries ago? Historical ecologist and forester Thomas Siccama used original land surveys for the northern half of Vermont and the first lotting surveys for Chittenden County to try to find out. In the 1780s, town-line surveyors blazed one "bearing tree" per mile to mark their lines. When they came to a corner, they drove in a stake and marked the nearest tree as a "witness tree." These were recorded, and became the basis of Siccama's study.

He found that the presettlement forest had about 142 trees per acre in hardwood forests, almost exactly what there are today. So while we do not know how tall those trees were, we know they were no thicker than they are now. The main difference between the presettlement forest and the forest

### VERMONT NATIVES

Harold Meeks found that the most common species of trees in the state are:

**Deciduous**
Beech
Yellow Birch
Paper Birch (White Birch)
Gray Birch
White Ash
Black Ash
Hop Hornbeam ("Hardhack")
Bigtooth Aspen ("Popple")
Quaking Aspen ("Popple")
Black Cherry
Northern Red Oak
Black Willow
Basswood
American Elm
Red Maple
Sugar Maple
Silver Maple

**Coniferous**
Balsam Fir
Tamarack
Black Spruce
Red Spruce
White Pine
Canada Yew

of today lies in their composition. The forest of two centuries ago was made up of the same trees we see today, but in different proportions. It had far more beech trees, and only half as many maples; the cutting of the original forest helps to account for the brilliant fall color we see today, because it increased the numbers of maple trees. Beech rejuvenates far more slowly than maple, so this may account for its decline. Spruce and birch were more common in the mountains; today, spruce has almost been logged away in Chittenden County, while birch is still commonplace. Another change is that the tree cover has become more diverse in the twentieth century, as people have planted many new varieties of ornamental trees. But even before European settlement, another force for change was afoot in the mountains.

**COMPOSITION OF PRESETTLEMENT AND PRESENT FORESTS (%)**

| *Tree* | NORTHERN VERMONT *Presettlement* | CHITTENDEN CO. *Presettlement* | CHITTENDEN CO. *Present* |
|---|---|---|---|
| Beech | 30.4 | 40.4 | 4.7 |
| Maple | 15.4 | 15.8 | 23.8 |
| Spruce | 16.4 | 5.6 | 1.9 |
| Birch | 11.0 | 5.1 | 16.2 |
| Hemlock | 10.8 | 7.3 | 11.0 |
| Pine | 1.2 | 6.3 | 12.0 |
| Oak | .6 | 2.8 | 5.6 |
| *TOTALS* | *91.2* | *83.3* | *75.1* |
| Other Species | 8.8 | 16.7 | 24.9 |

Siccama, p. 161 and Meeks, *Land and Resources*, p. 235

## ENVIRONMENT AND CULTURE

The glaciers had brought more than ice to North America. Starting as early as 18,000 years ago, Asian people were able to cross a land bridge at the Bering Strait in Alaska and make their way onto this continent for the first time. Over the next 10,000 years these ancestors of the Native Americans managed to reach from coast to coast, and from the Arctic to Tierra del Fuego. The Paleoindians, as these first settlers are called, arrived in what was to become Vermont around 9000 B.C., perhaps drawn by the abundant marine life of that fecund oceanic estuary, the Champlain Sea. The sea would soon turn to fresh water, but it remained an attractive source of food for human settlers. The surrounding tundra was full of game. People had come to stay in Vermont.

Archaeologists furnish us with most of what we know about the prehistory of indigenous peoples, and we must never forget the sparse and fragmentary nature of their evidence. Imagine having to reconstruct our own culture from nothing more than the human remains of a few cemeteries, broken dishes, and rusted metal. How would they characterize our age? The Embalming Era? The Plastic Worshippers? The Junk Car Cult? Archaeologists look at physical evidence that does not necessarily consist of what the culture itself might have valued most, and extrapolate from what is known of the variations of human cultures in the present. This is where archaeology and anthropology converge, as scholars look at living cultures—food gatherers like the Inuit, for example—and see analogies with the tools produced by food gatherers living in similar climates thousands of years ago.

It is awkward to write about Native American people in a chapter that has so far been concerned with rocks and trees, as if they, too, were a "natural" feature of the landscape. This romantic way of seeing can lead to two questionable assumptions. The first is the idea that Native Americans had no effect upon the environment, leaving it exactly as it was in all circumstances. This is not true, although their environmental impact was certainly different than that of their European contemporaries. The other is the condescending implication that their ability to live in harmony with their environment came about "instinctively," rather than as the result of an enormous acquisition of knowledge and intellectual understanding of the land they turned to their use. After all, human beings were not "indigenous" to the North American landscape in the way they were in Africa. "Native" Americans were also immigrants to this continent, although much earlier ones. They created cultures of great richness and wisdom, innovating where necessary as they interacted with their environments. They thought things out as thoroughly as did their European conquerors. They just came to different conclusions.

In the presettlement forest, American beeches were the most common tree, giving autumn the predominantly burnished golden color shown at top. Today we are more familiar with the red of a maple-dominated forest (bottom).

A. Blake Gardner

## PALEOINDIANS IN A COLD LAND

High on a bluff overlooking a river, the short, strong men sit on the sand and wait. Below them, Arctic tundra spreads out as far as they can see, its scrubby grasses broken only by a few small shrubs. The river runs beneath, toward the cold, salty lake and the tall blue mountains beyond. The mammoths must come to drink. The men have time to wait. The autumn sun has little warmth, yet to the southwest, it is blinding. Then they see the giant elephantine mammoths, rounding the hill and heading toward the river. They quietly lift their spears and move together down the path.

This scene, or one very much like it, probably took place near what would later be called East Highgate, in northwestern Vermont, around 9000 B.C. The first human beings to make their homes on this land were confronted with the same mountains we see today, but the climate, plants, and animals they knew were very different. Their culture helped them to find a way to live in the Vermont they were given. Hunting was the main way they put their hands to the land.

The Paleoindians who arrived in Vermont at the end of the Ice Age found a patchy tundra-like environment, with scrubby plants and outcroppings of small spruce, that looked much like the Arctic tundra does today. They lived here in the damp, stark chill of the post-glacial landscape for about 2,000 years, from 9000 B.C. to 7000 B.C. Moving ice had scraped the land bare, but the seeds of tough grasses, mosses, and lichens soon sprouted. The

## VERMONT'S ALPINE ENVIRONMENTS

Imagine a land so cold and windy that trees cannot survive. 100-mile-an-hour winds are a frequent occurence here, sucking the moisture from every growing thing. The winter temperature rarely gets above zero and the summer growing season is less than 90 days. Most of the soil has been blown away, exposing the bare rock. It is a desert—but a frigid one. This forbidding environment exists in Vermont.

Botanists say that, on a mountain, every 400-foot rise in elevation is like a 100-mile drive to the north, as far as the plants are concerned. In Vermont, the northern hardwood forests predominate to an elevation of about 2,400 feet. Moving upwards, the boreal, or spruce-fir, forest begins to appear (sooner on colder north-facing slopes, later on warm, southerly ones). At around 4,000 feet you reach the tree line. The evergreens begin to get smaller and more twisted as conditions become harsher. This is called the *Krummholz*—German for "twisted wood"—where the few remaining trees are stunted and hug the ground, almost cowering from the hard conditions. Then the trees give up and alpine conditions begin.

Vermont has two of these alpine regions, atop Mount Mansfield and Camel's Hump. Their total area is under 300 acres, but they help to contribute to the great diversity of the state's flora. The plants hug the ground, clinging to whatever soil they can find in cracks out of the wind. Heath plants, grasses, and sedges cling to the slopes. Lichens cover the rocks. Colorful alpine flowers quiver in the June winds. Mountain cranberry, alpine bilberry, and mountain sandwort find their homes in this inhospitable climate. All have the ability to retain the moisture that the wind is so determined to wick away.

If you go to see them, it is recommended that you stay on the trails and keep well away from the plants. This is one of our most fragile environments.

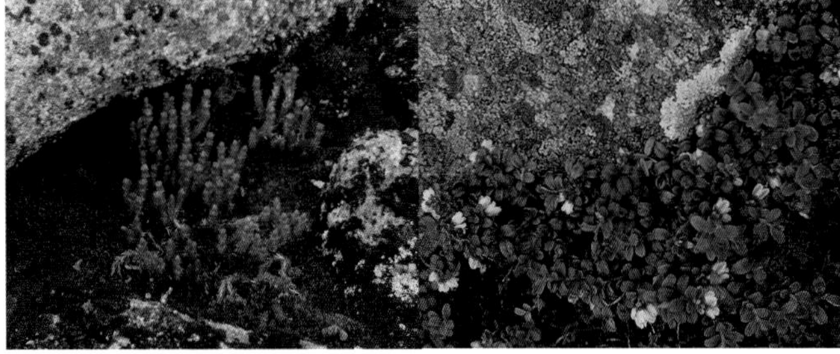

**The top of Camel's Hump, shown above looking south, is home to 10 fragile acres of tundra and can receive up to 100 inches of precipitation a year. Among the alpine plants growing there are (right) fir club moss and mountain cranberries.**

ground was wet and springy, with ponds and puddles of glacial melt water everywhere. As the land began to dry, the mosses were followed by sparse woodlands of hearty fir and spruce, scraggly and widely spaced. On the large, grassy sub-Arctic plains of North America, in all likelihood including the land that would become Vermont, herds of bison and caribou began to roam. Woolly mammoths, musk oxen, and mastodon wandered through the returning forests. There were bear and deer and a giant beaver that grew to six feet long. Smaller animals also made their way into the region: shrews, snowshoe rabbits, mice, ptarmigan, and grouse.

The Paleoindians ate a diet that would be a modern cardiologist's nightmare; it was heavily geared toward red meat (although recent evidence suggests that there was more dietary supplementation than previously thought, with berries, plants, small game, marine creatures, and birds). The game was probably tame and unsuspicious, and the Paleoindians were adept hunters. Because the post-glacial environment was initially geared to large herd animals, hunters worked in groups, stabbing the huge creatures with wooden spears tipped with stone. The classic Paleoindian spear tip was the Clovis-style fluted point, some two inches long with a small groove that may have served to make prey bleed heavily and die more quickly. The fluted points used in Vermont were almost always made of a stone called chert, which flakes similarly to flint. Tied to the end of long wooden spears, these made efficient hunting tools that worked as long as large game survived.

But big game lasted for less than 2,000 years after the final glacier melted. Mammoths and mastodons became extinct, and other animals, like the musk ox, moved north with the retreating tundra. We have no definitive answer for why so many species died out. A warming climate was leading to the growth of thicker, deciduous forests that were not conducive to large animal survival. But another intriguing possibility is the growth of the human population. The scrubby spruce parkland could not support very many people. (Similar cold environments have been found to have densities of around 10 people per 100 square kilometers.) The Paleoindians had relied upon animal resources more exclusively than people in any other period, pushing them to their limits. Mammoths and mastodons may well have been the first large species hunted to extinction by man.

We know little about their social patterns, but the Paleoindians seem to have spent their time either in large base camps, probably composed of a number of families, or in more intimate seasonal residential camps. They seem to have moved frequently over long distances, following the large game animals from place to place. Nomads travel light, but what they carried was varied and of high quality: spears, fluted points, specialized knives and meat scrapers, and fur clothing. Some of the materials used to make these tools came from as far as northern Maine and southern Pennsylvania. We know almost nothing about what these people believed. But it is intriguing to think that at some time in the distant past, in a place that is now your backyard, a woolly mammoth may have met its final spear, and early people may have eaten it there while they told tales of the hunt.

The Paleoindian era ended around 7000 B.C., as a distinct change in climate initiated a series of adaptations in their way of life. What they had to

Paleoindian big-game hunters fashioned weapons and tools out of a flint-like stone called chert; the resulting piles of stone waste or "chips" (top) are often encountered by archaeologists. These were found at the Reagan Site in East Highgate. Post-glacial Vermont was covered with a cold, open, tundra-like environment, much like that found in this view of Alaska's Denali National Park today (bottom).

Top: Tad Merrick/Bixby Library, Vergennes, Vermont; bottom: © CORBIS/Alissa Crandall

BIG GAME HUNTING IN VERMONT: LIFE AT THE REAGAN SITE, 8000 B.C.

**The first Paleoindian artifacts ever found in New England were discovered in the 1920s on a plateau overlooking the Missisquoi River in East Highgate. The Reagan Site, as it is known, caused a great deal of excitement, for it confirmed that Paleoindians had lived in post-glacial Vermont. It also strongly suggested that the earliest Vermonters were hunting large game, like caribou, as well as exploiting many other plant and small animal resources.**

**The plateau was a perfect place for the hunters to watch the movements of the big game herds on the patchy vegatation below. After killing their prey, the hunters might have hauled their mastodon or caribou to this spot. Stone knives and scrapers (like the one above) found here were used to butcher the kills and remove the meat from the hides. Charcoal-blackened hearths remain from where early people then roasted their game. Their feasts may have had celebratory or spiritual significance, for rare talc and soapstone objects (such as those above) were found in the dirt. They seem to have been worn as necklaces, and are the only Paleoindian objects of personal adornment so far found anywhere in North America.**

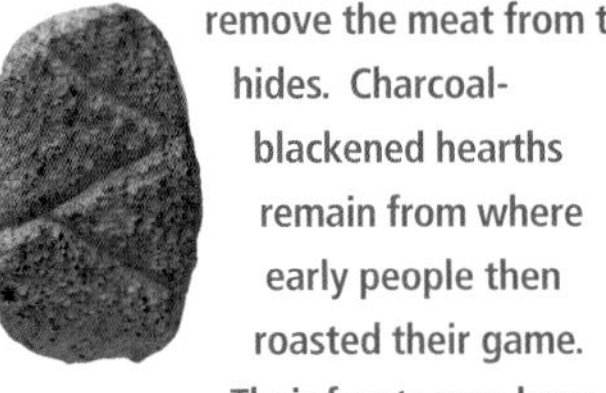

confront was an ancient, and thoroughly natural, case of global warming. The earth was beginning to warm up again, melting more of the huge cap of glacial ice. Patchy sprucelands retreated to the north as deciduous forests full of beech, birch, oak, and hickory slowly covered the valleys and foothills. By 5000 B.C., the climate had become substantially, if temporarily, warmer than it is today. Grasslands that had supported large roaming herd animals were gone, replaced by deciduous forests that were slowly moving north. There, among the trees and clearings, a far greater diversity of plants and animals could be found. Many demanded more human skill if they were to be put to use. Human beings had to adapt to this new environment or die.

## THE MYTH OF "NO INDIANS IN VERMONT"

One of the great truisms of Vermont history, as it was taught in the state's schools right up until the last several decades, was the idea that there had traditionally been "no Indians in Vermont." For whatever contemporary cultural reasons, some Vermonters were reluctant to acknowledge a long-term Native American presence in the region. The many Native artifacts that had been found in the state over 300 years were explained away as having belonged to Canadian or other Native people who were "just passing through." This attitude probably has more to do with a lack of knowledge of the culture of people who moved with the seasons than anything else. Contemporary Vermonters, like their settler ancestors, did not understand that you do not have to claim land, erect boundaries, and build permanent dwellings and villages to reside upon it. Different cultures can adapt to the same environment in very different ways; a moving village can be a movable feast. But it is important to say at the beginning that the current evidence for there having been a continuous, resident Native population in Vermont from prehistory to the present is overwhelming.

The span of Native history running until the first contact with Europeans is generally divided into three periods: the Paleoindian (9000–7000 B.C.), the Archaic (7000 B.C.–900 B.C.), and the Woodland (900 B.C.–1600 A.D.). The Archaic era saw the development of hunting and gathering societies adapted to new northern hardwood forests. The Woodland period is defined by the introduction of pottery, agriculture, increased trade, and mortuary ceremonialism. For thousands of years, Native people lived on their favored lands in Vermont: on bluffs over the Otter Creek, Missisquoi, Lamoille, and Winooski Rivers, from the Northeast Kingdom to the Taconics, from the shores of Lake Champlain to the tops of the Green Mountains.

Did the Paleoindians beget the Archaic and Woodland Indians, and are they the parents of today's predominant Vermont tribe, the Western Abenaki? Thirty years ago we knew almost nothing about the origins of the

Tad Merrick/Bixby Library, Vergennes, Vermont

## ARCHAIC DEER CAMP, 6000 B.C.

One fall, about 8,100 years ago, a family of Archaic Indians spied a fine place to pitch their camp, near what is today John's Bridge in Swanton. There was autumn hunting and good fishing—bullheads and catfish. This was all hungry work, and there are many signs of cooking and eating. The group probably included some children, because there were four miniature spear points like those known to have been put on toy spears by later Native people in Vermont.

Projectile points were made here; this is where the "Swanton corner-notched" point was first encountered. Other hunting tools were also being chipped; archaeologists found 23,000 flakes of stone that had been discarded in carving points and tools. They were made of local chert or quartz, more quickly and crudely than those of their Paleoindian predecessors. Another part of the site was devoted to butchering animals, while in a nearby spot, hides were scraped clean.

**Archaic Indian hunting parties, like that shown in this diorama from the New York State Museum in Albany, used specialized tools to cut elk or other large game into pieces that were easy to transport back to their base camps.**



Vermont Native population or the lives of the Abenaki before the Europeans arrived. Now, Gordon Day, William Haviland and Marjorie Power, James Petersen, and others have provided lively overviews of Abenaki culture and cosmology. They make a strong case for the continuous cultural development of the Native population in the region, from Paleoindian times until the present.

### ARCHAIC VERMONT AND THE GROWTH OF THE BIG WOODS

As the scrubby, cool, wet tundra and barren mountains slowly turned green and lush, new animals began to find homes in the forest—bear, fox, raccoon, hare, and white-tailed deer. Some of them joined man in a feast of acorns, walnuts, elderberries, and other new vegetable bounty. The world of trees offered diversity the Paleoindians had not enjoyed, and yet the early people found the hunting here far more challenging. Woolly mammoth and mastodon were relatively slow, docile, and easy to track. Once it had been

## VERMONT'S "OLD GROWTH" FORESTS

Above, left: In the presettlement forest, red pines were common, especially in upland areas. The Roy Mountain Wildlife Area, in the upper Connecticut Valley, has a 57-acre stand of native red pines, including those shown here.

In Gifford Woods National Natural Landmark (right), east of Rutland, a rare stand of virgin hardwoods stretches to the sky. Some, like these sugar maples, are over 300 years old.

One of the hottest debates in forestry concerns the definition of the term "old growth forest." A lot of things can affect such a forest—and such a definition. What if many of the trees were blown down in a wind storm but allowed to rejuvenate naturally? Would it still be an old growth forest, even if the actual trees were young regrowth? What about species of trees that only live for about 150 years? If stands of those have not been touched, would they be old growth? How old does a forest have to be to qualify? Different definitions can lead to wildly varying estimates of how many acres of original forest remain.

Vermont's Charles Cogbill has suggested that old growth is long enough for a forest's trees to reach a mean age of 150 years. By this definition, a forest need not have been untouched since settlement, but it has to have been undisturbed long enough to have achieved replacement by a second generation of undisturbed growth. This would tend to take 150–200 years for many species.

Actually laying eyes on such a forest can be difficult. If you ask a Vermont naturalist, "Where can I see a stand of old growth trees in Vermont?," the reply is often a sly smile and, "I know, but I'm not telling." Old growth forests are so rare that people can become very protective of them.

Small stands of very old trees exist on private lands throughout the state; scattered "witness trees" can still be seen on old boundary lines. But the easiest place to see old forests is in a designated "State Natural Area," within state forests and parks. These are defined as areas "which have retained their wilderness character, although not necessarily completely natural and undisturbed, or have rare or vanishing species of plant or animal life."

taken, a large mammal could feed the whole hunting party for a week, or a month. The new small animals of the forest were quicker and smarter, and the land offered more places to hide. The work of catching them could be more entertaining, but once they were brought down they only provided a meal or two (although on the lucky days when they got a moose or an elk, Archaic Indians might still enjoy over 600 pounds of meat). Hunting generally had to be done more often, and plant foods helped the people over the lean times. Hunting and gathering require a highly specialized knowledge of the rhythms of the natural world, and this the Archaic Indians, like their Paleo-predecessors, were able to acquire. The lore that makes successful hunting and gathering possible is gained over scores of generations, and forms the basis of a vital education for each new wave of children.

During the Archaic period, people began to settle down in one place longer. Bands made up of extended families still moved around, but within more strictly defined territories. A rising population was putting pressure on Vermont's lowlands. Several hundred members of a band might settle on a spot along the Winooski or the Missisquoi, scattered among a number of family houses. Here they would live in the winter and summer. In spring and fall, hunting parties left the villages, often going into the Green Mountains to look for the varied game of the deciduous and boreal forests. While these camps came to seem like little villages, they were not permanent. The next year the base camp might be in a completely different place. There was still so much travel that it did not make sense to acquire possessions that would only become burdens when it came time to follow the deer.

As among most hunters and gatherers, there was a fairly rigid division of labor by gender, with men doing the hunting and women the gathering, child care, and clothing-making. Like their Paleo-predecessors, the men spent a lot of their time in camp making stone projectile points for use in hunting. The old Paleoindian Clovis points—so perfect for killing a caribou or a bear—would not work against the smaller, faster, and more crafty game that hid in the woods. You cannot spear a rabbit with a Clovis, any more than you would shoot a mouse with a shotgun. The Archaic tool-makers came up with a corner-notched spear point archaeologists call the "Swanton point," which would be used successfully against smaller game for thousands of years. Another technological innovation of this period was the atlatl (although Paleoindians had known a type of spear-thrower). This wooden device weighted with a stone provided the hunter with greater leverage when he threw his weapon. It also gave the spear more speed and spring, helping it to kill game efficiently—a very useful addition to the hunter's repertoire.

Around 3500 B.C., when the Sumerians were inventing cuneiform writing in Mesopotamia and Europe was entering the Bronze Age, there was

**WHERE TO FIND OLD GROWTH**

The Vermont Department of Forests, Parks and Recreation publishes a list of State Natural Areas. Among the most important old stands on the list:

**Cambridge Natural Area**, Cambridge State Forest, Cambridge. Old growth white pine and hemlock.

**Camel's Hump Natural Area**, Camel's Hump State Park, many towns. Alpine tundra and more than 5,000 acres of undisturbed alpine boreal forest.

**Fisher-Scott Memorial Pines**, Arlington. Old growth white pine, among the tallest in the state.

**Gifford Woods Natural Area**, Sherburne. Vermont's most famous old growth stand.

**Granville Gulf Spruce-Hemlock Stand**, Granville. Very old and large.

**Lake Carmi Bog Natural Area**, Franklin. Unusually large old stand of spruce-tamarack forest.

**Lords Hill Natural Area**, Marshfield. Old growth hemlock-northern hardwood.

**Mt. Mansfield Natural Area**. Largest alpine tundra in Vermont. Krummholz.

**Quechee Gorge**, Quechee. Some untouched mixed forest, growing on the ledges.

**Roy Mountain Wildlife Area**, Barnet. Native red pine.

also a flowering of culture in North America. Now known as the Vergennes Archaic, this was an era when the Native people began making a variety of new and useful tools for hunting and dressing meat. Burial customs became more elaborate, indicating a deepening spirituality. Trading networks were also developing, as they had in the Paleoindian period, and stones and metals for making tools often came from great distances. Some found in Vermont were made of rhyolite, from near Moosehead Lake in Maine, and others of Onondaga chert from western New York State. A Caribbean conch shell found in an early burial site must have come through trade. It certainly did not wash up on the shore of Isle la Motte.

The Archaic people were also inventing other technologies. They learned to make two styles of canoes—heavy dugouts that were left on the same body of water all the time, and lighter birch bark canoes that could be portaged easily. Elaborately braided cordage, woven textiles, snowshoes, toboggans, and beautiful baskets appeared in the Archaic. All these aesthetically pleasing objects were also useful.

But people who were constantly on the move did not acquire very many possessions, especially those that were bulky to transport. They did not develop written languages, for they had no need for them. Without surpluses to create distinctions of wealth and status between people, these societies were stateless and relatively egalitarian. People might have been revered as leaders, but they earned that distinction through personal qualities like long life, successful hunting, and wise judgment. Hunting and gathering societies generally support low-population densities, but within that limitation, their culture provided more leisure time than we have today. The fewer a culture's needs, the more easily they can be satisfied.

## ARCHAICS INTO ABENAKI: LIFE IN THE WOODLAND TIME

As Jesus walked the dusty roads of Palestine, the Native people of Vermont were establishing a pattern of life that was to survive until the Abenaki first faced European Christians in the seventeenth century. Settlements tended to be larger, particularly along the Winooski, Lamoille, and Missisquoi Rivers, the Otter Creek, and in the Coos region of the upper Connecticut Valley. The climate had cooled from its post-glacial warm-up, favoring maple, beech, and evergreens at the expense of oak and hickory. The Woodland period is the first to find people living in a Vermont climate much like ours, and in forests very similar to those we see today.

But there were changes afoot in the north woods. As Europe entered what have been called the Dark Ages, the centuries after 600 A.D. were also a period of cultural decline among the northern Indians. The lively Archaic trade networks dried up, and most implements were again made only of local stone. The hunters had switched from the spear to the bow and arrow at about the time of Christ, and this used a light point called a Levanna. There is little evidence of further innovation in tool-making.

## THE WOODLAND PEOPLE TAKE UP AGRICULTURE

The riches of the northern forests, and Abenaki success at exploiting them, had provided a varied diet before the appearance of agriculture. The cultivation of corn, beans, and squash had begun in Central America around 5000 B.C., and by 1500 B.C. the ancestors of the Aztecs and Mayans were living in small towns and building temples. Agriculture, and the more sedentary life pattern it requires, were well-established in Arizona, New Mexico, and the Midwest by 1000 B.C. It took another 2,000 years for the planting of crops to come to New England. Agriculture soon became vital to Native culture in Massachusetts and Connecticut, where it had long been established when Squanto taught the Pilgrims to grow corn. At the same time, around 1000 A.D., it was first established in Vermont.

For most of this narrative, the major developments in the history of Vermont's indigenous people were centered in the Champlain Valley. But bean/corn/squash agriculture in Vermont is first evidenced in the Connecticut Valley around 1100 A.D., at the Skitchewaug site in Springfield. Farming later appeared up and down the Connecticut Valley and throughout the Champlain Basin. On the lower Winooski River, the earliest evidence of corn and bean cultivation dates back to 1450.

The Archaic and Woodland periods saw continuing innovations in projectile point technology, as evidenced in these examples. The largest point (top), made of quartzite, was dropped at the mouth of Otter Creek during the Archaic Period, and would have gone on the end of a spear. The next largest (middle), an Archaic Swanton point, was also used with a spear, but was lighter and easier to maneuver. By the Woodland Period, the bow and arrow had been developed, and required even smaller tips, like the Levanna point (bottom). It has been estimated that a skilled carver could make one of these in about 15 minutes.

Tad Merrick/Bixby Library, Vergennes, Vermont

Agriculture came slightly later to the northern forest, and it was never as important to the Abenaki as it was in southern New England. Here in the north, the growing season was so short that it did not pay to become too dependent on growing food. Many hunter/gatherer cultures experience the move toward agriculture as a step backwards, and undertake it only when population pressures, a loss of resource diversity, or a desire to stay in one place make it worthwhile. After all, farming is harder work, puts you more at the mercy of the elements, and provides less entertainment than hunting and gathering.

Yet even on a small scale, the introduction of agriculture represented a genuine mental and physical reorganization for the Woodland people and their landscape. To make farming possible, land had to be cleared (usually by burning) and some portion of the tribe had to commit to staying by the fields throughout the growing season. Seeds had to be collected and preserved from year to year, in order to make specific plants grow in places where they would not have grown wild. How magical it must have seemed for a hunter and gatherer to learn how to make a plant she wanted to eat appear right where she wanted it, rather than having to hunt for it in the woods. Slowly, over generations, such fine points as rotating fields or using fertilizers were discovered. Animals that had been friends in the forests—deer, raccoons, woodchucks, birds—became pests in the garden, inspiring a new wish for human domination over the environment.

Agricultural societies tend to acquire new social tendencies as well. Here, as in most early cultures, "hoe" agriculture, as it is called, was largely considered women's work. (The later, and heavier, "plow" agriculture would become the purview of men.) While the women gardened, men spent much of the summer hunting nearby and enjoying leisure pursuits.

The more settled lifestyle associated with agriculture has, in many cultures, led to a new materialism, as people who did not need to move regularly were able to amass more goods. Ultimately intensive agriculture leads to hierarchies, ranked societies, and bureaucracies, and makes the growth of cities possible. But most of these developments still lay in the future when Europeans first faced the Abenaki in the land that would become Vermont. The Woodland people of the northern forests eventually developed year-round settlements, but not everyone stayed in them all the time. The amassing of goods—and any accompanying accrual of unequal social status—had not yet fully developed by the time of first contact.

## THE ABENAKI WORLD IN 1600

These Indians came to be known as the Western Abenaki; their territory covered most of Vermont, New Hampshire, and a portion of western Maine and southern Québec. They spoke an Algonquian language, like their cousins, the Eastern Abenaki, who lived from Maine to Nova Scotia. (Algonquian is a language group, not to be confused with the tribe called Algonquin. The Algonquins spoke an Algonquian language, but so did many other tribes.) As is so often the case with names, "Abenaki" was not what they called themselves, but was what they were dubbed by a neighboring tribe, the Montagnais. It means "Dawn Land People," because to the Montagnais the Abenaki came from the east. The Abenaki called themselves the Alnôbak, which means the "Ordinary People."

In Vermont in 1600, the largest Western Abenaki village was at Missisquoi (Swanton), with others at the mouths of the Otter Creek and the Winooski and Lamoille Rivers. Both "Missisquoi" and "Winooski" are corruptions of Abenaki words, meaning, respectively, "at the Flint" (because of the chert source at Swanton) and "at a place with wild onions." The band of Western Abenaki living near present-day Newbury, on the Connecticut River, were the Cowasucks; those around Bellows Falls were the Sokokis.

The Abenakis' sacred Rock Dunder lies in the right foreground of this photo, near Lake Champlain's Viper Island. The best evidence that the Champlain Basin is the ancestral home of the Abenaki is that all their most vital myths are centered on its shores. Here, Odzihózo shaped the mountains and laid out the rivers' courses, making the lake last, as his masterpiece. Then he turned himself to stone off Shelburne Point and sits forever as Rock Dunder, admiring his creation.

Paul O. Boisvert

Their neighbors to the immediate west spoke a language no closer to theirs than Chinese is to English. These Mohawk, a tribe of the Iroquois who lived on the New York side of Lake Champlain, were relatively recent arrivals. Vermont also had some Mahicans living in the southwest, throughout the Taconics. By about 2000 B.C., Iroquoian- and Algonquian-speakers faced each other across the Lake with great suspicion, as they would still 3,600 years later when Samuel de Champlain arrived to put his French name to their watery border.

## DAWN LAND CULTURE

By 1600, the Abenaki culture had found many ways of living in relative comfort in the forest environment. The trend toward staying in one place longer

Among the artifacts from the Boucher Site are this twined fabric bag (top), three inches wide and probably made of basswood fibers; its bright aqua-colored copper may have come all the way from the Lake Superior region. The shells of the Atlantic marginella were found connected by a cord (bottom), which indicates they were probably used as a necklace. They are also long-distance trade items, originating on the Florida and Carolina coasts.

## THE WOODLAND WAY OF DEATH

One of the most powerful ties human beings have to the land is that this is where we often bury our dead. Around 1000 B.C., Vermont aboriginal people began to bury their loved ones with more ceremony than ever before. The "Middlesex mortuary complex," as anthropologists have named it, has left its signature burial practices all over the Northeast, from eastern New York through New England to Québec to the Canadian Maritimes. These burials have remained in an uncommon state of preservation for up to three millennia because they included copper beads, which have the capacity to kill fungus and bacteria, preserving organic matter.

The most important prehistoric cemetery in Vermont is the Boucher Site, on the Missisquoi River in the northwestern corner of the state. It is larger than most early burial grounds—the remains of at least 84 bodies are here—and shows a high degree of ceremonialism. Bodies were either cremated or buried; those who died in warm weather may have been buried there directly, while those who died when the ground was frozen were cremated elsewhere and later interred. Those who were buried were placed on their sides with knees drawn up into a flexed position and hands near their cheeks, then placed into a round pit and stained with red or yellow ochre. Many graves contained the remains of babies and small children, indicating an infant mortality rate of 19 percent for children below two years of age. Almost no one appears to have lived to be older than 45.

Graves contained a variety of precious goods, many acquired from distant places. Copper and shell beads, stone pendants and knife blades came from Ohio, Indiana, Maine, and Laborador. Clothing, thongs, and bags can still be identified, the latter believed to be medicine bags containing fish hooks and animal remains. Infants were buried with honor, in little leather shirts and strings of copper beads. Fibers show elaborately twisted cordage, some dyed indigo blue. Other textiles were carefully woven, with geometric designs made of moose or beaver hair. Three pots were broken, or "killed," and buried with the dead at Boucher, perhaps for use in an afterlife. There were few signs of special status for anyone, denoting the egalitarianism that is typical of hunter-gatherer societies.

---

and growing crops was now well advanced. Villages had about 500 to 1,000 residents during the winter months, giving a total Vermont Abenaki population of perhaps 4,000 in the Champlain Valley and 2,000 in the Connecticut Valley. (This was probably about one-seventh the population density of southern New England, where more intensive Native farming could support more people.) They had generally given up living in easily movable round huts (only big enough for one nuclear family) in favor of long houses. These could be up to 100 feet long and 30 feet wide, made of wooden poles

James Petersen and Michael Heckenberger

clad in birch bark. All the residents of a long house were relatives, often an older couple living with their grown children and grandchildren. The houses were divided into rooms, each of which housed a nuclear family, living around its own fire.

Abenaki social organization was less elaborate than that of their neighbors, the Iroquois. There was no Abenaki "League" or nation identification, as the Iroquois to the west developed in the sixteenth century. Although both Iroquois and Abenaki lived in villages of long houses, the closest Iroquois tribe, the Mohawk, were far more dependent on agriculture. And like most agriculturists, the Mohawk were reportedly more warlike than their hunting and gathering Abenaki counterparts. Agriculture tends to lead to ownership and the predatory behaviors that cause war. The Abenaki could also be brave warriors, but like most hunter-gatherers they probably did not go looking for trouble. For the Iroquois, exhibiting bravery in war—and having the ability to force your neighbors to pay a "tribute"—was an essential part of the male self-image in a way it was not for the Abenaki.

In April of 1997, divers made a spectacular find in 50 feet of water off Thompson's Point in Charlotte: an almost perfect example of Native American earthenware. The Thompson's Point Pot is just under seven inches tall; its shape and decoration show that it dates from approximately 200 B.C.–400 A.D. Traces of black carbon were found inside, indicating that it was probably used as a cooking pot over a long period of time.



Since family bore so much of the burden of social and economic life for the Abenaki, the choice of marriage partners was important. When a young man saw a woman he wished to marry, he would send an older relative to her house to give her a present. If she kept it, he would go off on a hunt to bring her game, showing what a good provider he would make. Upon his return, he and his fiancee would engage in a practice much like the "bundling" of Europeans at the same period, sleeping in the same bed, but with impediments to sexual relations. (Europeans put a "bundling board" between them, while courting Abenaki slept head to foot.) This took place at the woman's parents' house, and if they found themselves able to get along well they were married before their band with much dancing and feasting. The usual pattern was then to move in with the groom's parents, but they sometimes stayed with the bride's family if circumstances made that more sensible. Most couples soon became parents, and the Abenaki are known for having been particularly indulgent toward their children.

## THE ABENAKI CALENDAR ON THE EVE OF CONTACT

For many early Abenaki, the great, unwritten calendar was the seasonal food cycle. Anthropologists who study the Abenaki—Peter Thomas, Haviland and Power, and others—have provided us with a vivid picture of the yearly pattern as it existed at the time of European contact. If you could follow an Abenaki family through the year, you would notice an enormous amount of seasonal variation. During the cold period from January until April they would stay in their lowland villages (perhaps at the mouth of the Lamoille River), eating stored foods like corn, butternuts, dried raspberries, and smoked meat. Late in February, as days began to grow longer, grandparents, parents, and children headed for their hunting grounds in the Green Mountains. They paddled their birch bark canoes upriver as far as they could, then walked forest paths to the hunting grounds, perhaps on the side of Mount Mansfield.

The Abenaki did not "own" property in any Western sense of the word, but it had become traditional for families to claim specific areas as hunting territories (as the Cree do today). A hunting ground was usually centered on a tributary of the river you called home. Haviland and Power have suggested that a family's sense of identification with this place was so strong that it would not be an exaggeration to say that they thought they belonged to the hunting ground, rather than the reverse. Each family band had a totemic animal helper who was supposed to support family members in the hunt: a raccoon, for example. They would hang an image of a raccoon on their house in the village, use its picture to mark their territories in the forest, and carry a raccoon charm with them, to encourage success in the hunt.

The Abenaki showed a high degree of understanding of control of animal populations. Each season they might hunt only one-quarter of their territory, so that game had a chance to make a comeback. Anthropologists call this living at 25 percent of "carrying capacity." In other words, this land could conceivably provide for four times as many people as it was supporting. This left the Abenaki less vulnerable to starvation. In the dense forests of the harsh north, it was far more vital that they maintain this margin than it would have been for Native peoples in Massachusetts or Connecticut. Southerners could better rely on agriculture during a bad hunting season; in the northern forest an early frost might spell disaster if they depended too much on their produce.

When the time for the hunt came, the hunters left camp on snowshoes, armed with spears and trained dogs. Large animals, like deer and moose, were easy to track and lacked mobility in the snow. Smaller mammals, like squirrels and hares, were also good prey this time of year. It was also a great advantage of winter hunting that meat could be frozen in large wooden troughs, then pulled by toboggan over the snow to camp. There the women spent their time cooking and making clothing.

Late in the winter, everyone moved back to the villages, where the women were in charge of tapping the maple trees and making syrup. The taps were reeds, the pails were birch bark, and the boiling was done in pottery vessels, but there was nothing in the process that would look completely unfamiliar to the modern eye.

The fish started to spawn in April; hunters could take scores of alewives and salmon. The tributaries of the Connecticut River were particularly full of salmon, and the Abenaki would gorge themselves on this richness. There was also good bird hunting, as migration began; passenger pigeons were killed by the thousands. Almost nothing else was eaten while this spring bounty was at hand.

The focus turned to the women in May, when it was time to plant the fields. This tied everyone close to the village, where the men fished and the women tilled the soil and gathered wild plants. The shift to agriculture had enormous ramifications for women's lives, as all its work was considered to be their responsibility. From summer through the fall harvest, the men relaxed, while the women worked intensively all day.

The autumn saw great preparations for the harsh weather ahead. Once the corn, beans, nuts, berries, and up to 200 different medicinal plants had

## THE SHORT TOUGH LIFE OF AN ARCHAIC WIFE

Alan Jakubek

She was only 5'3", although that was not short in 980 B.C., and she had a groove etched into her forehead from a thong that had held heavy loads on her back. Though she was about 45 when she died, there was no sign of tooth decay. (This is commonly the case with meat-eating people. You can tell when carbohydrates come into Native diets, because teeth begin to rot.) There had been a couple of periods of hunger in her life—they showed in her teeth and her ribs—but neither had lasted for long. Her bones show signs of arthritis and osteoporosis, both of which plagued many Archaic people by their 40s.

She had suffered two serious blows at some time in her life—one to the side of the head from a wedge-shaped object and one to the eighth right rib. Accidents? Violence? How long had it taken her wounds to heal?

Her whole skeleton had been distorted by a terrible disease. Lesions had formed all over her skull and joints. Modern radiologists have diagnosed bone tuberculosis, or something like it. She suffered from it for a long time.

Archaic healers tried to help her by making an incision in her skull. Was this supposed to cure her, or let out demons? It healed and she lived another year. Then they tried it again, boring a small hole in her left temple. That, or the disease itself, finished her life.

Her body showed that she had borne at least one child. A 9-year-old, probably a boy, was found nearby. He had died of the same devastating disease.

Only the right sides of their bodies were stained with red ochre, the color symbolizing life and emotion to the early Native people.

*—Forensic archaeology by Robert L. Blakely and Richard Woodworth.*

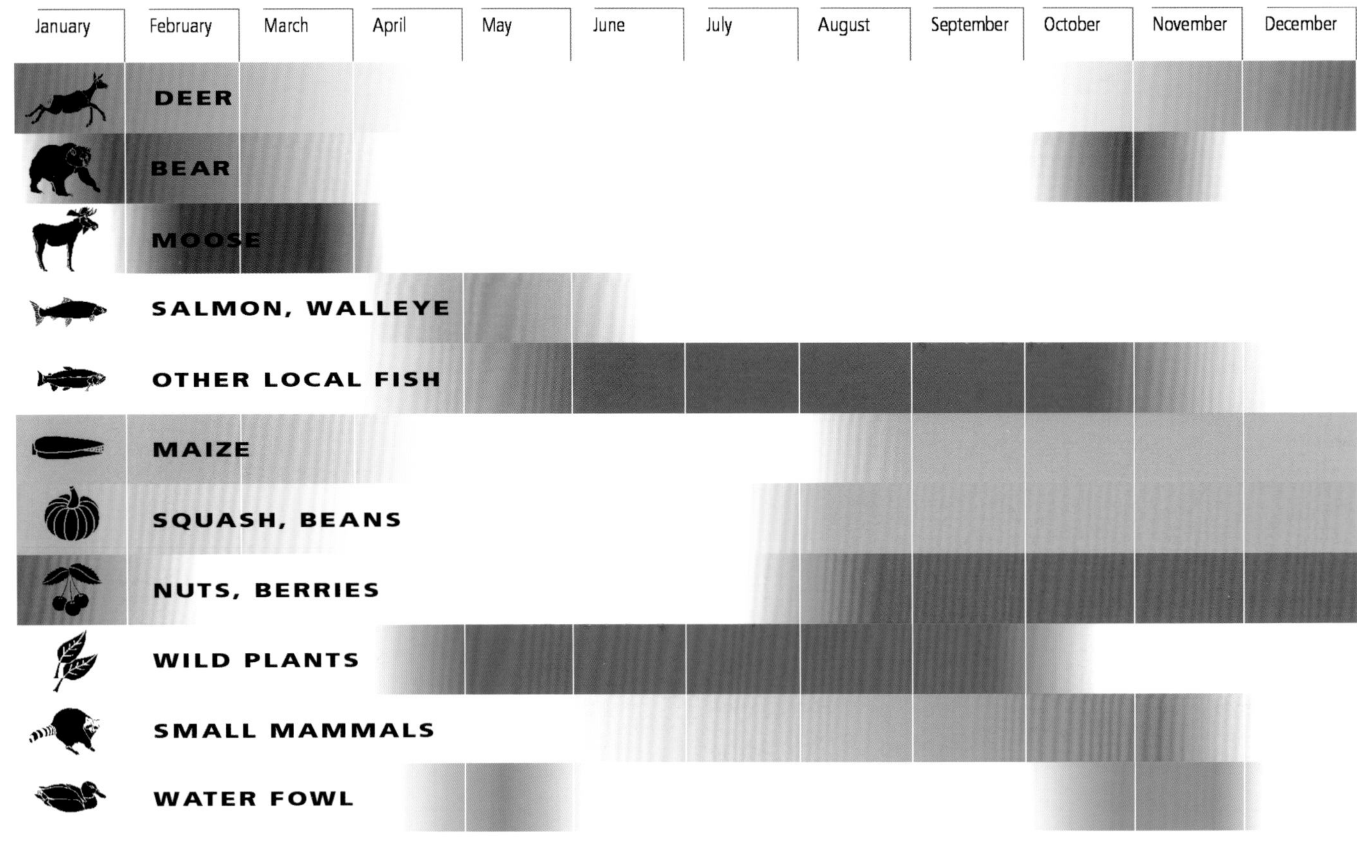


Native diets varied enormously with the seasons. The colored blocks on this calendar show the months of the year in which various food sources were available to Native people.

been dried and stored for winter, the people again left their villages for deer camp. On the slopes of Camel's Hump or the paths through Lincoln Gap, they returned to their hunting territories to try to take enough game to last until February. The focus was on hunting deer and moose, and trapping fur-bearing animals; it was as important to get warm hides to wear through the winter as it was to dry or smoke enough meat. When the snow came, it was back to the village to begin the cycle again.

The Abenaki may have spent much of their time adapting to nature, rather than adapting nature to themselves. But they were also creating landscapes. The fields where they grew their corn and squash were cleared by cutting and burning. Because some game, like deer, prefer to live on the edge of the forest, it is likely that the Abenaki, like other Indians, used burning to open forest clearings. They made paths through the woods to help them to their hunting grounds and utilized the earth's resources—animal foods, animal hides, clay for pottery, and birch bark for canoes. But virtually everything they used was what we would term "biodegradable"; as far as we know, little was used to excess. The absence of any drive for acquisition helped to minimize the Abenaki's environmental impact. All that we can find of their landscapes today are woodland paths and the remains of small objects, hidden deeply within the earth.

### GOD THE ONLY OWNER: THE SPIRITUAL LIFE OF THE ABENAKI

In many societies, religion is at the heart of people's ideas about nature and land use. While seventeenth-century Europeans believed in a God who threw people out of the Garden to live in a wilderness, their Abenaki counterparts also found gods among the animals, rocks, and trees. It would be wrong to assume that there was a single Native American religion. Native tribes could differ greatly in their approaches to spirituality. The Abenaki did not believe the same things as their Mohawk neighbors. While Mohawk tales, like those of their fellow Iroquois, tended toward recurring themes of aggression, sorcery, and cannibalism, the Abenaki had a gentler ethos.

The Abenaki thought that almost all objects in the world, living or inert, were animate in some way (and were shocked to find that Europeans disagreed). Human beings and animals, they believed, had both a physical body and a life force, or vital self. The source of this life force was the Earth, Our Grandmother, who gave everything life when warmed by the sun. Like most hunting people, they placed high value on animal life. Many hunters, even today, argue that they love animals more than other people because they know and respect them through having hunted them; this belief was common among the Abenaki. Animal bones had to be treated with respect and returned to where the animal had lived, if possible. Concern for the animal dead was considered vital, for it was believed that, as Haviland and Power have put it, "Failure to respect the rights of animals would result in their no longer being willing to be killed."

The Western Abenaki had no creation myth for the physical world, because they believed that it had always existed. The role of creator was taken by Gluskabe (sometimes called Tabaldak), known to the Ordinary People by the intriguing title of "the Owner." In a culture that set almost no store by personal ownership of property, it is revealing to find that the only being designated as an owner was the Creator. What little was considered to be personal property was held in trust for the family or band. Amassing material goods was unnecessary because everything was already possessed by the Owner. This is a spiritual view of the landscape that stresses the unity of all life, and stewardship rather than ownership.

Gluskabe had made all living things, including men and women. In their case, he made them first from stone, which symbolized ancient power,

### NATIVE AMERICAN NAMES ON THE LAND

Vermont has retained fewer Indian names than almost any state in the Union. The only city or town in Vermont with an Abenaki name is Winooski, which means "a place with wild onions." A few tiny villages have Indian names: Bomoseen ("keeper of the ceremonial fire"), Passumpsic ("stream over clear sandy bottom"), Ascutney ("at the end of the river fork"), and Quechee ("swift mountain stream").

As early as 1794, historian Samuel Williams was lamenting that the Indian names "are mostly lost," and arguing that "On account of their originality, antiquity, signification, singularity, and sound, these names ought to be carefully preserved. In every respect they are far preferable to the unmeaning application, and constant repetition of an improper English name."

**The Winooski River, named for the Abenaki word meaning "a place with wild onions."**

Paul. O Boisvert

but they did not please him. Then he made them again of living wood, and this made him so happy that they became the ancestors of the first Native people. The Owner also cared deeply for two of the most important elements of a hunter-gatherer's existence: the animals of the hunt and plants with medicinal properties.

Gluskabe had a helper, Odzihózo, who was able to create himself from some dust that had been touched by the Owner. Odzihózo is often thought of as the Transformer, because he had the power to alter the shape of the land that would be Vermont. He personified all the unknown forces of plate tectonics, botany, and biology, heaping dirt to make the mountains, carving the rivers, planting the trees, and altering the animals so they could be more easily hunted by man. His last, and greatest, creation was Lake Champlain, which he loved so much that he decided to stay there and admire it for eternity. The Abenaki believed that Rock Dunder, in Burlington Bay, was actually Odzihózo enjoying his handiwork. All these myths and stories helped to bridge the gap between human experience and knowledge at a time when science did not exist to answer questions about how the world worked. They are firmly rooted in the joys and anxieties of life in Vermont's forests before the coming of the Christians.

On a rock next to the Connecticut River in Brattleboro, Abenaki petroglyphs probably show that this was once a holy spot. Here the community's holy leaders, or shamans, went into trances in which they were believed to communicate with the spirit world. These carvings are thought to depict the faces of the keepers of game, who were believed to reside underwater.

Sara Gregg

## ABENAKIS ON THE LANDSCAPE

The Abenaki pattern of life seems to have been as successful as many others in the early seventeenth century. As Haviland and Power have noted, in 1600 infant mortality was no higher here than it was in Europe. There was also almost no difference in Native American and European life expectancies, both of which averaged around 37 in this era. Of course, many people who grew to adulthood lived to far greater ages, and circumstantial evidence suggests that this was more often true among Native American populations than for Europeans.

In his provocative book, *Changes in the Land: Indians, Colonists and the Ecology of New England*, historian William Cronon has shown that the idea that America was an untamed "wilderness" before the coming of the Europeans is a myth. Native Americans had already been shaping the landscape for their own purposes for thousands of years. Long before the colonists came, the Natives of New England had cleared great tracts of trees through burning. They preferred that the forest be park-like, with widely spaced trees and little underbrush, for this made moving through the forest much easier.

Vermont's Native population got a larger proportion of their diet from hunting and gathering until a later date than did their counterparts in southern New England. Because they almost always lived on rivers or lakes, and for many millennia had relied on canoes to get around, a fire-opened forest was less necessary, although there were some well-defined paths through the forest leading to hunting grounds in the mountains. But the coming of agriculture eventually brought burning to the forests of Vermont, New Hampshire, and Maine, as well. And the summer miracle of tiny seeds becoming head-high corn and fat pumpkins imparted a new sense of power over nature.

Even without a great deal of fire-cleared land, it would be inaccurate to argue that Vermont was a "wilderness" when the first white people arrived. A land is only "wild" to those who do not know how to survive in it. To its indigenous people, it had been home for thousands of years. As long as they enjoyed free access to the land, they could live in relative comfort among its trees and plants, animals and birds, fish and fields.

Land and climate may put constraints on all people who might ever live here, but they do not dictate that cultures develop in only one direction. Early Native people lived here differently than the Europeans who would follow them. The history of the Abenaki and their ancestors shows one way of turning a hand to this land. They did it with a light touch, and without great numbers of technological innovations. This is not to say that they did not leave their marks—the village clearings, paths in the woods, the bones of dead bear. It may well be wise to avoid romanticizing lives that were often short and full of physical hardship. But there was an inner richness to Native life that animated the mind through long hours spent coiling pottery or watching silently for deer in the clearing. The myths were big enough to explain both the beauties and the hardships of a life spent in nature.

Yankee Vermonters looked at Mount Mansfield and saw a face. The Abenaki looked at Rock Dunder and saw a god with a human shape. It is a peculiarity of human consciousness that we experience nature as being outside ourselves, and yet we cannot look at it without projecting ourselves into its center.

There is nothing wrong with finding human meaning in the landscape. There is great beauty and comfort in this. But we have to remind ourselves that we are not the only agents of change in the environment. As you read this, the rock beneath you is either pushing up or wearing down. Ice may be forming at the poles in preparation for a return trip south. The seeds of trees are sitting on the earth nearby and will either fan into branching life or rot on the ground according to whether they find the right mixture of climate and soil. Lightning may burn the forest, ice may make the trees crack like matchsticks, or tornadoes may blow them away. Nature has never been any more stable than we are. Knowing how to behave in this great garden must start with rightly seeing ourselves as only one among the millions of blowing, growing, pushing, burning, changing actors in nature.

## CHAMPLAIN'S BATTLE WITH THE MOHAWK

A view of Champlain's battle of 1609, first published in Paris four years later. It shows Champlain and his Native American allies defeating the Mohawk. There is some question over whether this took place at the future site of Crown Point or Fort Ticonderoga, although the latter seems more credible. The engraving was certainly not drawn by anyone who was present—or is this the only recorded instance of northern Natives fighting naked amidst palm trees?

Collections of Vermont Historical Society

CHAPTER 2

# CLAIMING THE LAND, 1609-1791

*I marched on until I was within some thirty yards of the enemy, who as soon as they caught sight of me halted and gazed at me and I at them. When I saw them make a move to draw their bows upon us, I took aim with my arquebus and shot straight at one of the three chiefs, and with this shot two fell to the ground and one of their companions was wounded who died thereof a little later. ...The Iroquois were much astonished that two men should have been killed so quickly, although they were provided with shields made of cotton thread woven together and wood, which were proof against their arrows. This frightened them greatly. ...seeing their chiefs dead, they lost courage and took to flight, abandoning the field and their fort, and fleeing into the depth of the forest, whither I pursued them and laid low still more of them. ...The place where this attack took place is in 43 degrees and some minutes of latitude, and was named Lake Champlain.*

—SAMUEL DE CHAMPLAIN, *Works*, 1609

On a July morning in 1609, the brilliant French adventurer Samuel de Champlain found himself in a dangerous melee with the native inhabitants on the western shore of a lake he would soon claim with his own name. This was nothing new for Champlain. In his 42 years, this ship captain's son from Brouage, France had already sailed the West Indies and made the long, rough trek overland to Mexico City. (His suggestion that a canal could be built through the Isthmus of Panama went unheeded, for the present.)

Now he was the first white man to venture into the great wooded valley that ran south from the St. Lawrence into the mountains. Champlain hoped to mitigate the Iroquois

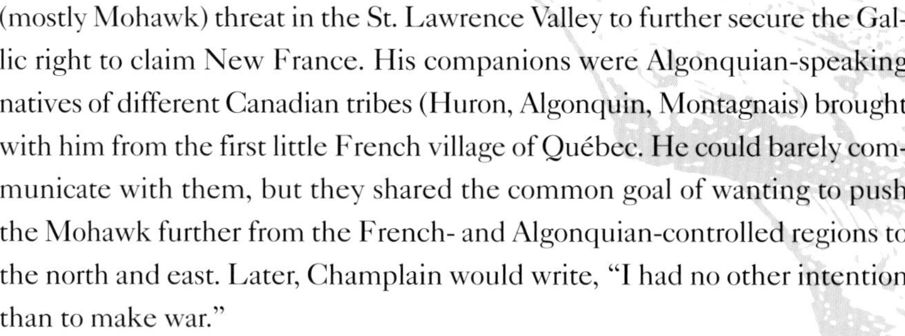

(mostly Mohawk) threat in the St. Lawrence Valley to further secure the Gallic right to claim New France. His companions were Algonquian-speaking natives of different Canadian tribes (Huron, Algonquin, Montagnais) brought with him from the first little French village of Québec. He could barely communicate with them, but they shared the common goal of wanting to push the Mohawk further from the French- and Algonquian-controlled regions to the north and east. Later, Champlain would write, "I had no other intention than to make war."

Champlain used a wheel-lock arquebus much like this one in his battle with the Mohawk. Its ingenious firing mechanism was invented in Germany around 1515; Champlain brought a German model with him to the New World.

When the Algonquians led him to confront about 200 Mohawk on the night of July 29 near the present site of Ticonderoga, New York, Champlain "promised them to do all in my power, and told them that I was very sorry they could not understand me, so that I might direct their method of attacking the enemy." After hiding and watching the catcalling rituals of Indian warfare for some time, Champlain revealed himself, marched forward in his glinting silver armor, and lit the fuse of his arquebus, the precursor to the musket. The first shots of gunpowder ever to explode in battle in this land echoed from the Adirondacks to the Green Mountains and ripped through the cloth armor of the Mohawk chiefs, killing them with stunning dispatch. Warriors in woven tunics were no match for the European killing machines. Seeing their chiefs so strangely killed, most of the enemy warriors ran into the forests in terror. The victors crossed the lake to the mouth of Otter Creek, where Champlain danced and sang with his native comrades in arms to celebrate the victory. Indian and Frenchman alike knew that fighting was, in some way, about who would possess the land. Yet, on that summer night by the lakeshore, Champlain's Algonquian allies had no more understanding of Western conceptions of private property than the Mohawks had of arquebuses. Champlain formally claimed the land and the lake for France.

Champlain's battle with the Mohawk was the first shot in a century and a half of bloodshed over the part of North America that would become Vermont. The way we choose to interpret this incident has a lot to tell us about how we see our place on the land. The old school of history would argue that the northern forest was a wilderness full of savages until it was "discovered" by great explorers like Champlain, the forerunner of Christian civilization in this godless land. For these scholars, the Vermont landscape essentially had no history until the European settlers arrived, displaced the murdering heathens, and transformed the wilderness into productive farmland. More recent historians have lamented Champlain's encounter with the Mohawk as the symbolic beginning of the end for the northern wilderness and its more ecologically sensitive native inhabitants. For them, a superior way of living in nature was cruelly destroyed by Western violence and greed. The reality was more complicated than either version of the story suggests.

## CLAIMING THE LAND

The first battle of Lake Champlain was a minor skirmish in the history of warfare, but it foreshadowed the long initial phase of the European occupation of North America. For the next 150 years, the future Vermont lay as a green and rugged no man's land between the more comfortable settlements of New England and New France. The Indians, the French, and the English would all fight to lay claim to this long tract of the north woods. For each of these three groups, the landscape held a different meaning, and that is where this story must begin.

For before European settlers could turn their hands to the land, they had to get their hands on the land. The period from 1689 to 1760 saw an almost continual state of war, as the French and their Algonquian allies (including the Abenaki) and British, with the Iroquois (Mohawk), played out their conflicts over who was to control the seemingly boundless resources of the great northern forest. Until the final large battles, these were mostly wars of small-scale raids and counter-raids—guerrilla warfare in the woods. Decade after decade, settlements were ambushed, their inhabitants scalped or force-marched to New France as prisoners. This is a significant topic for the study of the landscape, because the winner was to determine both the look and the use of this land.

Many states began in struggle, but the circumstances of Vermont's birth were more protracted and peculiar than most. In the remote reaches of the future Vermont, forbidding topography, a harsh climate, European conflict, native resistance, ill-controlled land speculation, and revolution would all act as barriers to large-scale white settlement. From 1609 until statehood in 1791, people of European ancestry struggled to claim the land that would become Vermont in a free-for-all that would delay the creation of organized community life. Their struggles would also heighten the first great wave of environmental destruction.

What did it mean to "claim"? The Abenaki had felt no need to claim the land at all; Europeans, meanwhile, felt they had a right—or even a duty—to do so. Does working the land give people a right to claim it? What does claiming have to do with transforming the landscape and the creation of communities? Claiming happens on many levels. First, on the global level, the superpowers of the early modern world, France and England, fought for a century over who would claim the future Vermont. When that was settled, the struggle became more localized, with New Hampshire and New York grappling to gain supremacy. Vermont finally became its own Republic, then decided to join the new United States. At the same time, on the personal level, thousands of people poured into the region to clear their "stakes"—the area between actual stakes marking out claims to portions of land.

### WAS CHAMPLAIN THE FIRST EUROPEAN TO SEE "CHAMP"?

Samuel de Champlain not only gave his name to the great lake, but also to its fabled sea monster, Champ. The Indians told him of a 10-foot-long creature they called "Chaousarou," although the largest one he saw himself was a mere five feet long. The creature was allegedly imbued with unusual properties, some of them medicinal. Its mouth was said to be filled with needle-sharp teeth, and in his *Journal*, Champlain relates that:

*The point of the snout is like that of a hog. ...The Indians gave me a head of it, which they prize highly saying, when they have a headache they let blood with the teeth of this fish at the seat of the pain which immediately goes away.*

**One representation (left) of the kind of "monster" believed by some to be an inhabitant of Lake Champlain; other versions depict it as a long-necked plesiosaur-type creature. Legends about such a fabulous beast have persisted for hundreds of years.**

At the dawn of white expansion, the trees grew thick in the land that would become Vermont. There were a few clearings along the shores of lakes and rivers, where native people had practiced agriculture. Some of these meadows were filling up with brush, for the women who had cleared them had fled to the mountains or were dead of the smallpox. The roads were water roads, bubbling quietly beneath the arching trees. On land, ancient paths ran from the water to the mountains, to territories marked with the symbols of their human stewards. The salmon ran strong and the mammals scurried at the edge of the woods. It was a quiet world, of snapping twigs and trilling birds and the soft thudding of suede-covered feet on dirt trails. No one then alive could anticipate how quickly such a world could be lost.

## SPIRITS ON THE LAND: THE NATIVES AND NATURE

*Gluskabe looked around for something else to make human beings. He saw the ash trees. They were tall and slender and they danced gracefully in the wind. Then Gluskabe made the shapes of men and women in the trunks of the ash trees. He took out his long bow and arrows and shot the arrows into the ashes. Where each arrow went in a person stepped forth, straight and tall. Those people had hearts which were growing and green. They were the first Abenakis. To this day those who remember this story call the ash trees their relatives.*

—ABENAKI CREATION STORY, as told by Joseph Bruchac

These drawings of seventeenth-century Abenaki and Montagnais Indians, first published in Paris in 1612, are said to be based on accounts of Samuel de Champlain. The classical garb, however, is more likely the product of a French artist's imagination.

Indian attitudes toward the land were largely an outgrowth of their spiritual beliefs. As their creation story shows, in their view, human beings shared a oneness with the trees and contained within themselves a green heart. The Abenaki, along with other tribes of the northern woodlands, saw "personhood" in many inanimate objects, and this sense imbued rocks, trees, and animals with discernible spirits. Because objects had personhood, they also had the right to own themselves. If humans needed to kill animals or plants for their use, they had to do so with respect and in a spirit of social responsibility. There is no northeastern Indian equivalent for the European notion of "claiming." To the Abenaki, private property held no meaning. Their fledgling experiments with agriculture had not yet led them to stay in one place, claim their fields, or amass property. Communities were based upon the shared joys and frustrations of hunting, gathering, and farming; social and political hierarchies, as Europeans understood them, did not exist.

The fur trade soon introduced new elements into Native American life. One early observer, Nicholas Denys, had found that the northern Indians traditionally "killed animals only in proportion as they had need of them. They never made an accumulation of skins of Moose, Beaver, Otter, or others, but only so far as they needed them for personal use." But despite a traditional respect for nature, they were quick to embrace the technological marvels Europeans had to offer. In exchange for iron pots, cloth, and wampum, Indians were willingly recruited to hunt fur-bearing mammals to near-extinction. The Abenaki's restraint in the taking of game proved impossible to sustain when they were tempted by unprecedented opportunities for trade. In one small example, as early as 1670, Denys found that the northern Indians had become dependent upon the Europeans' unbreakable iron cookware, and had "abandoned all their own utensils." In a century, most of the beaver in the north woods would be gone, but goods, guns, and alcohol would become permanent features of Native life.

## TRANSFORMING THE LAND: THE EUROPEANS AND NATURE

*The fear of you and the dread of you shall be upon every beast of the earth, and upon every fowl of the air, upon all that moveth upon the earth, and upon all the fishes of the sea; into your hand are they delivered. Every moving thing that liveth shall be meat for you.*

—GENESIS, IX. 2-3

For seventeenth-century Europeans, religion also lay at the heart of conceptions of man's relation to the environment. In Christianity, only human beings had personhood, and therefore only people could have spirits. Western culture made a sharp distinction between people and all other objects, so a rock was only a rock and a tree was only a tree. Because the Christian God created people—and only people—in his own image, human beings had certain rights in relation to the rest of the world that other creatures and objects did not have. The land, therefore, had been created for man's use. People could take what they wanted from the land, and nature would always provide enough. The most highly respected people were usually those with the greatest command of the world's resources.

For Europeans, the human domination of nature was the basis of civilization, and it was precisely this that led them to judge the Native Americans to be "uncivilized." Their own culture was based upon conquering the natural world. The result was an attitude toward nature that was almost entirely unsentimental in the early modern period. It also meant that human beings had to hold themselves apart from—and above—those parts of their own natures that they defined as "animal." Christianity was the great bastion against man's physical nature, helping to elevate him above the beasts who served him. Man had to conquer the beast in himself as surely as he would conquer the wilderness. In northern New England in the seventeenth century, a possessive view of nature began to force itself upon a sustaining view of nature.

Fanciful early depictions of beavers, which were to become so vital to French trappers and traders in the New World. Likely done by someone who had never seen them in the flesh, these illustrations show industrious animals looking like busy, water-loving dogs, their dam so symmetrical it could be made of cinder blocks.

The Indians of the northern forests were coming to understand something of the Europeans through the fur trade, but they had yet to see them in their most domineering role of all, as agriculturists. They certainly had no forewarning of the ramifications European farming might have for their own cultures. Centuries of intensive agriculture meant that Europeans had to count on retaining the land that supported their families. Farming also had a profound effect upon the shape of the landscape, as people cleared and plowed and molded it to their use. And because Europeans lived in permanent settlements, they were able to amass material goods. These led to differences in social status, the creation of hierarchies, and the development of elaborate political systems. Private property held profound meaning in European cultures, so claiming resources was a way of protecting and promoting the family's—and the nation's—interests. Community grew out of shared political, social, economic, and religious values.

## FUR, FORTS, AND THE FRENCH

While all Europeans had a similar view of man's place in nature, cultural differences affected how they dealt with the alien North American environment. For the French, the great attraction was extraction, particularly of the hides of fur-bearing mammals; communities might come later. Extractive

## A YOUNG PRIEST'S FIRST HORRIFYING WINTER ON ISLE LA MOTTE, 1665–66: FRANÇOIS DOLLIER DE CASSON

In the terrible winter of 1665–66, a young French Sulpician monk, François Dollier de Casson, agreed to minister to the soldiers stationed at the future Vermont's first fort, St. Anne, on Isle la Motte. His coming offered many the only joy remaining to them—the hope of receiving last rites:

*M. La Motte, the commander...immediately rushed out with all the officers and men not absolutely needed to guard the fort and came to meet me with unspeakable joy, embracing me with so tender an affection I cannot describe it. "Welcome!" they all said. "What a pity you did not arrive a little earlier! How the two soldiers who have just died longed for you! What joy your coming will bring to all our sick. How the news of your coming cheers them! How grateful we are to you for coming!"*

*It was high time I came, for of the sixty soldiers in the fort, forty had scurvy, and seemed near death. They well were afraid of the contagion, especially as they had no vegetables—only bacon and bread made of flour damaged in ocean transit. ...They also had a cask of vinegar that would have been excellent for their malady, but unluckily it all leaked out.*

*...This sickness lasted three whole months. The death agony lasted eight days, during which the stench was so great that it reached almost to the center of the fort, although the patients were shut up in their rooms. The dying were so far gone that no one dared so much as go near them, except the priest and a surgeon named Forestier...*

*The neglected sick hit upon a successful way to get help from some comrade. They set about making elaborate wills, as if they had been very rich, saying, "I give so much to so and so because he helped me in my last illness, when I was forsaken." Every day saw such wills made. Those who saw through the device smiled at the resource of these poor fellows, who did not have a cent in the world.*

**Isle la Motte remains a wind-swept and desolate place in winter, as it was in the harshest season of 1665–66.**

enterprises—fur trapping, lumbering, mining—often hold out the hope of fast profits. They also have the potential to cause great environmental harm, as resources are squandered and ecosystems despoiled. In seventeenth-century North America, nature's bounty could be converted swiftly into cash; the French hoped to keep this treasure chest for themselves. To do so, they learned to survive in the forest in much the same way the Native Americans did, conforming to the demands of climate and topography. There is some truth to those old images of the hearty voyageurs paddling their birch bark canoes through the wilderness, singing lusty choruses of "Auprès de ma Blonde." From the early seventeenth century, the French were establishing trading outposts geared to serving the European rage for hats made of beaver pelts.

Louis XV of France, shown here as a youth who had just come to the throne, was known for his self-indulgence. By the end of his reign, he was deeply unpopular—and doomed to be remembered as the monarch who lost New France.

The French quickly came to realize that they needed a resident population to maintain their claim to the Champlain Valley, but before that could happen the land had to be secured by military personnel. When war threatened the Abenakis, the traditional course had been to withdraw; but when war threatened Europeans, their solution was to build fortifications. So now, deep in a forest full of trees, plants, and animals they did not fully comprehend, they began to build forts to defend...what? Nothing that would seem familiar to the people back home—no formal gardens, no neat hedgerows, no cabinetmakers's shops, no boat-crowded Seine.

Wilderness forts were the first bastions of European civilization, places that both defined and defended the borders of those who sought to claim territory. Forts are about power and saying to your rivals, "Everything behind this point of land is ours. We will stop you if you come past here." In contested territory, they are the precursors to community—artificial assemblies of temporary occupants, sent at the authority of a foreign state, whose presence is meant to ensure their citizens the right to turn this landscape to their own use. The Europeans understood that part of claiming land was clearing it of all your enemies. The Indians who helped the Europeans in the wars would not see the implications of this for themselves until it was too late.

On July 26, 1666, a diverse group of 60 French soldiers, fur traders, and Jesuit missionaries assembled to dedicate a new fort to Sainte Anne, on the northern tip of Isle la Motte in Lake Champlain. It was the first European settlement in Vermont, constructed under the eye of Pierre de St. Paul, Sieur de la Motte, as a launching pad against the obstreperous Mohawks. The place must have seemed a secure refuge against any forest dangers, on that balmy summer afternoon. But by the middle of its first winter, it had become a chamber of horrors, as the unprepared Frenchmen got their first—and for many their last—taste of winter in the wilderness. Their sufferings appear in the writings of François Dollier de Casson, an earnest young

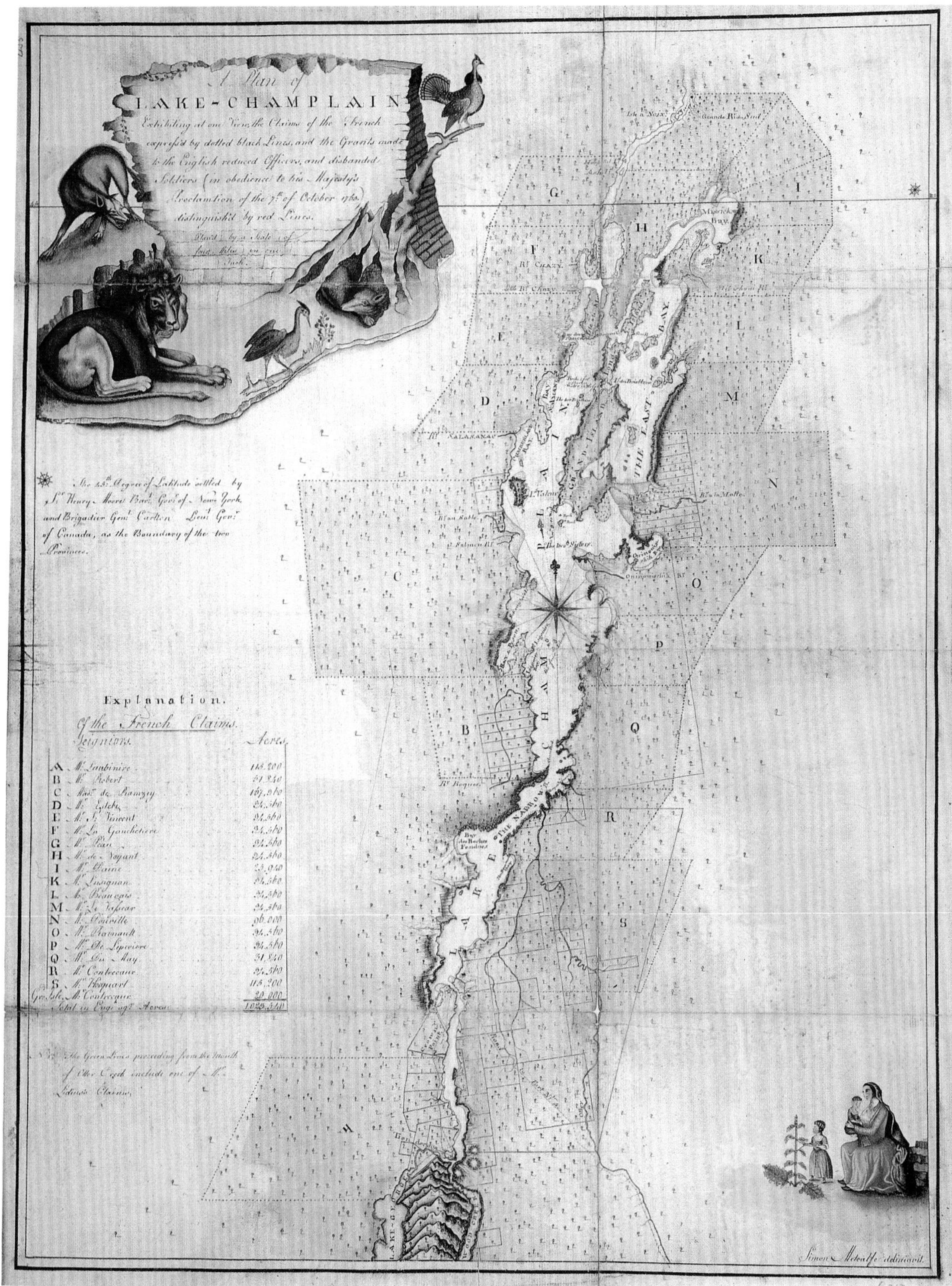


"A Plan of Lake Champlain," by Simon Metcalfe. The French seigneuries, or land grants, are shown on this map from 1767 by cartographer Simon Metcalfe, who depicted the status of French claims in the Champlain Valley at the time of the French and Indian Wars. French grantees were notoriously lax about promoting settlement on their lands; the only substantial settlements to come from this system were those at Chimney Point and Swanton Falls, both of which disappeared with the British victories of 1759–60.

Sulpician monk who arrived from France to minister to the sick and dying. We glimpse the young monk running around in the snow in order to fight off disease ("Anyone who saw me would have althought me crazy"), saying his breviary as he dashed from one duty to another ("but I had no other time"), and joking with Monsieur La Motte over how few men he had fit for combat, telling him, "Prepare me some wheeled stretchers and we'll take them to whatever bastion you say. They are brave now; they won't run away as they did." His robust constitution, lively intelligence, and unfailing good humor must have helped everyone tough it out in that toughest of all years.

Forts could hold the land temporarily, but only settlers could retain it. Back in Paris, that unpopular sensualist, Louis XV, took a moment from his amours to examine the various options for retaining and advancing New France. It was time to extend the French system of land tenure to the shores of Lake Champlain.

### SEIGNEURIES AND SETTLEMENTS

Imagine that you are in a boat on Lake Champlain, slowly making your way down the eastern shore. You round a corner and there, set back from the bank in an immaculate garden, lies a large eighteenth-century stone farmhouse. Its steeply pitched roof and broad front porch belie its French origins. Beyond it are miles of fields full of crops and animals, tended by the *habitants*, or farmers, who have their land from the great *seigneur*. The seigneur is not here often; he chooses to live in a mansion in Montréal, where his family can enjoy a measure of civilization. A few miles further along, another impressive mini-chateau hugs the shore of the lake; the pattern repeats itself along the banks. There is a snug tidiness to this whole section of New France.

This was the fantasy the French government hoped to make manifest in the Champlain Valley. The French had been slow to switch from an economy of extraction and trade to one of production and development. By the early eighteenth century, the English, by contrast, were threatening to get the upper hand in North America precisely because thousands of English farmers were willing to come here to stay. England no longer had to bring all its military recruits across the Atlantic, because it could tap the boys of Massachusetts and Connecticut. In the 1730s, the French began taking the idea of settling the future Vermont more seriously.

Settlement would not be possible without trade and protection, so the French decided to refurbish an abandoned trading post built at Chimney Point by a Dutchman from the Hudson Valley in 1690. In 1731 they made it into a real stockade, 100 feet square, and called it the Fort at Pointe à la Chevelure. Opposite this, they would build a large fort on the Crown Point (New York) side of the lake, so the two posts could guard Champlain

Thomas Davies, a professional soldier and Sunday painter, was with Sir Jeffrey Amherst when he took over Fort St. Frédéric in 1759. He tossed off this watercolor, thought to be an accurate depiction of the condition of the French fort at the time of the British occupation.

at its narrowest point. The plan was to use the seigneurial system to develop communities around the two forts; by 1734, the western complex, now called Fort St. Frédéric, was imposing.

The seigneurial system—used throughout New France—provided a land grant in exchange for promising the king loyalty, military service, corvée (days of service to maintain the king's roads), and taxes. The seigneur was also required to create subgrants, to populate the region. During the mid-1730s, Louis XV granted 16 seigneuries in the Champlain Valley on both sides of the lake. Each was very large; the southern one on the Vermont side, granted to the king's enterprising bureaucrat, Gilles Hocquart, Intendant of Canada, boasted 12 miles of frontage on the lake and ran 15 miles inland. Outlines of the seigneuries can be seen on Simon Metcalfe's 1767 map of Lake Champlain.

What would the architecture of the Champlain Valley have looked like if the seigneuries had been settled successfully? The lakeshore probably would have been dotted with houses in the eighteenth-century French-Canadian style, like this one located near Montréal. Typically, these were built of stone and featured steeply pitched gabled roofs and tall, narrow windows.

Unfortunately for France's future prospects in the region, only two tiny communities emerged from this system. In Alburg, the Seigneury of Foucault soon had a number of inhabitants, a stone windmill, and a Catholic chapel. At Chimney Point, where the Champlain Bridge alights on the Vermont side of the lake today, a little settlement grew up, consisting largely of retired soldiers from the fort, who were given land by the king to settle there with their families. Here, land on the lakeshore had been cleared and settled for a distance of three to four miles going north from the fort, and most settlers lived in rough wooden houses with stone chimneys.

In 1749, a young Swedish naturalist, Peter Kalm, was sent to North America to search for useful new plants that would be hardy in his homeland's cold climate. Visiting Fort St. Frédéric, he turned his botanist's eye for detail onto the local residents:

> *The soldiers had built houses round the fort on grounds allotted to them, but most of these habitations were no more than wretched cottages...of boards, standing perpendicularly close to each other. The roofs were of wood. The crevices were stopped up with clay to keep the room warm. The floor was commonly clay, or a black limestone, except the place where the fire was to lie, which was made of grey stones. ...Dampers had never been used here and the people had no glass in their windows.*

Despite the poor state of the housing, the French Crown knew what most governments know when they send soldiers to lonely and remote outposts: you have to make it worth their while. Kalm was amazed by the perquisites:

> *The soldiers enjoy such advantages here as they are not allowed in every part of the world. Those who formed the garrison of this place had a very plentiful allowance from their government. They get every day a pound and a half of wheat bread. They likewise get pease, bacon, and salt meat in plenty. ...The soldiers had each a small garden without the fort...and some of them had built summer-houses in them, and planted all kinds of pot-herbs. ...the lake close by is full of fish, and the woods abound with birds and animals, those amongst them who choose to be diligent may live extremely well and very grand in regard to food. ...the King presents each dismissed soldier with a piece of land.*

By the 1740s, there were probably around a thousand French living in the Champlain Valley, but an old soldiers' haven was not what the King had in mind when he granted the seigneuries. The plan had been a dismal failure. Louis XV could not persuade his seigneurs to settle a hundred miles from nowhere, and the seigneurs seemed to have little luck finding settlers who were willing to reproduce the land tenure of France in the Champlain Valley. Fees paid to seigneurs were low, but French immigrants preferred to stay in more settled areas rather than clear land for a lord. The main thrust of French expansion remained tied to the fur trade. Most of the grants were revoked in 1741, but the ghosts of the seigneuries remained on the land. As late as the mid-nineteenth century, it was said that on the Addison shore "the remnants of old cellars and gardens [are] still to be seen." There, a number of long, rectangular lots of the French sort go back from the lake: the last vestiges of the seigneuries. The age of great estates on the lake would have to wait until families like the Webbs, at Shelburne Farms, built their compounds in the nineteenth century.

It is still possible to see the ruins of Fort St. Frédéric and Sir Jeffrey Amherst's subsequent establishment at Crown Point. The photos here show a section of the French bastions (top) and the nearby ruins of the Crown Point British officers' quarters (bottom). Most of the fort burned in a 1773 fire—just before it might have done the British some good in the American Revolution.

Sara Gregg

## JOHN BULL'S WILDERNESS: THE ENGLISH IN NATURE

> *The brute creation are his property,*
> *Subservient to his will, and for him made.*
> *As hurtful these he kills, as useful those*
> *Preserves; their sole and arbitrary king.*
>
> —William Somervile, 1735

While the French sought to recreate traditional reciprocal land tenure arrangements in North America with little success, the English turned to their own very different traditions. Secure in their God-given mandate to transform the earth to suit man's needs, they had always made colonization their top priority. A Frenchman looking at the wilderness was often content to go hunting there, while an Englishman tended to be more eager to carve it into productive units of settlement, whatever its topography might be. The English came in groups intent upon transforming the wilderness into farming communities, and only then looked around for what they might extract on the way.

As the French and Indian Wars heated up, the English colonists, realizing they could not compete with the Native facility for forest fighting, fell back on their own military traditions. If France was going to fortify the Champlain Valley and encourage settlement on the seigneuries, England would parallel them on the east by fortifying the Connecticut River Valley. They began by building Fort Dummer in the summer of 1724, the first permanent English settlement in the future Vermont. Built by Lieutenant Timothy Dwight, the fort was located on the western shore of the Connecticut River, well-situated for protecting the English settlements in northern Massachusetts. It boasted a wooden blockhouse, 180 feet square, and soon bustled with fur traders, forest scouts, Indians, and local settlers. Under its protection, a few adventurous settlers began moving into the Connecticut River Valley in the 1730s. This may have been premature, for they were very vulnerable to attack.

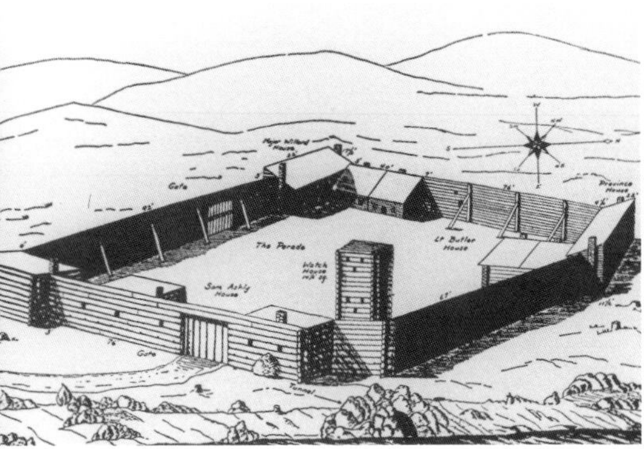

The first long-term English settlement in the future Vermont was Fort Dummer, built in 1724 by Lieutenant Timothy Dwight, whose son would later become the president of Yale College. The Brattleboro site of the Fort was consigned to a watery grave when the Vernon Dam was built in 1908.

For some of these English families, their home really was their castle, doubling as a fortress in times of turmoil. Native people felt they were fighting to retain their traditional way of life in the face of European encroachment. To the settlers, equally convinced of their rights to an "empty" land no one seemed to own, the Indians were black devils, the stuff of nightmares, the fearsome "other." Vermont's great compiler of settlement narratives, Abby Hemenway, relayed the story of the Kilburns in her account of the history of Rockingham:

> *John Kilburn's house which partook somewhat of the nature of a fort without being one, was nearly two miles further north, located on the low terrace. A desperate Indian fight occurred here Aug. 17, 1755. Four hundred Indians demanded of Kilburn that he and his party should surrender. But, although his force, all told, consisted of but four men and two women, he indignantly refused to surrender, and in reply to the chief who promised "good quarter," he replied, "Begone, you black rascal, or I'll quarter you!"*
>
> *The fight immediately commenced. The Indians fired on the house from the high terrace on the east, and the roof was soon completely riddled. The women worked with a will loading the guns, of which they had a number, and casting bullets. They melted up their*

> *pewter spoons and dishes, and when these were exhausted they suspended blankets in the chamber to catch the Indian balls which were sent back with deadly effect into the savage ranks. The unequal contest continued all the afternoon till nearly dark, when the Indians, thinking that Kilburn must have a regiment of men in the house, gave up the fight and returned to Canada.*

While this account rings with B-movie exaggeration, the settlers often faced real danger. Frontier life—even within the walls of a fort—could not offer enough protection when the number of settlers was so small, yet larger numbers could not be persuaded to come without more protection. The English came to realize that the only way to gain security for settlement was to win their claim to the land once and for all. Their strengthening position in southern New England had made them ready for total war.

Sir Jeffrey Amherst was the famously methodical British general in command of the army that finally defeated the French in Canada and the Champlain Valley in 1759–1760.

It was the English success in settling their colonies in southern New England that finally gave them the advantage over the French. The speed with which they accomplished this may have been due to the simplicity of the English system of land tenure in her colonies. Strong believers in the absolute property rights of the landowner, the English divided the land into lots, used various ways of doling it out to individuals, and then gave them the right to do what they wanted on their own ground. It was a method of land distribution that offered incentives to transform the most land in the shortest period of time. It also provided the English with a large body of potential militiamen within a couple of hundred miles of the fighting.

Spearheading the English military arrangements was the appropriately methodical General Sir Jeffrey Amherst. While the French might be good at guerrilla warfare, roughing it in the wilderness was not Amherst's cup of tea; his strategy was simply to assemble as much power as possible before going forward to claim his ultimate victory. In this spirit, after capturing the French superfort at Ticonderoga in 1759, Amherst began two major building projects to help ensure British domination of the northern woodlands. One was a huge new fort at Crown Point, the largest the British ever built on the North American continent (although it was never to be used in war). The greater accomplishment, begun in 1759, was the building of the Crown Point Military Road. It provides a perfect example of the bullish British attitude toward the landscape. Amherst was not one for learning woodland guerrilla warfare and found it inefficient to bring troops from lower New England up the Champlain Valley via Lake George. To fight in his accustomed manner, in October he ordered the building of the first road ever to breach the Green Mountains. It would connect the Connecticut River Valley with the Champlain Valley, running from the mouth of the Black River opposite the Fort at No. 4, following the Black River Valley up to the headwaters of the Otter Creek, then along the Creek to Brandon, where it split, with one branch going straight west to a spot near Larabee's Point, opposite Fort Ticonderoga, the other coming out at Chimney Point.

Building the road was an impressive feat of engineering, utilizing the simplest of tools. Major John Hawkes and 250 men with axes started tromping and hacking their way east from Chimney Point. Conditions on the road crew were appalling, with the men having to take long breaks because of lack of food. On November 6, 1759, Sergeant Robert Webster wrote despairingly in his journal, "Our bread is just gone. We haven't had but one biscuit a day this four or five days. ...This day we lay still whilst just night and then went to work without any bread to eat. Ammedown killed a beaver with my hatchet." Yet they made it most of the way, with the last 30 miles being finished by 800 soldiers coming west from the Connecticut River the following spring.

The Crown Point Military Road, still plainly visible in this late nineteenth-century photo, largely followed the course of a traditional Abenaki east–west route over the Green Mountains, near the paths of today's Routes 103 and 131.

As they were clearing mile after mile, only about three hundred Europeans were living in the future Vermont, all of them in the Connecticut River Valley between Fort Dummer and the Fort at No. 4. For people who knew the grinding difficulty of clearing even an acre, the sight of the great rough road cutting for mile after mile through the dark forests must have been awe-inspiring. But the Crown Point Military Road's significance would be less for the soldiers than for the settlers.

The final French defeat came on the Plains of Abraham at Québec City in September 1759; in the Treaty of Paris, signed in 1763, the French formally gave up their claim to North America. Military might had finally determined who had the power to clear this land of all intruders so that the victors could transform it in their own image. Even Louis XV's own trusted emissary in New France, Pierre François Xavier de Charlevoix, gave the moral victory to the English:

> *The English planter amasses wealth and never makes any superfluous expense; the French inhabitant...enjoys what he has acquired and often makes a parade of what he does not possess. The former labors for his posterity; the latter leaves his offspring facing the same necessities he was himself at his first setting out and to extricate themselves as best they can. English Americans are averse to war, because they have a great deal to lose; they take no care to manage the Indians from a belief that they stand in no need of them. French youth, for very different reasons, abominate all thoughts of peace and live well with the natives, whose esteem they easily gain in time of war, and whose friendship they hold at all times.*

Major Robert Rogers, looking in this contemporary portrait so coolly debonair, was a crafty Indian fighter who benefited from knowing the ways of his adversaries.

## MAJOR ROGERS GOES NATIVE

Many English settlers feared that the New England environment would make them "uncivilized" before they had a chance to "civilize" it. But those who were born on the eighteenth-century American frontier soon came to know that understanding native ways was their best hope for survival. Major Robert Rogers—leader of the crack wilderness fighters known as Rogers' Rangers and dubbed "The White Devil" by the Abenaki—credited the knowledge gleaned from his Native American enemies for much of his subsequent success:

*Such, in particular, was the situation of the place in which I received my early education, a frontier town in the province of New Hampshire, where I could hardly avoid obtaining some knowledge of the manners, customs, and language of the Indians, as many of them resided in the neighborhood, and daily conversed and dealt with the English. Between the years 1743 and 1755 my manner of life was such as led me to a general acquaintance both with the British and French settlements in North America, and especially with the uncultivated desert, the mountains, valleys, rivers, lakes, and several passes that lay between and contiguous to the said settlements. Nor did I content myself with the accounts I received from Indians, or the information of hunters, but traveled over large tracts of the country myself, which tended not more to gratify my curiosity, than to inure me to hardships, and, without vanity I may say, to qualify me for the very service I have since been employed in.*

---

The greatest losers in this conflict may not have been the French. The fortunes of their Abenaki allies were directly linked to the French cause. The Native people had fought alongside the French to retain control of their lands and their way of life with grim desperation, often retreating to Swanton, Missisquoi, and St. Francis, on the St. Lawrence in Québec, to regroup. They had spread terror for decades, successfully preventing mass English immigration into the future Vermont. Now Amherst sent his most trusted woodland fighters, Major Robert Rogers and his Rangers, to try to break the Abenaki for good. In the well-known Rogers Raid, the Rangers attacked the Abenaki settlement at Odanak (St. Francis) in southern Québec, killing men, women, and children and burning the village. It was a cruel blow for these embattled people.

The English triumphed in the French and Indian wars by sheer strength of numbers, organization, and technology; not by any fine-tuned understanding of the environment. They were able to claim this great tract of North America because their settlement in southern New England provided a seemingly endless supply of young fighters who had already beaten back the woods in their own farmyards. The British army won a European-style victory in a European-style battle in the town setting of Québec City precisely because they had already mastered the skills needed to give frontier America a European face.

The Commander of the British forces in northern New England in 1777 was the dashing "Gentleman Johnny" Burgoyne. After taking Fort Ticonderoga and terrorizing the Champlain Valley, his forces went down to defeat at the decisive battle of Saratoga. The handsome general later had a successful career as a London playwright. This romantic portrait by Sir Joshua Reynolds, painted circa 1766, shows John Burgoyne in the uniform of the 16th Light Dragoons, after he led an earlier, and more successful, campaign in Portugal in 1762.

## THE STAGES OF VERMONT SETTLEMENT

In the years after the French and Indian Wars, dinner tables all over southern New England were enlivened by conversation about going to the territory that would be Vermont. Fathers told their families they were going, brothers tried to talk brothers into going, fiancées wept at the suggestion of going. The prospect of having your own farm was tempting when Massachusetts and Connecticut had become so crowded.

Vermont was not settled at a steady rate between 1760 and 1791, but it is striking to realize that settlements had reached most of the state in the 40 short years between 1760 and 1800. New residents arrived in staggering numbers. The population went from a few thousand at the time of the peace in 1760 to 85,539 in 1791 and 154,465 in 1800. No wonder one historian has referred to this as the "swarming period."

The rapid increase in population is even more impressive considering that it came to a virtual halt for nearly a decade during the American Revolution. By 1775 the war had come to the Champlain Valley; fort-building was revived with the raising of Mount Independence. In 1777, when the British General John Burgoyne took Ticonderoga, the Valley was terrorized by, in the words of Middlebury's early historian, Samuel Swift, "foraging parties of British, Indians and Tories, who plundered and carried off all such moveable property as was left behind and desired by them." By then, most of the settlers in western Vermont had retreated south, often to the Massachusetts and Connecticut towns from which they had come, to wait out the war in greater safety.

Those who did not go were in for even bigger trouble the following year, when the British decided to clear the Champlain Valley of all settlers. The Vermont Council of Safety of the new Republic of Vermont announced in April that it could not hope to protect any settlers north of a line running between Pittsford and Castleton. Some heads of families decided to stay and defend their property; many more retreated south. In the cold of November, British Major Christopher Carleton, with 100 troops and 80 Indians, unleashed a reign of terror on the Valley. Addison County was nearly leveled. When they were finished, only three buildings were still standing unburnt in Middlebury, and all around the countryside farmers were taken prisoner, leaving women and children to fend for themselves.

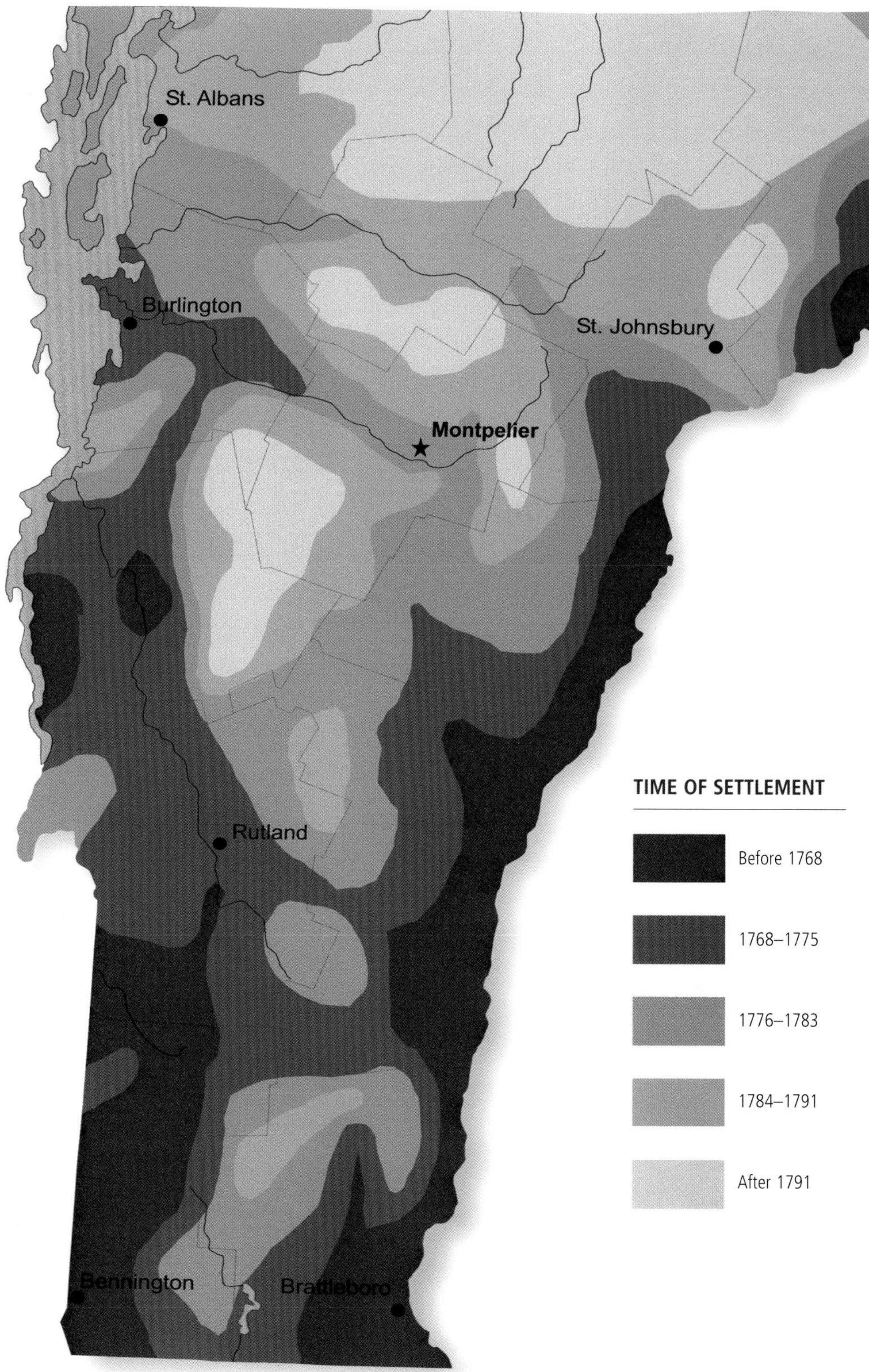


## HOW VERMONT WAS SETTLED

Vermont settlement generally moved from south to north, following the two traditional transportation routes into the state: the Taconic and Champlain Valleys on the west and the Connecticut Valley on the east. Settlers did not just hack their way into the forests willy-nilly, but tended to move out like ripples on a pond from wherever settlement had already taken place. There was also a tendency to settle valleys first, since rivers were so important to transportation in an age when Vermont could boast of only one road. It is not surprising that settlement came last to the high mountains in the middle of the state and the remote coniferous forests of the Northeast Kingdom.

When the Revolution was over, a significant new feature had been added to the landscape. In 1776 the crafty proprietor of Newbury, Colonel Jacob Bayley, managed to persuade George Washington that Vermont needed a second military road, this one running between Newbury, on the Connecticut River, and St. Jean, Québec. Bayley himself was put in charge of the project, more aware than his general of the added benefits that might accrue to him if a road was constructed that would later encourage settlers to come to his district. The road builders had got as far as Cabot when Washington realized that the route might speed enemies to them as well as friends. After the Saratoga defeat in 1777, the road again seemed plausible, and another local of some means, Colonel Moses Hazen, took over the project. This time it got as far as Hazen's Notch before the same worries overtook it. It was now 54 miles of the straightest road in Vermont, and led to a beautiful nowhere. As with the Crown Point road, the Bayley-Hazen's main significance was in encouraging settlement in the high mountains.

As the War wound down, the 1780s saw an unprecedented boom in population. Refugees who had gone south poured back into the Champlain Valley, soldiers who had worked on the Bayley-Hazen Military Road decided to return to settle, and the Republic of Vermont handed out new grants to towns like Canaan, Fayston, Glover, and Montpelier. Vermont seemed poised for greatness.

The Bayley-Hazen Military Road ended in a desolate wooded spot on the rocky ledges above Hazen's Notch. This 1935 photograph shows the terminal marker of what was, for more than a century, Vermont's straightest road.

## TO TAME THE WILDERNESS

Most Americans' knowledge of the settling of New England rests on traditional stories of the Pilgrims coming to Plymouth Rock in 1620, starting a community where they could worship together in freedom, learning to plant corn from their Indian friend, Squanto, and happily celebrating the first Thanksgiving. In the popular historical imagination, the next step saw Plymouth recreated all over New England in the form of perfect New England villages clustered around pretty greens, of clapboard houses under soaring church spires.

The settlement of Vermont, however, was different. When the first wave of settlers arrived in the north woods, Europeans had been living in southern New England for nearly 150 years—a longer time than that which separates us from the Civil War. The harsh climate, unforgiving topography, Indian terrors, and successive wars had delayed the settling of this region long past what might have been expected. (Although some wags have joked that if the Erie Canal had started taking people West in 1765 instead of 1825, there still would not be a soul living here.) Population pressures were building in southern New England, and the end of the French and Indian Wars meant that northern New England was the next place to open to settlers.

## ONE FAMILY'S TALE OF TERROR AND REUNION, 1777: THE STRONGS OF ADDISON

One of the most famous Vermont stories of the Revolution is that of John and Agnes Strong, whose post-war mansion on Lake Champlain is now owned by the D.A.R. In the summer of 1777, John was in Rutland procuring beef for an American army barely hanging on at Fort Ticonderoga. Agnes Strong was home in their lakeshore cabin when a neighbor ran in, shouting, "The Indians are coming and we are all flying! There are bateaux at the Point to take us off, and you must hurry!" The story continues:

**The elegant D.A.R. Strong House Mansion in Addison is now open to the public during the summer months.**

*Mrs. Strong was in very feeble health, totally unable to encounter hardship or fatigue; her husband away, her two oldest sons in the woods, and no one to warn or seek them. There was no way but to try and save the children that were with her. She took her youngest, a babe of six months (Cyrus), and putting him in a sack, with his head and shoulders out, fastened him on the back of her eldest daughter, and making up a bundle for each of the other children of the most necessary clothing, started them for the Point, charging them not to loiter or wait for her, and she would overtake them. After putting out the fire she closed the house, leaving the breakfast-table standing. ...She travelled on as fast as she was able until she came to the north bank of Hospital Creek. Here, entirely exhausted, she sat down, when Spalding, of Panton, who had waited to see all off, and also the approach of the foe, came riding at full gallop up the road, and seeing her sitting where she was, said, "Are you crazy? The Indians are in sight,—the lake is covered, and the woods are full of them!" She told him she could go no farther. He dismounted, and placing her on the pillion, remounted, and putting his horse to his speed, arrived just as the last bateau, containing her children, was putting off. ...*

*Asa and Samuel [the Strongs' two older boys], as they returned towards night, saw, by the columns of smoke coming up from every house, that the Indians must have been there. They hid themselves until dark, and then, cautiously approaching, found their house a blazing ruin. Believing that the family had escaped, they retraced their steps, and made the best of their way east towards Otter Creek...in about a week found their mother and the rest of the children. ...*

*After weeks of fruitless search, [John Strong] had almost despaired of finding them, when one evening, weary and footsore, he called at a log house in Dorset, Vt., for entertainment for the night. A flickering light from the dying embers only rendered things more indistinguishable. He had just taken a seat, when a smart little woman, with a pail of milk came in, and said: "Moses, can't you take the gentleman's hat?" That voice! He sprang towards her. "Agnes!" And she, with outstretched arms, "John, Oh John!"...Smiles of happiness and tears of joy mingled freely, for a father and husband was restored as from the dead.*

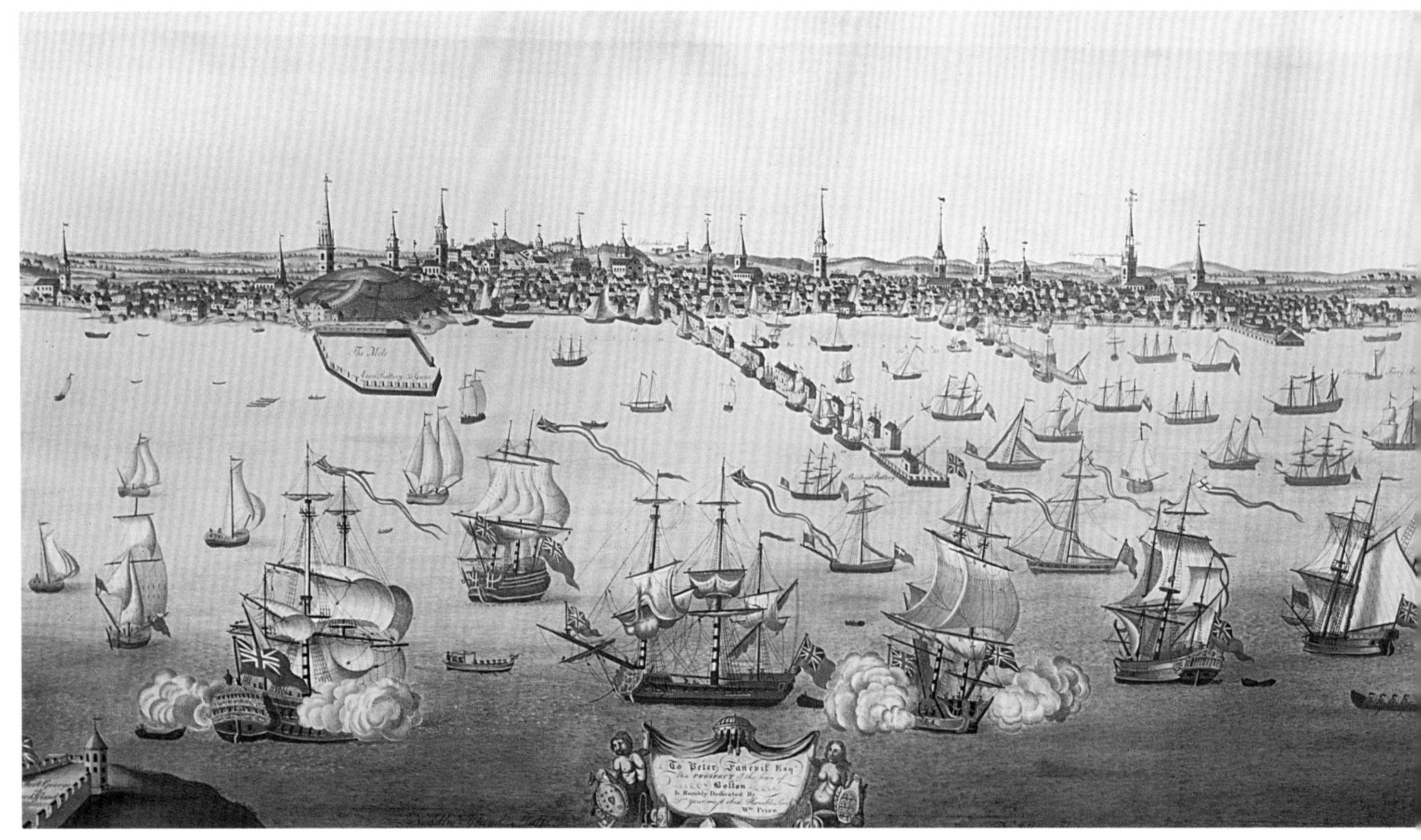

The world that many settlers were leaving behind in southern New England was becoming ever more crowded. One especially bustling port was captured by William Burgis in his 1723 "Southeast View of Ye Great Town of Boston."

Comparing eighteenth-century Vermont to the Massachusetts of 130 years earlier, it becomes apparent that assumptions had undergone a great shift. The first English in North America came in organized groups who had asked for grants in order to found church-based communities. They were expected to settle in towns, with everyone living close together so that both their external safety and their internal conduct could be strictly monitored. Fields were doled out on the outskirts of the village, in a pattern reminiscent of England, where farmers left their village homes and made their ways to the fields each morning. Home lots of less than four acres were laid out around a green space where the meeting house was built, signifying that the church was the center of the community. Initially, some fields were farmed in common, the residents deciding together what and when to plant. In these small towns, there was a distinct division between village and countryside. Villages were a physical representation of "community," as people clustered together to share their daily lives, moving outside only to work their fields.

Vermont grew otherwise, although the results look remarkably similar today. The large towns (or townships) of Vermont were granted to proprietors, people with political influence who hoped to turn a profit. Most

settlers purchased their stakes as individuals or in small units of family members, often near those of people from back home (especially in southern Vermont). Proprietors were bound to set aside designated lots for church, minister, and school, but the religious provision followed the settlement instead of preceding it. Some proprietors took an interest in the layout of the village, but others sold off lots as quickly as possible and left the settlers to sort things out. It quickly became clear that most settlers preferred to live in the countryside on their own fields, rather than waste time going out to them from a village each day. People wanted their own farms, and with many of these 50 to 100 acres in size, they were necessarily spread out on the landscape. No pretense of communal farming was proposed. The break between village and countryside was at first far less distinct than it had been in southern New England, as a village model of settlement was replaced with one that was distinctly rural. Early Vermonters escaped the hothouse atmosphere of the Puritan village, spreading out across the land in a more loose-knit fashion. Their new communities provided space for greater freedom and independence than they could have hoped to exercise in those they'd left. There was a spatial dimension to Vermont's early revolutionary republicanism.

The great Hudson River School painter, Thomas Cole, provided a vision of what settlers were creating in the wilderness of northern New England in his "Home in the Woods," painted in the mid-nineteenth century. The foreground acknowledges the environmental devastation they could wreak, but the tidy log house and robust family group imply that results were worth the cost. Cole often worked crosses into his paintings; here a homemade one can be seen at the base of the vine creeping up the cabin front, offering its own benediction on the scene.

Even though the place was now relatively safe, its geography filled late eighteenth-century European souls with a mixture of dread and excitement. Upon seeing Killington Peak, John Graham felt that it was "designed by nature more for the habitation of beasts of prey, than for the abode of man," and yet pronounced that "the top resembles a sugar loaf, and altogether it has an appearance of elegance and grandeur." To Luigi Castiglioni, an Italian nobleman traveling the Crown Point Road, "The tedium of that toilsome journey was increased by the gloom of the forest and by the disagreeable smell of the swamps." In battling all this fecund nature, historian Samuel Williams knew who would come out on top, for "In the formation of the mountains, rivers, vegetables, and animals, the powers of nature appear to rise in a steady and beautiful progress. This progress seems to be completed in the production of a rational, moral, and accountable animal. This animal is Man."

The men and women who settled Vermont had no doubt that it was right for people to claim the land. English philosophers like John Locke argued that God gave the land to mankind to be used, and working the land gave one an absolute right to own it. Since the Indians did not seem to be developing the countryside (out of what Europeans deemed a natural "laziness"), it was fair that someone else should come and make it productive. The English longed to see it covered in lush fields, cattle-bedecked pastures, and tidy farmhouses—the very features so many of us delight in here today. Why should the land sit empty, when it could be doing some good for a hardworking, well-meaning family? It was time to claim the land.

---

**John Locke (1632–1704), shown here in a French illustration, was a physician, a politician, and one of the greatest English philosophers of his age.**

## WORK IT AND IT IS YOURS: JOHN LOCKE AND PROPERTY

During the age of settlement, Europeans, so used to their own crowded and managed landscapes, were fascinated by the great expanses of seemingly empty land in the New World, which sparked provocative thoughts about how human civilizations, political systems, and economies had evolved from that original Eden they called "the state of nature." The influential English philosopher John Locke thought that in a place where there was land enough for all, you earned your right to property through labor. This also provided a rationalization for taking the land from the Indians, who had not "improved" it:

> *God gave the World to Men in Common; but since he gave it them for their benefit, and the greatest Conveniencies of Life they were capable to draw from it, it cannot be supposed he meant it should always remain common and uncultivated. He gave it to the use of the Industrious and Rational, (and Labour was to be his Title to it;) not to the Fancy or Covetousness of the Quarrelsom and Contentious. He that had as good left for his Improvement, as was already taken up, needed not complain, enough not to meddle with what was already improved by another's Labour.*
>
> —"Property," *Second Treatise on Government* (1690)

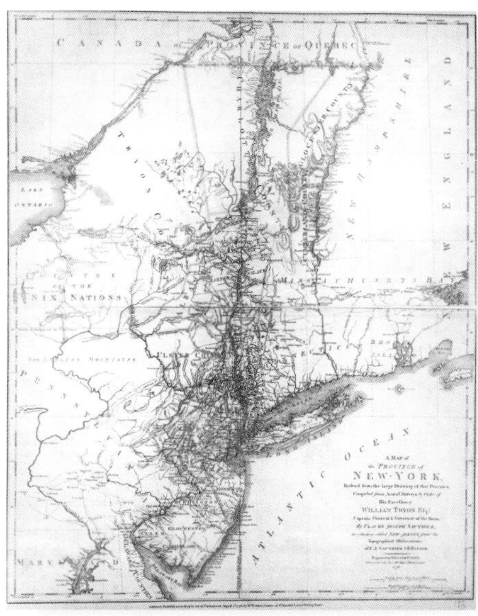


The map at left represents Governor Benning Wentworth's view of his universe, with a huge New Hampshire extending west to New York; the cartographers, Joseph Blanchard and Samuel Langdon, were forced to base much of their decidedly odd map on second-hand information. In contrast, the map above—produced for Governor William Tryon by renowned French cartographer Claude Joseph Sautier—shows the New York claim to the region in a fashion that is marginally more accurate.

## THE FIGHT OVER THE GRANTS

After 1760, the future Vermont was to become the latest of North America's "frontiers." But there was still one issue to be resolved before mass immigration could take place. Everyone agreed that the area was controlled by the English, but which English had the right to organize settlement? Few topics in Vermont history have received as much attention as the conflicts between the Green Mountain Boys and the "Yorkers" over whether Vermont was part of New Hampshire or New York. In simplest terms, it was a fight over who would get to control (and profit from) land speculation in these opening territories: the governor of New Hampshire or the governor of New York. For a young couple clearing a farm in Arlington or Brattleboro, there was disturbing uncertainty over whether they had clear title to their land. The resulting tension led to widespread social and political upheaval, the eventual declaration of Vermont independence, and, ultimately, Vermont's rebirth as the fourteenth state in the fledgling United States of America.

The fight over the grants meant that the future Vermont and New Hampshire were settled under the cloud of one of the greatest and most corrupt land distribution free-for-alls in North American history. This was partly a function of the timing of the settlement of northern New England. Vermont and New Hampshire were initially settled during the unstable period of time between the end of the French and Indian Wars and the American Revolution. This led to confusion over who had the authority to grant land, the amassing of huge tracts of land in the hands of speculators, and its disorderly distribution and uncontrolled growth.

The mechanics of how a Vermont grant was procured and distributed appeared simple. For example, on November 2, 1761, Benning Wentworth

## THE FIGHT OVER THE GRANTS; Or, a Short Summary of How a Large Stretch of Woods Became the State of Vermont

Governor Benning Wentworth of New Hampshire

**Before 1741.** New Hampshire, long a province of Massachusetts Bay, becomes a separate colony under its new governor, Benning Wentworth. He is unclear where New Hampshire's western boundary lies, but knows where he'd like to see it.

**1749–50.** Wentworth writes to New York asking where they consider their eastern boundary to be. Receiving no immediate reply, he grants a patent for the town of Bennington, at the extreme western edge of the disputed territory.

**1749–1764.** Wentworth grants nearly half of the land mass of the future Vermont—129 towns (113 of these are still towns).

**1764.** King George III finally replies that New York extends as far east as the Connecticut River—a real blow to the claims of New Hampshire, although the king did not actually invalidate grants already made. Wentworth's granting prospects seem to be worthless.

King George III of Great Britain

**1765.** New York plays hardball—making conflicting grants (called patents), telling those who have Wentworth grants that they will have to repurchase them, and sending out their own surveyors.

**1765–1776.** New York issues 107 patents in the future Vermont (only five of these are still towns).

**1766.** Benning Wentworth resigns in a corruption scandal and is replaced by his nephew, John Wentworth, as governor of New Hampshire.

**1767.** George III says New York cannot make grants until the territorial dispute is settled.

**1768–1772.** New York starts creating counties in Vermont, angering the Hampshire supporters, including the Allen brothers.

**1770.** New York courts refuse to honor the rights of the New Hampshire grant owners. The Green Mountain Boys, led by Ethan Allen, organize in Bennington and Arlington to resist the claims of the Yorkers—by force, if necessary. Beginning of period of threats and confrontations between the Green Mountain Boys and the Yorkers. Green Mountain signed a grant turning over 25,040 acres of land to 62 Connecticut-based proprietors who proposed the building of a town to be called New Haven. The proprietors were given five years to find settlers who would cultivate at least 10 percent of their acreage. It also conveyed the right to hold a market and two fairs, while requiring that the proprietors "carefully preserve" all white and other pine trees suitable for ship masts for the Royal Navy, set aside a tract of land in the center of the township to create a village, pay rents of one ear of Indian corn annually, and, for 10 years, one shilling per 100 acres annually. They were required also to reserve five town lots for the Church of England (Wentworth was an Episcopalian), the Society for the Propagation of the Gospel in Foreign Parts (the Church's mission organization), the first settled

Boys throw Yorkers off their farms, rough up judges, scare off surveyors.

**1774.** The "Bloody Act" is declared by New York, giving carte blanche for Green Mountain Boys to be killed on sight.

**1775.** Americans turning against Britain. The Green Mountain Boys interested in how this conflict might help get the Yorkers out of Vermont. Clashes get violent when two settlers opposing the convening of the New York court in the Grants are shot and killed in the "Westminster Massacre." Ethan Allen and the Green Mountain Boys take Fort Ticonderoga for the rebels. First convention to discuss Vermont independence held at Dorset.

**1776.** Vermont not safe for Tories.

**1777.** Sixth Convention at Westminster finally declares Vermont an independent state.

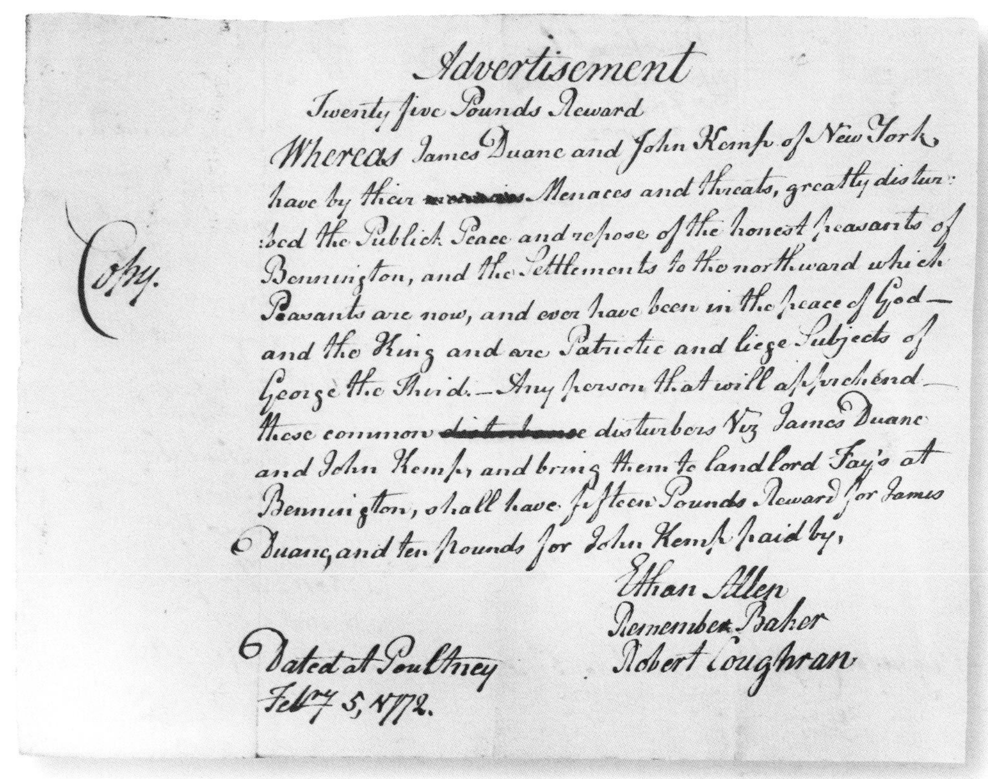

Advertisement
Twenty five Pounds Reward
Whereas James Duane and John Kemp of New York have by their Menaces and threats, greatly disturbed the Publick Peace and repose of the honest peasants of Bennington, and the Settlements to the northward which peasants are now, and ever have been in the peace of God and the King and are Patriotic and liege Subjects of George the Third.— Any person that will apprehend these common disturbers Viz James Duane and John Kemp, and bring them to landlord Fay's at Bennington, shall have fifteen Pounds Reward for James Duane and ten pounds for John Kemp paid by,

Ethan Allen
Remember Baker
Robert Cochran

Dated at Poultney Feb 5, 1772.

Copy.

**1778.** Thomas Chittenden is elected the first governor of the independent state of Vermont.

**1780.** United States Congress will not honor Vermont's independence or give her military aid. Disgruntled Allen brothers start secret negotiations to join Vermont to Canada and ally with Britain.

**1790.** Fight with the Yorkers finally ends with Vermont paying $30,000 to settle all claims under the New York patents.

**The Green Mountain Boys offered bounties on their Yorker enemies, attorney James Duane and General John Tabor Kemp, New York Attorney General.**

## IRA ALLEN: MARKETER OF ALL HE SURVEYED

This likeness of Ira Allen comes from a 1797 locket miniature, painted in watercolor on ivory; the artist is believed to have been Edward Greene Malbone. We do not know what Ethan Allen looked like, since no contemporary views of him have survived.

Modern marketers might learn a trick or two from Ira Allen. As a land speculator, he knew all the ins and outs and was not in the least ashamed of bragging about it. In his *Autobiography*, he tells of how, in the fall of 1772, he fleeced a group of proprietors into buying a tract of worthless farmland called "Mansfield," the future site of Stowe and Underhill:

*My next object was to make a map of the township of Mansfield, with the allotments & survey bills thereof. I so completed the map; but turning my attention to the field books, that Captain Remember Baker and I had kept, a difficulty arose in my mind, for my object was to sell out of Mansfield and if possible get the ninety pounds for the survey. A great proportion of the corners of said lots were made on spruce or fir timber, and if I described them as such, it would show the poorness of the town. In my survey bills, I*

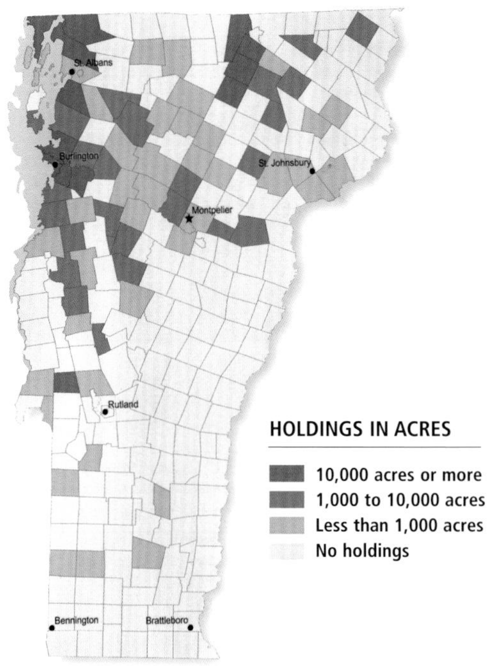


Through his Onion River Company, Ira Allen's landholdings once included the mammoth acreages depicted on this map.

minister, schools, and a particularly good lot for Governor Wentworth himself (he eventually amassed about 65,000 acres through all of his grants).

Proprietors should not be confused with settlers. In New Haven, a few proprietors lived in the township, but that was not the usual scenario. Most proprietors were rich out-of-staters, land speculators hoping to make a fast return on their investments by selling land to homesteaders. In New Haven, each proprietor got about 346 acres of land, and all their holdings were laid out in 50- or 100-acre lots (Luther Evarts was paid 40 acres for doing the surveying). These they would sell to potential settlers down in Connecticut for whatever they could get for them. (The going rate for good Vermont farmland was about a dollar an acre in this period, half payable in cash up front and half in farm produce in two years, with interest.) New Haven was ready to go on the market.

*called spruce and fir gumwood, a name not known by the people of Sharon [Connecticut], where the proprietors lived. They asked what kind of timber gumwood was. I told them tall straight trees that had a gum... I took aside the brother of one of the principal proprietors, who was an ignorant fellow and owned two rights. I tried to buy his rights, but he dared not sell them without first consulting his brother. By this the proprietors all got the alarm that I wished to purchase, and land in Mansfield was considered of consequence. I was urged to sell back to the proprietors the twenty rights I had bought, which I did, and obtained the ninety pounds for the survey, &c., which I considered of more consequence than the whole town. I returned to my brothers and had a hearty laugh with Heman and Zimri, on informing them respecting the gumwood.*

## GOOD BORDERS MAKE GOOD NEIGHBORS: SURVEYING THE LAND

In the fall of 1786, a young man named Eben Judd was given the job of making the first survey of Vermont's wildest corner, Essex County. It would be hard to find tougher work, walking the bounds of the property in a perfectly straight line no matter where they led, through dark forests, over jagged rocks, through clouds of blood-sucking black flies. Even the provisions could be dangerous: lodging at one house along their route, Judd and his assistants had to "eat old hasty pudding that the old man had made a week before." The surveyors blazed marks on trees as they went, with "witness trees" to mark the corners. It was physically taxing but also exhilarating work, as they were the first non-natives to see some of Vermont's now-fabled views.

Despite the physical hardships, the greatest danger to surveyors often came from settlers who had staked their claims and begun to clear before official boundaries had been set. Many settlers came up to Vermont without having bought land and proceeded to clear a spot for themselves, unknowingly following the dictates of philosopher John Locke, earning a right to the land by making it productive. When the results of a survey were revealed, people often stood to lose all or part of the land they had been working so hard to clear. This often led to threats of violence against the surveyors. Judd ran into just this problem during his survey of Maidstone, when "Just at sunset met a company of men on a piece of land that Mr. Shoff lived on. They held our chainmen, and said if we went on they would break our heads." He and his crew were physically detained by these disgruntled settlers, until Judd promised that he would speak to the proprietor on their behalf: "We compromised and they agreed to delay the matter till after the Surveyor's meeting, by our promising to use our influence to have each settler have 20 acres of meadow and 80 acres of upland."

The risks of surveying were richly rewarded. The proprietors often paid for the service in land; it is not surprising that the wiliest of the surveyors also became land speculators. The surveyor of Barnet made £139.6 for his pains in 1773. Other surveyors chose to take their pay in land, as Luther Evarts did in New Haven. And like him, many surveyors were also proprietors, despite an inherent conflict of interest.

The uncontrolled state of land speculation in the region allowed a number of surveyor/proprietors to amass great holdings, as exemplified in the career of that extraordinary character, Ira Allen. His brother Ethan is best known in his role as founder of the Green Mountain Boys, but it is arguable that Ira exerted far more influence as a speculator. Born in Connecticut, Ira was the youngest of the six Allen brothers and caught the fever for land in the New Hampshire grants. After deciding that it might be lucrative to learn surveying, he used this skill and his political wiles to amass huge numbers of acres for himself. By the spring of 1773, the 22-year-old Ira, Ethan, and three other partners had decided that the Champlain Valley held great commercial promise and managed to procure proprietorial rights to 45,000 acres of it under the name of the Onion River Company ("onion" being the translation of the Indian word *Winooski*). Within the next few years, Ira Allen became Vermont's Treasurer and its first Surveyor-General, which gave him even more scope for his freehanded wheeling and dealing. He soon gained even more land through rewards for political service, shady purchases of land confiscated for non-payment of taxes (so what if no one had bothered to advertise these public offerings?), and the development of earlier purchases. He would eventually control over 300,000 acres of the fledgling Vermont.

Despite his civic virtues as a founder of the University of Vermont and a promoter of the state, Ira's lackadaisical relationship to the law finally caught up with him. In 1795 he was tried in London for running guns for the Vermont militia. The case spilled over to Paris, where he was imprisoned for two years. Fighting all these charges took enormous amounts of money. Upon his return to Vermont, he was sued by the heirs of the other partners of the Onion River Company and lost most of his remaining assets. He had already been removed from his post as Surveyor-General for corruption—no mean feat in an era where standards were not high. By 1803, the man who had once been the most powerful in the state was forced into debtor's prison in Burlington. He escaped and left Vermont forever, dying almost forgotten in Philadelphia in 1814. It was a career that could only have happened in upper New England, with its easily abused patterns of land distribution and lack of legal and communal controls.

Asher B. Durand's "View of Rutland, Vermont, 1837" (above) shows a landscape as idyllic as the one Rowley described.

### COME TO VERMONT!

*The land included within [Vermont's borders], is of a very fertile nature, fitted for all the purposes and productions of agriculture. The soil is deep, and of a dark color; rich, moist, warm, and loamy. It bears corn and other kinds of grain, in large quantities, as soon as it is cleared of the wood, without any ploughing or preparation.*

—Samuel Williams, 1794

Once a grant was procured and land surveyed, proprietors were eager to find settlers to purchase it. The marketing of Vermont as a bucolic paradise has a long history. To encourage settlers to come to a place with a rugged and forbidding reputation, Vermont's earliest spin doctors were working overtime in the late eighteenth century. Samuel Williams's description of the soil would probably not be accurate anywhere east of Ohio. His contemporary, John

## AN EARLY ATTEMPT AT MARKETING VERMONT

In the early 1770s, a popular Rutland poet and promoter, Thomas Rowley, decided that a civic poem might inspire more people to move to the Rutland area. It was obviously produced in a time before there were laws about truth in advertising.

TO RUTLAND GO

West of the Mountain Green
Lies Rutland fair;
The best that e'er was seen
For soil and air:
Kind zephyr's pleasant breeze,
Whispers among the trees,
Where men may live at ease,
With prudent care.

Here cows give milk to eat,
By nature fed;
Our fields afford good wheat,
And corn for bread.
Here sugar trees they stand,
Which sweeten all our land,
We have them at our hand,
Be not afraid.

The pigeon, goose, and duck
They fill our beds
The beaver, coon, and fox,
They crown our heads.
The harmless moose and deer,
Are food and clothes to wear;
Nature could do no more
For any land.

There's many a pleasant town
Lies in this vale,
Where you may settle down;
You need not fail
To make a fine estate,
If you are not too late,
You need not fear the fate,
But come along.

Graham, enthused that in Bennington, "The soil is excellent, and raises vast supplies of wheat, Indian corn, red and white clover, and herd's grass. Butter, cheese, pork, and poultry, are every where produced in such abundance, as besides supplying the wants of the inhabitants even to profusion, enables them to export considerable quantities."

Propagandist and poet Thomas Rowley took these themes even further, portraying greater Rutland as an Edenic paradise of pleasant breezes and agricultural abundance, all ringed round by user-friendly forests full of "harmless" animals. The propaganda poured out in newspapers, books, letters, and, most of all, by word of mouth. In the crowded towns of southern New England, thousands of young people with few prospects decided to try their hands in this green and pleasant land.

The first settlers were overwhelmingly Yankees from southern New England. When Vermont entered the United States in 1791, it has been estimated that 95 percent of its residents were of English ancestry. Most were people whose families had first come to southern New England during the Great Migration of the seventeenth century. In general, people from western Massachusetts and Connecticut migrated into western Vermont, and people from southeastern New England entered Vermont through the Connecticut River Valley. Some had bought their lots sight unseen; like later purchasers of Florida swampland, they often got bad surprises. The more careful came north and looked until they found a spot they believed to be productive. Many came with family members, some with neighbors from back home, others alone and isolated from those around them. They were young, the population averaging 26 years old in the 1800 census. Their motivations were not often religious, like those of their Puritan fathers; some were probably trying to put some distance between themselves and stern fathers of just that sort. Most came simply to make life better for their families.

Settlers' stories often have a conventional quality, variations on the same themes. Yet some ended up making great successes of their gamble on the wilderness, while others ended in misery. Two such men were Jonathan Carpenter, who left a detailed journal of his satisfying experiences as a settler in Pomfret and Randolph, and Seth Hubbell of Wolcott, who met with more than his fair share of misery.

## MAKING IT IN VERMONT: THE STORY OF JONATHAN CARPENTER

*Mar. 27th [1780] I sot out in Company with David Carpenter to travil to the Northward Country to seek my fortune.*

— *Journal of Jonathan Carpenter*

In the early spring of 1780, a 22-year-old Revolutionary War veteran from Rehoboth, Massachusetts said goodbye to his parents and headed off on foot with his cousin, David Carpenter, to try his luck in the newly opening land in the north woods. Young Jonathan was typical of Vermont's pioneer generation in a number of respects. He had been a young man in the war, and had seen a bit of the world outside his home town. He was of old Yankee stock, from a family that had come to America in1638. Like most young men of his age, he had grown up "at home at my Fathers who gave me a Common Education & I worked at farming business." Now, like those ancestors who had left England to make their way in a new land, Jonathan was setting off for his own wilderness. But while they were spurred on by a search for freedom of worship, Jonathan could take that for granted. His motivation was as common as it was mundane. As he left the melting snow of Massachusetts behind, along with all that was familiar, he wanted only to "seek his fortune." So he worked 10 days for a man named Remember Kent, made enough to buy himself an ax and a "calfskin for a pair of shoes," and headed out for the long walk north.

For three weeks, he and his cousin tramped through Massachusetts and New Hampshire (averaging an astonishing 25 miles a day), stopping to work for farmers for room, board, or a little money. They were lucky to be moving during maple sugaring season, when their services were in demand for gathering and boiling sap. As they walked, Jonathan noted the land, topography, and trees, as if sharpening his eye for choosing his own land at the end of the journey. On April 22, they "crossed ye ferry at fort Dummer," seeing "sandy pine plaine oak Thro' Brattleborough to Guilford. ...uneveaven but good land, Maple hemlock and Settled 17 y'r."

On May 13, after a week of slogging through mountain snows, looking at land with the most eminent landowner in Pomfret, John Winchester Dana, the cousins were ready to make a decision. Jonathan records, "Then I & David Carpenter Bargaind for & bought a lot of 100 acres of Land (for 12s pr acre) of John Winchester Dana Esq'r of Pomfret having travild about 416 miles in 21 days." The proud new landowners wasted no time, for two days later, "We began to chop and made the first stump on our land."

That summer they put in long weeks of hard work, alternating days of clearing and planting (Indian corn) with days of working for "Esq'r Dana" to pay off part of their land debt. Jonathan's ax was not up to the task, and after two tries at mending it in mid-June, he wrote that "I have bad luck I broke my ax again & tis finally spoiled." It was obviously replaced, because by July 10 he wrote, wryly, that he and David had "chopt about 8 acres of [our] own land in 6 weeks successively which has almost tired me of that fun, no wonder neither, ha..." They were now in a position to do some quicker

## A POEM IN THE CLEARING

*On our wild land we've work'd a week*
*have built a house that's Strong & Neat*
*and it will Serve tho' it is low,*
*for kitchen, hall, & Palace too—*
*Planted Potatoes corn & Beans which*
*some may take for foolish schemes.*

—Written by Jonathan Carpenter, a week into clearing his stake in Randolph, May 20, 1780

**Jonathan Carpenter's tavern of 1798 is shown on the left in this photograph, with its barn on the right. It was located on the road running from Carpenter's beloved Randolph Center to Brookfield; sadly, it burned in 1930.**

clearing with fire, and on July 27, "We burnt our ground over." But all this clearing was to be in vain, for while traveling with the Pomfret militia on Indian duty that summer, Jonathan passed through Randolph Center and saw the place of his dreams for the first time, "having march'd over as fine level a tract of land as I have Seen in this Country."

The idea of settling on the beautiful, flat ground he had seen in Randolph Center had stayed with him, and in October 1782 he took out a note to pay Jabez Careys £37.10s for a "1/2 Right of Land" in that town, to be paid in "neat stock," or cattle. After this major investment, he returned to Rehoboth for the winter, describing himself as "Home poor merry & wise." He kept his original farm for the time being and was able to marry his Pomfret sweetheart, Olive Sessions (niece of "Esq'r Dana") in May 1784, when both were 27 years old. Conveniently, David Carpenter married Olive's sister, Betsey, and the sisters were to live close to one another for the rest of their lives. Jonathan and Olive were able to take up their rough new cabin in Randolph in March 1785, pulling their little baby, Fannie, to the site across the snow on a sled. David and Betsey joined them in the town two years later. By 1790, nine Carpenters (including one of Jonathan's brothers and many cousins) had taken stakes in Randolph.

Jedediah Hyde, Jr. built this log cabin in 1800 on the corner of Hyde and Reynolds Roads in Grand Isle. In 1946, local residents moved the well-preserved structure to a more visible spot on Route 2, where it remains open to the public.

Jonathan's diary ends in 1789, but we know he went on to fashion a rewarding life for himself in his beloved Randolph Center. He was town clerk there for three years and joined the Baptists, who met in a rough log school north of town. In later life, he operated a successful tavern, taking it teetotal when the temperance movement hit in 1830. He and Olive had eight children, seven of whom survived infancy. They did well in adulthood. Fannie married Sereno Wright, publisher of Vermont's biggest newspaper, the *Weekly Wanderer*, in the early nineteenth century. Others became local dignitaries, and the third generation included a judge, a state senator, and a doctor. Jonathan died in 1837, 80 years old, and Olive lived on to 91, their great Vermont dream having paid off to their satisfaction.

### THE SAD SUFFERINGS OF SETH HUBBELL

Jonathan Carpenter had the advantages of starting young, with few familial encumbrances, sharing work with another young man, sufficient financial backing, and plenty of luck. Others began in much the same way, but through personal failings or bad luck were unable to turn the landscape to their advantage. In the aptly named settler's reminiscence, *A Narrative of the Sufferings of Seth Hubbell & Family*, the author recorded the story of his coming from Norwalk, Connecticut to Wolcott, in Lamoille County, in the cold February of 1789. The trip north was slow, as he was travelling with his wife and their five daughters (all under the age of 10), two oxen, and a horse. Once they arrived, the isolation was almost unimaginable: "To the east of us it was eighteen miles to inhabitants, and no road but marked trees: to the south, about twenty, where there was infant settlements, but no communication with us; and to the north, it was almost indefinite, or to the regions of Canada."

Reaching his stake, Hubbell had no money and "...not a mouthful of meat or kernel of grain for my family." They lived three weeks with nothing to eat except some moose meat they got from an Indian. Hubbell had left Connecticut "with the expectation of having fifty acres of land given me when I came on, but this I was disappointed of." He was forced to sell his ox and his horse to buy his stake, leaving him with only one cow, "and this I had the misfortune to loose [lose] the next winter." The litany of bad luck with animals continued, for once he finally had been able to purchase another cow, it was "killed by a singular accident," and "its fine heifer calf...I lost by being choaked."

Seth had little better luck at cropping. He tells us that "When I came into Wolcott my farming tools consisted of one ax and an old hoe." He cleared two acres completely by hand the first year and was often "too faint to labour, for want of food." After he planted corn and potatoes, an early frost killed his

## CHANGES IN THE LAND

**This set of dioramas, located at the Harvard University Forest in Petersham, Massachusetts, was made to show the changes that might have taken place in the New England landscape over time.**

**1700 ■ The Virgin Forest**
On the eve of European settlement, the great trees of the virgin forest tower over the land. Note how the height and density of the forest obscure the topography, so that the outline of a mountain is only hinted at between the trees. It is a closed-in landscape, with almost no vistas.

**1780 ■ Clearing the Land**
The diorama lists this scene as taking place in 1740, accurate for parts of Massachusetts, but not for Vermont until around 1780. Small clearings appear amidst the great forest, as settlers enjoy an initial period of agricultural bounty from soil enriched by centuries of untouched organic accretion.

**1830 ■ The Denuded Countryside**
The great forest has given way to an elegant house, a substantial barn, and a higher standard of living for the farm family. Stripped of its trees, this is a landscape of airy vistas that show off the contours of the land's undulating topography.

crops; he was only able to get grain for his family by buying on credit. Once he began to grow grain successfully, "I had to carry it twelve miles to mill on my back. ...this I had constantly to do once a week."

The Hubbell family was never to experience much reward for all their pains. In 1806, sickness hit the family, and "In this sickness I lost my wife, the partner of my darkest days, who bore her share of our misfortunes with becoming fortitude." One daughter died, too, and another was made an invalid. Without their hands to labor, "This grievous calamity involved me in debts that terminated in the loss of my farm, my little all; but by the indulgence of my feeling relatives I am still permitted to stay on it." To support himself, he turned to his pen, writing the tale of their sufferings. His narrative was first published in 1824 and went through a few editions, its small profits helping to keep Seth Hubbell's head above water for the few years remaining to him.

Hubbell had started with some liabilities—including no male help and five girls too small to work, almost no money, and no luck. He certainly deserves credit for retaining a positive attitude in the face of all the odds. But were his problems due to bad luck or bad judgment? How did he get duped out of the land he had been promised? Why did he bring his whole penniless family up in winter before he had cleared any ground or made a shelter?

## WOMEN IN THE WILDERNESS

Corbis/Bettmann

Women's labor was badly needed on the northern frontier, and yet most Vermont settlements were seriously short of females. A few towns offered inducements; in Brookfield, "Mrs. Cross was the first woman who entered the place, and therefore was the recipient of the hundred acres of land so chivalrously bestowed by each town according to custom in its fair pioneer settlement." The Ryegate Scots were also getting lonely, James Whitelaw writing home in 1774:

*We shall have a flourishing colony here in a short time, but we are at a loss for young women, as we have here about a dozen young fellows and only one girl, and we shall never multiply and replenish this western world as we ought, without help-meets for us, and as this is an excellent flax country, a parcel of your spinners would be the very making of the place.*

When the Reverend Nathan Perkins of Connecticut toured Vermont in 1789, he gave the females what could only be termed a backhanded compliment:

*"I ask myself are these women of ye same species with our fine Ladies? tough are they, brawny their limbs,—their young girls unpolished—& will wear work as well as mules."*

## OFF THE BEATEN PATH WITH THE HUBBELL FAMILY

A family's first trip to reach its land was often lonely, arduous, and harrowing. Years later, Seth Hubble described his brood's ordeal as they made their way to Wolcott, in north central Vermont:

*In the latter part of February, 1789, I set out from the town of Norwalk, in Connecticut, on my journey for Wolcott to commence a settlement; family consisting of my wife and five children, they all being girls, the eldest nine or ten years old. My team was a yoke of oxen and a horse. After I had proceeded on my journey to within about one hundred miles of Wolcott, one of my oxen failed, but I however kept him yoked with the other end of the yoke myself, and proceeded on in that manner with my load to about fourteen miles of my journey's end, when I could get the sick ox no further. ...*

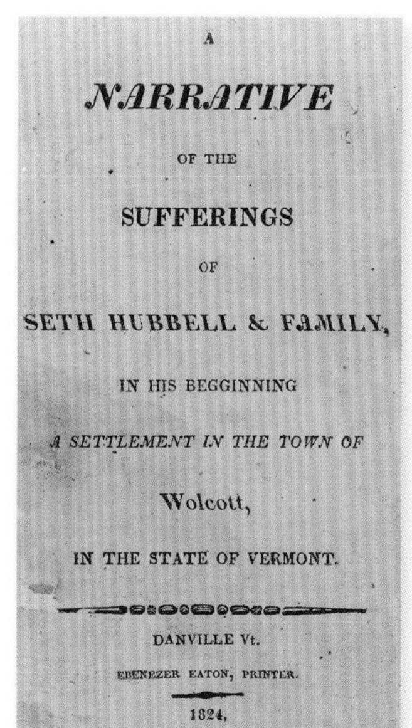
A NARRATIVE OF THE SUFFERINGS OF SETH HUBBELL & FAMILY, IN HIS BEGGINNING A SETTLEMENT IN THE TOWN OF Wolcott, IN THE STATE OF VERMONT.

DANVILLE Vt. EBENEZER EATON, PRINTER. 1824.

Seth Hubbell's *Sufferings* went through several editions, helping to support him in his old age. The axhead (right), used to clear land for a farm in Lincoln, would have been similar to one used by Hubbell.

*I then proceeded on with some help to Esq. McDaniel's in Hydepark: this brought me to about eight miles of Wolcott, and to the end of the road. It was now about the 20th of March; the snow not far from four feet deep; no hay to be had for my team, and no way for them to subsist but by browse. ...*

*On the 6th of April I set out from Esq. McDaniel's his being the last house for my intended residence in Wolcott, with my wife and two oldest children. We had eight miles to travel on snow-shoes, by marked trees—no road being cut: my wife had to try this new mode of traveling and she performed the journey remarkably well.*

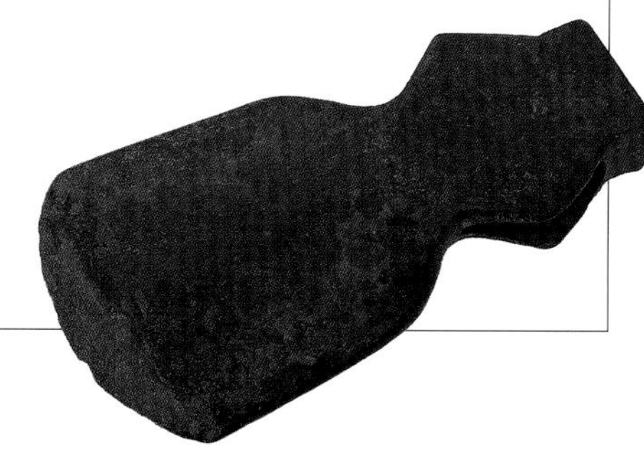

Why did so many of his animals die? Life in the wilderness had a way of taking the measure of a person.

### THE SETTLER'S LOT IN VERMONT

*...in May 1775 my Farther, my self in my 14th year, with 2 hired men, set out for Peacham. no road, nothing but a spotted line with know and then a bush, cut 20 miles from the settlement in Newbury. my Farther led his horse loded with Provisions. we drove a yoak of oxen and a cow. ...and when we got on to the ground we found on the lot adjoining the one my Farther had pitched, Robert Cour in a small camp whair we pitched till we bilt a log house and bound it with bark.*

*...in the fall we all retreated to Haverhill, N.H. ...the next spring...my Farther thought it a good time to go on with the first*

*company to Peacham and prepare for making shugar, and I with him. he took his old pung with his Provisions & Blankets & Snowshoes.*

—Reminiscences of Jonathan Elkins

When the Elkins family took up their claim in Peacham, they followed a pattern much like that of Jonathan Carpenter and other Vermont settlers. The men and older boys went out in the spring to stake a pitch. There were many theories about what sort of land was best. One common misconception was that hilltop land was richer than valley land. The first permanent settler in Andover, Moses Warner, did not want land in the Connecticut Valley because "early settlers then regarded river lands as almost worthless." Instead, he "selected his farm in Andover, because, as he said, it was free from stones; but he soon found that there were plenty underneath the leaves, and the farm is today the most stony one in town." In Dover, some settlers picked spots on the tops of the hills, thinking that the skimpiness of the trees there would make the land easier to clear and offer more warning of approaching danger. Many others had a sharp eye for the rich clay of the Champlain Valley.

### ROUGH AND SIMPLE HOUSES

The first year was usually spent in clearing a spot to plant and building a log house. The houses that were being scattered in country clearings and grouped in the villages were overwhelmingly made of logs in the prestatehood period. Many settlers and their families went through a three-house progression: rustic shelter (used for only a year or two) to snug log house to more elegant frame house. When Jabez Fitch and his three sons arrived on their stake in Hyde Park in June of 1788, he wrote that "After dinner we applied ourselves to cutting, timber, and building a camp or hut, which we covered with bark to shelter us from the inclemency of the weather, till we can get our house built." They lived in its primitive grandeur for a few days that summer while they were erecting a more substantial log house. (At least they retained their senses of humor, not to mention their creativity; Jabez recorded that one night, "We repaired to our hut as usual, and fortified ourselves against the mosquitoes, with fire and smoke, and the boys diverted themselves somewhat by rhyming on our present situation.")

Most settlers retreated back to their families in southern New England in the winter, although some, like Brandon's first settler, Amos Cutler, spent the cold, dark period in his cabin "accompanied only by his faithful dog." The following year they returned for good, often with their wives and younger children in tow. Then, as Frederic Palmer Wells, the historian of Barnet, describes, bark shelters would give way to comfortable log houses:

## NATURE'S FIRST LAW: A TEENAGER'S PARENT WILL ALWAYS BE IRRITATING

Young Elias Smith found himself pulled from a comfortable home in Lyme, Connecticut to the pitch his father had begun clearing in Woodstock, Vermont. His reactions will strike a chord in teenagers everywhere:

*After many sweats and hard pulls, my father pointed us to the house, about forty rods ahead, the sight of which struck a damp on my spirits, as it appeared to me only an abode of wretchedness. After going to it and taking a general view of the house and land around, before the team came up, I determined within myself to return to Connecticut; thinking it better to be there to dig clams for my living than to be in such a place. I was disappointed, grieved, vexed and mad. Though I was some over thirteen years, I cried.*

*With this fixed determination to return, I went down to the team, and passed by the team down the steep and dismal hill as fast as possible. My father, observing my rapid course, called after me, asking me where I was going; and commanded me to return to him. I obeyed with great reluctance, as it appeared better to die than be confined to such a place.*

Vermont's first settlers were often shocked to find that, once they had cleared their land of trees, what remained were thin-soiled, boulder-strewn fields much like this one in Bennington.

*The dwelling place stood on the north side of a very large hill, half a mile from any house. Around the house (as it was called) there were twelve acres of land. The trees were cut down and lay in different directions, excepting a small place where the house stood. there was no way to look, to see far, without looking up, as the trees around prevented seeing any house or cleared land, in any direction whatever.*

*The house was made of split basswood logs, locked together at the corners. There was no floor to the house, nore was there any roof to it. The grass had grown up within these wooden walls, and there was one large stump in the middle of the house, which, to heighten my trouble my father said would do for a* light stand.

—Elias Smith, 1782

Cynthia Locklin

In this charming drawing, writer and author Rowland Robinson envisioned the world of his settler grandparents as they cleared stumps to open their land for plowing.

*In Barnet, as in all new towns, the first houses were built of logs and when properly constructed such houses were warm and comfortable. The materials for building them were at hand and they could be put together with such tools as every pioneer had. At first they were huts roofed with bark, but more care was soon taken in their construction. Sometimes, but not perhaps in Barnet, the logs were squared, the corners mortised and the outsides clapboarded.*

Log houses remained a prominent feature of the Vermont landscape until well into the nineteenth century. The first frame houses could not be built until there was a convenient sawmill nearby, and then their appearances became a cause of local pride. Shrewsbury was settled by 1761 but did not see a frame house built until 1792. Rutland got its first settler in 1769, but had no frame houses until 1777. Orwell saw nothing more elegant than a log cabin until the 1790s.

The extensive surveys of the architecture of Addison and Rutland Counties that have been undertaken by the Vermont Division for Historic Preservation give a glimpse into the surviving housing stock from before 1791 in two counties that were settled relatively early. A total of 27 pre-1791 houses remain in Rutland County, with the largest numbers in Poultney, Rutland, and Tinmouth. Addison County has 18 homes from this era, with a few each in Middlebury, Addison, and Cornwall. In both counties, the overwhelming number of survivals are built in the classic Cape Cod style. This does not necessarily mean that Cape Cod houses were the predominant style being built, but their convenient floor plans have certainly helped them to survive in greater numbers. Yet the low numbers of any houses from this era reinforces the sense that the Republic of Vermont was overwhelmingly a country of log homes.

We can read some messages in the siting of those frame houses that remain to us. They often turn their backs on mountain views, placing a higher priority on facing south to catch as much sun as possible on long winter days. Most houses cannot be said to be facing anywhere at all, for their windows are too small for easy viewing. Windows were designed to draw in light and conserve heat, rather than to draw the eye outwards. Who wanted to gaze out at a forest whose clearing presented the prospect of years of back-breaking work? In eastern Vermont, the farmhouse was often connected to the barn, sometimes with other outbuildings added to the line. This was a common eastern Connecticut pattern and is rarely seen west of the Green Mountains.

Vermonters were not all lacking in refinement. Bennington was home to a number of elegant houses before 1791 and regarded itself as a center of culture in the little republic. When the Reverend Nathan Perkins of Hartford, Connecticut made a preaching tour through Vermont in1789, he said of Bennington, that it was "a good town of land, people, proud—scornful—conceited & somewhat polished—small meeting house—considerably thick-settled, as many, as can possibly get a living;—no stone;—no fencing timber;—some elegant building;—a County town; —a tolerable Court-house & jail;—a good grammar school." Scattered examples of elegant living were also being built in a few places in the countryside. In 1784 Jonas Case erected the first brick house in Addison County on Lake Street in Addison, firing the bricks in the yard. It remains a striking example of the vernacular Georgian style. There was hope in some quarters for a better architectural showing in the future. On a tour through Sunderland, John Graham fantasized

## THE CLASSIC CAPE: VERMONT'S FIRST FRAME HOUSE STYLE

As Vermont's settlers moved from log shelters to frame houses, many chose to build in the Cape Cod style they had known so well in southern New England. Capes were very common in Vermont in the late 1700s and early 1800s.

The form was (and remains) very adaptable, appearing in larger and smaller versions according to a family's means and space requirements. Of course, not all houses of this era were Capes, but many early Capes remain on the landscape because of the strength of their design, and because they still work for families today.

There were many variations on this form, but the most common characteristics of a classic Cape include:

- One and a half stories in height
- Large central chimney
- Steeply pitched roof
- Plain, symmetrical facade
- Five bays wide, with the door in the middle
- Steep stairs up to an attic space under the roof

A simple Cape Cod house in Middlebury (top), built around the end of the eighteenth century. Note the central chimney, steep roof, and symmetrical facade. The only ornamentation is the fanlight over the door.

This early Cape (middle) has a more extended facade and a saltbox roofline. It is probably the oldest house in Middlebury, and was built by one of the town's founders, John Chipman, around1784.

The Capes built by wealthy families sometime took more elaborate forms. This once elegant gambrel-roofed house (bottom) was built in Poultney around 1790 for Dr. Jonas Stafford, a Renaissance man who practiced medicine, law, and politics in the area.

Jan Albers

about a day when "Yes, on those majestic hills, within the bosoms of ever-verdant woods, what palaces, and what delightful villas are destined to rise." But the great age of Vermont building belongs to the next chapter.

## TREES AND ASHES

After a lot had been purchased and a house built, the primal act of claiming the land was clearing it of its trees. It was hard work. A well-muscled young man could only hope to clear about three acres a year. James Whitelaw, one of the Scottish settlers of Ryegate and Vermont's second Surveyor General, described how "There are several ways of clearing land in this country such as girdling, cutting and grubbing. Girdling is only cutting a notch about an inch deep, and two inches wide round the root of the tree which makes it die." A girdled tree had to stand for a few years, until its root system died, and it could be removed. Grubbing was the slow process of digging out the roots of girdled trees; the roots were often used for fences. In the late eighteenth century it became more common to cut trees, let them lie over the winter and burn them as soon as they were dry. This cleared the land faster, while stripping more nutrients from the soil than girdling. But land could then be turned to agriculture more quickly.

Trees held a financial bonus for the settlers, because they could be turned into potash and sold for a good price. For now, potash and timber were the only real export industries Vermont had. Potash (potassium carbonate) was a chemical derived from the ashes of burned trees that was used for making lye, gunpowder, soap, glass, and in the "fulling" (a finishing process) of cloth. England's booming textile industry had a huge demand for potash, and the Old Country was too deforested to make its own in any quantity. In a small Republic that had started out 95-percent forested and wanted to make the move to agriculture, potash and its more refined form, pearl ash (baking soda), was a perfect industry. It required little equipment or expertise. Trees were burned and water was poured over the ashes to leach out the lye. The lye was boiled in a large kettle until a dry, salty residue remained. This was packaged in wooden boxes as potash. From little clearings in Addison and Arlington, Panton and Peacham, the trees were burned, the potash was collected, and sent to England to fuel the Industrial Revolution, allowing many Vermont families to simultaneously clear and pay off their land.

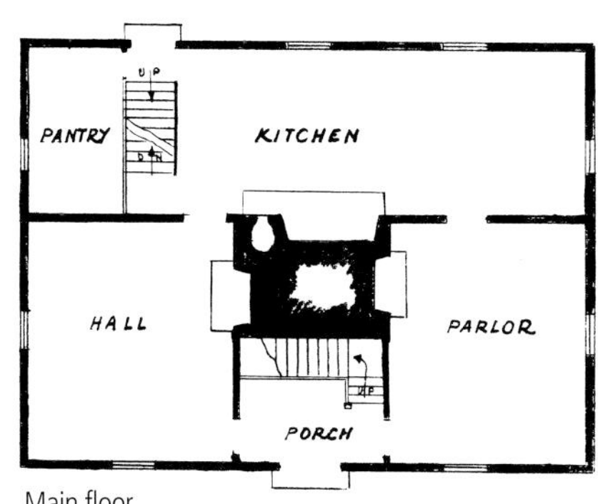

Main floor

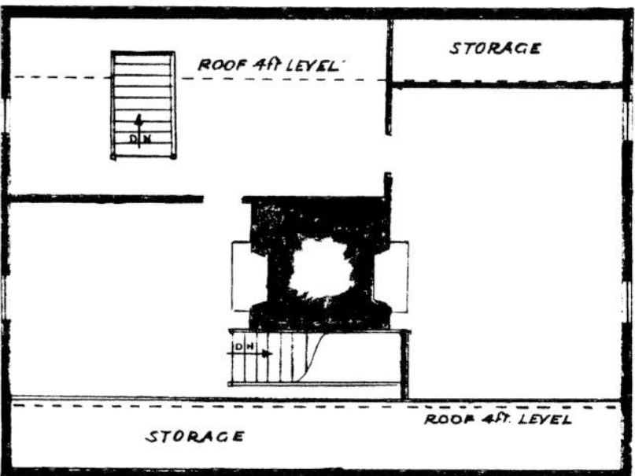

Attic

**A typical Cape house floor plan from Henry Lionel Williams and Ottalie K. Williams, *Old American Houses, 1700–1850,* Bonanza Books (New York, 1967), page 67.**

## THE FIRST AGE OF EUROPEAN AGRICULTURE

The heart and bread and life of the Republic of Vermont lay in agriculture. Here, as in so many places in North America, the first crops after clearing seemed to promise miracles. For thousands of years, nutrients had been building up on the forest floors, creating a layer of rich and fertile soil. The first crops planted in this earth produced great yields. Asa Burton, of Norwich, later wrote that "The land was fertile, and as soon as cleared and sown or planted, it yielded from 20 to 30 bushels of wheat or rye to the acres, and from 40 to 50 bushels of corn; and some rich meadow land produced from 70 to 80 bushels of good, sound corn. Oats grew very rank, generally as high as a person is tall of full middling stature. ...To such produce I have been an eyewitness." At Dover, the corn ran 25–40 bushels to the acre. In Pownal, "although some of the land is stony, yet it yields great crops of wheat, corn, rye, oats, pease and beans." The farmers of Clarendon were said to produce 200 to 500 tons of excellent hay per season.

Livestock was imported in large numbers, and with the animals came fences in some towns. In Dorset, the industrious inhabitants "enclose their land with strong fences of stone walls and timber; yet they are terribly annoyed by wolves, which pour down from the mountains and often destroy whole flocks in a single night." Around Dover, "Beef, pork, butter, and cheese, are here in vast abundance." In many towns, the stock walked freely, and most farmers had registered earmarks on their cattle after a law of 1779 required their use "To prevent disputes." Southern Vermont was already supporting important dairy and beef industries in the late eighteenth century. English Devon red cattle were the first preferred breed, for they were large and sturdy. Pigs rooted in the farmyards, a few sheep were appearing on the hillsides, and chickens pecked in the gardens of the log houses.

Agriculture was slowly transforming parts of Vermont's landscape from a forbidding wilderness into something approaching a Yankee's vision of a bucolic paradise. John Graham summed up this transformation in a word that, to him, encapsulated a valuable aesthetic: "neatness." Writing of the farmers of Rupert, he found that:

> *The inhabitants are good husbandmen, and keep their farms, barns, and stalls in the best order, and in a manner that proves Industry loves to reside amongst them. I do not know any thing more creditable to a country than that neatness, which, without doors as well as within, is a sure sign of chearfulness, content, and plenty; for I believe it is generally found that they go hand in hand, and that the people (in whatever country) who assiduously cultivate the protection of the household and rural deities, possess at the same time, liberal and generous sentiments; while disorder and filth, assuredly characterize sloth and a groveling meanness of intellect.*

We can glimpse here the beginnings of a new Vermont, one that had been tamed and tidied. Natural order was giving way to human organization.

Royal Ontario Museum, Toronto

Thomas Davies, the officer and artist who painted the great fort at Crown Point for General Amherst (see page 75), was also asked to investigate other useful sites. When Amherst wanted a waterfall to power a sawmill, he sent Davies to find one. The result was the first mill on Otter Creek, located at the great falls in what is now Vergennes. The mill Davies painted in "The Falls of Otter Creek, Lake Champlain, with a Saw Mill, 1766" (above) was burned down by the Green Mountain Boys in 1773, for the hamlet was a hotbed of Yorkers. Undaunted, the citizens of little Vergennes had enough faith in the potential of its natural setting to incorporate as a city in 1788. Today, Vergennes is the smallest incorporated city in the United States.

## PLANS ON THE LAND

As each family of settlers learned the boundaries of its acreage, made a clearing, and laid out fields, these actions created larger patterns on the land. The surveyors' work in the wilderness—the straight lines and witness trees—was now being made manifest on the land by the armies of choppers, girdlers, builders, and planters. The thudding of axes and crackling of fires muffled the quick rustling of the fleeing bear and bird and hare as man turned the full force of his hands onto the land.

Cultures, and the times in which they develop, can put a stamp as distinctive as a thumb print on the land. In Vermont, those patterns began to form in earnest between 1760 and 1791. The human imprint on the land begins as an imprint on the brain, and the patterns Vermont's first settlers knew from their childhoods can still be discerned on the landscape. Stewart

### THE IMPRINTS OF CULTURE ON THE LAND

Stewart McHenry has identified five main eighteenth-century field patterns whose outlines can still be traced on the land:

**DUTCH**
Dutch settlers from the Hudson Valley settled in Pownal in the 1720s, and some of the early settlers of Rupert and Pawlet had Dutch surnames. The field patterns of parts of Bennington County are more similar to those of New York State than to the rest of Vermont. Their distinguishing features include a strong preference for farms on the valley floor, avoidance of hills, few tree lines between fields, small fields in the flood plain, and a general orientation to the river. The farmsteads tended to cluster together.

**MASSACHUSETTS YANKEE**
The Massachusetts Yankee pattern is particularly strong in the Connecticut River Valley. It has the familiar patchwork quality that is so common in southern New England. There are many irregularly shaped fields in the valleys, a few remote farms halfway up the hillsides, with trees on the high places. Fields are divided by tree lines or stone walls, are oriented to each other or the road rather than the rivers, and often have sharp angles in their corners. Farmsteads tended to be isolated from one another.

**CONNECTICUT YANKEE**
Common in the Champlain Valley, these patterns look quite different from their Massachusetts counterparts. Fields are more regular, laid out in squares or rectangles. There are some tree lines, but few stone walls; all are oriented to grids. They can be anywhere from 3–20 acres in size; their shapes remain close to those on original lot surveys.

McHenry's work has distinguished five predominant types of eighteenth-century field patterns, based upon the ethnic origins of the settlers. He identified a set of traits that appear in the landscape, including such factors as the locations of villages, field sizes and shapes, evidence of abandonment of fields, relationship of fields to bodies of water, placement of dwellings and farm buildings, and presence or absence of field dividers like stone walls or tree lines. Aerial photographs of fields reveal patterns often linked to the ethnic origins of their settlers.

## VERMONT'S EARLY TOWN PLANS

The patterns that were appearing on the land were predominantly agricultural, but here and there villages were already being laid out. The original grants had posited communities similar to an English village—lots laid around

**NEW HAMPSHIRE YANKEE**
This pattern can be found in the rolling country of eastern Vermont. Most of the fields are small, more regular in shape than the Massachusetts ones, but the topography makes them less square than the Connecticut examples. Many have been consolidated, with their tree lines removed. They go right up the sides of the hills and are oriented to the roads. Many have stone fences and rock piles in the middle of the fields, which are also commonly found in New Hampshire.

**FRENCH CANADIAN COLONIAL**
The fields follow the pattern of long, narrow, rectangular strips so common in rural Québec. They run from the water's edge, and have distinct tree lines. Most are large at 10–20 acres. Houses are close together, along the narrow ends of the strips.

a common space set aside for a church, with other lots retained for schools. Beyond this, the plan—or lack of a plan—for the community was up to the proprietors. Some had grandiose schemes, while others had no preconceptions. Given the fact that most proprietors knew nothing of the topography of their land before they unloaded it on settlers, the results were mixed. Twentieth-century Shoreham, for example, is still laid out in a pattern remarkably similar to that proposed by the original proprietors. By contrast, proprietor Ezra Stiles (who would eventually be the president of Yale) sat in his study and made a plan for Sherburne (then, and now again, called Killington) that was a perfect reproduction of the rigid grid pattern in the center of New Haven, Connecticut. What looked so lovely on paper was completely ill-suited to the topography of the township's rugged V-shaped valley, and the settlers gave it no mind.

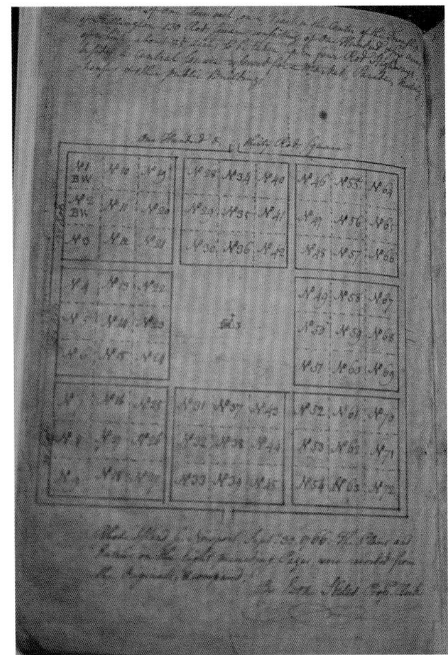

The original Sherburne town plan, in proprietor Ezra Stiles' hand (top), was unrealistically geometric, not conforming to the reality of the topography; Stiles had never seen the land where he was trying to plan a town. Today's Sherburne (bottom), which readopted its original name of Killington in 1999, actually wanders along its narrow valley in a very different, but far more practical, fashion.

Throughout seventeenth- and eighteenth-century New England, towns tended to be laid out in one of two ways. Most had a linear, or organic, configuration, in which virtually everything was clustered along one long street, which often rambled, conforming itself to the topography. Sherburne is an example of a linear village, as are Middlebury and Bennington. Still other towns were laid out in a more geometric pattern, or grid, like Fair Haven or Bristol.

Twentieth-century Vermont is famous for its "typical New England villages," laid out around greens or commons, but these were delayed developments here, and most of the examples we think of were largely products of the early nineteenth century. Because Vermont was parceled out by speculators, there was little incentive for proprietors to set aside common space. The age of grazing on the common was already past throughout New England (and had never existed in many places), so most villages had no economic need for greens and proprietors were anxious to sell as much land as possible. Their charters insisted upon reserving a lot for a church, however, and in many cases this also became the town green.

Before statehood in 1791, most of the churches that would grace these lots had not yet been built, and the greens themselves were notorious for being blighted by rotting, abandoned trees. Even people who were usually too busy to pay much attention to aesthetics were offended by environmental devastation when they saw it in the center of a village. In Rutland, in this era, "The large green was a great hemlock swamp, full of high stumps." In Middlebury, for decades anyone who was being held in the village jail was required to dig out stumps on the green, in the hope that the green would someday be attractive. This persistence of stumps was also a continuing problem because stumps from virgin hardwoods were so dense that they could take 50 years to rot. And because the Republic, as it then was, had been

Settlers coming from the rolling hills and flat fields of southern New England had little experience with a landscape that included terrain as forbidding as that found in the higher reaches of the Green Mountains. Killington Peak (above) retains much of its original grandeur.

granted in large, dispersed chunks of land, many villages went for years with no center at all.

### CREATING COMMUNITY

As late as 1791, Vermont was struggling to overcome the peculiar features of her origins. Frenzied land speculation and absentee proprietorships had tended to encourage individual rights over community-building. People came to Vermont to make it for themselves and their own families, and once they had secured their lots, there were few limitations on what they could do on them. It is this unregulated atmosphere that gives the history of early Vermont much of its attractive outlaw quality, as dashing individualists like the Allen brothers made their own law. To their credit, they successfully set up the political machinery for closer-knit communities: town meetings, select boards, town officers like fenceviewers and haywards. But even the Allen boys seem less romantic when we realize that many of their activities were aimed at protecting their own enormous landholdings.

While life on all frontiers can be isolated, early Vermont seems to have had more than its share of loneliness. Many people set their stakes in the countryside, a good walk from their nearest neighbors, unlike their Puritan ancestors whose habit of living in villages meant they would see their neighbors every day. The lots most charters mandated for churches and schools were set aside, but their proposed institutions could remain unbuilt for decades as citizens fought over which denomination was to get the appointment. As historian Michael Bellesiles says, "The settlers' cultural diversity produced a fairly contentious civic life and impeded the formation of any sort of collective identity." As a result, Vermont's early villages often lacked the amenities that were considered to be the foundations of community life in southern New England. The gap between first settlement and the provisions of these basics could be surprisingly long.

Most of Vermont's early mills and industrial buildings were rude wooden structures, but with the coming of community there would also be construction of more elaborate industrial sites. The Whipple Mill in South Shaftsbury (above) survives as an example of a small early nineteenth-century factory, where Eagle Square forged steel carpenter's squares were produced.

Springfield got its first European settlers in 1751, but had no real village until Eureka was developed in 1772. The Congregational Church was not built until 1781 (although a number of taverns had sprung up earlier, many serving as community meeting places). Eureka Schoolhouse went up in 1785 and remains the oldest in Vermont. In Eureka, as in many villages, a sense of community was centered on one family's house. John Little, the only proprietor to move to the grant, had the first large frame house there, and it soon served as tavern, store, and church as well. Peacham had settlers by 1775, a gristmill in 1781, a tavern in 1787, but no church until 1794.

The lack of churches in early Vermont may have been worrisome to some people, but it did not mean there was no religion. The freedom that marked so many aspects of early Vermont life extended to this area; the region soon became a hotbed of religious diversity and divisiveness, described by historians Jeff Potash, John Brooke, Randy Roth, and others. People were always glad to hear a visiting preacher and in some places met for worship in private homes. Many towns built simple log churches. In Danville, the residents spent a number of years after 1788 worshipping in the "bark meeting house." Similar simple places of worship appeared at Newbury, Barnet, and many other spots around Vermont. But having religion as one concern out of many rather than as a first priority set Vermont apart from the earlier New England colonies to the south.

There was some sense of community in the Republic of Vermont as people shared the common purposes of organizing their towns and regulating matters of daily life such as fence upkeep and thistle cutting; but it was seldom formalized in the sense of being centered around churches or other institutions. Neighbors helped neighbors; without such help many settlers never would have survived their first winter. The Reverend Nathan Perkins found that "Woods make people love one another & kind & obliging and

UVM Special Collections

One of the oldest schools in the state still stands in the village of Eureka, on the outskirts of Springfield. Built in 1785, the Eureka School House closed to students in 1900 (above, large photo), but is open to the public today, moved and restored (inset).

good natured. They set much more by one another than in ye old settlements." Samuel Williams also saw a special closeness among people in the wilderness:

> *That benevolent friendly disposition, which man should bear to man, will appear under different forms, in different stages of societies. In the first combinations of mankind, when all are exposed to danger, sufferings, and want, it appears in one of its most amiable forms, and has been called hospitality. In this form it exists among the people who are subjected to the common danger, fatigue and sufferings, which attend the forming of new settlements. Feeling every moment their own wants and dangers, they are led by their situation, to assist each other in their difficulties and danger.*

This does not mean that no one had fun. When the Reverend Asa Burton received a call to be minister in Thetford, he found that "Many heads of families were intemperate, hard drinkers of ardent spirits. They were very fond of amusements; especially such as visiting each other for the sake of vain and merry conversation, and drinking. They were very fond of what was at that day called frolicks, but now Balls; and of playing cards." (Significantly, the next section of Burton's autobiography bears the title "I Pitch My Tent in Satan's Camp.") The early Vermonters were a rough and ready bunch who could make fast friends with their fellow settlers. But while communities were developing, the classic shape of Vermont village life still lay in the future in most parts of the state.

## THE INDUSTRIES OF SETTLEMENT

Most hamlets had sawmills and gristmills long before they had churches, taverns, or any public spaces. The virtue of this progression is understandable. A sawmill was a necessity if anything was to be built of boards instead of logs. Gristmills were also highly desirable, for they were vital for making the wheat bread that the settlers craved. Many proprietors offered incentives to settlers who would promise to build a mill within an allotted period of time. In Athens, west of Bellows Falls, Samuel Bayley and Micah Read

---

## ONE MAN'S FRUITLESS SEARCH FOR CIVILITY IN VERMONT

The Reverend Nathan Perkins, by all appearances a rather Puritanical type, was appalled at the "wretched" conditions he found while touring late eighteenth-century Vermont.

In 1789, the Rev. Nathan Perkins, Princeton graduate and pastor of the Third Church of West Hartford, Connecticut, undertook a missionary tour of the heathen settlements of Vermont. The rather effete pastor's diary records his shock at the condition of life here with unusual frankness:

**Pownal:** "A bad appearance at ye entrance, Pownal ye first town, poor land—very unpleasant—very uneven—miserable set of inhabitants—no religion."

**Middletown:** "Put up at Mr. Minor's, a kind man,—a kind wife,—wretched fare,—wretched bed,—eat up with fleas,—no hay,—my horse starving."

**Brandon:** "Lodged at Mr. Flint's in Brandon,—meanest of all lodging,—dirty,—fleas without number."

**Jericho:** "Had no comfortable refreshment—was almost starved because I could not eat ye coarse fare provided for me—no candles pine splinters used in lieu of them—bed poor & full of flees."

**Burlington:** "Arrived at Onion-river falls & passed by Ethan Allyn's grave. An awful Infidel, one of ye wickedest men yt ever walked this guilty globe. I stopped & looked at his grave with a pious horror."

**Burlington Bay:** "One of ye most delightful places in nature."

**Vermont:** "Scarcely any politeness in ye State."

appeared in town during the second year of settlement and within two years had built a sawmill and a gristmill. They were rewarded with 168 acres of land from the proprietors.

What little industry there was often predated other amenities. Villages were always happy to get a blacksmith, as Rutland did in 1779 and Shrewsbury in 1785. Vermont was even developing a small iron industry, starting with an ironworks in Fair Haven by 1785. Pittsford was making pig iron in the year Vermont became a state. There was a great deal of interest in encouraging the iron industry, because of the demand for hardware and nails for house building. (The earliest houses had used wooden nails, called "trenails.") John Graham said that in Bennington, "Industry every where lifts up its chearful voice, and health, competence, independence, and content, smile around the fascinating scene." Yet he could list only a few sawmills, gristmills, and an iron works to account for this alleged miniature Industrial Revolution. He foresaw a marble industry in the future, but "at present, they have not the art of polishing it so highly [as in Europe]." Samuel Williams would also have liked to report more industry, but admitted that, after agriculture, the manufactures are "Chiefly of a domestic kind, designed to procure clothing for families." Vermont's initial development was not to be based on industry, but its early boosters thought it would be, some day in the near future. Nature would be broken, and industry would turn it to man's use.

## THE AWFUL POWER OF NATURE

The idea that nature had an intrinsic beauty that was to be "appreciated" was largely a product of the Romantic movement of the early nineteenth century and had, as its prerequisite, a growing sense of human mastery over the environment. Vermont's first settlers have provided us with a number of arduous accounts of homesteading; in almost all these, nature is more cause for cursing than delight. The work of clearing, house building, and tilling was inherently practical rather than contemplative and allowed little time for aesthetic reflection.

A few early Vermonters commented on the natural bounty of their new world. A Mrs. Thomas Moore of Chelsea found so many speckled trout in the stream outside her log house that she "could easily catch enough for breakfast during a few moments of the early morning." An early settler of Clarendon told Samuel Williams how "The number of pigeons was immense. Twenty five nests were frequently to be found on one beech tree. ...For an hundred acres together, the ground was covered with their dung, to the depth of two inches. Their noise in the evening was extremely troublesome, and so great that the traveler could not get any sleep, where their nests

Early settlers viewed the forests of northern New England as wild and uncivilized places, full of unknown terrors. This view would change to a more romantic one as forest tracts diminished; but here, a campfire provides the only respite from a dark and forbidding landscape.

were thick." The feature of the landscape that excited most comment was, as one would expect, the forest. John Graham was awed to find that "Some of the pines are of the enormous dimensions of six feet in diameter." It is interesting that most of the appreciation of trees comes in the 1790s, when the first great wave of clearing was finished.

Those who lived in the early forest felt more of its terror than its beauty, and their accounts of what lurked in its darkness were straight from the Brothers Grimm. Settlers faced wild animals with alarming frequency, if the number of mentions is any indication. Every settler seems to have had a bear story. Abby Hemenway tells us that in Randolph, Mr. Tracy, the first teacher, was coming to open the schoolhouse for the morning when, "He noticed the door was ajar, but although some of the boys were in advance of him, and pushing the door open, stood face to face with a huge bear, and two half-grown cubs. Here was a dilemma; but he sprang to the fire-place and caught a large shovel...and commenced a regular fight." He was only saved when "Diah Flint arrived, and, having a gun with him, soon dispatched the old bear and cubs, and then went for help to dress them." In celebration,

"The whole district rejoiced in a fine feast of bear meat for their suppers."

An inordinate number of these confrontations involved women, showing that their reluctance to come north may not have been entirely unwarranted. Marcy Robinson of Bennington, known for her intellectual bent, was also strong and brave. "When living in their log house, while her husband was in England, and her children, David, Jonathan, and Anna, were with her, wolves came at night, and tried to obtain entrance at the doors and windows. She knocked upon the door to frighten them away, then seized firebrands from the fire, opened the door, and waved them and shouted with all her strength." The wolves ran, unlikely to mess with a bluestocking again.

Clearing was destroying habitat at a staggering pace, and this had to have seriously affected animals' food supplies. Samuel Williams was soon to note, not too reassuringly, that the bear "is not an animal of the most fierce, and carnivorous disposition. There have been instances, in which children have been devoured by the bear; but it is only when it is much irritated, or suffering with hunger, that it makes any attack upon the human race."

What all these stories suggest is that the settlers were—or believed themselves to be—locked in a battle with nature that they had to win to survive. For the Yankee pioneers, there could be no truce with the wilderness. No friendly animal spirit guided and protected them in the forest. There was no confidence about where safety could be found out of doors. There was just a simple house to stand as a barrier, a safety zone, from nature. They sought protection from the natural world until they could transform it into a place of order, predictability, and profit.

The great American artist and naturalist, John James Audubon, painted the passenger pigeon, probably the most plentiful bird in North America in settlement times. Hunted throughout the nineteenth century, the species became extinct in 1914, when the last of its kind died in a Cincinnati zoo.

## SAMUEL WILLIAMS AND THE WITHDRAWAL OF NATURE

An army of young Yankees, armed only with shiny axes, had managed to wreak havoc on an aeons-old natural world within a few short decades. But the clearing of large tracts of the north woods had repercussions far beyond what most settlers could see at the time. As environmental historian William Cronon has written, "The colonists themselves understood what they were doing almost wholly in positive terms, not as 'deforestation,' but as 'the progress of cultivation.' " Yet even they saw some signs of nature's response—marauding bears at the cabin doors, packs of wolves in the farmyards, a "plague of worms" that devastated crops in eastern Vermont in 1771, leaving people in "terror and dismay."

In his *Natural and Civil History of Vermont*, published in 1794, Samuel Williams enumerated the environmental changes taking place in Vermont at great length. He noticed that the climate, which most people regarded as fixed, seemed to be changing as a result of the clearing of the forests:

*When the settlers move into a new township, their first business is to cut down the trees, clear up the lands, and sow them with grain. The earth is no sooner laid open to the influence of the sun and winds, than the effects of cultivation begin to appear. The surface of the earth becomes more warm and dry. As the settlements increase, these effects become more extensive.*

Williams and his fellow New England naturalists were accurate in saying that clearing the forests made the land warmer and drier. Trees are great conservators of moisture and help to moderate temperatures. Without their protection, the actions of sun and wind soon dried out the land, although Williams assumed that the climate itself had been changed, rather than the land's reaction to it.

The increase of settlements, with its attendant clearing, meant that this drying was having an effect on local water supplies. "Many of the small streams and brooks are dried up: Mills, which at the first settlement of the country, were plentifully supplied with water from small rivers, have ceased to be useful." While devastating to the millers, this could have a positive side as well, for "Miry places, and large swamps, are become among the richest of our arable lands." These considerable changes were accomplished within a speedy two to three years of clearing.

**The settlement era saw the loss of vast tracts of "miry places," swamps, and bogs when the cutting of forests caused land to dry out. Development poses a continuing threat to wetlands in our own day. This wetland (opposite) is on Mount Pisgah, in the Willoughby State Forest.**

## SAMUEL WILLIAMS: VERMONT'S FIRST NATURALIST

The Rev. Samuel Williams (1743–1817) was widely regarded as the most profound Vermont scholar of his day. He graduated from Harvard at the age of 18, was ordained into the Congregational ministry, and received a prestigious appointment as Hollis Professor of Mathematics and Natural Philosophy at Harvard in 1780.

Yet in 1789 he resigned his professorship and moved to the rustic community of Rutland, Vermont. The facts are unclear, though the Rev. Nathan Perkins, who met him in Rutland in 1789, says that Williams had been "Guilty of forgery & resigned."

Williams proved to be an enormous asset to his new home. He bought the local newspaper and changed its name to the *Rutland Herald,* conducted numerous scientific experiments in natural history, lectured at the University of Vermont, and preached in Burlington. John Graham, a fellow resident of Rutland, said of him, "He is the most enlightened man in the state in every branch of philosophy and polite learning." He was the first scholar to give systematic attention to the problems of Vermont's forest, and his carefully constructed experiments and depth of understanding of environmental forces were far in advance of most of his contemporaries.

Williams was also intrigued by the variety of Vermont's animal life, and realized that sharp declines were already taking place within some of their populations. He wrote with insight about the habits of bears, wolves, catamounts, deer, fox, moose, and many other creatures of the forests. Ironically, his highest praise was saved for the animal that had already been the most severely taxed by man for nearly two centuries in these woods—the beaver. They seemed to him to exhibit the longest list of settler-like traits—living in complex societies, constructing log houses, employing engineering skills, taking the initiative. He noted sadly that "The beaver has deserted all the southern parts of Vermont, and is now to be found only in the most northern, and uncultivated parts of the state." Otters, too, once abounded in their eponymous Creek and around Lake Champlain, but had become "scarce." The thousands of pigeon nests were now only remembered in the talk of the oldtimers.

Williams' explanations for these changes show a good measure of ambivalence. The beaver has "deserted" certain regions, rather than having been hunted to near-extinction. The pigeons are not dead, for settlement only "drove them further to the northward." Faced with explaining what has become of each beloved animal, Williams concludes that all seem somehow to be withdrawing from humans of their own accord. He had to believe they were still out there, somewhere farther away. And even while granting that the pattern of clearing that attended settlement was having enormous environmental consequences, Williams would never have doubted that it was all worthwhile to make a garden of the forest.

## VERMONT IN 1791

Imagine a bird's eye view of Vermont, 31 years after the French withdrew to the north. Between 1760 and 1791, sections of this land have been claimed by England, Massachusetts Bay, New Hampshire, and New York. Now the area has finally assumed a stable identity, marrying into the United States. Looking down, green is still the predominant color, but not the only one.

The changes that have taken place since 1760 are almost unbelievable—an extraordinary achievement if you are a human, a habitat holocaust if you are a bear. In the southeast, along the Connecticut River, there are many clearings. Some have fields planted into crops, in some the dead and girdled trees stand to rot, others shelter simple log houses and their kitchen gardens, with maybe a boiling potash pot in the yard. In places the houses are clustered into little towns with an exurban aura—large lots with agriculture on them exist even near the green. There are a few frame houses here, mostly simple Capes with large central chimneys requiring many cords of the land's free logs to stay warm. The villages have many empty lots—some

An anonymous 1808 sketch, "First Bridge at Bellows Falls," shows the world the settler generation was beginning to achieve, with its substantial houses, places of commerce, and a soaring new bridge to link them to their neighbors and a more comfortable future. Inherent in this image is a sense of civilization rising from the teeming waters, rocks, and plants of nature.

still covered with trees and others marking fledgling greens still filled with stumps as the residents busy themselves with getting their own places in order. A few rustic churches and schools exist, most of them indistinguishable from the log houses that surround them.

At Bellows Falls, a marvel of engineering has created the first bridge over the Connecticut River, and farther north numerous ferries cross to New Hampshire. Small roads have been cut through the forests to the north along the river and west to Bennington. At Springfield, the best of them, the Crown Point Military Road, heads off to the northwest, its route a string of settlements and their clearings. People can make some time on this road, with its "stringer bridges" of two logs thrown over the stream with boards nailed across. But on the Connecticut River, the farther north we go, the more the forest seems to take charge, except for some concentrations of population where the Bayley-Hazen Road heads northwest from Newport. We finally reach a clearing in Lunenburg where the northernmost families listen for the wolves from inside their log houses.

Heading west over the Green Mountains, we can see that a few settlers have recently made it into Orleans and Lamoille Counties, and many of their log houses are of the earliest and most primitive designs. The closer we come to Lake Champlain and her large tributaries in Franklin and Chittenden Counties, the more clearings appear. But only one substantial dirt track runs from Canada, through St. Albans, coming out near the home of the recently departed Ethan Allen, on the north edge of Burlington. All along the lake, it is a regular string of clearings, with a few small towns on the way. Little roads, running parallel to the mountains, connect the towns of Addison, Rutland, and Bennington Counties. As the big lake narrows to the south, ferries now carry the Yorkers and the Vermonters back and forth in peace. On the shore itself, a new little community is growing up near the French ruins at Chimney Point; but Fort Amherst is a sad pile of rubble, burned down by a chimney fire in 1773. Fort Ticonderoga and Mount Independence remain, but in disrepair.

At the time of statehood in 1791, Vermont's largest city was the now sleepy hamlet of Guilford.

### THE FIVE LARGEST TOWNS IN 1791:

| | |
|---|---|
| 1. Guilford | 2,432 |
| 2. Bennington | 2,377 |
| 3. Shaftsbury | 1,999 |
| 4. Putney | 1,848 |
| 5. Pownal | 1,746 |

In the southwest, most of the biggest settlements nestle in the Valley of Vermont—Pawlet, Manchester, Arlington, Shaftsbury, Bennington, Pownal. The farms in the valley are almost continuous, although most of the settlers have not yet managed to clear their whole acreages. Some of the larger villages have meeting houses, although most are simple. Log homes predominate, but there are more frame dwellings than we have seen before; on the hill in Bennington are a few that even a sophisticated visitor from Boston or Philadelphia might pronounce "fine."

But most of early Vermont is not a pretty, or a healthy, place. With little regulation, growth has been fast and ugly. The soil has been robbed of its nutrients, the mountain streams are drying up, stumps are everywhere. Wood smoke is always darkening the air, and sewage is seeping into the creeks. The birth of every farm is the death of another habitat. The undesirable animals—bear, wolves, catamounts—are being systematically exterminated. Even the friendly ones have been hunted to near-extinction or have nowhere to go. You will not see many passenger pigeons now, or beaver, or deer. Those who remain alive are hiding in the forests of the north.

From the coming of Champlain to statehood, successive waves of people of European ancestry claimed the land that would be Vermont. For three decades, Vermont was New England's Wild West, as earnest young families and the last-chance middle-aged made their way to the new Eden. If any New Englanders doubted that the Puritan dream of settled religious communities was dead, they needed only to come to this place to see the creations of the land sharks, the "towns" that were not towns. While there were exceptions like Bennington, many Vermont settlements were hamlets with no centers, no greens, no churches, filling willy-nilly with dispersed farms, each its own kingdom. But the framework of town government was now in place; soon it would provide a solid base for the building of the classic Vermont village community.

The sense of individual rights over the land would be repeated in territory after territory as America moved West. The ability to stake and chop and cut your own pattern out of the land, with few institutional restraints, seemed like freedom after the hothouse atmosphere of southern New England. No wonder that this place, like the Dodge Cities of the next century, made rugged individualists like the Allen brothers into its popular heroes.

But something was missing in Vermont in 1791, and it was not just the trees and the little streams that used to water them and the beaver dams. It was not just the Abenaki, many of whom had been forced over the border into Québec. Early Vermont was a lonely place full of scattered clearings in the woods, where the men were always out working and the strong, bear-fighting women could not spy the lights of other people through the trees. A few towns had something to offer, but if you went to most of the names on an early map you would find no "there" there. Claiming was not going to be enough, in a place whose proprietors had made little provision for the amenities of social life. Vermonters had learned to pull farms out of the forest, but once this had been done there was time to miss the amenities they had left behind in southern New England. A lack of understanding of their environmental impact, scattered settlement, and the slow emergence of legal restraints were having a devastating effect upon the landscape. Creating stronger communities with greater powers of regulating individual actions would be one of the first great tasks of the fourteenth state.

CHAPTER 3

# THE CLASSIC AGRARIAN LANDSCAPE, 1791-1860

*Putney lies like Dummerston on elevated ground, but exhibits a pleasanter surface along the road. On a stream which turns several mills in the neighborhood of some well-appearing houses, a beautiful winding valley opens toward the west. The acclivities [slopes] on both sides of the valley are very handsome, and present a succession of rich farms under good cultivation. Several good houses and a decent church add to the cheerfulness of the prospect.*

—TIMOTHY DWIGHT, *Travels in New England and New York* (1803)

On a misty September morning in 1803, the Reverend Timothy Dwight, president of Yale College, on a horseback tour of Vermont, stopped to record his first admiring glimpse of the picturesque village of Putney. His description contains many of the classic landscape features that have become near-clichés in our own day: the pretty little community with its white church spire, ringed by perfect farms, nestled amidst the sheltering mountains. It is a postcard—before there were postcards—of much that people in the next two centuries would come to value about the Vermont landscape.

But there was something genuinely striking, almost radical, in Timothy Dwight's word picture that is hard for us to grasp now that such descriptions have become conventional. We picture what we know of classic Vermont villages today—Arlington, Orwell, Craftsbury Common. In our fantasies (and often, now, in reality), New England villages have always been made up of trim clapboard houses and white church spires

The Bennington Museum

In the 1790s, the new state of Vermont's most elegant and "civilized" village was Bennington, shown here in this "Landscape View of Old Bennington," painted by the traveling Connecticut artist Ralph Earl. The idealization of the classical—and class-ridden—village is apparent in the way Earl has focused on the hamlet's most elegant houses. The large dwelling in the mid-foreground was that of Governor Isaac Tichenor; behind it is the courthouse. The homes of other prominent citizens are included—perhaps in the hope of inspiring more commissions for the artist, who has also painted himself and his son in the lower left corner.

soaring above clipped and weedless greens. But what was Dwight really seeing? This Putney enjoyed a physical setting that had only recently been hacked out of the woods. Its sawmills were up and running, so the original smattering of log houses was slowly being replaced by more substantial frame dwellings—but without the patina of age we appreciate in houses of that era today. Only the most pretentious had any paint; most were bare wood just beginning to weather to light gray. There was still sawdust in the cracks of the new church, significantly constructed after the tavern, which had been up and running for a number of years. Stroll on the surrounding green, and you risked stumbling over stumps and spending the evening picking burdocks off your pants.

The most striking thing about Dwight's description is that it was an evocation of a "landscape" rather than a simple enumeration of what could be found on the land. He painted a picture of the scene for his reader, and then invested it with aesthetic and moral judgments, much as a painter might. Dwight carried an ideal village in his mind, a place embodying all the virtues of community, and Putney was lucky enough to conform. There was every

---

## FRANCIS PARKMAN DISCOVERS THE FIRESIDE ECONOMY OF ESSEX COUNTY, 1842

The uneven pace of Vermont's development can be seen in this passage from Francis Parkman's account of a trip along the northern Vermont border in July and August 1842. While much of the state was now covered with farms and commercial villages, the more remote sections were still in the clearing stage.

Parkman, who later went on to be considered nineteenth-century America's greatest historian for his monumental study of the French and Indian Wars, *France and England in North America*, was an undergraduate at Harvard when he wrote of slogging through the forests to Canaan, where he and his friend were fed at the table of a family of subsistence farmers:

*Now and then there would be a clearing with its charred stumps, its boundary of frowning woods, and its log cabin; but, for the most part, the forest was in its original state. The average depth of the mud in the path was one foot. Scarce a ray of sunlight had ever reached there through the thick boughs. The streams had no bridges, and most of them preferred the artificial channel afforded by our path to the one they had worked for themselves among the mossy stones and decayed trunks of the forest. We emerged upon a broader path—practicable to a stout wagon. We stopped at a log cabin at three o'clock and asked for dinner. A decent one was given us. During the process of eating, the "girls" were working at the spinning wheel and giggling among themselves, the boys sat still and upright in their chairs—homemade—and contemplated us with great attention.*

*"How far to the next clearing?" we asked.*

*"Eight mile!" and a long eight miles it was to us—dismal slough of despond the whole way—mud to the knees.*

—Francis Parkman, quoted in T.D.S. Bassett, *Outsiders Inside Vermont* sign of its being a real community. It may not have been the archetypal "City on a Hill" that John Winthrop and his Puritan companions had meant to build in Massachusetts Bay, but at least it was built on "elevated ground." Early Putney's situation was "pleasanter" than that of some other villages, some of its houses were "well-appearing" and "good," its farms were "rich," its church was "decent," and the whole "prospect" made the viewer feel "cheerful."

This was a way of reading the landscape that required an educated eye and a level of sophistication that had not often been applied to pioneer Vermont before Timothy Dwight turned his considerable intellect to the north. To see this scene as he did required a certain distance from life on the land, the eyes of a man with smooth hands and clean fingernails, who takes the role of a detached observer. Timothy Dwight was describing a brave new world that was finally, to his southern New England eyes, beginning to look "civilized." To him, landscape order represented moral order.

Dwight's description is as interesting for what it leaves out as for what it includes. The growing prosperity of the countryside was making a real village possible, but it was still a village in utero. He mentioned no shops, no general store, no bustling professional community. Such amenities require customers with something to sell or trade in exchange for goods and services. Apart from the sawmills, there were no manufactures. The economy that would support them was barely coming into existence as neighboring farmers struggled to transform the wilderness and master the arts of subsistence. As the first frantic scramble of hand-to-mouth subsided, people began to create central places, more controlled environments where they could find a sense of community that transcended town meetings, barn-raising, and help with the haying. The structures of community—taverns, schools, churches, lawyers' offices, and general stores—were beginning to appear, usually in about that order. The growth of village communities would gradually lead to greater restraints on exploitation of the land.

The more sophisticated rural craftsmen often used pattern books to get ideas for fulfilling their building commissions. The magnificent East Poultney Baptist Church (bottom) was erected in 1805 by a brilliant Connecticut master builder, Elisha Scott. The design was based on a Federal church pattern in Asher Benjamin's *The Country Builder's Assistant* (top), although it could be argued that the rural builder improved on the original design.

## LANDSCAPE AND COMMUNITY

*No group sets out to create a landscape, of course. What it sets out to do is to create a community, and the landscape as its visible manifestation is simply the by-product of people working and living, sometimes coming together, sometimes staying apart, but always recognizing their inter-dependence.*

—John Brinckerhoff Jackson, *Discovering the Vernacular Landscape*

If you could freeze-frame a landscape for a single moment (for landscapes are always changing), what you would see would represent the sum total of all the decisions—individual and communal—that have been made about that

A successful landscape, like that of Island Pond (above), often looks as if it has grown organically from its physical environment. In a sense, it has, because most of its old buildings were necessarily made of local materials, wood and stone.

particular physical setting up to that moment. Some of those decisions enhance the landscape, others detract from it. The standards by which landscapes are judged are also always changing, as people alter the land for usefulness, beauty, or profit.

Landscapes are the physical repository of society's deepest beliefs and saddest mistakes; history has a lot to tell us about what has and has not worked on the land. If you know the signs, most landscapes show the tensions between communal values and private interests. These competing priorities have a long history. As we have seen, the Vermont of the settlement era was characterized by the predominance of private interests, although the political structures of public life were taking form. In a context of radical republican individualism, lack of environmental awareness, and minimal regulation, early Vermont's ecology was severely taxed.

The following period brought more structured communities, more control, and the beginnings of a greater environmental understanding. One of the best compliments we can give to our predecessors is a desire to retain what they have bequeathed to us. Preservation is an acknowledgement that some of their decisions were good ones. Many of the landscape features that still resonate for us in Vermont—the stern clapboard farmhouses, white church steeples, elegant brick town buildings, and rolling green pastures—remain from the first half of the nineteenth century. How did people living then come to so many successful, and some unsuccessful, decisions about what they would do on the land?

We can try to answer that question by looking at the development that had more impact upon landscape decisions in this period than any other: the transition from the simple subsistence economy of the first settlers, with its slim pickings and reliance on barter, to a more commercial capitalist economy, based on producing a surplus, using money, and trading in shops or with distant markets. This transition made its impact in several key ways. In agriculture, the pressure was on for farmers to become more "scientific" and specialize in producing one product in order to gain a larger surplus. The new capitalism led a few entrepreneurs to try developing industries ranging from textiles to tourism, all in the context of an underdeveloped transportation system. Commercial development helped stimulate the growth of community life by providing the wealth needed to build civic amenities like churches, schools, taverns, and stores where people could come together and forge bonds. Finally, life in the state's new villages helped to develop more sophisticated ethical, ecological, and aesthetic understandings of the land that were to have an enormous impact upon land use.

## TRANSFORMING THE LAND

*Could we exhibit to the world the phenomenon which has never yet appeared on earth, that of a nation of husbandmen, making commerce and the arts wholly subservient to the interest of agriculture, we might indulge more sanguine hopes of the immortal duration of our republic. But our national habits must be changed...And our husbandmen and other citizens must bestow that money which they pay for useless luxuries, and that time which they spend in running after these luxuries and contriving how they shall elevate to importance and to power a favorite partizan, in efforts by which they may increase the productive powers of the soil.*

—Leonard E. Lathrop, *The Farmer's Library, or Essays, Designed to Encourage the Pursuits & Promote the Science of Agriculture* (Rutland, 1825)

The classical agrarian Republic saw farming as the moral bedrock of a democratic state that rejected the materialistic degeneracy of the Old World. Agriculture would instill virtue in the people while it tamed the land. In the new landscape of the early 1800s, the trees pleased most when they stood at a distance, as flecks of red on an autumn hillside or a swath of dark green on a snowy winter horizon. The foreground, preferably, would be open and, in a favored attribute of the period, "airy." It would bear patterns produced by the productive hand of man, with lawnlike pastures and the straight stripes of crops ripening in the sun. The sylvan temples of the forest were a great place to visit, as long as one could be assured of returning by nightfall to the neat safety of home.

The life story of John Whittemore (1796–1885) is a classic American rags-to-riches tale of a boy who went from an impoverished childhood in a log cabin to prosperity as a farmer and respected community member in rural St. Albans. His biography demonstrates that it was possible to make it in Vermont if you had intelligence, ambition, and plenty of luck.

In Vermont, as in the whole new nation, the land was the place on which all future dreams of greatness must be based, and farmers were the chosen people. The sudden transformation of the landscape occurring in the first century of settlement had been a flood of Yankee immigrants who tried to control the environment for their own gain. But now a great change was taking place in the Vermont economy, as people moved from subsistence farming to commercially driven forms of agriculture and industry. This development would alter Vermont beyond either recognition or restoration.

The changes did not happen everywhere at once. Much of northern Vermont and the high mountains of the central spine of the state were still in the pine-cutting and potash phase in the early nineteenth century. Even in southern Vermont a traveller, as late as 1832, could write that on his way to Burlington, "I passed through many pleasant villages & some in which it did not appear to me to be decided whether man or nature was to rule." But while the timetable differed, the pattern remained the same, moving from clearing to subsistence farming to a new world of commercial farming and light industry.

## FAMILY FINANCE AS THE BASIS OF RURAL CHANGE, OR HOW JOHN WHITTEMORE SHOWED HIS NEIGHBORS WHAT'S WHAT

Vermont, like many developing countries today, was experiencing the changeover from self-sufficiency, where families grew or manufactured almost everything they needed on their own farms and bartered for most of their other goods, to a commercial economy, where they grew or manufactured more than they needed and sold the surplus to buy ready-made goods. Trade and access to outside markets became increasingly important, money and forms of credit were more widely used, and everywhere there was evidence of rising expectations. New "wants" created markets, as people strove to acquire whatever would pull them above subsistence.

The great transformation was actually very personal, happening in thousands of log cabins and clapboard houses around the state at different times in different places. One man's story will stand for the others, because it is typical of countless tales. The difference is that John Whittemore sat down as an old man and wrote a little autobiography describing a life that moved from the most painful subsistence to capitalist comfort in rural Vermont. Whittemore was born in Lynn, Massachusetts, in 1796 and had the dimmest early childhood memories of being brought north through the deep snow to homestead with his parents in St. Albans. He remembered their first hut, "a rude structure, hastily built," where he and his siblings would lie upon the floor and be "much amused by seeing the squirrels run around upon the timbers over our heads."

Young John's father, a shoemaker by trade and a farmer by necessity, got off to a good start in the neighborhood, but this short period of familial happiness and adjustment was brought to a shocking end when he died of a fast-moving fever. Mrs. Whittemore was left with four children under 12 "and scanty means for their support." She began taking in sewing, and the children farmed as best they could. They lived the barest of subsistences: "It may well be supposed we were poor and needy, and often in need of the comforts of life." Winters brought particular suffering. Years later, John remembered how it felt "To rise in the morning and see the ground covered with snow and no wood to make a fire, and no clothing to keep me warm, and no shoes for my feets, but old worn out ones of my mother's—all these together made it so gloomy that I would almost give up in despair."

The Whittemores got some help from family, but it is clear that they were alone through most of their sufferings. One glimpses almost no evidence of community in those early years; John was well into his teens when "About this time society began to settle down into something like order. A number of first-class families had settled in the village." There was now a Congregational Church to go to in St. Albans, and some friends for commiseration.

When he was 16, John's sister married an industrious young farmer and cooper named Josiah Smith, who began to teach him a way of farming that might help them both get ahead in life. Here is John's description of one boy's change from scratching out a bare subsistence to rudimentary captalist farming practices:

> *[Josiah] had team and tools, and he would prepare my ground in the spring and furnish seed, and I would work for him in return. We now began to succeed. We raised some corn and all the potatoes we needed and some to sell.*

> *Up to this time I wore old clothes, second-hand, such as had been cast off by other boys, but now I could furnish myself with new clothes, new shoes or new boots. These were luxuries indeed, which I could well appreciate.*

There are both method and motive here, as the young man worked hard to raise a surplus that could then be sold for the ready money that would buy a few of the luxuries we would term necessities.

John worked so hard that Josiah gave him a share in an 80-acre farm he was buying. They got off to a rocky start, for they planted their first crops on it in 1816, "the year without a summer," when Vermont saw freakish killing frost in every month. Luckily, their creditors cut them some slack, and they were able to make a go of the farm in the coming years. John could now afford a decent house for his mother and younger siblings:

> *We moved in sometime in October, bidding adieu to the old place and all its painful associations. We began at once setting up beds, arranging furniture, and putting our house in order, and then sat down to enjoy the contrast.*

Village greens or commons—like this classic example in the eponymous Craftsbury Common—are beloved features of many Vermont villages today, but their similarity to those in southern New England is often only superficial. The land speculation that characterized Vermont settlement meant that common land was seldom set aside for grazing in the first age of settlement. Many Vermont greens are products of the early nineteenth century, when villages began to spring up in the clearings. The commons were often developed on part of the church lot and used as landscape features from the start, rather than in their more traditional role as communal livestock grazing areas.

*A bright fire was blazing on the hearth, and shone out upon the floor; white and smooth, upon new plastered walls and broad well-lighted windows. All which taken together afforded a sensation of pleasure, I could not describe. I walked the floor with emotions of pleasure I was almost ashamed to acknowledge, yet could not suppress. I was pleased to see my mother contented, my grandmother comfortable, and my sisters with a home they were not ashamed of.*

*I had now entered upon a new era. We had risen from abject want to competence and comfort. The whole face of nature had changed its shady aspects for one more clear and pleasant, and we were well prepared to enjoy it.*

John, now 21, celebrated by courting and winning the hand of a young lady, "possessed of a well-balanced mind and a fair exterior," only recently come to the neighborhood. The day Aluna Kingsbury agreed to be his wife would be remembered as one of the happiest days of his life; she proved to be an excellent choice. They had to wait three years before they had enough money to marry, when John was in a position to look for his own place.

He was soon offered an old hill farm, 100 acres east of St. Albans on the road to Fairfield. The price was right, but "The farm was in low repute. Several families had tried to live on it, but had to leave to save their lives, and I thought but little of it—in fact, had a strong prejudice against it." But after seeing it for himself, he began to think its potential had been badly managed. He bought it for $1,100, payable at $200 yearly in good horses, signing the deed in October 1821.

When he was destitute and could have used a community, it barely existed; now, community values—in the form of naysaying—were all too prevalent:

> *I was now fairly launched on the sea of life and whether I should sink or swim remained to be seen. There were many obstacles in the way of success. The farm was rough and uncultivated with a soil that would yield to nothing but the hardest labor. I had no sympathy from without. All prophesied that I should fail and many hoped that I should. ...I resolved the Lord helping me I would make them change their tune.*

His first impulse was to tidy up the farm, something the settler generation had set little store by; for one by-product of community was a new appreciation for the look of the landscape. The new generation took pride in creating order:

> *I began work on the farm. The barn...was in a dilapidated state. I went to work to repair it and soon it had a new appearance, and in fact it changed the aspect of the entire place. I repaired fences. There were nooks and corners which were covered with briers and thistles, left to grow through carelessness or neglect. I went at such places with my oxen and plow, and soon had them subdued and fit for the seed. These little things gave a new appearance to the place, and in fact was working out a contrast which was noticed before long by those passing by.*

He threw himself into clearing fields and growing grain, later writing, "I cannot describe the sensation of pleasure which I felt when I saw the rich blades of wheat." His great success prompted a poor boy's enjoyment in proving himself to his critics: "The clamor was hushed. Not a dog to move his tongue. All were surprised, some pleased with my success and willing to acknowledge they were mistaken in the farm. But the most part fell back into sullen silence, having nothing to say."

The numbers of acres in production, the cattle herd, and the little family all continued to grow. Whittemore made a killing by selling a large potato crop to one of the new middle men who were shipping produce on

## LOVE AND DEATH IN EARLY ROYALTON: ERASTUS WILLIAMS

*Erastus Williams was a young farmer just starting out in life in the 1830s. He kept a diary of his daily activities, recording the great variety in a farmer's life in this, and every, age. These selections begin when he was 24 and just about to set up housekeeping with his new wife, Charlotte Safford, in an age when the fates could steal a young couple's happiness with little warning.*

**1835.** [Apr.] 7th. Finished cleaning the old house for the present, have been to work on it for three weeks, have just got it comfortable to live in. 12 Sun. For the first time my wife went to meeting with me. 13th. Mended fence some, brought water some, run after the sheep and geese some, and did other chores. May 6. Paid Charles Clapp 23 dollars for the stove. Isabel came to make me a visit, the first time she was ever in my house—my house—and have I a house of my own? Yes, I am a slave to no one but myself now. Jun. 3. Sheared sheep for Capt. Dutton. 15th. Worked on the road; my tax this year is almost six dollars. Aug. 25th. I threshed Indian whet. 26th. Cleaned up the buckwheat and threshed 2 bushels of Rye. Sept. 2. Went to tunbridge with Charlotte. 19th. [Militia] training, met at Mr. Fox's. 22nd. Went to father's, he and mother were gone a visiting so we children visited together. 23rd. Cut and bound corn. [Nov.] 17th. Set out apple trees. 21st. Finished ploughing the wheat stubble. [Dec.] 16th. The coldest day I ever saw.

**1836.** ...Feb. 21. Went to meeting and set in our pew for the first time. [Mar.] 31st. Hay and grain are gone but the snow is not. Today I began to tap the sugar place. [Apr. 24] I staid at home to take care of my lambs, the old sow eat up one this morning. May 1. Warm and pleasant, nature smiles and earth rejoices—grass has grown fast.

**1837.** [Apr] 16 Sun. I went to meeting—old Mr. Washburn preached, he was rather tedious but was the fault in him or me?

**1838.** Oct. 17. My wife and I this day buried our only son, he was 10 weeks old the day he died—he was a large babe, was always well and grew fast—he was pleasant, he gained our hearts, we loved him, never shall I forget his looks and actions. Last Friday he appeared in perfect health—Friday night he was restless—next morning the fatal disease showed itself—whooping cough.

*The grieving father did not write in his diary again for three years.*

Lake Champlain. Other crops did well, and the young couple were able to pay off their farm faster than they had ever hoped to do. He and Aluna "now began to feel that we could supply ourselves with some of the comforts of life." They bought a fine horse and "comfortable vehicles to ride in."

Whittemore also played a part in that great early capitalist development, the closing of the commons. All over New England, common land was parceled out and put into production. This happened quickly in Vermont,

**Erastus Williams lived in the scenic village of Royalton. This view (above), from Hosea Doton's 1855 "Map of Windsor County," shows the center of the village, with William Skinner's house and store flanking the Royalton Hotel.**

where the history of settlement by land speculation meant that little land had ever been set aside for common use. Here, farmers assumed a right to use any land not being developed, and often ran their cattle on land owned by distant proprietors. This was Whittemore's situation in St. Albans, where he had decided it would be most profitable to specialize in cattle production. He was steadily increasing his herd because "The summering...would cost us nothing as they could run on the common that lay adjoining us." When rumors began that this "common" land was for sale, he jumped at the chance to buy 65 acres for just under $400. He kept purchasing adjoining farms, and after 14 years on the hill he was master of more than 250 acres.

Prosperity fueled the Whittemores' desire for community, and they decided that "the time had come which we had been looking for when we could leave the hill for some place more convenient to society and schools."

---

## 1816: THE YEAR WITHOUT A SUMMER

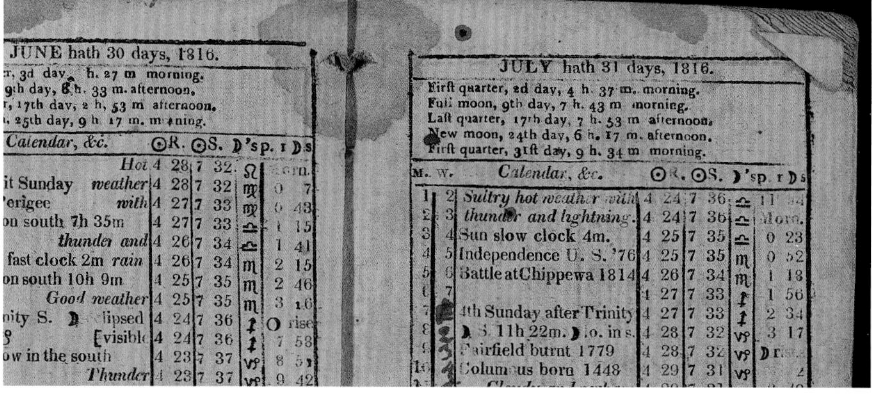

JUNE hath 30 days, 1816.

r, 3d day, h. 27 m morning.
9th day, 8 h. 33 m. afternoon.
r, 17th day, 2 h, 53 m afternoon.
, 25th day, 9 h 17 m. morning.

| Calendar, &c. | ☉R. | | ☉S. | | ☽'s p. | ☽ r/s | |
|---|---|---|---|---|---|---|---|
| Hot | 4 | 28 | 7 | 32 | ♌ | morn. | |
| it Sunday weather | 4 | 28 | 7 | 32 | ♍ | 0 | 7 |
| 'erigee with | 4 | 27 | 7 | 33 | ♍ | 0 | 43 |
| on south 7h 35m | 4 | 27 | 7 | 33 | ♎ | 1 | 15 |
| thunder and | 4 | 26 | 7 | 34 | ♎ | 1 | 41 |
| fast clock 2m rain | 4 | 26 | 7 | 34 | ♏ | 2 | 15 |
| on south 10h 9m | 4 | 25 | 7 | 35 | ♏ | 2 | 46 |
| Good weather | 4 | 25 | 7 | 35 | ♏ | 3 | 16 |
| nity S. ☽ eclipsed | 4 | 24 | 7 | 36 | ♐ | ☉ rise | |
| [visible | 4 | 24 | 7 | 36 | ♐ | 7 | 58 |
| ow in the south | 4 | 23 | 7 | 37 | ♑ | 8 | 5 |
| Thunder | 4 | 23 | 7 | 37 | ♑ | 9 | 42 |

JULY hath 31 days, 1816.

First quarter, 2d day, 4 h. 37 m. morning.
Full moon, 9th day, 7 h. 43 m morning.
Last quarter, 17th day, 7 h. 53 m afternoon.
New moon, 24th day, 6 h. 17 m. afternoon.
First quarter, 31st day, 9 h. 34 m morning.

| M. | W. | Calendar, &c. | ☉R. | | ☉S. | | ☽'s p. | r ☽ s | |
|---|---|---|---|---|---|---|---|---|---|
| 1 | 2 | Sultry hot weather with | 4 | 24 | 7 | 36 | ♎ | 11 | 34 |
| 2 | 3 | thunder and lightning. | 4 | 24 | 7 | 36 | ♎ | Morn. | |
| 3 | 4 | Sun slow clock 4m. | 4 | 25 | 7 | 35 | ♎ | 0 | 23 |
| 4 | 5 | Independence U. S. '76 | 4 | 25 | 7 | 35 | ♏ | 0 | 52 |
| 5 | 6 | Battle at Chippewa 1814 | 4 | 26 | 7 | 34 | ♏ | 1 | 18 |
| 6 | 7 | | 4 | 27 | 7 | 33 | ♐ | 1 | 56 |
| 7 | | 4th Sunday after Trinity | 4 | 27 | 7 | 33 | ♐ | 2 | 34 |
| 8 | 2 | ☽ S. 11h 22m. ☽ lo. in s. | 4 | 28 | 7 | 32 | ♑ | 3 | 17 |
| 9 | 3 | Fairfield burnt 1779 | 4 | 28 | 7 | 32 | ♑ | ☽ rises | |
| 10 | 4 | Columbus born 1448 | 4 | 29 | 7 | 31 | ♑ | | |

Imagine a year in which temperatures drop below freezing in every month. It happened in Vermont in 1816, known by the locals variously as "the year without a summer," "the scase [scarce] year," and "eighteen hundred and froze to death." On the night of June 5–6, temperatures dropped by nearly 50 degrees, and during the next day a wet snow began to fall all over the state. On June 7, a genuine blizzard struck northern Vermont, with five to six inches in the valleys and twelve inches on Craftsbury Common. Hard freezes continued through the 10th. July, August, and September all had cold periods, ending with an early frost.

A teenaged boy, James Winchester, described how his uncle went out to tend some sheep in the back pasture and disappeared for three days in the great snowstorm in June:

*On the forenoon of the third day the searchers found my uncle buried in the snow a mile from the pasture, in almost an opposite direction from home. He was almost frozen stiff.*

*He had evidently become bewildered in the blinding storm and had wandered about until he succumbed to fatigue and cold. It seems a most improbable thing that a person ever fell victim to a snow storm in the middle of June in this latitude, but such a thing was only too true.*

—quoted in David Ludlum, *The Vermont Weather Book*

The freakish weather resulted in the failure of a whole summer's crops, leading to widespread hunger and economic hardship all over the state, particularly during the following winter.

What caused the frigid summer of 1816? Meteorologists are still not sure. The 1810s were the coldest decade of a cold period that has been dubbed the Little Ice Age. In 1816 itself, sunspots were reported and there was an unexplained amount of dust in the upper atmosphere, possibly from an erupting volcano.

UVM Special Collections

During a chance meeting in a store in St. Albans (for there were now a few stores), John heard of a rich valley farm for sale and quickly bought it on credit for $3,000. But Aluna was not to enjoy the increasing pleasures of village society, for before they could move in she was diagnosed with a fatal wasting disease. Her loving husband wrote that "a life so precious and one so much needed it was hard to give up," but there was to be no choice. She died at 39, and John was left with five small children, the youngest 18 months old.

John Whittemore was to live for 40 more years, dying at 89 in 1885. His children were raised by a housekeeper, who gave them "motherly care." They seem to have turned out well, making good marriages and becoming productive citizens. His son Rodney married the girl next door, and they took over the farm and lived in harmony under the same roof with John until his death. Whittemore's capitalist adventure had paid off; his family was comfortable and free from serious worry. He finished his narrative with the satisfaction that he had enjoyed "a happy family, harmonious in all our relations," and an existence in which, following Psalms, "goodness and mercy have followed me all the days of my life."

John Whittemore's story is the story of the growth of rural capitalism; it was paralleled by thousands of Vermont families in the early nineteenth century. They began in the poverty of the settlement period, scraping a subsistence through diverse enterprises: growing some crops, keeping a few head of cattle, boiling potash, trying a little maple sugaring. Many in the settlement generation lived as much through foraging the state's natural resources as they did by farming. For the smart ones, or maybe just the lucky ones, there came a transition time when farming began to yield a surplus, middle men bought that surplus for cash money, and they started to get ahead. The bigger operators began to specialize, as Whittemore did, and bought up the land that had been deemed common, turning it to their private use. For them, the new villages held the enticements of shopping and society. For the others, those who foraged long past the days of good pickings, there would be less and less to keep them in Vermont.

## THE VIRTUOUS YEOMAN TRANSFORMS THE LAND

*Has not the farmer more than all others converted the wilderness into arable, productive farms, covered with waving grain, fruits, flowers, and the grasses that give sustenance to millions of domestic animals that give food and raiment and serve for domestic labor and for the pleasure of all? Who so much as the farmers have built these roads and canals, those colleges and institutions of learning, those public and private edifices that adorn the country? In fine does not a large*

Thomas Durant Visser, *Field Guide to New England Barns and Farm Buildings* (1997)

## VERMONT'S ENGLISH BARNS

Early barns survive today in far fewer numbers than early houses. Barns have tended to fall victim to shoddy construction and their own practical natures.

From 1620 to the early 1800s, the standard barn design in New England was the one that first settlers brought with them from home. These "English barns" were rectangular, often 30 feet by 40 feet, had large double doors in the middle of the long sides, and were divided into three bays, with animals on one end, hay storage on the other, and an open threshing floor in the middle. Farm wagons could be driven onto the threshing floor and out the other side. Other features might include:

- Transom ( a row of little windows) above the door to let in light.
- Large hand-cut inner timbers showing ax marks.
- Hand-wrought nails or early machine-cut nails.
- Wide sheathing boards on walls made from first-cut timber.
- Often placed north of the house to cut winter winds, with a sunny farmyard in front facing to the south.

*majority of taxes for all purposes come from the pocket of the Vermont farmer? Where else on earth can be found so many elegant and commodious dwellings, adorned with trees and flowers and everything to make home desirable, such convenient roads, so many churches and public schools so well supported, where such deep and general devotion to religion, and where else do the morals and intelligence of the community come up to those of the rural districts of our own Vermont?*

—Henry Lester, "*Man Made for Agriculture*," his Premium Essay, awarded five dollars by the Rutland County Society at their fair held at Poultney, September 1853

For Henry Lester, and other less articulate farmers of his day, agriculture was the backbone of America. Without farming, there would not only be a lack of food and clothing, there would also be no schools, no transport, no homes, no communities, no morals, and no freedom.

Today, when farmers make up such a small proportion of the population, even in Vermont, it is difficult to imagine a world in which almost everyone was a farmer. This does not, of course, mean that everyone was suited to be a farmer or was good at being one. It just means that there were few alternatives. Tom Bassett has estimated that in 1840, 80 percent of the families in Vermont were living and working on a farm. Not all the farms were good. It has been estimated that less than half of all land in Vermont turned out to be suitable for cultivation, and of that a large share could only support grazing. Only one-sixth of Vermont has first-rate agricultural land, and almost all of that is either in the Champlain Valley or Orleans County. Yet the whole state was full of farms, and in the early nineteenth century most of them were providing a subsistence. Farms were large enough to be viable, many averaging between 50 and 100 acres.

On the thin and rocky soil of the hill farms, farmers could still make a go of it in the first seasons of cultivation because the soil retained thousands of years of leaf-mould fertility. In the valleys, the first settlers had been able to grow that most prized bread grain, wheat, despite its high demands upon the fertility of the soil. In his history of Addison County, Samuel Swift recalled how in the early decades of statehood, "the valley of Lake Champlain and Otter Creek...was as celebrated for the production of wheat as Western New York has since been. It was the principal staple among the productions of the County." But here, as elsewhere, "the insects, rust and frost have, in late years, greatly diminished the crop and discouraged the farmers." Wheat was particularly prone to disease, and it was many years before farmers could prevent their wheat crop from becoming "blasted" and useless. The Coos region of the northern Connecticut Valley was Vermont's foremost wheat district while its soil fertility lasted. When wheat failed, as it almost always did in a few years without proper crop rotation or manuring, farm families turned to rye bread until the coming of the railroads brought cheap wheat imports from the West.

Early Vermonters were soon growing a variety of food crops. There was Indian corn for man and beast; in 1818 a Cavendish farmer named Salmon Dutton developed an extremely high-yielding variety that was soon being grown throughout the state. The settlers had been familiar with what were called "Indian vegetables" in southern New England, and so brought

## BARTER AND BUYING IN WEYBRIDGE

This early anonymous pen drawing, "A View of Middlebury in the State of Vermont" (1808), shows that the village the Weybridge ladies knew so well was already gaining a number of civic amenities—elegant churches, pretty houses, fledgling shops, thriving mills, the county courthouse, a state bank, a female seminary, and a small college.

UVM Special Collections

The responsibility for getting food usually fell to the women in early Vermont, and as the economy moved from barter to cash purchases there was a period when both systems overlapped. Sylvia Drake, a Weybridge seamstress who lived with her "lady friend," Charity Bryant, often mentioned food in her diary. She was in the culinarily advantageous position of performing a service in a farming district, where she was often paid for her sewing in foodstuffs. The women also had the shopping advantages of living near one of Vermont's earlier commercial towns, Middlebury, in the 1820s.

*Barter and swapping among neighbors were very common:*

TUESDAY [APRIL 10, 1821]. Ed[win] brings us milk & eggs. I give him meal. Mrs. H[aga]r gives us bacon. Sister sends us a box of sugar by Miss Pratt. Isaac brings us pork, give him sage and honey.

*Sylvia also did a great deal of baking:*

SATURDAY [APRIL 27, 1822]. ...make crackers & bake them.

MONDAY [APRIL 29]. Bake cookeys, ginger bread, &c.

*Many food gifts and payments are recorded in the diary:*

WEDNESDAY MAY 1. Laura comes, brings milk, grapes, &c. Emma comes in the afternoon, brings us two pyes, a loaf of bread. Takes tea here.

*Sometimes Sylvia's food does not seem to have agreed with her:*

SATURDAY, MAY 4. No better. Take tarter sufficient to puke me. Mrs. Kellog brings us a custard pye, Mr. Nor[cross] an apple pye.

*Sylvia's partner, Charity Bryant, went to Middlebury once a week to purchase more exotic goods:*

MONDAY [APRIL 18, 1822]. Miss B[ryant] goes to Middlebury. ...Purchase tea, molasses, bed ticking & brandy.

SATURDAY [JUNE 7, 1823]. My dear C[harity] goes to Middlebury. Purchases calico for Mother, a gown, tea, rice, snuff &c.

with them pumpkins, squash, and beans. Maple trees were tapped in the spring, with most of their sap turned into maple sugar rather than syrup. There were burgeoning fruit orchards in the Connecticut River basin as early as the 1790s; farmers soon realized that apples were particularly well-suited to the valleys of the state. A good share of their harvest went into making hard cider, although that new industry received a setback when, after 1830, thousands of apple trees were pulled up under pressure from the temperance movement.

How did the farmers of the early statehood period actually work the land? The original settlers had only a few hand tools—axes, saws, adzes, carpentry equipment, spades, and hoes. Once the land had been cleared, farming could be done on a somewhat larger scale with larger tools. A Middlebury blacksmith's apprentice named John Deere moved to Illinois and invented every farmer's dream, the steel self-scouring plow. It not only managed to "break the plains," but also accomplished the more difficult task of cutting through the thick clay of Addison County without getting stuck. Most farmers coveted a plow, and the few lucky enough to own one could make good money doing custom plowing for other farmers once their own work was done. Horse-drawn rakes, reapers, mowers, and cultivators also conserved human energy. But most of these new inventions could only be purchased by wealthier farmers. Access to inventions was increasingly separating the wheat from the chaff as marginal farmers found themselves unable to compete.

In the rich valley farmland, the more "scientific" farmers of the early nineteenth century soon reached an ecological equilibrium, recognizing that they had to add as many nutrients to the soil as they took out if they were to survive. All farms were organic farms then, and many farmers succeeded. But the situation was different for the hill farmers. In their thin and rocky soil, fertility from vegetable matter accumulated over a millenium was depleted in a generation or two. Despite attempts at crop rotation and manuring, it soon became painfully obvious that many of Vermont's soils were not meant for intensive crop farming.

What really seemed to do well here was hay. When the settlers came, the valleys and riverfronts were often waving with rich native grasses, but these were quickly eaten by livestock. More nutritious English varieties replaced them, many of which we still see in Vermont fields: timothy, redtop, red and white clover. Grazing seemed like a better idea than cropping, and Vermont's early farmers were particularly enthusiastic about raising livestock.

In the first few decades after settlement, most Vermont farm families aimed for the diversity prized by those who were forced to be self-sufficient. They tried to keep a couple of cows, a horse or ox, and a few sheep for making woolen clothing. Pigs and poultry were also appreciated both for their

The first settlers soon found that Vermont was a good place to grow hay. They quickly replaced native grasses with English varieties similar to those being grown in this modern hayfield (above) near Tunbridge.

John Deere (right) was born in Rutland in 1804; at 17 he began his career as a blacksmith's apprentice in the boomtown of Middlebury. In 1837, like many young Vermonters of his era, he headed west to Illinois, where a year later he invented "the plow that broke the plains." Plowing the loam of the Midwest was probably a breeze after his experience with the sticky clay of his home state. Until his death in 1886, Deere remained president of the extraordinarily successful company that still bears his name.

Above: Alan Jakubek; far right: Deere & Company

meat and for their ability to take care of feeding themselves by rooting around in the yard.

As farmers gained experience on the Vermont landscape, the better ones began to make surpluses that could be bartered or sold for profit. In 1800, Uriah Bingham of Bakersfield proudly wrote to his rich brother-in-law back in Massachusetts to tell him his Vermont mixed farming venture was going well. In one year, he had raised 40 bushels of wheat, 65 of corn, 200 of potatoes, and 50 of flax: "Enough to support My Family and Some to Sell— I improved about 7 acres of Land last year and I expect this year to improve about 14 acres—My Stock is a good yoak of Oxen two Cows and a yearling Heifer a likely Breeding Sow 10 Hens and 2 Hunting Cats."

All over Vermont, the more successful farmers were slowly beginning to get ahead—clearing a few more acres and increasing their herds in order to gain a little profit. But it was almost impossible to make any serious money farming in a state suffering from a shortage of currency, poor or depleted soils, a rudimentary transportation system, and a resulting lack of access to distant markets. Vermont farmers had two choices. They could retain their tradition of mixed farming, following the classic conservative practice of not putting all your eggs in one basket. This was the safer, more traditional option, and had the advantage of saving the farmer from the whims of a distant market. On the other hand, it did not lead to great profits, because the farmer never had a large surplus of any one product. Other farmers believed that the new and scientific approach to agriculture required that the farm family focus its efforts on one product, which would yield a greater surplus, and therefore a larger profit. But what could they specialize in? It was a question for families

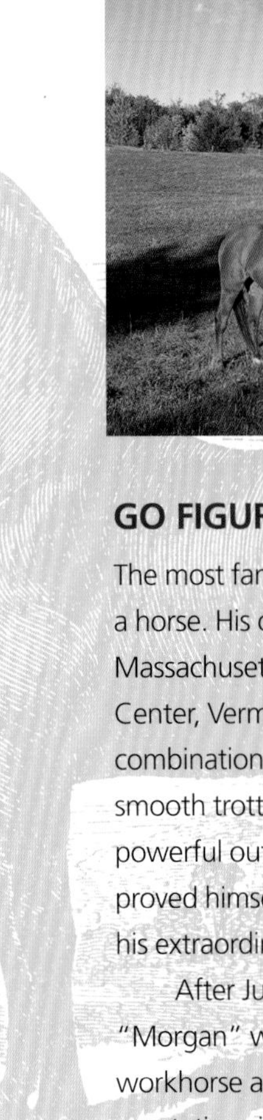

The genetic mutation that produced the strong, sturdy shape of the original Morgan horse, shown in this contemporary etching of Justin Morgan's Figure, can still be traced in these modern Morgans (left). The Morgan horse is now Vermont's official state animal.

## GO FIGURE

The most famous Vermonter of the early nineteenth century may well have been a horse. His owner, Justin Morgan, acquired him in West Springfield, Massachusetts, in the 1790s and brought him along when he moved to Randolph Center, Vermont. The horse, named Figure, soon began to exhibit a remarkable combination of qualities: strength, intelligence, speed, stamina, fast walking, smooth trotting, and a willing temperament. Sporting a dark bay coat, he was powerful out of all proportion to his moderate height and build. Figure soon proved himself to be both a genetic mutation and a revelation, able to pass along his extraordinary qualities to any number of progeny.

After Justin Morgan's death, his name passed to his horse, and the first "Morgan" went through a succession of owners, enjoying a long life as a farm workhorse and successful stud. Figure's Morgan progeny soon gained sterling reputations in a horse-mad age, going on to distinguished careers pulling the horse cars on New York's Sixth Avenue, hauling heavy loads over the Rockies, and carrying Union troops into battle in the Civil War.

UVM Morgan Horse Farm; inset: Paul O. Boisvert

all over Vermont. Ironically, this remote, underdeveloped, and democratic place in the New World was about to receive help from the King of Spain.

## THE GREAT MERINO CRAZE

When the summer sun was turning Madrid into a desert, the Spanish kings would retreat into the coolness of the high and arid hills that ring the city. There, around their stark palace complex at El Escorial, the royal farms had developed a breed of sheep with some of the longest, most luxuriant fleeces in the world. The Merinos were so famed that the Spanish nobility had long been hoarding the breed to prevent competition. But during the political upheaval surrounding Napoleon's invasion of Spain during the Peninsular War (1802–1813), the American consul in Lisbon, William Jarvis, was able to talk the Spanish royals into selling him a flock of their finest Merinos. In 1811 he sent 400 of them, along with a Spanish shepherd and "a noble shepherd dog," to his new farm on the great oxbow of the Connecticut River in Weathersfield. Here, the good grazing and cold winters made the fleeces even heavier than they had been in the hills of Spain.

In the ovine equivalent of a fish story, this early woodcut shows William Jarvis (right), the original importer of Spanish Merinos, trying to sell a man a ram that is bigger than a barn.

Jarvis was generous with his new flock, selling breeding stock to farmers around the state. At first, they were treated as a curiosity, but the Merino industry began to take off when Congress put a tariff on imported woolen cloth in 1824. This came just at a time when the soils of many Vermont farms were losing fertility. Governor Silas H. Jenison gave an address at the Addison County fair in 1844, in which he reminisced about the recent history of farming in the area:

> *During the next period of ten years, bringing us to 1830, the agriculture of the County appears to have been in a transition state. While some of the farmers had, as a main business of the farm, embarked in rearing cattle, and others in increasing their sheep, many had not abandoned the idea, that wheat might still be a staple product of the County for exportation. ...When the wheat crop failed [due to infestation by the wheat midge], those engaged in the business had to resort to some other branch of farming. The tenacious quality of much of the soil of the County, forbid the cultivation of hoed crops, and the raising of port, as a substitute...[but] the Merino sheep...spread through the County with wonderful rapidity. Indeed, so rapidly was the character of the flocks changed, that as early as 1824, in many towns, a considerable flock of native sheep could not be found.*

Sheep can graze on almost anything, and whether the soil was rocks or clay, there was hard cash to be made from Merinos. The rate of growth of the industry was astonishing. By 1840, at the height of the boom, there were

1,681,000 sheep in Vermont—six times the human population. Nearly all the state's towns were home to sizable flocks of sheep, although they were not evenly distributed. But the greatest concentrations of sheep were in precisely those parts of the state that had already been found to be the richest and best-suited to other agricultural enterprises: the Champlain Valley, the Connecticut Valley, and Orange County. For while sheep can graze anywhere, they still do best where the grass is greenest. Farmers whose previous success gave them a little more capital had enough money to make the original investments in prize Merinos.

The sheep boom reached its most astonishing proportions in Addison County, which then had more sheep per capita (11) and produced more wool per acre than any county in America. The sheep of kings had become the king of sheep, and Addison County was soon known for having some of the greatest Merinos in the world. By 1840 there were 41,000 sheep in the town of Shoreham alone. The sheep were also increasing in productivity. Breeders like the Binghams of Cornwall, the Jewetts of Weybridge, and the Wilcoxes of Orwell made enormous advances in the density of the fleeces, so that the weight of a single clip from a sheep that had averaged 1.8 pounds in 1839

Drawings of Merinos, like the one below, were usually done for advertising purposes, so the animals were made to look huge. The real thing (inset) is certainly noble, but considerably smaller.

William Jarvis (top right) had led a cosmopolitan life as a European diplomat before moving to Vermont to promote the Merino breed. His indirect influence on the Vermont landscape was enormous, for the sheep he introduced were to be the foundation of the state's first great economic boom.

weighed 2.4 pounds in 1849, and some prize breeding rams had fleeces that weighed as much as 12 pounds.

This wave of specialization meant the death of traditional mixed farming for many who lived in the sheep regions. The big farmers were anxious to maximize their profits, and the best way to do that was to expand. One old-timer from near Jarvis' sheep farm in Weathersfield remembered how his father sold out to a rich sheep-farming neighbor in 1826 and went to settle a new stake in the far north of the state. He recalled how back then, "men counted their flocks by thousands, and as they grew more and more rich in money and sheep, they bought farm after farm adjoining their own and turned them into pasturage." Many small operators had no choice but to sell out to their more prosperous neighbors and join the great wave of people leaving the state to try their hands elsewhere. A *Vermont Chronicle* editorialist in Windsor exhorted in 1834, "Beware of the 'western fever' and above all, sell not your farms to your rich neighbors for sheep pastures." Throughout the Champlain and Connecticut Valleys, signs of sheep riches were everywhere—large fields, new white clapboard farmhouses, a proliferation of fancy carriages on the roads. It was difficult for traditional subsistence

## BUYER BEWARE: IT'S THE "CORNWALL FINISH"

By the mid-1800s, there was so much money to be made from Merino breeding stock that unscrupulous owners of inferior quality sheep were tempted to find ways to pass off their own as the real thing.

A distinguishing feature of first-rate Merinos was their heavy "yolk," a greasy lanolin-like substance that covered the wool and made the fleece weigh more at shearing time. Since fleeces were sold by weight, this characteristic was very desirable to the sheep-owner.

A few sharpsters learned to concoct a mixture of linseed oil, burnt umber, and lampblack that closely mimicked the look, smell, and feel of the yolk of a prize Merino. Known as the "Cornwall finish," it was so convincing that almost no one could detect it. Wearing their greasy new coats, the stock would bring top dollar at the Ohio markets. By the time the first rainfall washed the substance off, the sellers would be laughing their way home.

In deference to our friends in Cornwall, the ruse probably was not invented there, but rather attempted to imitate Cornwall's legitimately superior stock. Who was using the "Cornwall finish"? New Yorkers, no doubt.

farmers to compete in the shadow of a sheep czar's rising mansion.

The traditional mixed farming adherents who survived had the last laugh, for within a few years many of their wealthy neighbors would see the bottom drop out of the sheep industry with stunning rapidity. Agricultural specialization could lead to great wealth, but its fledgling entrepreneurs did not always anticipate the dangers of having all of their fleeces in one basket. In 1840, at its height, it seemed as if the sheep miracle would never end; by 1850 it was almost over. There were two main reasons why sheep ceased to be economically viable in Vermont. First, the tariffs on wool were relaxed in 1841 and 1846, so that the higher grades in which Vermont specialized faced new, and cheaper, competition. Second, it had been hoped that the coming of the railroads would create better markets for the state's wool, but rails run both ways, and New England was soon swamped with cheaper wool from out West. It could cost nearly $2 a head to keep a sheep in the East for a year, while the Western cost was less than half that. By the late 1840s, the price Vermont farmers could charge for their fleeces had fallen below the cost of production. Merinos make tough lamb chops, so there was no hope of retrieval there. Many farmers would gladly have driven their sheep over a cliff, and in the late 1840s there were instances of owners slaughtering whole flocks because they could not afford to keep feeding them. Up to two-thirds of the state's sheep are estimated to have been killed between 1846 and 1850.

Only the biggest operators were able to survive, and that was because many of them were able to switch to selling fine breeding stock rather than wool. By the mid-century, Vermont farmers were known to have the finest Merino breeding stock in the world and could export them to places where sheep raising was more economically viable. Addison County breeders sold their stock for fabulous sums out West. Samuel Swift recorded that in an eight-month period in 1853–1854, Alonzo Bingham of Cornwall sold $43,302 worth of prize Merinos to customers who came to his farm from as far away as Michigan and Virginia. Some of his flock were producing 20 pounds of wool in each clip—over five times the weight of the fleeces of William Jarvis' original El Escorial herd. The greatest Merino rams could bring over $10,000, and a year's stud fees alone could run $2,000 to $3,000.

High-class Merino breeding was only an option for some of the biggest farmers. By the mid-nineteenth century, the agricultural picture in Vermont was mixed. Many thousands of farmers, particularly in the northern counties and on the hill farms that clung to the spine of the Green Mountains, were still struggling along with subsistence farming. Others were trying specializations in various crops and breeds of livestock: corn, hogs, and horses, among them. The deleterious effects of the railroads on the sheep industry

### THE MANSION MERINOS MADE: THE WILCOX-CUTTS HOUSE

**Some of Vermont's Merino breeders made considerable sums of money and were anxious to display their new-found wealth and taste. In 1843, a successful sheep man in Orwell named Linus Wilcox engaged a Shoreham builder, James Lamb, to transform his farmhouse into one of the most extraordinary Greek Revival mansions in the state. By the time it was finished, it had cost the fabulous sum of $30,000. Its classical elegance subsequently helped Lamb to get commissions for the still stunning Congregational churches in Orwell and Shoreham, which he adapted from patterns in Asher Benjamin's book, *The Practice of Architecture* (1833). The Wilcox-Cutts House (right), currently known as Historic Brookside Farms, is now one of Vermont's most elegant bed-and-breakfast establishments.**

Sara Gregg

would be compensated for by the possibilities that refrigerated railroad cars presented for transporting dairy products. The soft bleating of thousands of sheep would soon be replaced by the snorting and lowing of the dairy herds.

### COLORS ON THE LANDSCAPE

It was agriculture, more than all other changes put together, that altered the look of the Vermont landscape in the first half of the nineteenth century. It was farmers who chopped down trees, cleared out brush, built houses and barns, planted the crops, created the meadows, and scattered them with sheep and horses and cows. A landscape that had once been overwhelmingly green and dark and dense with trees was now open and swathed with all the colors of crops—light greens and dark, golden wheat, blue flax, and red

In Jerome Thompson's "The Haymakers, Mount Mansfield, Vermont" (1859), a farm family and their helpers cut a rich crop of hay on a hilltop farm. This agricultural Eden, bathed in golden light, shows humans in control of their environment, with the sublime form of Mount Mansfield towering over all, a contrast to the productive home created from the wilderness. Ironically, many hill farms would soon prove unprofitable; by the end of the century, many farm families lost these farms to the forces of a reemerging nature.

clover. Each color represented a choice that someone had made about how to use the land.

Clearing had also created new vistas that human beings had never seen before. Now one could see the forest for the trees, and the long lines of the mountains and the new spires of churches and the next farm. Where there had been the close flatness of the forest, there was now a depth of field that offered the mind a different and, in its way, more profound perspective. These great new vistas gave men and women the feeling that a view with more breadth was also a view with depth, as they looked at the land and saw the products of their own hands. A new beauty had been created that was not the beauty of the wilderness.

But not everyone had the talent, the luck, or the means to succeed as a farmer. As the population grew and competition for land intensified, many parents were looking for new ways to employ children who could not hope to inherit a viable share of the family farm. If the transition to capitalism meant specialization in the countryside, it meant diversification in other sectors of the economy that were being encouraged by the use of money and the growth of markets. There had to be new ways to make a living in Vermont, and prospectors, inventors, and entrepreneurs were determined to find them.

### THE SEARCH FOR BURIED TREASURE

*There are those in the community who are...seized with a mania to dig for...some reputed hidden treasure...with a legend connected therewith. ...It is curious, yet painful, to observe with what tenacity a visionary schemer, who has supposed that a fortune was buried and in store for him, adheres to his preconceived opinions. ...If the amount of money expended in fruitless researches for coal, iron and the precious metals, were counted together, it would give a sum much larger than all the profits ever realized in the State by the working of metals.*

—ALBERT HAGER, State Geologist (1861)

The long hours of repetitious physical labor involved in clearing, plowing, and planting the land left the mind free for fantasizing. And as some families began to make it big on the farm, others realized they were scratching in vain. A hopeful settler arrived on his stake only to find that it was hilly, rocky, and unsuitable for agriculture. Another grew enough to get by, but could see no way to provide a livelihood for his many growing children. It is understandable that they might begin to entertain hopes that their stony ground was hiding a rich lode of valuable minerals. Such dreams were the lottery wins or publisher's sweepstakes imaginings of the day. In the early statehood period, hundreds of reports of mineral strikes were reported in Vermont. Most of them did not pan out.

The first generation of settlers had foraged the land to the point of near-exhaustion, and their hungry descendants also hoped to be able to extract something of value from the state's often forbidding landscape. Early Vermonters, like people in many ages and places, were hoping to find gold in the hills. Most of what they uncovered was "fool's gold," or pyrite, but just enough of the real thing turned up to feed people's hopes. Excitement over the possibility of striking gold in Vermont began in 1826 with the discovery of the "Newfane lump," an impressive 8.5-ounce nugget that whipped the public into a fever. Only years later did it come out that this prize had not been pulled from the earth, but was dropped by a gang of counterfeiters.

Until the truth was known, the race was on to find more in the "Vermont Gold Rush." Vermonters began forming small companies and laying out money in sluices. Scattered groups kept up the search until the end of the nineteenth century. Some managed to find just enough dust to keep going, but there would be no gold millionaires in Vermont.

Orange County has no oranges, but for a century it was orange with the state's most lucrative ore, copper. A rich lode was found in Vershire around 1820, and an excited group of locals, known as the "Farmer's Company" (lest we doubt how they had been making their livings), tried to work it. They were singularly unsuccessful, being farmers, not miners. The mine only began to make money in the 1850s when Captain Thomas Pollard, "an intelligent and experienced Cornish miner," took over the operation "with the

Vermont's own small nineteenth-century Industrial Revolution left behind many evocative ruins. The state was rich in limestone, which could be burned in kilns to make industrial chemicals; the romantic edifice (above left) is all that remain of a Leicester lime kiln. Vermont had the three things needed for an iron industry: iron ore, limestone, and charcoal derived from trees. When a "charge" of these materials was put into a blast furnace, iron was the result. This impressive example of a blast furnace (above right) at Forest Dale near Brandon was roofed in 1991 by the Vermont Division for Historic Preservation to prevent further deterioration; iron-making at this site dates back to a forge operation in 1810.

most gratifying results." Under the Englishman's command, this mine, along with others in Corinth and Richford, would soon produce over half of all the copper in the United States.

### VERMONT'S STONE AGE

Early settlers, walking the stream beds or exploring the woods, found fine stone thrusting up through the vegetation—stone that could compete with that from anywhere in the world. The first purported "marble" quarry was on Isle la Motte, where the cutting of dark Chazy limestone, or "Black Marble," had begun by 1761. This black "marble" was shipped up the Lake and graced Montréal's mantles until the Champlain Canal of 1823 sent this trade, as it had so many others, south to New York and Philadelphia. A similar dark

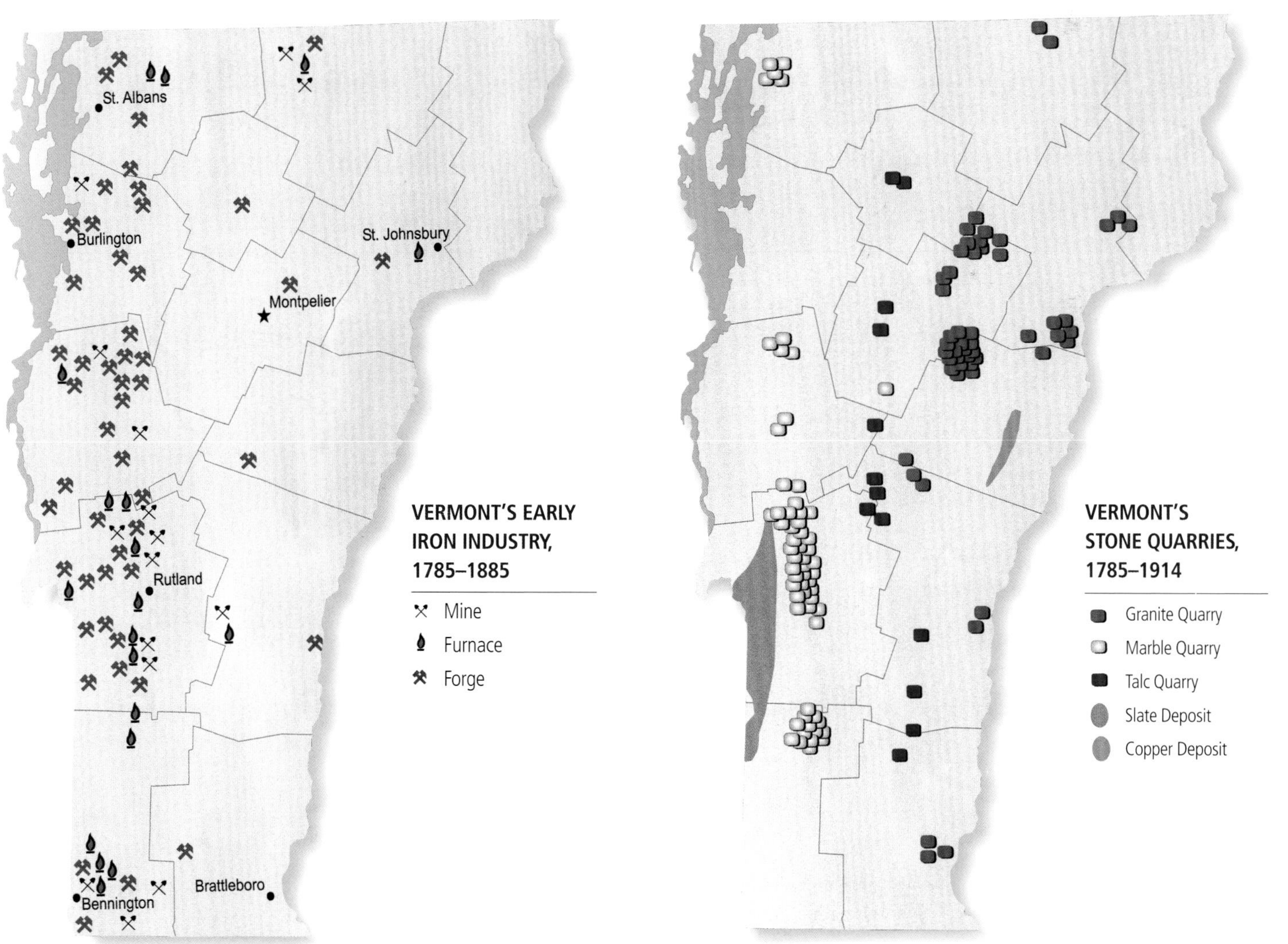

# MARBLE.

**The Proprietors of the Middlebury Marble Manu-**facturing Company, continue to carry on extensively, the business of sawing, polishing, cutting and carving Marble, at their Factory, at Middlebury Falls, Vermont, where may be had at all times,

## MARBLE TOMB-STONES,

### *TOMB-TABLES AND*

### MONUMENTS,

of all dimensions:—Also, Slabs, for facing Fire-places, Russian Stoves, Side-boards, &c. Jambs, Mantles, Hearths, Window and Door Caps and Sills, Curriers' Tables, Paint-Stones, &c. &c.

The Proprietors acknowledge the many favors they have received of their customers, and ask a continuance of them so long as orders are executed to their satisfaction.

Any gentlemen living at a distance from the Factory, who may wish for articles in our line of business, by forwarding their orders, by mail or otherwise, may depend on having them at the established prices of the Factory, the same as if they applied personally.

The Middlebury Marble is very fine, compact and hard—it receives a brilliant polish, and is warranted to withstand the effects of the weather for centuries.

The Proprietors, in all cases, where the pieces are finished at the Factory, warrant them free from breakage to any part of the world.

E. W. JUDD, *Agent of said Company.*

*Middlebury, July* 1, 1815

**We certify, that the Marble found in Middlebury,** and manufactured by the Middlebury Marble Manufacturing Company, is very fine, susceptible of a beautiful polish, and we have never known an instance of its decomposing by the action of the air or water.

H. DAVIS, *President.*
F. HALL, *Prof. Math. & Nat. Phil.*
JOHN HOUGH, *Prof. Languages.*
JOEL H. LINSLEY, *Tutor.*

*Middlebury College, June* 30, 1815.

WM. SLADE, JUN'S PRINT—MIDDLEBURY.

In the first decade of the 1800s, Eben Judd's Middlebury Marble Manufacturing Company (advertised at right) grew into a major supplier of gravestones, mantles, lintels, and other decorative objects. Timothy Dwight, the President of Yale, pronounced the glowing grey-veined white marble from the falls of Otter Creek to be of "an elegance not surpassed on this side of the Atlantic." It was soon making its way as far as New York and London. Judd (above) was able to build himself one of the most elegant brick houses in the village, now open to the public as the Sheldon Museum.

Courtesy Sheldon Museum, Middlebury, Vermont

green marble-like serpentine has been quarried and polished in Cavendish, Rochester, and Roxbury since the mid-1830s.

But the most beautiful and valuable stone was the marble of western Vermont, its luminous, cool, milky whiteness lightly veined with the palest grey. This precious marble lay in a long, thin belt from Middlebury south to Manchester; to the enterprising eyes of the early Republic, with its Neoclassicist love of white, it was perfectly suited to adorn a graceful fireplace or commemorate a worthy burial. The earliest large-scale operation was that of Eben Judd in Middlebury, who started a marble factory on the west shore of Otter Creek, just below the falls, in 1802. There he (or, rumor has it, a local 10-year-old mechanical genius named Isaac Markham) developed the technology to cut marble with water-cooled saws. A contemporary wrote that Judd was making "Tomb stones, currier's tables, jambs, mantle pieces, hearths, window and door caps and sills, side boards, tables, sinks and various other kinds of furniture. These articles are transported to Montréal, Québec, Boston, New York and even Georgia." A six-inch square marble hitching post went for $1.50 and a six-foot high cemetery obelisk cost $6. To put this in perspective, a skilled marble workman made between 50 and 90 cents for a 12-hour day. Judd's company closed upon his death in 1837.

Although no extractive industries became economically vital to the Vermont economy in this period, something new was happening on the land. Groups of people were working toward innovative, non-agricultural enterprises, and in the course of these operations they were transforming the landscape in unprecedented ways. All these activities were still having a small fraction of the impact of agriculture, but they foreshadowed later, more large-scale environmental changes.

## THE FIRST COMMERCIAL CLEAR CUTS

The settlement generation had seen trees as impediments and enthusiastically wasted them to reach the soil beneath. But while most sawmills served only the local building trades, a few began to harvest timber on a larger scale,

Until the time came for the drive downstream, logs were often piled on the banks of rivers, as demonstrated in this mid-nineteenth-century photograph taken on Otter Creek near Brandon. Note the contrast between the huge piles of logs and the almost denuded landscape that surrounds them.

Collections of Vermont Historical Society

heralding the state's first major non-agricultural industry, logging. As the settlers girdled and burned their way through the woods, a few people began to realize that there might be a market for the forests in the growing towns of the St. Lawrence Valley. A Colchester man, Stephen Mallet (of Mallet's Bay, rumoured to be a "retired pirate"), assembled the first shipment of oak in 1794 and sent it north on the Lake to Québec.

Before the railroads, almost all logs had to be moved by water in large rafts that were collected over the winter months. The Lake Champlain lumber rafts were floated north until 1823, when the Champlain Canal, joining the southern tip of the Lake and the Hudson River, spun shipping in a 180-degree turn to the south. The rafts were huge, with tents and log cabins sitting on top to provide homes for the crew on the way to market. Jefferson's Embargo of 1807 against Canada slowed the Canadian trade until loggers realized that smuggling to the north was reasonably safe and very lucrative. It has been estimated that the white pine and oak logs that went over the Canadian border in 1810 alone were worth $600,000—and that at the height of the Embargo. The lumber trade in western Vermont helped to make Burlington the third largest lumber port in the nation by the end of this period. Its success was such that marketable trees had been virtually eliminated from the Champlain Valley by 1840, and the natives were being forced to import wood. In *Danvis Tales*, one of writer Rowland Robinson's characters caught the mind set behind this commercial spirit. To him, a majestic old-growth tree was only an assemblage of potential products: "...more than the symmetry or majesty of a tree he saw the axe helves in the hickory, the baskets in the ash, the plant in the hemlock and pine, and the medicinal virtues of the prettiest plant were more to him than its beauty."

**Although furniture-makers could be found all over the state, concentrations of people in the trade were found in Bennington, Brattleboro, Burlington, Danville, Middlebury, Montpelier, Rutland, St. Albans, and the industry's high-end capital, Windsor County. This particularly elegant chest of drawers was built by George Stedman of Norwich and Chester. In the summer of 1998, a similar Vermont-made chest with a bombé front from the early 1820s was sold at auction for $25,000.**

A. Blake Gardner, Bennington Museum

### AN AMBIVALENCE TOWARD "ARTIFICE"

It was difficult to find anyone who had a good word to say about manufacturing in the Federal period. Thomas Jefferson saw no reason for industrialists to exist in a country with enough land to allow everyone to be a farmer. Believing that wage labor led to Old World decadence and servile dependency, he urged his fellow Americans to "let our workshops remain in Europe." Jefferson was not alone in revering the farmer and reviling the manufacturer. The very word his contemporaries used to describe industry, "artifice," retains its negative ring. Many would happily have had Americans buy all their manufactured goods from Europe forever, fearing that manufacturing introduced into society a "degree of corruption."

A more sympathetic Alexander Hamilton did not place a value upon industry in its own right; instead, he urged its acceptance because he felt that it might allow a farmer more time in which to farm better:

*If instead of a farmer and artificer, there were a farmer only, he would be under the necessity of devoting a part of his labour to the fabrication of clothing and other articles...and he would be able to devote less labor to the cultivation of his farm; and would draw from it a proportionable less product.*

It would be difficult to devise a less supportive intellectual climate for the development of manufacturing. But imagine a society in which there is only one occupational option. Not everyone was cut out to be a farmer. Pressure was building to diversify the economy so that some of the settlers' children would have non-agricultural options.

By 1791, a number of small industrial enterprises were appearing on the land. They were to grow and diversify as forms of monetary exchange became more sophisticated and the transport system improved. In the early 1800s Vermont's small-scale Industrial Revolution seemed to have a good chance of success. But by 1860 it would become clear that it was impossible for the state to become a major industrial force in New England.

The Windsor machine-tool industry began with Asahel Hubbard's invention of a rotary pump in the 1830s and flourished in part because of his use of a captive labor force: the inmates at Windsor State Prison (above). The hydraulic pumps made by Hubbard's National Hydraulic Company were so well-crafted that one supplying Hubbard's brother's kitchen sink was said to be still working a century-and-a-half after it was installed.

### A SMALL INDUSTRIAL REVOLUTION

Cloth-making provides a good example of the promises and problems involved in developing industry in Vermont in this period. In Britain, the Industrial Revolution had been founded on the mechanization of the textile industry, and Vermont women were as anxious as their European sisters to be relieved of the many burdensome steps in making cloth. The state had Merino wool, potash for fulling, streams for power, and a ready labor force. It was a short leap for local entrepreneurs to try the trade.

The textile industry did not begin with full-blown factories taking in fleeces and spitting out finished cloth. Textile-making involves a number of complex steps, and the original mills only provided part of the process. The first were fulling mills, which performed a finishing process, exposing textiles to chemicals (derived from potash) that helped to clean, shrink, and soften the cloth. Home-spinners brought their cloth to the fulling mill, where it was treated and greatly improved. The next part of the process to be mechanized was carding, combing raw wool to prepare it for home-spinning. By 1809, Vermont had 58 fulling mills and 28 carding mills scattered around the state. And because the water needed to generate power is usually stronger lower down the mountain, this helped to spur what was to become a common Vermont pattern: the movement of industry and population away from the hilltops and into the valleys.

By the 1820s, English-style textile factories were beginning to appear in Vermont, some with more than 100 workers. Women had always been the

## ABBY HEMENWAY'S NEW STOVE

Brandon's nascent iron industry got a shot in the arm in 1796, when John Conant arrived from Massachusetts and became, in local parlance, a "captain of industry." Possessed of both financial and mechanical acumen, he invented the Conant stove, the first stove manufactured in the state, and a design improvement of considerable ingenuity, incorporating an oven, a broiler, and a griddle. In 1877, Abby Hemenway recalled her family's purchase of this amazing new appliance:

*It was the wonder of the farmer's kitchen and sold in all the villages around, and abroad. ...It was the first stove we ever saw—our father bought one and brought it home as a surprise—and never was anything brought into the house that created such an interest. It was the inauguration of a new era in the culinary kingdom—the pleasant old fireplace with its swinging crane of well-filled pots and kettles; hearth-spiders with legs, and bake-kettles and tin-bakers to stand before the blazing logs and bake custard pies in—all went down at once and disappeared before that first stove, without so much as a passing struggle.*

cloth-makers at home; now textiles became their first industrial occupation off the farm. The largest early operation was David Page's cotton mill in Middlebury, employing 130 people at 80 power looms making 10,000 yards of cloth a week in 1825. By 1850 there were 156 textile operations scattered around the state, the biggest in Bennington, Colchester (Winooski), Springfield, Cavendish, Middlebury, Bethel, Northfield, Pawlet, and Waterville. But lest our mental picture of Vermont in 1850 begins to become too industrial, it must be remembered that the total number of men, women, and children employed in Vermont's biggest non-agricultural industry, textiles, was about 2,300 workers out of a population of 314,120, or only about three-quarters of 1 percent of the total population. And most of these would soon find themselves unable to compete with the textile giants of Fall River and Lowell, Massachusetts, where thousands of farm girls from Vermont would go to work long hours in exchange for a new freedom.

### MADE IN VERMONT

The Vermont economy remained overwhelmingly farm-based, but growing demands for goods stimulated the "artificers" to try to produce them locally. Families moving from log cabins to clapboard houses were ready and able to have more things around them. And local entrepreneurs were gaining the expertise to turn the state's natural resources into more elaborate manufactured articles.

The building trades were booming in this period, spurring many auxiliary industries. Blast furnaces fed their product to local blacksmiths or small factories making nails, latches, door handles, and other household hardware in towns like Vergennes, Ludlow, Shaftsbury, Bennington, and Brandon. The state was known for its excellent stoves from the early nineteenth century, the Conant version from Brandon being the most innovative. (Its inventor, John Conant, became very wealthy, and was said to drive around the village "with his coachman on the high seat, himself in the rear, with his ruffled shirt, diamond pin and cane...a true aristocrat.") The state's glass-making industry began with the Lake Dunmore Glass Company, started in 1813 to provide window glass for the many new homes being built in the state. It prospered under the creative management of Henry Schoolcraft, later famed as one of America's most noted Midwestern explorers and Indian agents. The firm was forced out of business by the 1840s when, like so many Vermont products of the era, its goods could not compete with cheaper glass from outside the state.

The housing boom also created a need for new furniture; Vermont has a particularly strong tradition from this period. Some 900 cabinetmakers, chairmakers, and furniture-makers were at work in Vermont before 1855. The majority were self-employed, farming in summer and making furniture in the

In 1815, Major Joseph Fairbanks came to St. Johnsbury from Massachusetts and spent $300 for a mill site on the Sleepers River. Fifteen years later, his son, Thaddeus (above), invented the platform scale, the foundation of the family's fortunes.

By the mid-nineteenth century the E. and T. Fairbanks Company's platform scale (above) had revolutionized railway shipping. The lithograph (top) shows the company in full operation at the height of the railway age.

Shelburne Museum, Shelburne, Vermont

S. H. Washburn's mid-nineteenth-century painting, "Falls at Vergennes, Vermont" (above), stands in sharp contrast to Thomas Davies' pristine view, recorded for General Amherst (see page 108). The power of the falls was now being put to use by a number of industrial firms, including (left to right) the factory of Hayes, Falardo, and Parker, makers of doors and other construction supplies; the Keeler tannery, its chimney belching smoke; Hawley's sawmill (on the site of the present pumphouse); the Norton gristmill; and on the far right, the Holland and Maxfield furniture factory, which produced 300 chamber suites a month.

slack season during Vermont's long winters. They worked in a variety of local and exotic woods: pine, cherry, maple, birch, butternut, rosewood, and mahogany being particularly popular. The trade took its toll on the environment; by the early 1800s the most desirable woods, like walnut and black cherry, had almost disappeared from the forests of upper New England.

The Connecticut Valley towns of Windsor and Guildhall became centers for the machine-tool industry. In the 1830s, Asahel Hubbard of West Windsor perfected a rotary pump with interchangeable parts. His National Hydraulic Company boomed for a few years. He was, conveniently enough, also warden of the local prison, but even his captive labor pool could not keep the company from going bust in the mid-1850s. In St. Johnsbury in 1830, Thaddeus Fairbanks invented the first platform scale, making it easy to weigh bulky goods. In one of the few long-term success stories in Vermont manufacturing, the scales were so useful and of such high quality that the company was making three-quarters of the platform scales sold in America as late as the 1950s. Vermont also had many other small firms, making bricks, paint, whiskey, ships, paper, and other useful articles. But for many of these manufacturing enterprises, success was to be fleeting, as Vermont manufactures succumbed to Western competition.

There is little documentation of the impact these industries were having on the environment. Clearing by fire, potash-making, heating with wood, and the charcoal fires of the blast furnaces were certainly creating unprecedented levels of air pollution. Mill wheels clogged streams, preventing fish from making their spawning journeys. Many industrial processes involved chemicals: the softening agents of the fulling mills and lead-based paint among them. Since the only source of power was water, these chemicals, sewage, and other forms of waste were often dumped into the adjacent, once pristine streams. From the copper pits to the clear cuts, extractive industries were leaving scars on the landscape. Vermont, along with most of the rest of the world, was not yet attuned to seeing human relationship to the earth as a reciprocal arrangement.

## TAKING THE CURE: VERMONT'S FIRST TOURISM BOOM

Back in the stressful year of 1776, a mystic in Clarendon named Asa Smith claimed to have had a dream in which his scrofulous skin condition was cured by the waters issuing from a spring in the nearby forests. The dream was so realistic that the next day he dragged his weakened body to the woods, found his dream spring, drank its "chalybeate water impregnated with lime," and allegedly was cured instantly. Five years later, his crafty neighbor, George Round, had a waking vision that he might be able to make a lot of money off

An inn has stood on this site in Manchester since 1769, but it was Franklin H. Orvis who made the Equinox House (above) into a world-class resort, a status it continues to hold today. By the mid-1800s, it was attracting long summer visits from Mary Todd Lincoln, among other notables.

The Clarendon Springs Hotel, shown above in James Hope's "View of Clarendon Springs, Vermont" (1853), was one of the most well-known spas in New England in the mid-1800s. The site's mineral waters were rumored to cure numerous maladies, and the lovely setting attracted both the sick and those seeking the curative properties of "resting" among their social equals.

The Missisquoi Springs Hotel in Sheldon (above) began as a small establishment, growing to this size in the 1860s, thanks to the judiciously placed rumor that its waters had cured a cancer patient.

this little Lourdes. Round built a log cabin at the side of the mineral spring, took in his first guests, and watched the money roll in. His success led him to build a substantial clapboard hotel in 1798, and Clarendon Springs was soon known to the quality and the quacks of the whole Eastern seaboard. Here lay the roots of Vermont's tourism industry.

Early tourism was closely tied to health in an era when disease remained largely uncontrollable. Calling your summer holiday a necessary "cure" mitigated any lingering Puritan guilt about taking time for leisure and recreation. And many people did, quite sincerely, believe that mineral waters could cure almost anything. Their medicinal properties were so apparent—the horrid smell, the ghastly taste—that they had to be doing something. When Dr. Theophilus Clark tried the water at Middletown Spring, he pronounced that it must have value because "the waters acted powerfully on the urinary organs." The gap in time between a sip and a cure could be reassuringly short. At Clarendon in 1800, a man named Shaw put mud from the spring on a cancer and it was almost instantly cured. Cataracts, kidney trouble, and consumption were said to have disappeared in a few days. Even dwindling desire could be provoked, one man proudly reporting that the "waters you supplied have unleashed passions of great magnitude."

Spa hotels were soon springing up all around the state, imitating the lavish health resorts of England, France, and Germany. The waters acted as the bait, but the accommodations made the money. Soon hotels and rooming houses were catering to the upwardly mobile middle classes at places like Clarendon, Sheldon, Highgate, Newbury, Brunswick, Middletown Springs, Brattleboro, and Manchester. By the 1860s, Abby Hemenway listed over 20 spas in the state. The Franklin House in Highgate Springs had room for 125 visitors, and the Missisquoi Springs Hotel at Sheldon was almost as large. Most resorts tried for the greatest degree of elegance they could muster, with lush lobbies and elaborate landscaping to encourage strolling.

The spas attracted visitors from all over America, including a considerable number of Southerners eager to escape the summer heat in the decades before the Civil War. Visitors returned to the same places year after year, often staying for weeks at a time. Vermont could not hope to attract America's top-drawer elite, who spent their summers in Europe, or at the posh watering holes of Newport, Bar Harbor, and Saratoga; but the state was a magnet for the intelligentsia and middle-class luminaries. By the 1850s, the spartan Wesselhoeft Water Cure in Brattleboro could boast the most illustrious guest list, including Henry Wadsworth Longfellow, William Tecumseh Sherman, Julia Ward Howe, and Martin Van Buren.

Tourism was having the strange effect of stimulating a certain interest in restoring to nature some of the glory that had been destroyed during the

## SPAS CURE VISITORS, INFECT LOCALS

By the mid-1800s, Vermonters were worrying about the example those fast-living tourists from down country were having on the natives. From his room at Highgate Springs, Vermont lawyer and poet John Godfrey Saxe wrote a poem about the spa scene meant to answer the locals' most burning question, "What do they do at the Springs?"

In short—as it goes in the world  
They eat, and they drink,  
  and they sleep;  
They talk, and they walk,  
  and they woo;  
They sigh, and they ride,  
  and they dance  
(with other unspeakable things);  
They pray, and they play, and they pay,  
And that's what they do at  
  the Springs.

**The Franklin House in Highgate Springs (top) was first built in 1835. In its heyday, it could accommodate 125 people. Like many large hotels of this era, it later burned to the ground.**

Collections of Vermont Historical Society

## MYTH AND REALITY IN NINETEENTH-CENTURY VERMONT

Nineteenth-century Romantics passionately believed in the ideal of an unspoiled American wilderness, its surface barely brushed by the hand of man; Vermont—thanks to its occasionally difficult soil, terrain, and climate—remained in many regions stubbornly resistant to development, and so could present just such an "untouched" landscape to the eye of delighted philosophers, naturalists, travelers, writers, and artists such as Jerome B. Thompson, whose idyllic vignette of leisurely picnickers lounging in the Green Mountains near Rutland was painted in mid-century.

But while scenes such as those depicted by Thompson did, in fact, exist in Vermont, they do not tell the whole story. Side by side with Romanticism, the entrepreneurial spirit was alive and well; economic pressures were taking their toll. Lumbering operations like the one pictured here denuded vast tracts of forest throughout the state. And while much of Vermont has been reforested over the last century, the same sort of recovery has not been possible in places like Vershire (far right, in the 1880s), where the Ely mining company scraped copper from the ground with 97 percent waste, requiring a heavily polluting smelting process to concentrate the ore. Resulting clouds of sulfur dioxide created a highly concentrated acid rain that killed all neighboring vegetation; most varieties of trees still will not grow around Vershire over one hundred years later.

The hillside stripped of its forest to feed a Vermont sawmill (below, top) and the wasteland created by copper mining at the Ely Mine in Vershire (below, bottom) offer a stark contrast to the nature-worship of nineteenth-century Romanticism.

In his idyllic "Recreation," Jerome B. Thompson painted man in an ideal relationship to nature: as a visitor, enjoying its beauties, but leaving it virtually untouched.

Painting: Fine Arts Museum of San Francisco; photos: Collections of Vermont Historical Society rampant decades of settlement. A new awareness of the grandeur of mountain scenery was developing now that it could be observed from a comfortable and civilized distance. Albert Hager, the State Geologist, extolled the modern wonders of the luxurious Equinox House in Manchester in 1861. Where once the Abenaki had found more trout than they could ever eat, "An artificial trout pond...is located. Guests of the house are permitted to take out the speckled trout from this pond, and those weighing one and two pounds are not unfrequently caught." In place of the native forest, "Ornamental shade trees are set out, and a good carriage road is built around the pond." The old village of Manchester was no longer deemed adequate for a clientele that boasted such people of quality as Mary Todd Lincoln and her sons, so it had been fitted up with shade trees, smooth streets, and marble flagstones. Says Hager, "We claim that this great improvement of the village has resulted mainly from the magic dollar of the tourist who came here to live awhile amid the beautiful display of nature's handiwork." There was nature, but very different from the wilderness that had so recently preceded it.

John Winans (above) and his brother James came to Burlington in 1808, fresh from learning the steamboat business on the Hudson from Robert Fulton. John went on to build the *Vermont*, Lake Champlain's first steamer, and led numerous steamship operations over the next 30 years. The woodcut (opposite) is a copy of an 1830 postcard often said to show the *Vermont*. Its accuracy is doubtful, since the same image can be found with many other ships' names inscribed. The ship had genteel pretensions, its rules for passengers including the admonition that, for male passengers, "neatness and order are necessary. ...It is not permitted for any person to lie down in a berth with their boots or shoes on."

## THE GREAT WATER ROADS

Early nineteenth-century Vermonters were full of energy and ideas, but were often thwarted by an undeveloped transportation system. Local transport was sufficient in the subsistence period, when farmers made only an occasional trip to a mill or village. But capitalism required access to more distant markets. Farmers had to get their products to consumers, quarrymen could only sell heavy stones if they could be shipped, and tourists needed easy ways into the state. Vermont kept missing the boat.

The first roads were made of water, as the settlement narrative demonstrates. Water made the forest world accessible, so most initial sites for homesteading tended to be near those burbling escape routes in the wilderness. Even as roads sprang up, water transport was to remain preeminent for many decades as the only commercially viable means of transport for the export of bulky goods.

From the time of the Paleoindians, Lake Champlain and the Connecticut River had been the region's watery superhighways. And as the Champlain Valley turned into one of the richest agricultural and industrial regions of Vermont, the Lake was receiving ever more commercial use. Because the Lake flowed north, so did commerce, and Canada was anxious for many of the resources Vermont could supply. In eastern Vermont, the usefulness of the Connecticut River for transporting goods was hurt by the mighty rocks and racing water at Bellows Falls. In 1791, the first canal ever built in America was constructed to take shipping traffic around this natural barrier. From that time onwards, as the goods of western Vermont headed north, those on the eastern side of the mountains headed south to Boston and Hartford and New York.

On a June day in 1809, Captain John Winans, a devout Quaker and former assistant to steamship inventor Robert Fulton, stood on the deck of the steamship he had built as it puffed its way out of Burlington Bay for the first time. His little daughter Joanna was at his side amid the noise and smoke, cradling her frightened kitten. With this trip, his dream of building the world's first commercial steamship fleet on Lake Champlain became a reality. The premier vessel, a ship of Quaker-like starkness dubbed the *Vermont*, began running on a route that stretched from Whitehall in the south to St. Jean sur Richelieu in the north, a 24-hour voyage. The unfamiliar boiler induced terror in some of the passengers. One old lady was recorded as having spent hours badgering a fellow traveler on "whether we would die by hot water on deck or cold water below." Steamships would soon become more comfortable and even elegant, ruling the Lake until the coming of the railroads made them seem slow and cumbersome.

The long-anticipated southern shipping route appeared with the opening of the Champlain Canal in 1823. Stretching for 64 miles (46.5 of

UVM Special Collections

## CHARLES DICKENS STEAMS DOWN THE LAKE

A number of famous people wrote about traveling under steam on Lake Champlain, including Charles Dickens, who in 1836 journeyed aboard the *Burlington,* then the greatest steamship in the world:

*There is one American boat—the vessel which carried us on Lake Champlain, from St. Johns to Whitehall, which I praise very highly, but no more than it deserves, when I say that it is superior...to any other in the world. The steamboat, which is called the Burlington, is a perfectly exquisite achievement of neatness, elegance and order. The decks are drawingrooms; the cabins are boudoirs, choicely furnished and adorned with prints, pictures, and musical instruments; every nook and corner of the vessel is a perfect curiosity of graceful comfort and beautiful contrivance...*

*By means of this floating palace we were soon in the United States again, and called that evening at Burlington; a pretty town, where we lay an hour or so.*

—Cited in Ralph Nading Hill, *Lake Champlain* (1995)

them artificial canals) between Waterford, New York, on the Hudson, and Whitehall, the Canal meant that Vermont goods could now go to the more numerous markets to the south as easily as they went north. The cost of shipping from Burlington to Albany went down 80 percent almost overnight, and Vermont's trade turned from northern to southern markets.

But the Champlain Canal was to be another broken promise for many Vermonters. Access to markets meant access to competition, and Vermont firms were not distinguished by their efficiency in comparison to far-flung competitors. While the Canal was the making of Burlington, with its perfect harbor, smaller ports like Vergennes were quickly cut out of the picture. Water may not flow both ways, but water traffic can; the conduit that held so much promise of bringing Vermont goods to distant markets was soon flooding the state with lower-priced goods from other places. Many of Vermont's industries could not hope to compete.

### A MUD FOR ALL SEASONS: VERMONT'S EARLY ROAD SYSTEM

*In wet seasons every rain converts it into mud. Whenever the weather is dry, it is pulverized wherever mankind live and move; and the dust, being very fine and light, rises with every wind, fills the air with clouds, covers the houses, and soils the clothes with a dingy, dirty appearance. When the surface of well-made roads has become hard, a slight rain makes them so slippery as to be impassable with safety, unless with horses corked in the same manner as when they are to travel on ice.*

—Timothy Dwight on the muddy roads of the Champlain Valley

In the early 1800s, Vermont's road system was expanding in length, if not in quality. Local governments designated Surveyors of Highways, whose job was to try to get all able-bodied men to devote four days each year to the unpopular task of road-building. Non-compliance was so rampant that in 1797 the State authorized the creation of turnpike committees whose investors would build the roads and could then charge tolls. The first turnpike, from Middlebury to Woodstock, opened in 1800.

Over the next decade, 31 toll roads were built, and most were fairly well-maintained to the standards of the time. The tolls were hefty. In 1815 it cost $2.75 in tolls for a man in a cart with two horses to drive from Bennington to Brattleboro. Tolls this high were a disincentive to development. Most investors had hoped to make a killing on tolls, but between the "shunpikes," little detours around the toll booths, and the costs of maintenance, profits were seldom realized. It was a lose-lose situation for both operator and user.

In the end, the owners often begged the towns to take over the toll roads, and most were glad to oblige.

### THE IRON HORSE CLIMBS THE MOUNTAINS

*In most of life's products of excellent kind*
*Our state equals others, or leaves them behind;*
*If we cannot raise wheat quite as much as we please,*
*We can produce sugar, and butter and cheese;*
*We have wool in great plenty, and with it the power*
*To turn it to cash, and the cash into flour.*
*Our ore is too plenty of iron refined.*
*We have minerals many of excellent kind;*
*If markets are distant they'll surely be near*
*As soon as the railroads projected are here.*

—*The Vermont Watchman*, December 1849

Many Vermonters believed their recent economic doldrums would be solved in a flash when the railroads came to the state; naysayers who predicted doom

## THE DISAPPOINTING EFFECTS OF THE RAILROAD: THE VIEW FROM MONTPELIER

Writing in 1860, soon after the coming of the railway age in Vermont, Montpelier's historian, D.P. Thompson, captured the confusion people felt at the coming of the railroads:

*Here, again, however, another great mistake appears to have been made in regard to the class of community most to be benefited by the opening of the railroads. The inhabitants of the villages bordering the line of the road, supposing it would cause a large increase of the trade and business of their respective towns, taxed themselves to the utmost of their means, and often far beyond them, in contributing to the enterprise; while the farmers, seeing few or no prospective benefits from it in store for themselves, hung doubtfully back and took scarcely any stock, though, as the matter resulted they should have been the very ones to have taken the lead, and contribute the most liberally in the whole movement: for, if there is one thing more palpable than another in the business world, it is the fact, that the villages have built the railroads and the farmers have reapt all the great benefits.*

—D.P. Thompson,
*History of the Town of Montpelier, Vermont* (1860)

**The Woodstock Railway opened this dizzying matchstick bridge (above left) over Quechee Gorge in 1875; at 163 feet high, it was Vermont's tallest bridge for years.**

and gloom were considered out of step with the times. Elisha Sabin, who had left Vermont for Ohio, wrote to quash his mother's enthusiasm, "You speak of having a Rail Road in Vt. No doubt you will. It will in my opinion be a great curse to the State. All Monopolies are. Also all internal improvements have a tendency to make people unhappy."

Early railroading could be extremely hazardous. This stereoscopic view shows a wreck that took place at Brockway's Mills in Rockingham. The vintage image is captioned: "The down mail train of July 24th, 1869, was thrown from the track by a misplaced switch and narrowly escaped being precipitated from High Bridge 78 ft. upon the rocks below."



Railroads came to Vermont relatively late—in 1848, fully 17 years after trains had begun to run on the pioneering Albany and Schenectady line. The Canadians had managed to link Montréal with the Lake Champlain navigation at St. Jean sur Richelieu, a town halfway between the Vermont border and Montréal, by 1836. But in Vermont, one of the great obstacles to railroad building was the physical and psychological barrier presented by the Green Mountains. As the early historian of Montpelier, D. P. Thompson, wrote in 1860, "Ten years before the Central Vermont Railroad was commenced, there was not probably one man in a thousand in the State, who could have been brought to believe that a railroad could, or at least ever would, be constructed through this, the heart of the Green Mountains."

Vermont had a railroad race on before an engine ever touched the tracks, as the directors of the Rutland and Burlington Railway, running from Bellows Falls to Rutland and north, rushed to beat the Vermont Central, snaking up the east side from White River Junction to Montpelier to Burlington. Everyone knew that Burlington could support only one railroad. The Vermont Central won by skipping Burlington entirely, and connecting to the Canadian line at Essex Junction. And still the railwaymen kept building, over 500 miles of track at a cost of $26,000,000. Many of the investors would go bankrupt long before they ever showed a profit.

The railroads were to have a great impact upon Vermont, but not necessarily in the ways that people had envisioned. They were expected to help turn Vermont from agriculture to industry and commerce, and it was assumed that future prosperity would only be possible for towns on the railway lines. Within a few years of the coming of the railroad, the value of village and agricultural real estate near the lines doubled. Yet the iron horses often hurt manufacturing, for the high expenses incurred in making things in the north country and getting them to market were often not competitive. The Vermont economy was not strong enough to make many of its towns attractive railroad destinations. Ultimately, the lines just passed through Vermont, heading elsewhere. A lot of Vermonters jumped on for the ride.

## BOOM AND BUST IN VERMONT'S GOLDEN AGE

The first half of the nineteenth century was the best of times and the worst of times in Vermont, depending upon who you were. The apparent economic equality of the settlement period, when almost everyone seemed to be starting out with an even stake, quickly proved to be an illusion. Class distinctions were appearing as some made the transition from subsistence to capitalism more successfully than others. There were many fortunes made in early Vermont from sheep and lumber, copper and cloth, marble and machinery. A comfortable class of yeomen was also appearing, on both specialized and mixed farms, who made enough surplus to build substantial houses and set their children up in life. But the Vermont landscape was turning out to be inherently unforgiving for many families. A lot of things were going wrong for a lot of people between the War of 1812 and the Civil War.

First, national policies had an impact on the Vermont economy. Jefferson's embargo of Canada in 1807 and the War of 1812 dried up trade with Vermont's biggest trading partners, although this had the fortunate, if unforeseen, consequence of stimulating local manufactures. Many items that had been cheaper to import had to be made at home. Unfortunately for some, the peace brought the lifting of the wartime embargo, driving many of the new firms out of business. The imposition and lifting of tariffs also had serious repercussions for Vermont industries, like the decline in sheep farming when tariffs on wool were lifted in the early 1840s.

Second, almost all of Vermont's early industries were tied to the exploitation of the land. For this reason, the early economic boost they provided often became chimerical, as the ores and minerals and, especially, the once infinite trees began to give out. The exportation of nature's bounty does not make for an endlessly productive economy. Even on the farm, soil was being depleted, especially the thin soil of the hill farms, hurrying the trend described in the catchphrase, "everything's moving downhill." When the resources began to give out, so did the money.

Finally, many of the state's agricultural, industrial, and commercial problems could be traced to the transportation system. It was not that the system did not develop, but rather that it developed out of sync with the economy. At the dawn of the 1800s, when the economy was ready to boom, many industries found it difficult to get off the ground because home demand was still small and there were few economically viable ways to get products to distant markets. By the time new roads, the Champlain canal, and the railroads had alleviated some transport problems, Vermont's soils, natural resources, and commercial energies were all depressed. As Western goods flowed into Vermont on the rail lines, Vermonters flowed out on them to the West.

### VERMONT GOES WEST

In Vermont, the virgin land had seemed to promise infinite possibilities, but those who came after the early settlers were often faced with a rocky truth. All land places limits on human possibilities; in the first half of the nineteenth

### THE VERMONT FARMER AND THE MINNESOTA FARMER: AN EMIGRANT JOKE

Here is what contemporaries called "that old yarn of the Minnesota Vermonter":

*I know Vermont and I know Minnesota. My father had three sons and two of us came to Minnesota. Last year I went home to the old farm, and in the morning I went out to look at the fields. When I came in, I said to my brother, "How are you getting on, John?" "O," he answered, "we manage to get a living, and that is about all." "Why, John," I said, "I don't wonder that you are poor. If I had a man in my employ who would reap a field of oats and leave as much standing as there is in that field yonder, I would discharge him at once." "Why, Bill," exclaimed my brother, "that's the crop!"*

—Lewis Stilwell,
*Migration from Vermont* (1948)

## TWO WOMEN WRITE HOME ABOUT LEAVING VERMONT: SARAH WALBRIDGE WAY AND SALLY RICE

Historians have tended to write about those who migrated from Vermont as a bloc who voted with their feet, all leaving for the same reasons. In fact, people's motivations varied enormously. This was particularly true of married women, many of whom left reluctantly at their husbands' insistence. In the excerpts below, two women who emigrated write home to their mothers in Vermont, explaining their very different experiences of being out of state.

This portrait, taken in Vermont, shows the steady gaze of the young Sarah Walbridge Way shortly before she left her home state to homestead in the West.

### Sarah Walbridge Way

Sarah Walbridge grew up on a farm in Peacham and married a local boy, John Way. Bitten by wanderlust, in 1855 John informed his wife that they were moving to the remote frontier outpost of Northfield, Minnesota. Sarah grew to love it there, but as the 1856 account of her mother, Roxana, suggests, she did not begin her life there with enthusiasm:

*I got a letter from [Sarah] a few days ago she says they were in tolerable good health but she is not contented I expect they have seen some pretty hard times since they have been on their new place. They have built them a log house and the winter was so severe that they suffered very much with the cold. ...Sarah writes that it has been verry trying in minesota and the prospect for crops were not very flattering. I think it is rather a hard case for one to go from a cold Country to a colder one and have to suffer all the privations of beginning new faring hard and being homesick into the bargain as Sarah is she thinks she dont see anything there that is any better than in Vt and a good many things worse especially the Snakes she has to watch there to keep them out of the house and beds she says she killed as many as three a day for 3 weeks within 3 feet of her house. I don't believe she will ever be contented there.*

—Lynn A. Bonfield and Mary C. Morrison, *Roxana's Children:The Biography of a Nineteenth-Century Vermont Family* (1995)

### Sally Rice

Sally Rice grew up on a farm in Somerset, the youngest of five children. In 1838, at age 17, she went off to Union Village, New York, to work for another family. After a brief visit home, she wrote to explain why she never wanted to come back to Vermont to live:

*I can never be happy there in among so many mountains. ...I feel as though I have worn out shoes and strength enough riding and walking over the mountains. I think it would be more consistent to save my strength to raise my boys. I shall need all I have got and as for marrying and settling in that wilderness, I wont. ...I am most 19 years old. I must of course have something of my own before many more years have passed over my head. And where is that something coming from if I go home and earn nothing. What can we get off that rocky farm only 2 or 3 cows. It would be another thing if you kept 9 or 10 cows and could raise corn to sell. ...You may think me unkind but how can you blame me for wanting to stay here. I have but one life to live and I want to enjoy myself as well as I can while I live. ...Do come away dont lay our bones in that place I beg of you.*

—quoted in Nell W. Kull, "'I Can Never Be Happy There in Among So Many Mountains,'—The Letters of Sally Rice," *Vermont History*, 38,1 (Winter 1970), 49–57, 52.

ay Collection, courtesy of Lynn A. Bonfield

century, it was the land, more than anything else, that decided the Vermont population needed an adjustment.

The hardscrabble existence so many Vermonters were living after the early statehood boom went bust convinced many to head for the promise of an easier life out of state. For young women, the route was often to the textile mills of Massachusetts, while for young men, the road usually led west. The state's population grew at every census in this period, going from 85,425 in 1790 to 314,120 in 1850, but in the 1840s the rate of change was only up four percent in a decade. By 1860 half of the towns in Vermont were losing population.

Historian Lewis Stilwell's book *Migration from Vermont* (1948) recites a litany of "blows" that provided reasons for leaving the state. It is so long and disturbing that the reader begins to wonder why anyone stayed: Jefferson's Embargo of 1808, severe rains washing out mills in 1811, the War of 1812, an increase in tuberculosis, and finally, 1816: the year without a summer. There was a particularly large number of emigrants in 1816–1817, mainly young farmers heading West. But the greatest outpouring happened in the 1830s, at the height of the sheep craze. Small-scale farmers sold out and fledgling manufacturers gave up in disgust at trying to deal with Vermont's rudimentary transportation system. By the railroad age, in 1850, a total of 96,780 Vermont natives were living out of state, while 232,091 Vermonters remained at home. Stilwell concludes that Vermonters had "used up" Vermont and were now looking for the easy life in Michigan and Wisconsin and Minnesota.

It is part of the mythology of America to favor the frontier, under the assumption that "the best and the brightest," the most adventurous and vigorous of Vermont's young people, left for the West. In fact, it is just as likely that the opposite was the case. What incentive was there for leaving family and friends if you were getting on well in Vermont? Those who left were as likely to be the ones who had been unsuccessful here as they were to be those with a fire in the belly.

Hal Barron has written on those who did not emigrate from the town of Chelsea, in his study, *Those Who Stayed Behind* (1984). He argues against the idea that loss of population was related to severe economic decline, finding that the consolidation of sheep farms, for instance, was indicative of economic growth. In the Chelsea region, hill towns, industrial towns, and valley towns had all found a state of equilibrium that Barron believes is "normal" for many settled agrarian communities. Perhaps an absence of growth was not indicative of stagnation in early nineteenth-century Vermont. It just meant that the land was telling the people how many of them it could support under prevailing conditions. Small could be beautiful.

## THE CLASSIC VERMONT VILLAGE

*Brattleboro, Vt., June 30th ...There are many elegant private mansions and the buildings, mostly new and in good taste, have an air of neatness and comfort seldom met with. In the evening, scarcely passed a well looking house without hearing the pleasing and familiar sounds of the Piano in accompaniment with the cheerful laughter-loving voice of its fair possessor. On Sunday attended the Episcopal Church in the forenoon which has a handsome interior. The Presbyterian in the afternoon where we had a fine seat, a regular orthodox sermon, and pretty black eyes. But it is the scenery that makes the charming B [rattleboro]. 'Tis only too beautiful for the picturesque and romantic. The mountains extending and retreating in regular courses to the horizon, are covered with dense foliage of the richest green, and rolling with the gentle, swelling undulation of the ocean, lie in soft quiet repose upon the face of nature like the embodied fancies of a Poet's dream.*

—Charles William Eldridge (1833)

The Vermont of 1830 to 1860 has often been portrayed as a tragic place in which poor soil, bad weather, an antiquated transport system, and a weak business climate were driving its natives out by the thousands. But something very important is missing from that gloomy picture of the period. Charles William Eldridge, a dashing young miniature painter with an eye for beauty of all sorts, saw it when he traveled through in 1833. And we see its legacy today. Villages had appeared on the landscape, and as small as they were they had an air of culture and community. The "elegant" houses were filled with music, and the churches were "handsome" and "orthodox." There was comfort and laughter, in contrast to the heaving labor and physical discomfort of the settlement period. Surrounding them was a romantic, dreamlike mountain landscape that was gentle and tame, "lofty just enough to fill the eye." There were enough agricultural and industrial riches here to provide ease to more people than ever before.

All of this village neatness had its price. In the first half of the nineteenth century, the same process of consolidation and enlargement that allowed the Merino farmers to buy out their neighbors was also taking place in the villages. While few townsmen ever achieved the riches of Brandon's John Conant or the Fairbanks family of St. Johnsbury, the rich managed to get richer, while many of the poor clung on in silence or headed West.

It was an era of rising expectations. The plucky, self-sufficient settlers did not find their own lives as romantic as they have seemed to us in retrospect. Most wanted things easier, a chance "to enjoy myself as well as I can while I live," in the words of young Sally Rice, as she struggled to escape the

UVM Special Collections

Alvan Fisher's "Brattleboro, Vermont" (1830) is one of the earliest paintings of a Vermont village and a forerunner of the great age of American landscape painting that was to come in the next 30 years. It shows the prosperous little community, its surrounding fields bathed in golden light, while in the foreground the tree stumps of the conquered wilderness remind the viewer of what civilization has accomplished. The state's increasing refinement is exemplified by the elegant carriage leaving the village, pulled by a horse said to have been a son of "Figure," the first of the Morgan breed.

hill-farm poverty of her brief childhood. They wanted schools, churches, and warm houses with a bit of furniture. Those who could get that for themselves in Vermont were happy to stay. Those who could not got out or struggled on as their homesteading mothers and fathers had before them.

## THE BIRTH OF VILLAGE COMMERCE

*Windsor is a flourishing and beautiful town, the shire town of the county of Windsor, and plainly superior to any other in the state of Vermont on the eastern side of the Green Mountains. The houses in Windsor are generally good, and several of them are built in a handsome style. Very few inland towns in New England appear with equal advantage. The courthouse, which stands on the northeastern corner of the upper plain, is large and well appearing. ...Windsor contains a considerable number of stores, and among others one or two bookstores. Here are two printing offices. More mercantile and mechanical business is done here than in any town on the river north of Massachusetts, and it is said to be increasing.*

—Timothy Dwight (1797)

Some village centers never grew beyond an original settlement-era nucleus. In Addison, the church and town hall (below), along with a nearby general store, give focus to a far-flung agricultural community.

The pivotal Vermont development of the early statehood period was the appearance of commercial villages, with their new civic amenities. For Vermonters who had been leading lonely and isolated lives on distant stakes, these expanding villages were a convenience, a relief, and a revelation. In Yankee fashion, there was probably some suspicion of the sharpsters of Shelburne or the fleshpots of Putney or the tipplers of Tinmouth. But the villages brought new riches and a new richness to community life in Vermont.

The Vermont villages were not large, but they represented a distinct break with the surrounding countryside. Farmers might come to the village to do their business, but the villagers were not going out to work on the farms. The great change from an economy where people grew their own and bartered for the rest to one where they sold things for money and then bought what they needed was fueling the growth of villages all over the state. And in serving the unprecedented demands for trading and commerce, shipping and shopping, new non-agricultural vocational options were appearing that had been almost non-existent in the 1700s. Vermont was generating enough wealth to allow some folks to move off the farm and live lives more like the ones their ancestors from southern New England had left behind.

Around the time of statehood in 1791, the whole regional economy of New England was gaining steam. When John Lincklaen, a Dutch land agent, visited Vermont in that year, he found that "The settlements are new, but people begin to live at their ease." Farmers had greater surpluses to sell outside their own neighborhoods, creating a need for more cash transactions. When they had cash, they wanted local places to spend some of it, whether on tea at a general store or on chairs at the local cabinetmaker. As transportation improved on the turnpikes, goods could move more easily. Commercial villages sprang up to facilitate these new transactions. Both Middlebury and Springfield got their first shops in 1790.

Village economies began diversifying quickly under the Republic of Vermont. When a goldsmith named William Storer moved to Rutland in November of 1788, he found there three blacksmiths, a tanner, a master builder, a mason, a tailor, a merchant, two attorneys, two doctors, and an innkeeper. These were soon joined by more shops, cabinetmakers, silversmiths, and clockmakers. In Franklin County, Bakersfield had a gristmill, four sawmills, a potash factory, a tannery, a wool-carding mill, a starch factory, a brick kiln, and a whisky distillery by the early nineteenth century. In 1824, the shire town of Orange County, Chelsea, had two gristmills, five sawmills, two fulling mills, two clothier works, two carding machines, a small woolens factory, two trip-hammer shops, two tanneries, three stores, a tavern, two clergymen, three doctors, and three lawyers. All this was happening in villages that, just a decade or two before, could boast little more than a tavern.

## THE GLORY THAT WAS GREEK REVIVAL

Villages are not just places to live, work, and trade. They are also places where people express their aspirations and sense of self. Once the struggle of the settlement period was past, Vermonters, like many Americans of the early Republic, were desperate to show they had become "civilized." And what better way to do that than to build in the Federal or Greek Revival styles, with their echoes of the ultimate in civilization, the ancient world? Columns rose, temple-like pediments appeared, mini-Acropoli were scattered in village and sheep pasture alike. It was as if Vermonters were determined to tell a skeptical world that they were no longer pioneers; they were educated, tasteful people with a connection to history and culture. Even their white paint made a strong statement, shocking rural communities that had only seen houses in "natural" colors of yellow ochre, brown, dark red, or, more frequently, with no paint at all. White houses were an acquired taste; early critics complained they

## FANCY FEDERALS

This handsome Federal house in Hartland (top) shows the delicate detail so typical of the style. A brilliant local builder, Thomas Dake, designed another elegant Federal house (bottom) in Castleton around 1815.

In Vermont, as in much of the eastern United States, the preferred design for a house from the late 1700s through the 1830s was in the Federal style. A number of elegant examples remain in the state, many of them modeled from carpenters' handbooks like Asher Benjamin's *American Builder's Companion* (1806).

Federal houses were often center hall Colonials in their floor plans, with four rooms downstairs and four rooms up. Their trim was often delicate, modelled after Classical Roman design. They can be spotted sporting the following features:

- Symmetrical facades centered on an elaborate front door, often with an entryway leading into a hall.
- The front door may have sidelight windows extending halfway down, thin pilasters (flat columns made of wood) to the sides, and an elliptical fanlight over the door.
- Elaborate examples display delicate tracery designs, particularly along the cornice (eaveline) and around the door.
- Many have elegant Palladian windows on the second floor over the front door.
- The glass sidelights and semi-circular fanlights often have delicate leaded glass tracery designs.

Top: UVM Special Collections; bottom: Jan Albers

did not blend into the landscape (except in winter, of course). But that was exactly the point of white houses. They were meant to show that the denizens of a great culture had conquered the wilderness and created a civilization where people ruled over nature.

Not all buildings of the era contained high-style architectural details. In our fantasies of perfect villages, all the churches are good looking and all the houses are above average. In fact, architectural historians have shown that the large, stylish houses we admire were as exceptional in their own day as they are in ours. A New England study found that in 1798 one-story houses outnumbered two-story houses by a ratio of seven to one, yet two-thirds of the eighteenth-century houses that remain standing today are large, two-story buildings. Elegance may not be typical, but it endures. Houses with convenient floorplans (central hall Georgian plan, for example) are also more apt to have survived than houses without upstairs hallways, where you have

## GREEK REVIVAL FOR EVERYONE

Jan Albers

The next great architectural style to hit Vermont—and the one that still very much defines the austere beauty for which the state is known—was the Greek Revival. Popular from the 1830s to the 1870s, Greek Revival houses often had center hall Colonial floorplans very similar to those popularized in the Federal style. The greatest difference was in the details, which were becoming more monumental. Some characteristics of Greek Revival houses include:

- Heavy and stark wooden detailing: massive columns, pilasters, and cornices.
- Emphasis still on the main entry, which is often flanked by long sidelight windows and elaborate wooden trim.
- Some put the gable end to the street, surmounted by a heavy triangular pediment.
- The most elaborate look like little Parthenons or other Greek temples.
- Details are rectangular and heavy rather than light and decorative, as in the Federal style.

**By the mid-1800s, people in many price ranges could put some style into their new houses. For those of modest income, the Greek Revival influence is shown (left) in the heavy trim work, elaborate door treatment, and side hall plan. This one-and-a-half-story house in Weybridge was built around 1845. A prosperous middle class farmer in Waltham built his brick Greek Revival dream house (center) in 1830. It has sidelights, pilasters, and marble lintels and sills on the windows. For the truly wealthy, the style could be made as grand as they could afford. A spectacular Greek Revival pavilion with ells (right) was built in Castleton in 1848.**

to pass through one room to get to the next. (Although try buying an old Vermont farmhouse today, and you will soon become convinced that the opposite is true.) Houses improved in the next 50 years, but the ideal Vermont village composed solely of perfect elegant houses was never a full-fledged reality.

The lawyer and playwright Royall Tyler (top) could have found greater fame elsewhere. But this son of the Boston elite, author of a successful play, *The Contrast*—long considered the first truly American theatrical work—chose instead to be a big fish in the new little pond of Vermont. He quickly became state's attorney of Windham County and was eventually made Chief Justice of the Vermont Supreme Court. His modest home (bottom) shows him to have been a man of relatively simple tastes.

## THE GROWTH OF CIVILITY

The houses reflected, or perhaps helped to create, a growing civility in Vermont life. This was not only a village phenomenon, for some of the state's most elegant houses were in the countryside. But villages were particularly symbolic of culture because they were the places where most community relationships developed for both rural and village people—church, tavern, schoolhouse, workplace, the courts. The closeness of villages, in both a communal and a claustrophobic sense, seems to have brought about a certain reformation of manners. In 1821, the dour Reverend Asa Burton of Thetford gave much of the credit to religion, and he was not completely wrong in this:

> *The aspect of society is greatly altered. The inhabitants of this Town, who were few in number, very rude, ignorant, vicious, and uncivilized, in general, have increased greatly, and settled in every part; they have been improving gradually in knowledge, in property, in morals, and religion, until they have become as respectable, as distinguished, influential, and in all respects as regular in their habits, as perhaps any town nigh here. This great change has taken place within the period of 42 years. It has been effected by the grace and agency of God.*

Even the sons and daughters of the wild Green Mountain boys could eventually be tamed.

In 1791, America's first comic playwright, Royall Tyler, turned his back on literary success and moved to Guilford, Vermont, to settle down to life as a lawyer and family man. As a teenager, he had visited his Boston friends, the Palmers, to view their new baby daughter, and declared, "This child will become my wife." Now, 20 years later, Mary Palmer had been duly claimed, and in anticipation of his bride's arrival, he was busy selling her on the community she would be joining in Guilford:

> *If they have a social party, the whole neighborhood are invited. We have two merchants, the Messrs. Houghtons, two physicians, Dr. Stephens and Dr. Hyde, one lawyer, your humble servant, all men of education, and their wives and families well bred country people. There are several well-to-do mechanics who aim to treat company equally well. In fact, my dear, you will find it a truly primitive state*

Top: Alan Jakubek; bottom, left to right: Stuart McHenry,
Sara Gregg, Stuart McHenry, Sara Gregg

In our romantic view of American expansion, the pioneer generation is always plucky and self-controlled, but it has been shown in other parts of America that settlers actually had high rates of mental illness and suicide. Their children also felt the stresses, often expressed in religious fervor; the witchcraft accusations in Salem provide the most horrific, if extreme, example. Vermont was also hit with religious frenzy, consuming thousands of its citizens with a zeal equal to the anxieties that had preceded it. Wave after wave of revivals hit Vermont's villages; these particularly affected the young. From the turn of the century until the mid-1830s, many villages were acrimoniously divided as some people got religion and others, adamantly, did not. It was almost as if the act of living in closer proximity had created tensions that needed to be redressed.

Vermont had been founded in an atmosphere of disrespect for institutions, especially in the wilds west of the Green Mountains, where the Allens held sway. (It was observed that Connecticut Valley people tended to be more conservative and controlled.) The long lag between settlement and the coming of organized religion had left men and women to religious free thinking. It produced the mind of Joseph Smith and his Mormon cosmology, the free love philosophy of John Humphrey Noyes (later founder of the Perfectionist Oneida Community in central New York), and William Miller, who convinced his "Millerite" followers that the world was going to end in 1844. Yet with their eyes on the next world, none of them was able to make a life in Vermont's orderly new villages. There, a new mentality was arising that would profoundly alter the way in which people understood their role in the natural world.

With its tiny human beings dwarfed by the awesome beauty of nature, Sanford Robinson Gifford's painting, "Mount Mansfield" (circa 1858), is one of the last to show the scenery of Vermont in the sublime tradition of the Hudson River School. The great vista from Mount Mansfield's summit is obscured by pearly light, perhaps in hopes of making the scene look more wild than it had, by then, become. In the same decade, other artists were to focus on the more mundane and realistic aspects of the Vermont landscape.

## A NEW WAY OF SEEING

*All the hills blush; I think that autumn must be the best season to journey over even the Green Mountains. You frequently exclaim to yourself, what red maples! ...Tall and slender ash-trees, whose foliage is turned to a dark mulberry color, are frequent. The butternut, which is a remarkably spreading tree, is turned completely yellow thus proving its relation to the hickories. ...The sugar-maple is remarkable for its clean ankle. The groves of these trees looked like vast forest sheds, their branches stopping at a uniform height, four or five feet from the ground, like eaves, as if they had been trimmed by art, so that you could look under and through the whole grove with its leafy canopy, as under a tent whose curtain is raised.*

—HENRY DAVID THOREAU, on an autumn train journey through Vermont, 1850

George Walter Vincent Smith Art Museum

The end of the wilderness was the beginning of knowledge. All over the Eastern United States, the men and women of the neat fields and tidy villages were gaining a new ability to see the wilderness now that so much of it had gone. Instead of regarding trees only as stolid impediments to agriculture or promising numbers of board feet, Thoreau and his contemporaries were experiencing a new beauty in nature. But even here, it was not a nature completely apart from man. Thoreau's trees have "clean ankles" and look like "eaves" or a "tent," as neat as if a human hand had pruned them. The people of the early Republic looked at nature and saw themselves.

The Abenaki had seen themselves as humble beings who stood on the same level with nature. But the Christian God stood above and apart from nature, experiencing it only through a transcendent "seeing." Once the men and women of the settlement period had changed the land with God-like power, their children looked out on these new vistas with a transcendent eye and saw, for the first time, what had been lost.

## THE ASSAULT ON THE WILDERNESS

On June 5, 1850, a tall and angular native Vermonter, Zadock Thompson, rose to address a sophisticated audience at the Boston Society of Natural History. After many expressions of his unworthiness to speak to this distinguished company due to "the difficulties in the way of the cultivation of Natural History in country places," he proceeded to provide a painstaking overview of the effects of the hand of man on the Vermont wilderness. He would try to do better than his predecessor, Samuel Williams, but admitted he had

Zadock Thompson, Vermont's premiere naturalist of the early nineteenth century, was largely self-taught.



## ZADOCK THOMPSON: VERMONT'S FIRST NATIVE NATURALIST

Vermont seems to be home to one great naturalist in each generation. Zadock Thompson (1796–1856) was born on his father's farm in the rugged hills of Bridgewater between Killington and Woodstock. The family was so poor that he did not manage to finish putting himself through the University of Vermont until he was 27 years old. Little was offered in the study of natural history during his time there; Thompson learned about nature largely on his own. He became a schoolteacher, then was ordained an Episcopal deacon. When not doing substitute preaching, he devoted himself to writing a series of gazetteers (the first in 1824), a *Geography and History of Vermont* (1833) and then *The Natural History of Vermont* (1842). He worked on the geological survey of the state, was appointed State Naturalist, and taught at the University. His fame spread beyond Burlington after he analyzed, reconstructed, and wrote about the bones of an "elephant" (in 1848, later found to be a mammoth) and the Charlotte whale (1849).

Thompson's scholarship was not on the cutting edge; the combined resources available to him in the state of Vermont consisted merely of a few books and conversations with some fellow enthusiasts. He never had access to any scientific instruments, lacking even a microscope. But he did have what he once wished would someday be available to the schoolchildren of Vermont, "...the means and motives for understanding, appreciating, and enjoying what is real, and valuable, and beautiful in the productions of the natural world around them."

neither the laboratory resources nor the training to do research with the professionalism that the scientific community expected.

Thompson's speech was based on his own book, *The Natural History of Vermont* (1842, appended 1853). It was one acute observer's chronicle of the status of plant and animal life in Vermont in the face of relentless hunting by human beings. With studied precision, Thompson described the extermination of a variety of dangerous animals at the behest of state government. The black bear was "so plentiful at the present day, that our Legislature continues in force a law allowing a bounty of $5 each, for its destruction." (The State Treasurer reported paying out about 40 or 50 bounties per year.) Wolves "have always been so great an annoyance that much pains have been taken for their extermination, but at present, their number is so much reduced that comparatively very little damage is done by them in this state." The red fox was still in the hen house, so a bounty of 25 cents each remained in force. Catamounts "were formerly much more common in Vermont than at the present day," but the princely sum of $20 would go to anyone lucky enough to destroy one.

In these two charming illustrations from Rowland Robinson, nineteenth-century Vermonters confront nature —to nature's detriment. (Top) A hunter pauses before shooting what may be the last deer in the forest; (bottom) a group of men shoot their Thanksgiving turkey in a most unsportsmanlike manner.

Rokeby Museum

Other animals were being pursued for the money their pelts could bring. Mink, weasels, and red foxes brought 20–30 cents a pelt, and the precious skins of the fisher martin were worth 10 times that. A silver fox pelt brought in $15—almost as much as a catamount and without the danger—but just try to find one. Other less showy animals were being wiped out for sport. The once plentiful raccoon was now confined to the mountain forest lands. A wolverine had not been spotted for several years. Otters and lynx "were formerly much more common." Beavers were now "nearly or quite exterminated...the last...was killed, in Essex county, 12 years ago." Moose and elk had also been completely exterminated. Even the "common deer" had become uncommon and were now "exceedingly scarce." (They would soon disappear completely; those we see today are descended from Adirondack deer that were reintroduced to Vermont in a later period.) The hare was lucky to reproduce so prolifically, because "They are pursued and destroyed in great numbers, by men and dogs." Passenger pigeons were threatened and the wild turkey had "every where diminished." The salmon on which the Abenaki had gorged themselves each spring had been dammed out of existence and were now "so exceedingly rare a visitant that I have not been able to obtain a specimen taken in our waters."

The stew pot that had once been fragrant with venison was now reduced to squirrel. There was also no shortage of skunks, mice, and what Thompson called "chipmucks." Muskrat and woodchuck numbers were down, but there were still plenty to go around. The most rapidly increasing creature in Vermont was a recent introduction that had been carried in with the settlers—the Norway rat. Its cousin, the brown rat, was also exploding in population, and "is now the common rat in all the older parts of the state; and yet it is but a few years since it was said that none of these rats had ever been seen in the county of Orleans."

The same destruction was happening in the plant world. Red cedar was being cut in great numbers because it was so sturdy that it had been "standing in the common fences in Burlington and other places for 50 years...and as sound as when set." White pine had once been "very abundant" near Lake Champlain, "But in consequence of the indiscriminate havoc of our forest trees by the early settlers...white pine have mostly disappeared." Apple trees were threatened through political motives, because so much of their former bounty had been made into hard cider that had been the "everlasting ruin of many of our previously thrifty farmers."

Rowland Robinson (1833–1900), a Quaker farmer from Ferrisburgh, became a successful illustrator and devoted abolitionist, but his chief claim to fame was his novels, which poignantly capture how nineteenth-century Vermonters loved nature and yet could be ignorant of the roles they played in defiling it. A Robinson illustration (opposite) shows some more sensitive Vermonters striving to redress their ecological wrongs by stocking a stream with fish.

Thompson knew that environmental concerns could be random and ill-considered. The state of Vermont had been "paying liberal bounties for the destruction of catamounts, wolves, bears and foxes, while the wheat fly, from which we were sustaining far greater damage...has hardly received any attention." Man's attempts at ecological engineering often proved to be misguided: "We have even paid a bounty for the destruction of crows, while in consequence of that destruction our fields were suffering from the ravages of grubs, which the crows are designed to check." Thompson struggled to maintain an air of scientific objectivity, but his disgust with wholesale slaughter of nature sometimes came out: "We are of the opinion that all birds, without a single exception, are...friends to the farmer...and we cannot too severely reprobate the barbarous practice in which boys are permitted to indulge, of shooting birds for amusement." A first glimmer of contempt was appearing for those who hunted wastefully.

But boys were only a small part of the problem in early nineteenth-century Vermont. It would be difficult to exaggerate the carnage that took place in the natural world during the first century of settlement. This was a time that the native-born writer, Rowland Robinson of Ferrisburgh, captured with great passion in the stories of upland folk recently rereleased under the title of *Danvis Tales*. Robinson described a tough world, where men killed for sport and from boredom. He shared their love of hunting, yet grappled with a growing awareness of its price. His characters sit around the fire and wonder at not having seen a deer for five or ten years, when they used to be so plentiful. Writing in the Vermont dialect, Robinson told how the older and wiser ones look back in disgust at times when "critters 'at went on tew legs an' called 'emselves men...useter go aout in Febwary an' March an' murder the poor creeturs in their yards with clubs, twenty on 'em in a day, when they wa'n't with skinnin' fur their skins." Others rejoice in the killing of the wolves and repeat rumors that justified their demise: "When I was a boy you c'd hear 'em a-yowlin' up on the mountain, most any night, 'nough tu make yer back freeze. Naow an' ag'in they ysed tu kill folds, I s'pose. I never knowed o' their killin' anybody for sartain, but some on 'em 'lowed they killed Cephas Worth an' eta him clean up, an' then ag'in, some cal'lated they didn't." Robinson showed sensitivity to the tragedy at the heart of this carnage; yet he himself loved nothing better than the hunt. As Hayden Carruth puts it in his introduction to *Danvis Tales*, Robinson hoped that "the enforcement of the game laws...would preserve not only the 'balance of Nature' but the very means for keeping alive his beloved blood sport—the supply of killable animals."

But as accurate as Robinson was at describing the lost world of his boyhood before the Civil War, he was writing in the late nineteenth century,

---

## "THE PRIVILEGES OF EVERY FREEBORN AMERICAN": ROWLAND ROBINSON ON ECOLOGICAL ATTITUDES IN THE 1840s

In this passage from Rowland Robinson's *Danvis Tales*, Pelatiah Gove is hunting along the shores of Lake Champlain on a spring morning in the 1840s:

*Guns were booming all along the shores—the thin report of rifles spitting out their light charges, the bellow of muskets belching out their four fingers or powder, two wads, and "double B's," and giving one's shoulder a sympathetic twinge as he althought how the shooter's must be aching—all proclaimed that it was a sad day for the pickerel that had come on to Little Otter's marshes to spawn. Probably not one man of the fifty who were hunting them there had a althought of what the fish were there for, or would have cared if he had. There were too many pickerel, and always would be. There could be no exhaustion of the supply of them nor of any other fish. Any proposition to protect fish and game of any kind, to prescribe any method of taking, to limit the season of killing, would have been althought an attempt to introduce hated Old World laws and customs.*

*Hunting and fishing were the privileges of every freeborn American, to use or abuse whenever, wherever, and however he was disposed. And he could not live long enough to see the end of it, for why should there not always be fish and game as innumerable in all these unnumbered acres of water and marsh and woods? Alas! why not?*

with its more sophisticated understanding of the pressures that settlement had brought to bear on the environment. Hunting had stressed or exterminated some animal species, but probably more had been killed or driven out of the state by the loss of habitat. The destruction of the flora and fauna had also delivered a near death blow to the Abenaki. Their small remaining community was struggling to maintain their traditional migratory hunting patterns. And the forests continued to fall.

### THE LOST WORLD OF THE ABENAKI

With the destruction of their traditional landscape, the Abenaki were increasingly marginalized in the early nineteenth century. Many moved over the border to native villages in Québec. Others adopted agricultural practices. A few tried to maintain their traditional nomadic existence, and even in the mid-nineteenth century Rowland Robinson visited their seasonal encampments on the shores of Lake Champlain. Abby Hemenway recorded their sad plight in the north-central part of the state:

*Several families moved into Troy and Potton [Orleans County] in 1799, and in the winter of 1800, a small party of Indians, of whom the chief man was captain Susap, joined the colonists, built their camps on the river, and wintered near them. These Indians were represented as being in a necessitous and almost starving condition, which probably arose from the moose and deer (which formerly abounded here) being destroyed by the settlers. Their principal employment was making baskets, birch-bark cups and pails, and other Indian trinkets. They left in the spring and never returned.*

## THE LAW OF THE LAND

The first European residents of the northern forests had foraged at will, and were stunned to find how quickly the seemingly bottomless supplies of animals in the woods could actually be depleted. There had been attempts at regulation from a very early time. In 1777 the Constitution of the Republic of Vermont stipulated that the inhabitants had the right to fish any public waters "under proper regulations made by the General Assembly." Two years later they were trying to protect dwindling fish populations by forbidding the erection of dams and weirs on Vermont's rivers that were interfering with spawning. The fine was to be four pounds, with half going to the informer. 1779 also saw the beginning of the "bounty" system of animal management, as lawmakers moved to protect the populace from perceived predators by passing "An act to encourage the destroying of wolves and panthers." This legislation promised the substantial sum of eight pounds to anyone who could produce the head of one of these beasts (what State Archivist Gregory Sanford has dubbed "the ultimate in head taxes"). These regulations were renewed in 1797, and a poignant new regulation was added to protect the deer population. The great herds of deer that had sustained the Abenaki for centuries were almost wiped out by the first generation of settlers; a season was set for their protection.

In this transitional time, Vermonters, like their fellow New Englanders, alternated between asserting their dominance over those features of the landscape the new capitalist farmers deemed "noxious" and trying to save those they saw as "useful." Deer were to be protected, yet they were so rare that when one was sighted it would often rate a mention in the local newspapers. Their range tended to mimic that of moose in the twentieth century, being confined largely to the Northeast Kingdom and the spine of the Green Mountains. Moose themselves had grown even more elusive than deer by 1850. Meanwhile, bounties were extended to black bears (1828), red foxes (1839), and lynx (1856). Mastery of the environment for the convenience of mankind was sought, with as yet little understanding of ecological balance.

By the mid-nineteenth century, Vermonters were becoming more aware of the changes their behavior was wreaking on the landscape. This was

largely a result of the growth of a stronger sense of common interest. Historian Richard Judd has shown how the transition from a subsistence economy, sympathetic to foraging, to a regulated capitalist economy, with its stronger emphasis upon community values, was leading to calls for more regulation of fish and game. In 1828 the citizens of Shrewsbury were asking the state legislature to stop hunters from running down deer with dogs. Other towns moved to restock the fish that had been depleted in local streams.

The Vermont "wilderness" had been demoted from center stage to backdrop in a single human life span. As trees continued to crash and streams were snarled with weirs, even the untouched wild lands had been changed from the bounty of Abenaki days to an eerie quiet. The raucous whooing of passenger pigeons was seldom heard, no salmon swam frantically in the spring sunshine, and the last catamounts searched for safe cover. They had been replaced by the whispering grain and the bleating of the lambs.

Asher B. Durand has been called the "theologian" of the Hudson River school of painters, for he believed that wild nature was "fraught with lessons of high and holy meaning." In "Study From Nature, Stratton Notch, Vermont" (1853), the gnarled branches of a felled tree symbolize the "fallen" nature of mankind, while the sublime beauty of the unspoiled wilderness of Stratton Notch glows in the background.

B. F. Nutting's "View of Newbury, Vermont from Mount Pulaski" (circa 1850) presents a vision of landscape that is very different from that of Asher B. Durand shown on the previous page. Durand rejected the hand of man in favor of a God of the wilderness, while Nutting's view rejoices in the beauty wrought by humankind's transformation of nature. On the great loop of the Connecticut River's Oxbow, Newbury was built on what had once been the site of a thriving Abenaki community. Now the village's trim white buildings seem to rise organically from the tidy farm fields; a few trees in the foreground remind the viewer that this landscape was cut from the forest. In fact, the image is testimony to the effects of deforestation, showing a landscape far more open than the one we know today. In this green and pleasant land, the mountains are distant and unthreatening, for wild nature has been tamed and made productive by human hands. But sublimity is rapidly being replaced by domesticity—in life, as in art.

## THE ARTIST'S EYE

An American Eden was almost gone just at that moment when the young nation's artists were most determined to glorify the fierce beauty of the natural landscape. Again, the destruction of the wilderness seemed to provide the necessary precursor to its aesthetic appreciation. The dark and forbidding forests of Puritan New England were assuming a mantle of holiness, as they now seemed to have been the birthplace of American religion and democracy. Poet William Cullen Bryant wrote that "The groves were God's first temples," natural churches where mankind could worship the Creator's great bounty. The massive cutting of trees seemed to highlight those that remained. It was as if this new perception of God's power in nature could only be admitted once the black, moist, monster-ridden, fairy-tale forests of nightmare had been conquered.

The new artistic view of nature, infused with romanticism and that sense of power contemporaries referred to as the "sublime," appeared most famously in the work of Thomas Cole, Frederick Church, Asher B. Durand, and other painters of the Hudson River School. As landscape viewing became a spectator sport and a goad to tourism, this new way of seeing was making its way to Vermont. The state found itself at a disadvantage here, because its pastoral landscapes were considered too "tame" compared to those of the Catskills, White Mountains, and Lake George. Americans were craving "wildness" now that it had almost ceased to exist. In the words of Thomas Cole, "Those scenes of solitude from which the hand of nature has never been lifted, affect the mind with a more deep toned emotion than aught which the hand of man has touched."

Perhaps to show that Vermont retained a healthy measure of wildness, State Geologist Albert Hager published a *Report on the Geology of Vermont* in 1861, which promised to cover the "descriptive, theoretical, economical and scenographical." The text was accompanied by a series of lithographs by A.L. Rawson showing a new consiousness of what constituted worthy "scenery." They show a wild Vermont, largely devoid of people, farms, and villages. It is a Vermont of primeval forests, rushing waters, hulking boulders, and majestic mountain vistas. Only Manchester village was allowed to appear, a snug little jewel clustered under the great mute form of Equinox Mountain, luring the tourists to the comforts awaiting them in their search for the sublime.

## LIFE IN THE POLITICAL LANDSCAPE

The Vermonters of the early Republic embraced a stance of mastery over their environment because that was what they believed it took for them to survive as a species in their age. Where there are humans, there will be excesses. Were the results of all their physical toil worth the sacrifices they demanded of the natural world? The romantic answer—that the wilderness should have been allowed to stay wilderness—is too simple. The people who cut the forests saw their lives as predominantly creative rather than destructive.

## FIVE LARGEST VERMONT TOWNS IN 1820:

| | | |
|---|---|---|
| 1. | Middlebury | 3,170 |
| 2. | Burlington | 3,070 |
| 3. | Windsor | 2,956 |
| 4. | Springfield | 2,702 |
| 5. | Woodstock | 2,601 |

## FIVE LARGEST VERMONT TOWNS IN 1860:

| | | |
|---|---|---|
| 1. | Burlington | 7,713 |
| 2. | Rutland | 7,577 |
| 3. | Bennington | 4,389 |
| 4. | Northfield | 4,329 |
| 5. | Brattleboro | 3,855 |

The style of landscape they created in Vermont has sometimes been called the "political landscape," referring to all those landscape features commonly regulated by state and local governments: lot lines, boundaries, walls, roads, monuments, and public places. The settlers' Vermont had been a chaotic place of political division, amorphous land titles, and the casual claiming of undeveloped private land for common use. In an atmosphere of minimal regulation, foraging was rampant and private interest was checked by only a few almost unenforceable laws. The world that was now disappearing was the one John Whittemore described in his early years of farming, where fences and boundaries were so indistinct that "Some of [my haystack] would be taken off by the wind, but more by the neighbors' cattle which would be constantly breaking over in spite of all we could do." The newly rational landscape was based upon the protection of private property; legally and physically secure boundaries were the basic unit of a landscape that served to protect the exalted yeoman. When boundaries were upheld, people felt their hard work was also being protected. It was also a landscape that provided people with a larger measure of justice and community. In this new world, John Whittemore moved closer to the village to escape the loneliness of hill farm life.

The heart of the political landscape of the early 1800s was the need to dominate nature in the service of agriculture. Fields of imported cattle and fancy white houses were meant to tell the world that the wilderness was gone and had been replaced by a new civilization. It was a classical agrarian landscape for a Republic that was unlike any that had preceded it. It had already transformed the wilderness into a garden. And a people who had begun life scraping by and relying upon barter were now embracing specialized agriculture and burgeoning villages in a new commercial culture based on surplus production, hard cash, and serving distant markets.

The classical Vermont village of our fantasies—and our postcards—is a product of the early nineteenth century. It did not look as it does today; then the roads were dirt, the village greens were unclipped, and many houses wore no paint. Even the things we think we understand about this landscape are more our own projections than true reflections of its inhabitants' attitudes. Where we see the serenity of a village church, they were reminded of the heat and fervor of revival. We look at the Greek Revival designs of their homes and register a vague appreciation of tastefulness, while for them even village school educations encouraged an understanding of the classical that made those features more redolent of lost civilizations. We see the village set against the dark green foliage of the mountains and it looks merely beautiful to us, while they saw it set against their own barren hillsides and rejoiced in having wrested the earth from an awesome wilderness.

We love the pure visual landscape bounty this age bequeathed to us, with its white clapboards set against the scattered colors of its farmland. And we imbue the Vermont village with many of the same values Timothy Dwight saw in the description of Putney that opened this chapter: a comfortable melding of the human and natural world, a reassuring air of moral rectitude and a cheering sense of order. But we are not completely comfortable with the message that went into its creation. As Dwight put it, with the unwavering certainty of his vision:

> *The colonization of a wilderness by civilized men, where a regular government, mild manners, arts, learning, science, and Christianity have been interwoven in its progress from the beginning is a state of things of which the eastern continent and records of past ages furnish neither an example, nor a resemblance.*

While Dwight was right about the unprecendented nature of what had been done to the land in the New World, we wonder about its cost. And yet we, too, appreciate many of the same aspects of "civilization" he extolled. It is worth wondering which of us is the more honest about our own actions and motivations.

The classic agrarian landscape is one of our favorite dreamscapes, and the reason for that is not only its physical beauty. At its heart, we know that it is a symbol of community. The villages of the early Republic were created to defy the isolation of rural life by providing places where people could come together in churches, colleges, societies. Safe within those common boundaries, secure from the threat of the wilderness, they began to see their world with fresh eyes. This new communal vision was to lie at the heart of a healthier relationship to the land they had altered almost beyond recognition.

CHAPTER 4

# CREATING VERMONT'S YANKEE KINGDOM, 1860-1945

*Nature has provided against the absolute destruction of any of her elementary matter. ...But she has left it within the power of man irreparably to derange the combinations of inorganic matter and of organic life. ...The earth is fast becoming an unfit home for its noblest inhabitant, and another era of equal human crime and human improvidence, and of like duration with that through which traces of that crime and that improvidence extend, would reduce it to such a condition of impoverished productiveness, of shattered surface, of climatic excess, as to threaten the...extinction of the species.*

—GEORGE PERKINS MARSH, *Man and Nature* (1864)

The international environmental movement had its beginnings in the rock-strewn, clear-cut, soil-depleted fields of the state of Vermont, in the brilliant mind of a young boy named George Perkins Marsh. Born in 1801 into the Yankee aristocracy of Vermont's most patrician town of Woodstock, the young George had eyesight so poor that, even though he had been an early and voracious reader, he was forbidden to look at books for years at a time. His disability freed him for a life outdoors, roaming the shattered landscapes the settlers had left as a legacy to their children. The boy naturalist developed a passion for learning the names of the trees, birds, and animals with whom he shared the family's large farm, the boulder-strewn banks of the Ottauquechee, and the denuded slopes of

The nineteenth century saw most of Vermont's trees falling to the unrelenting clear-cutters. In this early photograph, Woodstock nestles among the barren hills that inspired the young George Perkins Marsh to question man's role in nature.

Woodstock Historical Society Archives

Mount Tom. This life in nature made him think about his place in the universe in a way that was, in his day, exceptional. As he later wrote, "the bubbling brook, the trees, the flowers, the wild animals were to me persons, not things." Forty years after the first Europeans had cleared this valley, a boy began his search for the world that had been lost.

George's father, the brilliant lawyer and dour Calvinist Charles Marsh, was something of a naturalist himself and encouraged his son's interest in learning about the countryside. Later, when he was a man, George had vivid memories of how the two of them had driven around the countryside in the family chaise, where

> *...to my mind, the whole earth lay spread out before me. My father pointed out the most striking trees as we passed them, and told me how to distinguish their varieties. I do not think I ever afterward failed to know one forest tree from another. He called my attention to the general configuration of the landscape, pointed out the direction of the different ranges of the hills, told me how the water gathered on them and ran down their sides, and where the mountain streams would likely be found. But what struck me, perhaps most of all, he stopped his horse on top of a steep hill, bade me notice how the water there flowed in different directions, and told me such a point was called a watershed. ...I never forgot that word, or any part of my father's talk that day.*

It was the beginning of Marsh's lifelong attempt to understand the complexities of mankind's effects on the natural world—an obsession that would culminate in the first epic of conservationism, *Man and Nature* (1864).

*Man and Nature* was published in the midst of that great American apocalypse, the Civil War, and Marsh's view of the war between the human and natural worlds was no less apocalyptic. At its heart lay the almost unprecedented idea that there are limits to nature's bounty, and whether humans realize it or not, they have the capacity to destroy the earth. Though he was not trained as a naturalist or a geographer, Marsh systematically examined the many ways man had altered the natural world. Cutting the trees had led to climatic warming, soil erosion, and a cycle of flash flood and drought in mountain streams. The more technology man developed, the greater was his capacity to destroy the environment.

These ideas do not seem radical to us today, and they were not unique in his own era, but Marsh's greatness lay in his being the first writer to reach a wide audience with them. After all, this was America, where nature's abundance had stretched from sea to shining sea. The new nation's resources had

### PAST AND PRESENT ON THE LAND: THE DEFORESTATION OF THE HILL FARMS

By the mid-1800s, the Vermont landscape had been transformed from a deep, majestic forest into a long series of barren deforested hilltops. The relentless axes of the hill farmers had first cut clearings—little islands in the forest. But as time went on, and the thin mountain soil was depleted, they cut more and more timber both for the lumber markets and to clear land for grazing. As the soil was exposed, even more of it eroded away in the violent spring rains. George Perkins Marsh was well aware of the effects of this clearing, writing in *Man and Nature*:

*The extension of agricultural and pastoral industry involves an enlargement of the sphere of man's domain, by encroachment upon the forests which once covered the greater part of the earth's surface otherwise adapted to his occupation. The felling of the woods has been attended with momentous consequences to the drainage of the soil, to the external configuration of its surface, and probably, also, to local climate; and the importance of human life as a transforming power is, perhaps, more clearly demonstrable in the influence man has thus exerted upon superficial geography than in any other result of his material effort.*

seemed limitless, and it was blasphemy to imply that they could be used up. Most of Marsh's contemporaries believed that since man was himself a part of nature, nature would always have the capacity to heal any damage man might cause. As Marsh told his publisher, "nothing is further from my belief, that man is a 'part of nature' or that his action is controlled by the laws of nature; in fact a leading spirit of the book is...that man, so far from being...a soul-less, will-less automaton, is a free moral agent working independently of nature." For people who felt that God had sent them to subdue and "civilize" this wild and savage continent, the idea that they were, in fact, its destroyers was both controversial and compelling.

---

## THE MANY LIVES OF GEORGE PERKINS MARSH

*George Perkins Marsh (1801–1882) had a life that was unusually varied and cosmopolitan for an American of his era, marked by colossal failures and great successes. Here is a final tally sheet for his various careers:*

**Failures:**

Attorney

Sheep farmer

Lumber baron

Woolen mill owner

Real estate speculator

Tool-making entrepreneur

Central Vermont Railway investor

Marble quarry owner

Ardent advocate for use of camels in the American West and author of an extended treatise on their virtues

Public lecturer (said to be a very dry speaker)

Father (one son died as a toddler and the other as a young man, resenting his highly demanding father)

*Statement to his wife after one notable failure:* "I shall hang my 'lecturing' on the same peg with my other failures and follies. It must be a long peg and a strong peg to hold them all."

**Successes:**

America's greatest scholar of Scandinavian languages

Noted linguist

Vermont congressman

U.S. Congressman for State of Vermont

Helped found the Smithsonian Institution

Architectural expertise gave him final say in designs for the Washington Monument and the Vermont State House

Amassed America's greatest collection of European engravings, later sold to the Smithsonian to pay his debts, and then lost in a fire there

Husband (beloved by two wives, the first of whom died young, the second an adored intellectual companion despite her having spent most of their marriage as an invalid)

**Marsh was such an intellectual prodigy that he was able to enter Dartmouth College at the age of 15. This portrait shows the young scholar at the time of his graduation four years later, in 1820.**

UVM Special Collections

U.S. Ambassador to Turkey

Vermont Railroad Commissioner, Fish Commissioner and Statehouse Commissioner

U.S. Ambassador to Italy

It was America's very abundance that helped to clarify the issue of man's place in nature. Marsh's career as a lawyer and diplomat had allowed him to spend long periods abroad, in Turkey, Scandinavia, and Italy. He was able to show that in Europe, landscapes had also been devastated since the days of ancient Greece and Rome; but the relative artificiality of European landscapes tended to obscure man's detrimental role, because almost all their land had been altered by human action. The wasting of America's pristine wilderness made humanity's power to destroy the environment more difficult to ignore. Man was seen to be outside nature, not a benign part of it. In Marsh's words, "Man is everywhere a disturbing agent. Wherever he plants his foot, the harmonies of nature are turned to discords."

George Perkins Marsh was not a purist like Thoreau, who thought that man was evil when he destroyed the wilderness. And he did not make a religion of nature, as John Muir and others who came after him would do. His approach was practical, but optimistic. People had the power to understand their actions and redress much of the damage they had done. If they were taught to see, they would behave rationally. Technology might save some of what it had destroyed. Many human alterations of the landscape were positive and necessary. But where they were not, government should step in and regulate the use of natural resources, even if that flew in the face of free enterprise. It was a radical message for an anxious age.

## VERMONT AND THE NEW VISION OF NATURE

The impact of Marsh's vision on Western thought about environmental issues would be hard to exaggerate. In the first two decades after the appearance of *Man and Nature*, it spurred a number of changes in the way the American government managed its forests and helped lead to the creation of the national park system. But more importantly, it jolted many people in many different countries into seeing that they had a responsibility to use their power in nature more prudently.

This new vision of nature was the outgrowth of the author's experiences in a small, rugged state in northern New England that most of Marsh's readers would have been hard-pressed to find on a map. And yet the Vermont landscape experience provided an excellent metaphor for the wasting of nature. Perhaps if Marsh had come from a more bountiful and forgiving state, his insights would have been slower in coming. But young George had grown up surrounded by evidence of man's use and abuse of nature. Growing up in the 1810s and 1820s, he could see the tree-barren outline of Mount Tom from his family's large brick house on the edge of Woodstock and watched its thin top soil carried away in each heavy rain. He had heard the old timers speak of the birds and animals that had lived in these mountains but were there no

longer. In his age, the cutting of the trees had led to the drying up of streams, and the hillsides still showed the hulks of mills abandoned when there was no longer water to turn their wheels. He himself could remember when most of the hills he knew were covered with trees, and yet when he returned home from his Burlington law practice to visit, he found them bare. As he told a farmers' group in Rutland in 1848, "Every middle-aged man who revisits his birth-place after a few years of absence, looks upon another landscape than that which formed the theatre of his youthful toils and pleasures." The Vermont landscape had provided its brilliant son with a picture of environmental damage so clear that he was able to extrapolate his findings to the rest of the world.

The difficult years of the nineteenth century were rich food for the imagination; they caused Vermonters to question themselves, their heritage, and their futures. George Perkins Marsh was the first of many voices urging them to consider their place on the land. While his fellow citizens reveled in

By the later nineteenth century, landscape awareness had grown to the point that it seemed a suitable subject for photography. In this image (above), the subject is photographing the Pogue, on Mount Tom near Woodstock, long rumored to have no bottom. But why was this act of recording recorded?

the glories of the man-built landscape, the young Marsh saw past them to a troubling end result: the lovely villages of adolescent Vermont lay on a scarred landscape. Marsh saw the benefits of culture and technology and had no desire to go back to an age when such comforts had not existed, and yet he could not help questioning their price. His purpose was to make people conscious of their place on the earth. How were human beings to live on the land without defiling it? How could they have the benefits of culture without destroying nature?

The period from the Civil War to World War II saw Vermonters struggling to come to terms with these issues. In the years after 1860 the landscape reached its lowest point, as the state's fragile soils gave out, deforestation ran rampant, the economy struggled in the face of competition from the opening West, and the population was hard-pressed to maintain itself. Vermont had never been a rich state, and now it was filled with the suffering of a growing poverty. Many farm families were forced to leave their lands, and many communities found it difficult to survive. But crisis can also be the well-spring of creativity, and new landscapes do not come into existence until someone can imagine how they could be. As we'll see, the later decades of the period saw the beginnings of a new and mythic Vermont born of a community awareness of landscape issues that would someday lead to environmental protections and the development of landscape-friendly industries.

### EULOGY FOR THE SHEEP LANDS

We are a nation of tree lovers, but many people who grew up in the deforested landscape of the sheep era missed its airy openness and tidy vistas when it was gone. As one Vermont farm woman remembered, looking back a number of decades from the 1930s:

*I grew up on a farm. Some day I hope farms will come back. I'm looking for the day. Oh, it makes me sick. All these hills were open country and a great many people had large flocks of sheep. And those pastures were grazed and so they were just like lawns. There was no brush scattered around. Well, all those hills are grown up now. No one who isn't very old can remember how they looked. The cattle and the sheep were turned out in spring and got in the fall and kept in barns through winter. You went once a week to salt them and they were all right. They were happy. But now it's all growing up to wilderness.*

—RUTH DUTTON, quoted in Scott E. Hastings, Jr. and Elsie R. Hastings, *Up in the Morning Early: Vermont Farm Families in the Thirties*

## THE GREAT CRISIS, 1860–1900

The awakening consciousness of the deterioration of the landscape only came with a growing concern about Vermont's economic decline. In his classic history, *The Hill Country of Northern New England*, Harold Wilson dubbed the late 1800s the "winter" of Vermont; there is some truth in that dreary assessment. The state's soil had always been marginal, and now it was giving out. There was a 92-percent drop in the nutrient-greedy wheat crop between 1869 and 1899. As late as 1863, Vermont Merinos took first prize in a competition in Germany, beating out 1,761 sheep from all over Europe. But the sheep industry was quickly going bust for all but the most elite producers. There were still 580,000 sheep in Vermont in 1870, but by the end of the century, their numbers were down to 297,000. Similar declines took place in many other branches of agriculture.

Yet the clearing continued. Vermont did not reach its all-time maximum number of farms until 1880, when 35,522 of them sprawled over the landscape. The previous decade had seen the state reach its highest-ever proportion of "improved" land, 68 percent in 1870. It is difficult to work out how completely deforested Vermont may have been at the high point, but this figure gives us a rough approximation. Where today we see a state that is about

Sheep were the only effective lawnmowers in nineteenth-century Vermont, as the close-cropping of this meadow (above) shows. The sheep landscape may have been largely deforested, but it also opened many beautiful vistas the likes of which will probably never be seen again by anyone alive today.



30-percent cleared and 70-percent forested, late nineteenth-century Vermonters would have seen its mirror image—70-percent cleared, 30-percent forested. Yet even with this much cleared land, the Vermont economy found it hard to compete with the West. In many parts of the state, the hillside sheep pastures were too played out for cows or crops, leaving the land free of trees but essentially useless.

## THE ROOTS OF FARM ABANDONMENT

When the soil eroded from the hill farms, so did the population, silting down into the valleys or out of state. The overall population posted gains so meager (from .1–4.9 percent per decade) as to be losses in a nation that was growing by nearly a quarter in most decades of the period from 1860–1940. In the 1860s, 34,238 men from Vermont marched off to the Civil War (about 10 percent of the population) and 5,224 of them died. Harold Wilson found that a greater part of the demographic slump was caused by soil depletion that rendered many upland farms unfarmable. This tended to ghost the pattern of first settlement, so that in the 1880s the old towns in Windham County suffered the greatest losses. Farms were increasingly abandoned, starting in the southern hills.

Many Vermont men, like these (above) from the Vermont 5th Regiment, saw the world the hard way during the Civil War. A Vermont soldier's chances of dying in the conflict were about one in seven.

Farmers were receiving less and less for their products. From 1865 to 1895, the price of wheat went down by 60 percent. At the same time, land prices dropped like a hill farm boulder. Farms that had sold for $100–200 an acre in 1874 were fetching $5–10 an acre close to town or $3–5 an acre in more remote areas by the end of the century. The combined valuation of Vermont's farms went from $135 million in 1870 to $100 million in 1890. For those who were left, the burden of taxation fell on farms far out of proportion to agricultural incomes. People who could not farm or sell out just up and left, heading West or, increasingly after 1880, to the industrial towns of southern New England, to make an easier living in a mill or a sweat shop. After 1870, over one-third of Vermont's natives had moved out of state; in the next 50 years the number of farms in the state dropped from 33,828 to 29,075.

Farms were abandoned by the thousands, but it would be misleading to suggest that their land became ownerless or lay fallow. Abandoned farms are ones that have ceased to be cultivated, and in many cases they reverted to woodlands. But these new woods or old pastures were often bought for a song by the adjoining neighbors who were still struggling to make a go of it. The amount of land owned stayed stable, but the amount of it that was "improved" by clearing for grazing or cultivation declined rapidly. In 1870,

67.9 percent of farmland was considered improved, while in 1920 only 39.9 percent was improved. With declining rural populations, the houses that had sheltered the hopes and disappointments of farm families were often abandoned to the advancing woods. Their lumber was stripped for other projects or slowly rotted in the elements. When you walk the high hills of Vermont today, you can often see where they once stood, marked by cellar holes and stone fences and lilac bushes that once brightened the view from long-gone kitchen windows.

Farm abandonments also led to the loss of community services in many rural areas. By 1926, Clarence H. Dempsey, Vermont's Commissioner of Education, was lamenting the sad condition of rural schools in declining districts:

> *When the family furniture is loaded in the wagon, the key is turned in the door and the boards are nailed over the windows, children do not come from that home. Thus many a school becomes lonesome, and many are closed because the children are gone. Oftentimes the small school which may be continued becomes lifeless, difficult and expensive to run. Its upkeep seems a burden. There is a strong temptation to cut*

In this photo (below), one derelict farm building is sadly evocative of the thousands of Vermont farms abandoned in the late nineteenth and early twentieth centuries.

Alan Jakubek

> *expenses—employ a cheap teacher, skimp on books and supplies, neglect repairs. Conditions then go from bad to worse, and discouragement, dissatisfaction and fault-finding are common.*

By the late 1800s, the folds of the Green Mountains were dotted with the sad signs of rural decline.

### THE SOFT MOOING OF SALVATION

Yet even in the desperate decades of the 1870s and 1880s, the vast majority of Vermont's farmers were able to keep going. Some were even to thrive as never before. Salvation came in the form of a large, four-legged creature with big dark eyes, quadruple stomachs, and an udder full of milk.

As upper New England lost its sheep, wheat, and small grain industries to Western competition, a new market for dairy products was appearing closer to home. The cities of the East—Boston, Providence, Hartford, New York—were industrial meccas in the late 1800s, their populations booming with workers and immigrants. Urban demand for dairy products meant the

---

### FARM ABANDONMENT

The ghosts of Vermont's abandoned farms can still be seen on the land. Deep in the woods, often high on a hill, abandoned roads often ease the hiking. Follow one and you may soon see stone walls running between the trees. (One estimate says that the rural areas of central New England still have 100,000 miles of stone walls, so it is easy to find them.) Many dated to the sheep boom of 1810–1840, but continued to be maintained and extended until they were replaced by barbed wire in the late 1800s.

One way of telling the original purpose of a stone-fenced field is to look at the size of the rocks that were used to make it. If the rocks are small, it means the farmer was trying to clear the land for growing crops. The rocks tend to be larger around pastures where animals were grazed, because then there was no need to bother with picking up every little stone. These walls represent a numbing amount of human labor. Even the best mason could only hope to progress about 15 feet in a day.

**There is still considerable grace in the lines of this farmhouse ruin in Addison County.**

There may be a rectangular depression in the earth that is lined with stone. This is the cellar hole of an old house. Some time after 1820, the idea of a "front yard" gained favor, and its shrubs often remain to bloom here a century or more after those who planted them have gone. Lilacs, old roses, orange day lilies, and hydrangeas were favored, along with apple trees and stately sugar maples. After 1870, exotic trees like black locusts and Lombardy poplars became popular.

Other signs of human occupation can also be found: the foundations of old mills and schools, boundary markers, the ruins of lime kilns and blast furnaces. Bearing witness to it all are the marble and granite stones of abandoned graveyards, some holding the bones of but a single family.

## THE DAIRY LANDSCAPE

The landscape most of us think of today as a "typically" rural one was produced by dairy farming. Dairying landscapes look very different from the land patterns that sheep leave behind. In late nineteenth-century Vermont, the high, barren, close-shorn sheep pastures so reminiscent of parts of the British Isles today were slowly reverting back to forest while cows made inroads in the valleys. Cows are not good mountain climbers and prefer a flat or gently rolling pasture. They also require a lot of hay and grain for the winter, meaning that farmers spent periods of intensive labor on the neighborly task of haying. Straight rows of corn break up the green monotony on the land and are then chopped for silage. The dairy landscape, with its gentle cows, geometric hay cuts, and large cattle- and hay-holding barns, is a particularly beautiful one and worth preserving.

This photo of an afternoon of threshing grain in Waitsfield in the late 1800s gives a clear picture of the transformation dairying was bringing to the land. A group of workers, probably consisting of the farmer's family and some neighbors, takes a break to pose for the photographer. On the steep and rocky hill behind, trees have sprung up on what may have been an old sheep meadow. The grain field itself is flat enough for easy farming. What appears to be a tidy and well-constructed barn sits nearby. It is the beginning of a prosperous new era for the Mad River Valley.

Collections of Vermont Historical Society

## THE FARM HUMOR OF GRAMP LYNDES

Stanley Horace Lyndes (1898–1975), later known to his family as "Gramp," grew up on family farms in Calais, Cabot, and Marshfield. He always loved drawing, and after graduating from the Montpelier Seminary in 1918, he went to the Pratt Institute in New York to study art. He later taught at prep schools and summer camps around New England.

The cartoons reproduced here were drawn for a school assignment at Pratt. They show the wry side of Vermont farm life as Lyndes had lived it in the years before the First World War. The drawings feature his father, Alp Lyndes, whose lack of enthusiasm for his agricultural profession comes through loud and clear.

"milkshed" was reaching further into the countryside than ever before, as the railroads made the rapid transport of milk, butter, and cheese realistic for the first time. At first, those farmers closest to the city furnished fluid milk, those an intermediate distance away sent butter, and the ones at the end of the line provided cheese. But by the 1880s refrigerated train cars had arrived, and fluid milk could be sent to southern New England from even the northernmost towns in Vermont.

The making of butter and cheese at home was labor-intensive and quality control was hard to enforce. Farmers soon began to band together to start creameries, where all the dairy farms in a given area could bring their milk to be made into cheese or butter under factory conditions. Vermont was an early promoter of butter creameries, the first one in New England opening in 1879 in Shelburne. Franklin County was a leader in dairying from early on, and Harold Meeks found that in the 1890s the St. Albans creamery was making an astonishing two million pounds of butter a year. Soon home cheesemaking was also almost a thing of the past, as local cheese plants were established.

But the biggest money and the least hassle for the dairy farmer came in shipping fluid milk. As more and more of this frothy white product was

In the late 1800s, artists travelled America, encapsulating civic pride in lithographs called "bird's-eye views" of America's towns. Edward Meilbek recorded this view (above) of Vermont's important dairying center and railroad terminus of St. Albans in 1877.

Vermont companies found new sources of revenue catering to a burgeoning dairy industry. In this advertisement for the Vermont Farm Machine Company (left), all sorts of arcane-looking tools and implements are on display.

A contemporary view of a Champlain-side orchard in Shelburne (above). Orchards were one alternative for farmers looking to diversify.

Maple sugaring was labor-intensive work, but it kept many hill farmers from going under in the latter part of the nineteenth century. Even children (right) could lend a hand.

loaded onto refrigerated rail cars, a great incentive was created for building large dairy farms near the rail lines. Farmers who were situated near the transport system were soon increasing their herds to sizes far above the two dozen head that had been common in the past. This led to the building of large and stately dairy barns, many of which can still be seen in the landscape today.

In spite of dairying's new and multiple advantages, no one who was making a good living with sheep was going to be enthusiastic about trading them in for cows. Apart from wild frenzies of activity during lambing and shearing seasons, sheep almost raised themselves. Shepherding was rather pleasant, sitting out on a hill with nature all around. And if there were no wild animals to threaten your flock, it was not as if you had to be with them every minute. There was something reassuringly relaxing about keeping sheep.

Cows were another story altogether. They were—and are—far more work than sheep could ever be. A cow tied a farmer down. Most of the year they could not be fed on pasture grasses alone, so there was the food hauling. Cows had to have rich hay to last them through the winter, so there was the intensive summer labor of haying. Corn also had to be grown for silage. But the most grinding aspect of dairy farming was the milking, for the farmer or his help had to be available twice each day—in early morning and late afternoon—to milk the herd. This had to be done 365 days a year, rain, sun, or snow. There was—and is—no easy method of dairy farming.

"Real Vermont Turkey" was a mainstay of Boston menus for years, even when no turkeys were being shipped from the state. In a resurgent economy, Vermont is again known for its high-quality birds.

But farmers needed alternatives, and Vermont's state government was firmly in favor of the move from sheep to dairy farming. In 1868, the Vermont Board of Agriculture published a report on the profits to be made in each field, concluding that five cows could bring in $357.50 a year, while 40 sheep would only net $210 annually. It was a persuasive argument; by 1900, Vermont was the leading butter producer in the nation, with 180 creameries scattered around the state.

Dairying was never the only type of farming going in Vermont. Many farmers still kept a variety of animals for family use. Maple sugaring had been popular in the region long before the European settlers arrived, and by the late 1800s Vermont led the nation in maple production, making over 14 million pounds in 1890. Maple products remained lucrative for hill farmers lucky enough to have a sugar bush, and some tapped over a thousand trees. This spring bonus required a lot of work, but it kept more than one farm family in business. Vermont was also becoming a leader in poultry raising, particularly turkeys. There was also a measure of truck gardening, led by the newly invented Vermont potato, the "Green Mountain," in the 1880s. Tobacco was grown in the southern Connecticut Valley. Apple orchards were appearing in the Champlain Valley, and seemed poised to gain in importance. But dairying appeared to be the wave of the future.

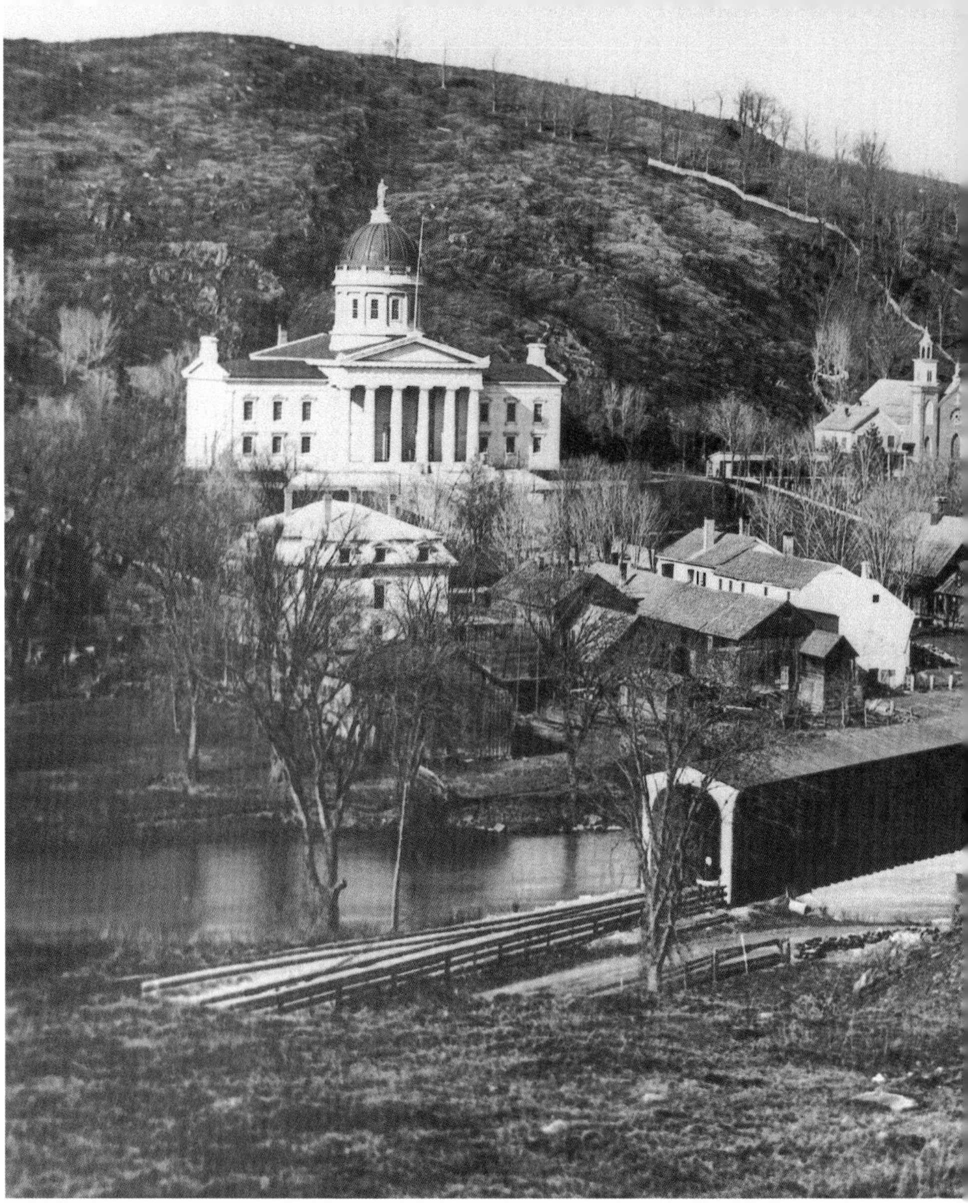

The starkness of Vermont's earlier landscapes even extended to the grounds of the State House itself. This photo of Montpelier in 1875 (above, right) provides quite a contrast, with its denuded hillside, when placed next to the lushness of the setting as it appears today (above).

## HILL FARM DIARY: THE CHILDHOOD OF WALTER RICE DAVENPORT

What was life like on a Vermont hill farm in the second half of the nineteenth century? Most farmers' diaries of the period are like those farmers have produced since literacy came in, concerned above all with that perennial obsession, the weather. The most complete accounts of the hill farms are memoirs written years later, usually suffused with a rosy glow. Nevertheless, they often provide a fascinating picture of the hardscrabble lives people were living on this rocky land.

In the late 1920s, Walter Rice Davenport wrote an account of his boyhood in the 1860s and 1870s in one of the highest of the hill towns, Williamstown, located between Montpelier and Randolph Center. Like old men in every age, he remembered "privations that were then cheerfully endured," asserting how much harder life had been for his contemporaries,

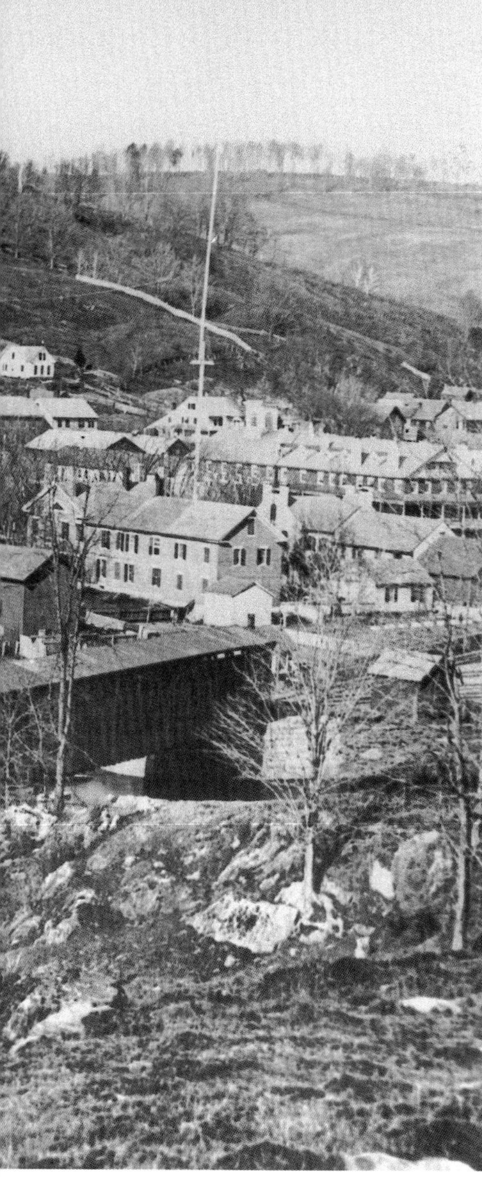

and yet how much better, too. His father's farm had about a hundred acres, and it "consisted of a series of hills slanting in every direction, corrugated and serrated by ledges and rocks of every kind."

When Walter was not engaged in the tedium of picking stones from the fields, his father could always find hard work for him to do. The family homestead had no running water, and hauling water a goodly distance from the well to the house was a frequent job: "When a boy has to carry all of the water by hand, a pail in each hand, he can vividly realize the difference between 'washing days' and 'baking days' and just common days." He long remembered his shock when he brought a requested dipper of water from the family barrel to a workman and watched him take a sip and waste the rest by tossing it onto the ground, for "I literally poured out my life to bring it day after day."

The greatest labors came with dairy farming, and the Davenports were trying hard to make a go of it on their rocky hillsides. It was difficult in the days before mechanization:

> *As I have intimated, the farm originally had no machinery of any kind indoors or out. Everything was done by hand. The farm was a "dairy farm" which meant cows, and cows meant milk, the milking all done by hand; and the milk meant cream, skimmed by hand; and the cream meant butter, churned by hand.*

Cows also required hay, and cutting and storing it was a major task of the agricultural year. The family could not handle it alone:

> *We had no mowing machine for the haying at first; that came later. My father used to hire in shoemakers and others from the village, and they would all come with their snaths and scythes and hand rakes and stay for several days, or weeks at a time. Shiftless farmers there were who made their brags that they hayed "until snow flew": not so my father who knew that such dilatoriness would waste the best of the nourishment in the hay, and lessen by just that much the butter product of the winter. Farmers always arose in the summer before five o'clock, and I remember working out a few days to help a neighbor finish his haying one season and he routed me out of bed at three-thirty A. M. the last morning, being determined to get the work finished that day.*

Haying was also a great cultural experience, because when farm work was being swapped, it meant the novelty of staying at neighbors' houses. For young people who hardly ever left the isolation of their own farms or families, even a night spent down the road seemed exciting:

## PASTURE SUCCESSION, OR WHAT HAPPENS ONCE THE SHEEP ARE GONE

Men and women are innovators, but nature is pretty regular in her habits. When the sheep pastures were abandoned, the land tended to go through predictable phases.

When pastures were overgrazed by sheep, the turf began to thin out, laying the soil open to the air, encouraging weed growth. Much of the exposed bedrock found in Vermont fields was once covered by a thin layer of top soil and was only exposed by the grazing of sheep

The weeds that colonized in these spots were basal rosettes (still common in New England lawns today), flat, broad-leafed weeds like plantain and sheep sorrel. They were perfectly suited to sheep pastures, because their flat shapes made it difficult for sheep to eat them.

—adapted from Tom Wessels, *Reading the Forested Landscape: A Natural History of New England*

*Indeed, the swapping of works by the farmers in haying time was a bit of adventure to an ambitious boy. He moved at least one farm away. He had one or more new boys with which to joke and work. He had new kinds of food at dinner time. He had a new set of rocks to work around, and new fields to mow and rake, and new barns to fill. It was almost all different, and while it was work, and hard work, it was a change. What flying across the Atlantic was to Lindbergh... changing works was to the farmer boys.*

This yearning to break from the isolation of rural life was often very acute for young people, and no doubt contributed to the great exodus from the farm. Walter Davenport's father was to find it hard to keep him down on the farm after he had seen Montpelier. He called this section of his memoir "Montpelier Vs. Heaven":

*I think my first trip to Montpelier must have been made some 63 or 64 years ago, just after the [Civil] war, or in the closing days of the struggle. We went, of course, by team, going through Berlin, as the "turnpike" through that town was a shorter cut than the route through Barre.*

*Up to that time Northfield was the largest village I had ever seen, and the Northfield of that day was much smaller than the thriving village of today. ...But when we reached the crest of Berlin hill overlooking the capital of the state and I saw the golden dome of the State House, the spires of the village churches, the seemingly majestic facades of the business blocks, and the meandering Onion, as it wound through the place, I was filled with unspeakable joy. If when my raptured eyes finally behold the New Jerusalem, it seems as wonderful to me, as did Montpelier as I saw it from the hills of Berlin, I shall be abundantly satisfied.*

For a boy living only at home, with no light except tallow candles, no carpets, no indoor taps, and so few books that he could know them all by heart, even this small taste of the outside world was a revelation.

### THE SCIENCE OF AGRICULTURE

The move to the specialization required by dairying acted as a great stimulus to the development of a more scientific approach to agriculture. Farmers all over New England were actively involved in new organizations that would help them learn better ways of choosing, feeding, and managing their dairy herds. Not incidentally, given the romantic imaginations of boys like Walter Davenport, there was also the hope that making farming "scientific" would keep the best and the brightest interested and at home. As one expert said in an address to the Vermont State Agricultural Society in Burlington in 1869:

> *...intelligent farming, farming that is really scientific, is also a source of mental culture. From a mere physical drudgery, it is thus converted into a work of intellectual growth and development. Make the boys feel this, and they will stay at home. It will take the monotony out of farm work. It will ennoble it. It you can not show a lad that there is something to farming beside development of mere brawn and muscle, you need not wonder if he grows restless and wants to escape to the machine shop, or to the excitement of traffic. But show him that there is philosophy in farming; that there is scope enough to develop all his faculties, mental and moral, as well as physical, and the gold regions of California and the broad prairies of the West will have fewer attractions for him.*

The idea that you could keep boys on the farm by making the work more interesting was repeated over and over in the second half of the nineteenth century. An 1873 treatise even managed to link this great theme to barn building:

> *By no other means can they so completely relieve their high and honorable calling from the odium which is attached to it because of the tedious and monotonous drudgery, in the labors about the barn especially in no way can they do more to induce their boys to adopt the calling as a business of life, and enter it with a zest and relish...than by building large, convenient barns.*

A similar piece from the same year bears the revealing title, "Opportunities and Rewards for the Application of Brain Work to Dairy Farming," and argues that "the great essential to improvement in the dairy business is *the application of more brain work to its development.*" The sheer volume of such exhortations makes the reader wonder whether they were inspired by the greater level of scientific sophistication involved in successful dairy farming or reflective of the difficulties of convincing young people to take up the life of drudgery it entailed. Sheep farming had never required such a hard sell.

From 1870 onwards, farm experts were unanimous in their view that science would return Vermont to the good old days of soil fertility and the rural prosperity it had brought to their grandparents' generation. As Dr. T. H. Hoskins, editor of the *Vermont Farmer*, put it in 1872:

> *With the coming of that time when any large proportion of our farmers shall believe in and understand scientific farming, will come the*

## A TALE OF TWO STATES: OR, WHY VERMONT'S FARMERS WERE IN TROUBLE

A fantasy of farming in Massachusetts is shown in this late nineteenth-century ad (below) for the Bullard Hay Tedder. The well-dressed farmer works his flat, rockless field with the latest horse-drawn equipment. His progressive approach to farming has already been rewarded with a snug Greek Revival homestead and miles of neat fencing.

The reality of Vermont farming was very different. In this early twentieth-century photo (above), the simply dressed farmer walks behind his plow over a hilly and barren landscape more like the moon than the earth.

## THE NEW DAIRY BARNS

Dairy cows required more elaborate barns than most other farm animals. Because they could not graze in winter, they had to have large supplies of hay. And since their manure was a valuable fertilizer, as they produced it in great quantities during the long winter, it had to be collected and stored for spreading on the fields in spring. Barn designs had to provide for all these uses.

One of the most popular styles throughout this period was the High-Drive Bank Barn. This was a three- or four-story structure built into a hillside (above). On the high end, a ramp led straight into the hayloft, and wagons could drive right in for unloading.

The cows lived on the middle and/or lower floors, making it simple to fork hay down to them from the loft. Some of these barns also had basements where manure could be collected and stored.

Round barns (left) enjoyed a short period of favor in the late nineteenth and early twentieth centuries. They usually functioned much like ramp barns, and many had a convenient central silo. They were somewhat cheaper to build than rectangular barns, and also saved the farmer steps.

The most common dairy barn remaining to us from the past is the ground-level stable barn (above). These barns came into vogue in the early twentieth century and were designed to combat some of the health problems that had plagued the dairy industry. Farmers found that storing manure in the barn with their milk cows could lead to the spread of tuberculosis, so that practice was going out of favor. They also now knew that sunlight was important to keeping bacteria levels down.

So these barns had only two floors: a hayloft upstairs (with a gambrel roof for maximum storage space) and a milking layout on the ground level. The floors were sanitary concrete and manure was hauled outside on a little trolley that ran down the center of the barn, between two rows of cows. Windows were larger and there was more ventilation. Many of these barns are still in use.

**The spectacular Tudor-style Breeding Barn at Shelburne Farms (above) was the centerpiece of a model-farm complex built in the nineteenth century by the Webb family, longtime Vermont enthusiasts and philanthropists (Electra Havemeyer Webb founded the Shelburne Museum). Shelburne Farms remains well-known today for, among other products, its specialty cheese, produced from its own dairy herd.**

**The Farm Barn at Shelburne Farms is shown here under construction in 1890.**

Left to right: Cynthia Lockin; Shelburne Farms Collections, Shelburne, Vermont; Collections of Vermont Historical Society; Courtesy James Watson Webb, Jr.

*time when the soils of Vermont, strong in natural fertility, will be restored to that high condition in which they were found by our pioneer ancestors, and kept there. Then, crops of fifty bushels of wheat to the acre will become common again.*

For many of the hill farms, this hope would not be realized.

In the true tale of how Mr. Morrill went to Washington (with movie star looks to rival James Stewart), Strafford native Justin Morrill represented his state for 44 years. He sponsored everything from the legislation that established the Land Grant Universities to that ensuring that the Washington Monument was finally completed. In what little spare time remained, he built a house in his home town that is one of Vermont's most distinguished examples of Gothic Revival architecture; it is now in the hands of the State Department of Historic Preservation and can be visited in the summer.

## A COMMUNITY OF SCIENTIFIC FARMERS

If farming was to require continuing education, farmers soon craved venues for the dissemination of new agricultural knowledge and practices. Agricultural associations of all sorts sprang up in rural Vermont in the post–Civil War era. Some were sponsored by the government, like the State Board of Agriculture that Vermont had established in 1872. These were made up of representatives of county agricultural societies, who in turn set up local Farmers' Institutes. Some organizations were primarily social, like the Farmers' Clubs and the Community Clubs, where farm couples might listen to a short educational program, and then move on to the more important work of chatting over a piece of pie. Such events were often well-attended, for they met in the winter, when even dairy farmers had a bit of free time, and provided agricultural education for the masses in an unpretentious atmosphere. Farmers also joined clubs for their specialties, like the American Ayrshire Breeders' Association, which was founded in Brandon in 1886 and has remained there for over a century. Other farm organizations, like the Grange, and later the Farm Bureau, were more politically and economically oriented and spent a lot of their time lobbying for such things as better agricultural education, improvements in rural roads, and ensuring the passing of tariffs that would damage the dairy farmers' great nemesis, oleomargarine. All gave farmers a new sense of pride and professionalism.

On another level, Vermonter Justin Morrill went to Washington, D.C. as a Representative; there he argued that if farming was to be a science there should be colleges to teach it. In 1862, Congress agreed, giving each state a tract of land from the national reserves to endow a college of "agriculture and the mechanical arts." Vermont chose to add agriculture to the curriculum of the established University of Vermont rather than build a separate college—a decision that would later lead to controversy here. But all over America, Morrill's "land grant" colleges and universities were to change the educational, and the agricultural, patterns of the nation. Their agricultural schools were soon in the vanguard of the move to scientific farming, pioneering in such areas as soil testing, livestock management, and agricultural economics.

## STEP RIGHT UP TO THE COUNTY FAIR

Anyone who has been trapped on a rural road behind a farmer who is examining the state of his neighbor's crops will recognize the agriculturalist's need to know what is happening over the fence. Modern agri-scientists who ran the County Agricultural Societies began to cater to that need early on by starting annual local agricultural fairs. In Addison County, the fair (a prime exemplar of the type) began as early as 1844 and was long held on the grounds of the court house in Middlebury. By the 1860s, it was well enough established that permanent buildings were put up to be used during fair time. Farm women had their "Floral Hall," where the results of the pie judgings could cool friendships until the snow flew. Over in the "Horticultural Building" similar dramas were played out over the firmness of Farmer Pratt's pumpkins or the sweetness of Farmer Hallock's honey.

The fair had something for everyone. It was a primarily a place for learning new farming and homemaking techniques and showing off the ones you had already mastered. In addition to the agricultural exhibits, circus acts and vaudeville performers could be seen (Addison County folk had never

## THE GRANGE HALL

The largest and most influential of all late nineteenth-century New England farm organizations was founded in St. Johnsbury, Vermont, in the early 1870s. The Grange was a secret society for farm men and women, established to promote the farmer's interest in political and economic causes. By 1875, 160 granges had appeared around the state and over 11,000 Vermonters had joined the movement.

One of the most notable things about the Grange was that, for the first time, women were full members. The new farm feminists were able to hold office and play a policy-making role in the organization.

It is testimony to the wealth and influence of the granges that in their heyday before the First World War they were able to raise enough money to custom-build occasionally elaborate meeting halls. This one (right) in Panton is a simpler example.

Paul O. Boisvert

**The turn of the twentieth century was the golden age of Vermont's county fairs, as evidenced by the huge crowds at the Addison County Agricultural Fair (top). Advertising posters for the fairs, like this one (bottom) from 1893, suggested the richness of farm life, but could also amuse.**

before known the likes of "The Four Panto-Mimics" or "Derenzo and Ladue's Comedy Revolving Pole Act"). Bicycle races came into vogue at the fair with the biking craze of the 1880s and drew large crowds. Young people were catered to with their own children's events, particularly after the founding of the local 4-H Club in 1905. Refreshments were available, and for the worried an ad for a booth run by Hartin's of Middlebury proclaimed, encouragingly, "At the Fair...Eat, Drink and be satisfied at Hartin's Under the Grand Stand...We Have No Flies."

The Addison County Agricultural Fair reflected the specialties of the area. Sheep exhibitions were important in the early years, although they became less prominent after the industry finally went bust in the 1890s. Cattle soon eclipsed them here as they had earlier done on most Vermont farms. Horse trotting events were popular in a country where the Morgan was revered, and the races got so frenzied that it was feared they would distract from the more "worthy" educational purposes of the gathering. Some worried that the fair was becoming too commercial, as businessmen jostled to advertise their wares for the assembled crowds. The most elaborate display ever seen at the Addison fair may have been that of the Piper & Boyett Furniture Firm in 1900, who built their own four-room "house" (conveniently connected to the Floral Hall), complete with a parlor, library, dining room, and bedroom full of furniture. It was also at the fair that many people had their first glimpses of new inventions—the sewing machine, the automobile, the radio.

The Addison County Fair did not survive the Depression of the 1930s, when its sponsoring organization, the County Agricultural Society, went bankrupt. It was replaced by a much smaller Farm Bureau Field Day exhibition that returned to its almost solely agricultural origins. The Addision County Field Days would not be revived until 1948, and then it would be years before it was again as large and diverse as the Addison County Fair—and its statewide counterparts—had been in its golden age before the First World War.

### THE NEW RURAL IMAGINATION

Landscapes begin in the human mind, and the net effect of all these rural changes, new farm organizations, informative publications, and agricultural exhibitions was to create a new rural imagination. No age can claim to be fully conscious of its own actions, but some have the ability to think about what they are doing more than others. And for societies, as well as individuals, crisis often creates a greater consciousness. When a farm couple sat through an address on "The Proper Tending of Rural Woodlots," or "Reclaiming Your Swampland," or "The Brain Work of Agriculture," it gave them something to think about after the pie was eaten and the lemonade was drained. They were no longer just reacting to each circumstance as it came up, the way their parents and predecessors had done. They were beginning to have a handle on the big picture. This belief provided a comforting feeling—or illusion—of control in an occupation where they were so often powerless in the face of the weather or the markets.

It was not that farm families understood their effects on the environment very well (most farmers had not, after all, read George Perkins Marsh). But they were beginning to give more thought to what they were doing. As a product of its age, this kind of thought did not lend itself to an ecologically balanced landscape, but rather to a morally balanced one. A moral landscape was a rational, productive, and well-maintained landscape, with a proper mix of elements presented in an attractive form. The tidiness of the classical villages of the previous age was now making its way into the countryside.

Advocates of the new agriculture often told farmers to take the time to plan out how to use each part of their farm to best advantage. As A. E. Jameson put it to a group of Vermont farmers in 1873, the farmer has such a knowledge of each square foot of his own ground that the relationship came to be "like the friendship of true friends." And like a friend, a farmer would do what was best for each part of his farm: planting trees on the rocky hills,

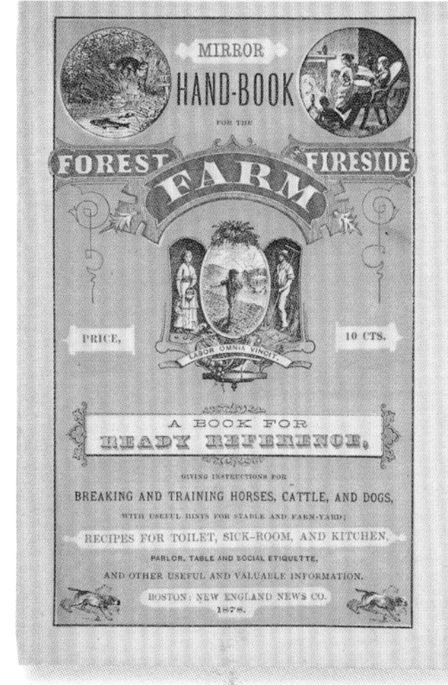

MIRROR
HAND-BOOK
FOR THE
FOREST
FARM
FIRESIDE
PRICE, 10 CTS.
LABOR OMNIA VINCIT.
A BOOK FOR
READY REFERENCE,
GIVING INSTRUCTIONS FOR
BREAKING AND TRAINING HORSES, CATTLE, AND DOGS,
WITH USEFUL HINTS FOR STABLE AND FARM-YARD;
RECIPES FOR TOILET, SICK-ROOM, AND KITCHEN,
PARLOR, TABLE AND SOCIAL ETIQUETTE,
AND OTHER USEFUL AND VALUABLE INFORMATION.
BOSTON: NEW ENGLAND NEWS CO.
1878.

**MIRROR HAND-BOOK FOR THE FOREST, FARM, AND FIRESIDE**

Earlier generations of Vermont farmers had been readers, but with the coming of "scientific" farming, the pursuit of agricultural advice increased. Farming periodicals had a long history in Vermont, dating at least to the *Rural Magazine or Vermont Repository* of 1795, and by the late nineteenth century there were many more sophisticated choices in pamphlets and periodicals for farm families. In this example (above), the inclusion of "Recipes for Toilet, Sick-Room and Kitchen" assumes that the women of the house read agricultural publications as well as the men.

tilling the flat, arable middle ground near the farmstead, and draining the "treacherous depths" of low-lying, swampy areas. The hand of man must take each natural feature and turn it to the good by imposing regularity and order.

Each farm must be exploited as thoroughly as possible for purely capitalistic ends, but at the same time there was a growing insistence that it be beautiful. A disorderly homestead was an immoral homestead and robbed the whole neighborhood of its enjoyment of the countryside. The whole farm must, in a sense, come under the moral sway of an American version of the Victorian cult of domesticity, where home and family lay at the heart of good citizenship. As *Facts for Farmers* (1868) put it in a section titled the "Influence of Dwelling Upon Character," attention to appearances was one of the most important moral lessons of childhood:

> *There is a debasing influence about a mean house upon the minds of children; while a good one, that has many points of beauty about it, makes them not only love to call it "home," but it always has an influence upon their minds to attract them away from places that might injuriously affect their morals, for it is a home that they love. ...One of the strongest and one of the most common inducements for the sons and daughters of farmers to leave the country for a city life, is the neglect of parents to beautify home, and teach children to love it because everything around it is more cheerful, more beautiful, more pleasant, more enticing than any other spot known to them.*

The growing emphasis on the moral importance of rural beautification was never more clearly illustrated than in these etchings from Solon Robinson's *Facts for Farmers; Also for the Family Circle* (1868). The two farms, the one on the left belonging to "Farmer Snug," the one on the right to "Farmer Slack," are ruthlessly compared—and judged.

Again, there was the threat that if things were not made attractive on the farm, children would leave for greener pastures.

This new concern with rural aesthetics also reflected growing class divisions in the countryside. When the settlers had arrived in fledgling Vermont, people had their pick of lands, and there was a rough equality in the size of stakes. A century later, distinctions in soil fertility and mental ability, access to capital and plain dumb luck had created far greater class distinctions. The poor hill farmers were getting poorer, while the rich dairy farmers of the valleys grew ever more prosperous. The neatness of a farm conveyed both the morality and the competency of its proprietors. A slovenly farm was thought to reflect the laziness and degeneracy of its owners.

Beauty, in this instance, lay in a message of total human control of the farm landscape. While the settlers had been happy just to survive, and their successors of the early nineteenth century built elegant houses in the midst of chaos, there was a growing feeling that by now your land should have been subdued. The stones should have been picked out of the fields, the tillable ground should have been flattened by the plow, the house should have a neat coat of paint, and the fences should run straight and true. A century was enough time to have gotten a handle on things. To be a part of the community, you had to adhere to its standards (although then, as now, some people were immune to these admonitions and did not wish to be told how to behave). Example after example trained the public's eye in how a farm should present itself—helping farm families to imagine so that they could make their visions manifest on the land. If America was to be an agrarian paradise, it was time it looked like one.

Vermont's farm folk were gaining a sense of mastery over the landscape in the late nineteenth century, but what did that say about their view of nature? Did farmers appreciate nature better than anyone because they worked with it every day, or were they too preoccupied with altering it to experience it for itself?

### MACHINES IN THE GARDEN

Agriculture may have molded the greater part of the landscape in the second half of the nineteenth century, but it was not the only way to make a living in Vermont. By the end of this period, it would not even be the state's main industry. In 1850, 52.5 percent of the state's population was engaged in agriculture, 14.2 percent in manufacturing, 3 percent in trade, 27.3 percent in personal services, 1.1 percent in quarrying, and .7 percent in transportation and utilities. By 1900, the percentage working in agriculture had dropped to 36.6. The state's 35,522 farms in 1880 had fallen to 32,890 by 1900. While 63 percent of Vermont's land was considered "improved" in 1850, that proportion

### FARM WOMEN ARE PRONE TO GET UPPITY

Many stories about the personalities of women who ran farm households reflect a strongly self-possessed quality. The following example comes from an East Corinth farm woman named Grace Hutchinson and took place when she and the twentieth century were very young:

*When you've planned for your big meal at noon you cooked potatoes enough so you could fry them for breakfast next day. The men folks didn't think they'd had breakfast unless they had potato. And not long before that lots of farmers' wives put out pie for breakfast. I had an aunt that her husband didn't think he'd had breakfast unless he had hot apple pie. She was sick once and he came in the barn one morning and the hired girl was bustling around trying to have a pie ready for breakfast. And he told her she didn't have to bother with pie for breakfast, that they could get along without it. And my aunt, she was in bed, but she heard him say so. So, she said to herself, "Old man, if the hired girl doesn't have to make pie, your wife don't have to." So he didn't get any more pie for breakfast. He'd get it for dinner and supper but not breakfast.*

**THE LAST CATAMOUNT**

On Thanksgiving Day, 1881, a Civil War veteran named Alexander Crowell had the dubious distinction of killing what may have been Vermont's last catamount. The creatures had been assumed to be extinct for 30 years, so when this 182-pound giant (above) was taken in Barnard, the news electrified the whole state.

had dropped to 45 percent by the turn of the century. Farms that had sold for $100–200 an acre in the 1870s were only worth $5 an acre in 1900. At the same time, manufacturing now employed 21.8 percent of Vermonters, trade had hit 8.8 percent, 22.3 percent provided personal services, 5.3 percent worked in quarrying, and 5.2 percent were in transportation and utilities. By 1930, agriculture was down to 27 percent, finally surpassed by manufacturing at 28.4 percent, with quarrying now down to 1.9 percent. Growing gaps between rich and poor could also be seen in more industrial occupations. Vermont was not to become a major industrial power, for it did not have the natural resources, labor force, capital, or location to suit most industries. But many of the industrial enterprises that had begun here in the early 1800s continued to be pursued.

Industrial Vermont was still centered on the exploitation of natural resources—extraction rather than production. As long as those natural resources held up, they could be systematically gathered, taken to transport, and shipped off to market. And as George Perkins Marsh had predicted, the more sophisticated technology became, the greater was its ability to destroy nature. The late nineteenth century showed that the power to make the land barren had reached a whole new level in Vermont. To borrow a phrase from historian Leo Marx, the machine was in the garden.

### THE WAR AGAINST THE TREES

The largest and most lucrative industry in post–Civil War Vermont was logging. Even as Marsh pleaded with his contemporaries to restore some of the lost trees before the ill effects of clear-cutting became irreparable, the trees were going down at an unprecedented pace. This was largely the result of two developments: the expansion of the railroads into remote forest areas and increasing demand by the wood products industries. Most Vermont wood factories were making small products called "treen"—wooden boxes, cartons, and the like; but after 1880, the paper companies came in with their capacity to use trees at an unprecedented rate. Steam engines were themselves great consumers of wood, running only 21 miles on each cord. Farmers all along their routes would bring cords of wood to the depot, where they could get $2.50–5 for each one from the railroad men.

Railways were not a cheap way to ship anything as bulky as trees, so it only made economic sense for Vermont to send finished lumber by rail rather than raw logs. Burlington took a lead in shipping lumber, and by the late 1860s it was the fourth largest lumber port in the United States. The boom in lumbering can be seen in the numbers: 20 million board feet cut in 1856 and 375 million board feet at the peak of production in 1889.

Not all the trees being sawed into lumber in Burlington came from the forests of Vermont. By the1870s, these forests were so depleted that most of

Burlington's raw stock came down from Canada. The massive white pines that had soared over the land in settler days were almost impossible to find by 1880, the same year in which Chittenden County is said to have been 80-percent deforested. (Satellite photography shows that in 1980 Vermont was only 16.8 percent open land without tree cover.) Clearing for agriculture had removed an enormous number of Vermont's trees in the previous century, but it has been estimated that even more were lost in the nineteenth century's third-quarter scramble for lumber.

One sympathetic glimpse of Vermont's lumber camps in this period can be found in the memoir and letters of the painter Edward Martin Taber, published as *Stowe Notes*. Taber (1863–1896) immigrated to Vermont from New York and was to die young, too soon to recover from his initial sense of wonder at the beauties of his adopted state. In a letter to his mother posted from Stowe in January 1891, he gave a rhapsodic account of his first trip to a lumber camp in the mountains. The thermometer hovered at zero as he and a friend drove their horse sled up through the deep snow.

> *We went up the mountain...through a region that was like Fairyland, where the evergreens were so densely coated with frost that hardly any suggestion of green remained to them. ...The choppers were about quitting work, so we offered them a lift back. They were very interesting—young fellows of about eighteen to twenty-five, the very picture of health and robustiousness. ...Passing places where a tree had been felled and the severed boughs trampled, the smell of the rushed leaves was very strong and fragrant.*
>
> *On returning we did not stop, but continued directly down the mountain. The last glimpse of the camp was an interesting picture—horses, oxen, and men grouped between the log barn and the little shanty; the bright colors of flannel shirts and toques conspicuous on the snow; the light gleaming on the axe-heads; the movement, bustle, and color against the background of the cold and darkening wood.*

The last catamount put on a lot of mileage after his demise, being exhibited all over Vermont (above). He finally ended up in a glass case at the Vermont Historical Society in Montpelier, where he can still be visited.



Taber was a city boy in love with the mountains. A less starry-eyed account of cutting timber in the 1930s comes from a longtime logger, Buck Heath. Heath was born in North Hyde Park, up in northern Vermont, in 1921, and by his mid-teens he was swinging an axe:

> *You got up in the morning and you got your breakfast into you, and you had to be all ready to go by half-past five. And we went every day, I don't care what the weather was or what the temperature was, or whether it was snowing or blowing, we went. And we'd be up on the mountain sometimes before it was daylight enough to see to cut the tree,*

Logging was carried on at a furious pace in the winter, with logs carried to the shores of rivers to wait for spring. The camps often included women, although one of the women and her children in this photo (above) seem to be wealthy visitors.

The bustling harbor visitors to Burlington had found so enchanting in the early 1800s was almost completely obscured by industry 100 years later. Lumber piled up on the shoreline nearly to the foot of the boathouse (right). Burlington would turn its back on the lake for decades, not rediscovering the beauty of its harbor until the waterfront cleanup of the late twentieth century.

Once the trees had been cut, they had to be turned into boards. Sawmills like this one could be found all around the state in the late nineteenth century.

> *and that was in crosscut saw days and you had to cut some logs. ...And we didn't cut no trees that the first log wouldn't go 100 feet. It wanted to be 14" the first log at the top end or we didn't cut it. ...And the average cut for a man was 4 to 5000 a day with a crosscut, board feet of logs.*

Buck chopped down a lot of trees in his career, but by the time he started, the first great age of Vermont forestry was long past. The first cut of trees, downed before 1850, had not started to come back in great numbers until after 1880, and it was another 40 years before the state's forest cover made it back to 50 percent. Concerns over the need for reforestation led to the creation of municipal forests in the 1920s. In 1927 alone, 17 Vermont towns committed themselves to planting 267,000 trees. Much of this planting was done by holding planting bees. In Sheffield, a village in Caledonia County, a planting bee in 1926 drew 126 men who planted 25,000 trees in a single day.

In the early twentieth century, logging was slowly becoming mechanized—here, under the watchful eyes of a horse who is in danger of losing his job.

But this second and third growth, where Buck Heath was to make his living, did not compare to first growth in either quantity or quality. Where Marsh had found that "The woods of North America are strikingly distinguished from those of Europe by the vastly greater variety of species they contain," this diversity was not to be found in the replanting, so that by Buck's day Vermont was no longer a major exporter of lumber. By the time of the Second World War, the trees were back, but the majesty and diversity of the wilderness would not come again.

## CARVING STONE

The railroads that had made it possible to ship lumber over long distances also meant that stone cutting and mining could be undertaken on a scale that would never have been viable in a world confined to the power of horses and humans. With the founding of Redfield Proctor's Vermont Marble Company in 1880, the Clarendon & Proctor Railroad was built to carry the great white stones. From that year until 1930, Vermont was the greatest marble producing state and a major player in the world marble industry. The consequence was that the value of marble quarried in Vermont increased seven-fold between 1860 and 1990. Vermont's most important marble source, the Imperial Quarry in Danby, opened in 1907, and now stretches underground over an area greater than 70 football fields. Other quarries spread across the surface of the earth, leaving gaping scars.

The railroads were even more important to exploiting granite. Granite was found early on in Vermont's history, but unlike marble, which was located along the waterways of the Champlain Valley, the granite seam was too far from anywhere to be shipped out without rails. Granite is also much harder and heavier than marble, so its cutting and shipping are more cumbersome. Yet by the 1870s and 1880s, Barre granite was already becoming well-known nationally. From that time, Vermont has generally been the first or second greatest producer in the United States. The huge Rock of Ages quarry in Barre was not begun until 1930.

Deep below the ground, the marble tunnel at Pittsford (above) is not for the claustrophobic.

The new granite industry offered work for the highly specialized jobs of skilled stonecutters, and many came from across the Atlantic to sign on. When stone workers in Scotland found that there were Scottish communities in Ryegate and Barnet, many were persuaded to move to the area. They flooded in during the 1880s, until Barre was 20 percent Scottish. The next decade saw the coming of the skilled Italians, especially in Rutland and Barre. They specialized in poignant funerary stone carvings, but also managed to chip away at Vermont's Yankee domination.

One of them was Angelo Ambrosini, a stone carver from Italy who arrived in Montpelier Junction on a winter night in 1901. He went on to open a carving business in Northfield, later moving his wife and children to Barre. His son later told his story:

> *There's one section in the cemetery where a lot of Italian families had their lots and there's a whole string of monuments that he cut. And every year I used to take my mother over...and she would tell me, "Pa cut this one and Pa cut that one."*
>
> *My father became ill with silicosis, it's a lung disease caused by inhaling the granite dust. In those days all the men stricken with silicosis went to the Washington County Sanitorium. ...And he was there for perhaps a year and a half. He died before I was seven so maybe I was only five and a half years old when he was still living at home.*

How ironic to die from carving cemetery monuments! The air filtration systems that were to save stone workers from this choking disease process were to appear in the 1920s, after a Bureau of Labor study condemned the industry for not protecting workers from the devastating health effects of stone dust.

Marble and granite were traditionally worked wet. The water, clearing off the dust and small particles, caused water pollution and environmental damage as it made its way back into neighboring streams. It was a great

Sheldon & Slason's Marble Quarry in West Rutland (shown above circa 1861) was one of Vermont's largest. This print shows the process of marble extraction. Marble has an inner structure conducive to being cut into blocks; once the cutters had drilled and split them, the blocks were removed from the quarry by a wooden lift and pulleys. On the surface, the enormous blocks were taken to the adjoining mill to be cut into smaller slabs for use in cemetery monuments. Marble from this quarry has been used to clad the Washington Monument (whose final design was largely determined by Vermonter George Perkins Marsh).

river killer, choking out fish, aquatic plants, and water insects. These damaging discharges wreaked havoc on the Stephens Branch of the Winooski River and many other streams until well after the Second World War.

A massive slate seam stretches south from Rutland, which also boomed with the new railroad transport. Here, the skilled workers came from Wales. In the early twentieth century Vermont's slate was worth almost as much as its granite; Vermont has been the nation's second largest slate producer, after Pennsylvania, since the 1880s. Cutting slate could be dangerous work, as related by a woman named Eleanor Evans McMorrow, who came to Poultney from Wales as a little girl in 1924. Looking back years later, she said:

> *I'm very happy I don't have anybody in the slate quarries anymore. We were brought up, get your bed made and your dishes done and your floor swept, in case somebody gets hurt, and they bring them home from the quarry. ...My father was hurt badly. He was unconscious for 21 days. They operated on his brain. He was home for nine years after it. He had to learn to write and everything over again, learn to talk.*
>
> *They have these big blocks that they send up. It was a bad day, it*

The massively scaled granite faces at the Rock of Ages Quarry in Barre, (above) show the striations caused by the chiselling process.

Vermont's marble industry has been supplying building details for over 200 years. This worker (left) is loading a monolithic column onto a box car. It was quarried from the Pittsford Valley tunnel and weighed over 50 tons.

Top: Alan Jakubek; bottom: UVM Special Collections

> *was sleeting. A block came out of the chain and hit him in the head. My father got $9.00 a week compensation. I don't know how they made ends meet, if they did.*

Much of the danger derived from the Vermont method of slate mining, which caused great damage both to the land and to the people who worked it:

> *But there were always injuries, broken legs, broken arms. Somebody was always getting killed, it was terrible. More so here than there was in Wales, I think, from what I've hear them tell. Over there the quarries were mined in shelves. And here, right down.*
>
> *Around the quarries are huge dumps of waste slate. Those are so dangerous. The man that was boarding with us, ten days after my father was hurt, this guy made him go and work in the same spot my father was in. These dumps get icy, they slide. And it slid and killed him. He was knocked right off the ledge and down into the quarry. He was killed ten days after my father was hurt. Today they wouldn't be able to allow that because of your safety codes. But they didn't have safety codes back then, in 1938.*

The copper miners of Ely stand for a somber portrait (below) against a backdrop of environmental devastation. Only 3 percent of what came out of the ground was copper, leaving mountains of waste whose outlines can still be seen today.

They did not have environmental codes, either. Quarrying any of these stones generally resulted in 60–80 percent waste, and this huge quantity of unusable rock had to go somewhere. Since only marble can be cut underground, most of the leftovers sat on the surface, open to view. All were unsightly, although the leavings of slate were probably the most dangerous because they were composed of large piles of small and slippery surfaces.

The most dramatic mineral story of late nineteenth-century Vermont concerned the strange career of the Vermont Copper Mining Company. In the mid-1860s, a New Yorker named Smith Ely had created a major copper boom at the mine in Vershire, a remote village in Orange County. By 1880, it employed 851 workers (about half of them Cornish and Irish), who scraped 3.2 million pounds of ore out of the ground in that most amazing year. The product came out of the ground with 97 percent waste, creating huge piles of dirt and requiring a heavily polluting smelting process to concentrate the ore before it could be shipped. The "roasting bed" featured fires fed by enormous amounts of wood, which emitted clouds of sulfur dioxide that killed all neighboring vegetation by creating very highly concentrated acid rain. The mine was forced out of business by falling prices and worker unrest in the "Ely War" of 1883; most varieties of trees still will not grow around Vershire over 100 years later.

### INDUSTRIES OF PRODUCTION

While the extractive industries wreaked their havoc on the environment and agriculture saw considerable farm abandonment, industry also went through a depressed period in late nineteenth-century Vermont. Even in the Gilded Age, Vermont was never an industrial powerhouse, but some types of manufacturing were thriving. Fortunes were made in Springfield and Windsor, towns that continued to specialize in precision tools, as they had since the early 1800s. Springfield was the heart of Vermont manufacturing on the eve of the First World War, with three thriving machine-tool companies serving a national market. All had an impact on the land, but because the state's manufacturing was so concentrated and small in scale, its impact on the countryside was negligible compared to the ravages of the industrial revolution in other parts of the country. The textile industry, which had expanded during the sheep boom years, now saw the closing of many redundant mills. The few that were left had to grow to survive after 1870. The biggest was the Colchester Mill, established in 1880, with 850 workers. Winooski, Ludlow, Hartford, and Cavendish also had large mills. Bennington had the most, making the greatest variety of products, but their inability to compete with the South's cheap labor put most of them out of business by 1945.

The late 1800s saw a consolidation of Vermont's woolen textile industry, with many smaller factories going out of business in the face of competition from a few large concerns like the Bridgewater Mill (top) near Woodstock and the huge American Woolen Company in Winooski (bottom). The latter was the biggest textile employer in the state by 1940, employing 2,500 workers.

Vermont was not to be an industrial state, and thousands of her sons and daughters were fated to leave to find factory work in the boom towns of southern New England and the West. Those who remained to work with their hands were more apt to be skilled craftspeople, plying their trades alone or in a small family business, doing carpentry or custom ironwork. Down in Manchester, the Orvis Company began making fishing rods and reels in 1857. In Brattleboro, the Jacob Estey Organ Company was turning out 600 elaborately carved organs a year by 1860. Bennington could boast of its pottery industry, and the Norton Pottery continued to make simple redware and stoneware that was the mainstay of general store crockery stock. Railroad cars were made in St. Albans. Furniture-making remained a Vermont specialty, although its practitioners now had to go further afield to find suitable hardwoods. The scale of these enterprises generally remained small and local.

### ELUSIVE URBANISM, OR WHY VERMONT HAS NO BIG CITIES

Vermont's relative lack of industrialization meant that there was little accompanying urbanization. Most of the state's towns and villages remained smaller than they had been in the early 1800s, and some of the hill towns virtually disappeared. The hill town of Granby had once been home to a thriving wood products business with scores of employees, yet once that closed, the town

## THE GOLF LINKS

Vermont's suffragette, pacifist, and humanitarian poet, Sarah Cleghorn (1876–1959), wrote this little poem, "The Golf Links," about how she saw the growing class divisions in her home town of Manchester long before it was dubbed a "Gold Town." It would become a celebrated national rallying cry in the war against child labor.

*The golf links lie so near the mill*
*That almost every day*
*The laboring children can look out*
*And see the men at play.*

The state had a number of industrial sites in operation in this period including the Stark Paper Mill in North Bennington (above).

Vermont had child laborers, as this photo (left) shows. The boy was Edward Marcotte, who worked as a backroper at the Chace Cotton Mill in Burlington. His picture was taken in 1909 by the famed photographer Lewis Hine for the activists of the National Child Labor Committee, who sought to eradicate the use of child workers.

Top: Images from the Past/Bennington, Vermont ; bottom: Robert Hull Fleming Museum, UVM was quickly reduced to one family. Between 1850 and 1930, the number of towns with a population of over 1,000 had dropped by roughly a third, to 102.

The stagnant population often rearranged itself closer to the rail lines because jobs followed the transport system. The railroads helped to create a few boom towns at crucial junctions, with Rutland, St. Albans, Ludlow, Bennington, White River Junction, Newport, Bellows Falls, and Northfield as a few examples. But what growth there was must still be kept in perspective. Of these, only Rutland approached 10,000 people in 1870, and the number of towns with over 5,000 did not need a whole hand to be counted. Rutland even surpassed Burlington in population in 1880, beating it 12,149 to 11,365. This falls short of a pattern that could be truly termed "urbanization."

Burlington was, and remains, Vermont's "big city," despite its relatively small scale. Over this period, Burlington grew decisively, more than doubling in size from 13,596 in 1870 to 27,686 in 1940; this would hardly be termed a city in most states. Burlington had first made it into the top five population centers in the state in 1820, and has been there ever since. It started with the enormous geographical advantage of its location on a good natural harbor on Lake Champlain, surrounded by the breadbasket of the Champlain Valley. Its strategic, and spectacular, setting had already secured it the state's university, medical college, steamship company, customs house, courts, retail center, and some small factories by the time of the Civil War. By then it was rapidly becoming the state's most diverse melting pot, with Irish railway workers, French Canadians in the lumberyards, and growing Italian and Jewish communities. Urbanism is a state of mind as well as a population figure, and Burlington's growing ethnicity gave the little city more of a citified air than it might have had otherwise. It was also acquiring amenities that were considered urban: luxury goods dealers and restaurants, saloons and saddlers. Whatever city things Vermont was destined to have would be found here.

Burlington's prime location on the transport system ensured its growth during the boom years of the lumber business, and a number of other small- and medium-sized manufacturing firms began there in this era. But Vermont still did not have enough of everything to support Burlington's growth into a city the size of Boston, or even Hartford or Providence. The lumber would play out, the last steamship would soon puff its way across the lake, and much of the city's manufacturing would be replaced by service-oriented industries like medicine and education after 1900.

So while America's great industrial age was in full swing to the south and west, Vermont's non-agricultural economic development remained small-scale, scattered, often family-owned and managed. The overall number of jobs off the farm was slowly increasing. Whether the small rate of industrial growth was a tragedy or a lucky break for the state depends upon your point

In this late nineteenth-century view of Bellows Falls, one can see how the railroads were an essential component of boom-town status.

UVM Special Collections

of view. For families who were being forced off the hill farms, it meant that there were few openings in other types of work in-state, and most were forced to leave the world they had known for a more frenzied pace elsewhere. Opportunities for other Vermonters to escape the tedium of dairy farming were also limited. For a majority of the population, late nineteenth-century Vermont was a land where wages were low, job choice was limited, and it was hard to pull yourself out of poverty.

On the other hand, in landscape terms, poverty is a powerful preservative. It is true that the state's extractive industries and its manufacturing plants were wreaking environmental havoc in this age of bully capitalism and almost non-existent regulation. Dyes and chemicals were dumped into the once-clear mountain streams; dirty smoke belched from factories and stone dust lay in sinister wait in cutters' lungs; the trees were stripped from the hill-sides a second time, leaving more of the soil to slide down into the lake. Eco-

## HENRY JAMES CONFRONTS THE QUEEN CITY

In 1870 Henry James turned his novelist's eye upon the fair city of Burlington. Here is what he told the readers of *The Nation*:

*The vast reach of the lake and this double mountain view go far to make Burlington a supremely beautiful town. I know of it only so much as I learned in an hour's stroll, after my arrival. The lower portion by the lake-side is savagely raw and shabby, but as it ascends the long hill, which it partly covers, it gradually becomes the most truly charming, I fancy, of New England country towns.*

*I followed a long street which leaves the hotel, crosses a rough, shallow ravine, which seems to divide it from the ugly poorness of the commercial quarter, and ascends a stately, shaded, residential avenue to no less a pinnacle of dignity than the University of Vermont. The university is a plain red building, with a cupola of beaten tin, shining like the dome*

*of a Greek church, modestly embowered in scholastic shade—shade as modest as the number of its last batch of graduates, which I wouldn't for the world repeat. It faced a small enclosed and planted common. The whole spot is full of civic greenness and stillness and sweetness. It pleased me deeply, considering what it was...On the summit of the hill, where it leaves the town, you embrace the whole circling presence of the distant mountains; you see Mount Mansfield looking over lake and land at Mount Marcy.*

*Equally with the view, though—I had been having views all day—I enjoyed, as I passed again along the avenue, the pleasant, solid American homes, with their blooming breadth of garden, sacred with peace and summer and twilight. I say "solid" with intent; the most of them seemed to have been tested and ripened by time. One of them there was—but of it I shall say nothing. I reserve it for its proper immortality in the first chapter of the great American novel.*

*It perhaps added a touch to my light impression of the old and the graceful that, as I wandered back to my hotel in the dusk, I heard repeatedly, as the home-faring laborers passed me in couples , the sound of a tongue of other than Yankee inflections. It was Canadian French.*

logical damage was here, as it was all over America. But where Vermont was lucky was in its scale. Agriculture and lumbering took their tolls, but in those areas there were signs of a more sophisticated understanding of environmental consequences. Farm abandonment caused a period of human dislocation, but also removed the human pressure from fragile soils and allowed the trees to reemerge. Industrial waste existed in Vermont, but its effects were mitigated in some measure by its small size and scattered siting.

As early as the 1870s it happened that Vermont was just about the most rural state in the Union. (This was thoroughly documented by the end of World War II, but had been assumed for decades earlier.) To some natives, this meant they were the biggest failures—almost no other place had seen the Industrial Revolution pass it by so decisively. The state was just a bunch of green mountains with trees coming back where there had once been productive farms, a bunch of once-beautiful Greek Revival farmhouses now unpainted and down on their luck, villages clustered around greens with churches and town halls, and hardly a smokestack in sight. In the valleys, Farmer Snug seemed to be gaining on Farmer Slack, but the Slacks were winning in the creases of the mountains. Not having seen what the rest of America was starting to look like, many Vermonters bemoaned their lack of slick modernity and suffered in their rural poverty.

In the 1860s and 1870s, Vermont was still trying to beat New Hampshire at its own game by generating images of the state that showed it looking as sublime and awe-inspiring as anywhere in the White Mountains. There was still the hope that Vermont could cash in on the elite tourist market, which saw the greatest beauty in those landscapes that created the most anxiety, as (above) in W. H. Linton's "Looking Toward Smuggler's Notch from the Nose" (1874).

At the same time, people started to come here from elsewhere and say that the air was so clean, and the mountains so beautiful that it looked like their state used to look. It had not changed because nobody had enough money to do much of anything to it. The state had been cleared and browsed down to the bone, and that was how it had stayed. People told Vermonters that they lived in a place outsiders could only visit in their imaginations, and they should find a way to take advantage of that. At first, Vermonters said, "You can't eat scenery!" But it was scenery—the remaining natural landscape that was, to the outsiders' eyes, relatively untouched—that would be Vermont's salvation.

## WHO WILL BUY VERMONT?

If it was to be a major player in the tourism market, Vermont would have to figure out what it was selling. There had been disappointments in this area in the past. In the early nineteenth century, the state had seen a small tourism boom, mainly centered around "medicinal tourism," as visitors flocked to resort hotels boasting of healing springs. But as people became more comfortable with the idea of vacations centered around relaxation and seeing new things, the spa model began to fall by the wayside.

Vermont was also at a disadvantage in attracting tourists in the 1860s and 1870s because it did not conform to the prevailing fashion for wild and

In his well-known image, "Chin From the Nose, Mansfield Mountain" (circa 1860–1870), photographer Frank F. Currier shows a group of tourists enjoying the view from the top of Mount Mansfield. Their clothing indicates that they were from the prosperous middle class, like most tourists of their era. Let us hope that the view at the top was "sublime" enough to repay them for hiking in these outfits.

"sublime" scenery as well as neighboring New Hampshire and New York. In an age that expected scenes of awesome grandeur, such as the educated tourists of the day saw in the paintings of the Hudson River School, Vermont was considered too tame. As the New York poet Will DeGrasse put it in 1866:

> *...there is scarcely a range of elevation in the state of Vermont, excepting Mount Mansfield, near the village of Stowe, which is truly worthy of the name of "a mountain." Truth demands that they should be called what they were first named, "The Green Hills of Vermont."*

His argument that they had once been called the "Green Hills" is inaccurate, but he had a point. Despite artistic attempts to convey the state's views with a proper sense of wonder, Vermont was not considered romantic or wild enough. It was too domesticated.

There were other barriers to tourism as well. The steamboats still plied Lake Champlain, depositing visitors at the United States Hotel at Larrabee's Point in Shoreham, and similar spots. But it was mountain scenery that was more in favor, and a few farsighted people were beginning to see it with an eye toward combining tourism and conservation. In 1870, Joseph Battell opened a popular resort called the Bread Loaf Inn in Ripton. Battell, a wealthy and eccentric bachelor from Middlebury, had fallen in love with the Green Mountains while he was a student at Middlebury College, and began buying up great tracts of mountain and forest land from Waterbury to Brandon. He had a horror of lumbering and was determined that the trees should be allowed to come back. Part of saving the landscape was bringing people in and teaching them to appreciate it.

Battell ran the Bread Loaf Inn for the rest of his life, combining it with his interests in conservation, Morgan horse breeding (he also started the Morgan Horse Farm in Weybridge), and acting as a trustee at Middlebury College. In 1910 he deeded Camel's Hump Mountain to the state of Vermont for the public's use; on his death, he gave the rest of his great holdings to Middlebury College. They kept the Inn and a large natural area that now serves as the College's cross-country and downhill skiing area, selling the remaining 20,000 acres to the U.S. government for the Green Mountain National Forest in 1936. It was to become a great resource for teaching both tourists and natives about preserving the landscape.

## THE SWEET LAND OF MEMORY

Battell was a pioneer, ahead of his time in realizing that, although Vermont was not wild, it had its own pastoral beauty because men and women had tamed it. It might not have big cities and major manufactures, but it had a

## THE BREAD LOAF INN

*Some folks pay $10,000 for a painting and hang it on the wall where their friends can see it, while I buy a whole mountain for that much money and it is hung up by nature where everybody can see it and it is infinitely more handsome than any picture ever painted.*

—Joseph Battell

**Middlebury philanthropist Joseph Battell (left); summer visitors arriving at his Bread Loaf Inn in Ripton (right). Battell always favored horses, and long after the automobile was becoming widespread he forbade guests to arrive in one.**

homely quality that had kept people there even in bad times. In the 1880s and 1890s, this growing understanding of the virtues of rural simplicity would change the way Vermonters saw themselves and presented themselves to potential visitors.

Down in Boston and New York, people who read *Scribners* or *The Atlantic Monthly* or other such publications were seeing a lot of articles about the decayed state of northern New England, with its abandoned farms and rural poverty. But they were also looking out their own windows at the dirt, the crowding, the unsettling anonymity, and the disquieting ethnic diversity of urban life in the new cities of the eastern seaboard. Was the world they had left still there, going on the way they remembered it? What would it be like to be able to go back to that time before the family had struck out in search of something bigger?

Northern New Englanders needed money, and they hoped they could get some from visitors. In an age of farm abandonment, it is significant that the state agency put in charge of luring tourists was the Vermont Board of Agriculture. They began putting out pamphlets meant to lure visitors, the first called *Resources and Attractions of Vermont* (1891). Two years later, they more explicitly tried to resettle abandoned farms by publishing *A List of Desirable Vermont Farms at Low Prices* (1893).

The marketing strategy was to mythologize a Golden Age of Old New England, when the values of the sturdy settlers had created a new democratic ideal amidst this rural paradise. This heritage was shared by all of New England, but was particularly true of Vermont, which remained the most rural state in the Union. Here, the old Yankee and Anglo-Saxon outlook still prevailed (buzzwords for those city folk who were still uncomfortable living in the melting pots of southern New England. No need to mention Vermont's own influx of French Canadians, Welsh, Italians, and other ethnic sorts). As the introduction to a Rutland Railroad Company advertising pamphlet put it in 1897:

> *The line of the Rutland railroad in southern Vermont...is older than any historical record. First an Indian trail, then a bridle-path for white settlers, then a military road, then a turnpike and stage route, it*

## THE LONG TRIP NORTH IN THE RAILWAY AGE

The railroads made northern New England a realistic vacation option in the late 1800s, but it was not an easy trip. A New Yorker named Cecil Dyer remembered how, as a boy, he and his family had made their way to the Willoughby Lake House in the Northeast Kingdom:

> *In the nineties Willoughby was a long day's journey from New York. ...One took the White Mountain Express which left Grand Central at 9 A.M. To a small boy the trip held absorbing interest: along the Sound to New Haven, up the Connecticut Valley, Hartford, Springfield, Greenfield, Brattleboro, White River Junction, and finally, about 5 P.M., Wells River. There we changed while the Express went on to New Hampshire. Then supper, and presently the train from Boston and the last lap to St. Johnsbury and West Burke, reached about 8:30. Followed then the final stage, a six-mile drive behind horses, with a lantern swung under the wagon, through the crisp coolness of a northern Vermont summer night, and arrival at the big lamplit hotel between nine and ten, pretty tired and sleepy. A long day indeed.*
>
> —CECIL DYER, "Lake Willoughby 60 Years Ago," *Vermont History* (1956)

**Trains quickly became a popular form of transportation for locals and outsiders alike, as the crowd on this platform shows.**

In the late nineteenth century, itinerant painter James Franklin Gilman captured many idealized views of the Barre-Montpelier area, showing the beauty of the Vermont landscape as it would soon become known to a wider world of tourists. In "The Joshua Thwing Homestead" (1887, above), even the small industrial hamlet of Thwingville, in North Barre, is bathed in a warm glow, with only a few suspicious wisps of smoke to suggest its commercial purpose.

*finally becomes the course of a great railway. ...Whether as a war path of savages, or guide to the pioneer, or channel of commerce, the history of this natural highway...runs through a country with a noble history; it carried the tourist into high altitudes where the oppressive heat of summer cannot follow, and where the mountains rich in minerals and the valley well cultivated are a continual source of delight. In fact, it opens up a land which Nature and the Yankee have cooperated in making famous.*

Vermont's advertising campaign soon began to show results, and by the late nineties the state had 650 hotels and farmhouses hosting over 50,000 tourists a year. Tourism was only an option for farmhouses that were in reasonably good repair, located in scenic spots, and large enough to have spare bedrooms; so the overall proportion of farms participating in tourism was always relatively small. Historian Dona Brown's work on Vermont tourism in this era has shown that farm visits were especially appealing to the new tourist market. Like modern bed and breakfast places, farm holidays were less

## THE FLOOD OF 1927: A LANDSCAPE RESCULPTED

The '27 Flood is still remembered as one of Vermont's most fabled natural disasters. The autumn of 1927 had been a particularly rainy one, so no one thought much about it when rain began again on November 3. But soon the storm had become torrential, and within 24 hours up to 15 inches had fallen on the spine of the Green Mountains, with 4–9 inches coming down in the valleys. The state's rivers and streams rose so rapidly that many people were trapped, and 85 lost their lives. Property damage topped $25 million, and was particularly severe in the Winooski and Lamoille River basins, with Montpelier, Bolton, Waterbury, Barre, Cambridge, and many other towns badly damaged.

Experts speculate that the same kind of thing could happen again if conditions were right, although now the property damage would be far greater. The one positive effect of the flood: many roads that had always been dirt were paved in the reconstruction that followed.

The Flood of '27 inundated many towns with water up to the second-story windows, as shown here in Windsor (top). Many buildings lost their footings, and were scattered over the landscape like Monopoly houses. The state had 1,258 bridges destroyed or severely damaged in the flooding. A makeshift structure (above) carried foot passengers across a swollen stream in Bethel.

expensive and more casual than hotel visits. Farm families usually charged between $3 and $12 a week for a family, while good hotels charged $3.50 a day. Most of this profit was plowed back into farm improvements.

Advertisements stress those aspects of farm life that most appealed to city folk. This one touches all the usual bases:

> *Mrs. A. S. Newcomb. Green Mountain View Farm, Wardsboro, Vt. Conveyance, stage or private team. Accommodates ten persons. Terms, $5 to $7 per week. Fine views. Nice shade trees. Best of spring water. Milk, cream and eggs. Vegetables and berries in season. Splendid drives and some good fishing.*

This pamphlet is typical of the sort of thing the Vermont Board of Agriculture was sending out in the 1890s. It was designed to interest out-of-staters in buying abandoned farms and making them into vacation homes.

Cooling shade, scenery, fresh country food—Mrs. Newcomb was running her own little Eden, with everything required for a restorative experience.

The whole idea of farm visits sounded perfect: hard-strapped farm families would make some money and city folk would get a healthy dose of country life. In reality, the arrangement could be a bit more complicated, as two groups with alien expectations met over the breakfast table. The Board of Agriculture quickly found out that the rural fantasies of the city slickers were not often in accordance with the reality of Vermont farm life.

The visitors found a lot to complain about. The views could only be seen from the far end of the back garden, not from their rooms, as they had imagined. The furniture was modern (bought to make the city people comfortable), although they had thought it would be old and quaint. And the food! To the city person, the highlight of a farm vacation was the thought of having fresh food at every meal: milk squirted from the cow that morning, vegetables picked from the garden in the afternoon, a chicken discreetly strangled and made ready for the pot just before cooking time. They would be eating the way those lucky farmers got to eat every day.

It turned out that Vermont farm families were not much into healthy food. They liked anything, as long as it was fried. The boarders wanted roast chicken, but the family liked fried pork. They expected fresh bread, but the landlady only had time to make lardy biscuits. They wanted a variety of fresh vegetables, but the farmer usually only grew potatoes and beans. A dessert of fresh-picked berries with cream might be nice, so the dried prune pie came as something of a shock. Farm wives all over Vermont felt humiliated and exhausted trying to please them, while the visitors believed they had been misled. The Board of Agriculture finally had to mediate the state-wide "food wars," sending out detailed instructions for farm wives on how and what to feed the city people. Following all these edicts made for a lot of extra work. As one exhausted rural hostess put it, witheringly:

*They find the morning so fresh after you have served their late breakfast, and the glass of milk so refreshing after their afternoon nap, and the cream is so delicious, and the piazza so cool, you think some day you would really like to enjoy it yourself for a few minutes.*

But when the visitors had gone and the house was their own again, there was money in the mattress for another winter. Many guests ended up enjoying themselves, and the hosts were enriched in more ways than one by having had this personal contact with the outside world.

This photo of tourists in New Londonderry circa 1910 demonstrates that the new forests of Vermont were so tame and welcoming that even well-dressed women and little children were safe there. Note the outfits of the boys in the foreground; the wild forest of the Abenaki now seemed like child's play.



### NO PLACE LIKE HOME

In 1899, the governor of New Hampshire, Frank Rollins, came up with a great gimmick for getting more people to come back to their home state for a visit, where they would, presumably, drop a little money along the way. Even more importantly, it would build self-esteem among those who had remained behind. The state chose official dates for an "Old Home Week," when towns would welcome back their native sons and daughters who had moved away. Once there, they would be welcomed and feted and reminded of their origins in a simpler, more pastoral community.

Old Home Week was one of the earliest and most successful organized tourism promotions in Vermont history. Many towns jumped on the bandwagon, like Chelsea (above), hoping to welcome back the state's legions of nineteenth-century expatriates.

Old Home Week caught on big, and for the next 20 years it was a staple of small-town tourism and civic celebration in northern New England. And even though it had been a New Hampshire idea, Vermont soon came to be the premier Old Home Week state. The images employed to promote these gatherings were blatantly nostalgic and sentimental: the old farm, the little red school, the old oaken bucket. All of them spoke of a childhood spent in the country, close to the land.

As much as the visitors enjoyed Old Home Week, it was the natives who found it most healing. Vermonters' crisis of confidence finally seemed to be coming to an end; as they put on the rose-colored glasses handed to them by the visitors, they began to believe that the state had something unique to offer: a precious past that other places had lost. They still had relatively clean air and fresh food, good values and civic virtues, and all the advantages of a life lived in daily interaction with the forces of the natural world. Those forces had given them a run for their money, but they had come through it together. From this era forward, leaving aside for a moment the issue of whether this insight represented their fantasy or their reality, many Vermonters would be imbued with a sense of their own uniqueness.

The preindustrial landscape seemed to have been largely preserved (if you did not remember the virgin forest). The new scientific farms were beginning to prosper, and many were looking spruce to welcome visitors. Summer houses were appearing on the Taconic lakes and in the Northeast Kingdom and at Thompson's Point on Lake Champlain. Summer camps for children were springing up on lakes and in the mountains. Things were looking better for this one segment of the state's economy.

By 1919, the Vermont Publicity Bureau (which had taken over the job from the Board of Agriculture) was promoting a new relationship between mankind and mountain:

> *To tired bodies and weary nerves, the Green Mountains bring peace and rest and renewed health. From the din and turmoil of the great city the transition to the quietness and repose of the mountains is almost like entering a new world. Here the visitor may look out over a far reaching expanse of mountain peaks, forest clad. ...He may listen to nature's great organ tones as the wind plays through the tops of the evergreen forests, and inhale the healing odors of balsam and cedar and pine.*

And while you enjoyed this mountain wonderland, you need not fear for your safety, for in Vermont even the Green Mountains possessed a comforting "hominess":

> *The Vermont mountains are easily accessible. One need not go a day's journey into the wilderness in order to reach them. They are not far removed from the comforts of civilization and the habitation of men. The highest peak of the Green Mountains is reached by a good carriage road. No peril to life or limb need be encountered in climbing most of the Green Mountain summits.*

The whole state was about to be made more accessible to tourists than it had ever been for the natives. The machine was about to meet the mountains.

## START YOUR ENGINES

In 1899, the first motorcar ever seen in Rutland County rolled off a railroad car and putted its way through town, drawing a crowd wherever it went. The same scene was taking place around the state as the new century came in. By 1906, Vermont had 860 cars registered—the new status symbol of the successful businessman. Not everyone was happy about the darned things. Up in Ripton, for example, Joseph Battell got hopping mad every time he saw one. Acting in line with his beliefs about conservation, he was to become one of Vermont's first and most vocal opponents of motor cars and would not allow any guests who arrived in an automobile to register at the Bread Loaf Inn. He also owned a newspaper, the *Middlebury Register*; some people thought he spent too many columns documenting the grisly details of every auto accident story that came his way. Much of his championing of the Morgan horse was due to his seeing this noble animal as the environmentally friendly alternative to the motor car. Yet even Battell could not have imagined the far-reaching cultural and environmental impacts these alien machines would have in the twentieth century.

In the early twentieth century, Vermonters were proud of their new cars. Auto-touring parties were all the rage, as shown (top) in this shot of a summer meeting at Kendrick's Hotel in Putney around 1910. Driving was a novelty for anyone in this period, but women drivers were so anomalous that everyone seemed to want to take a photo of a female performing this impossible feat (bottom).



In the post-War giddiness of the 1920s, the automobile represented freedom, and the number of cars registered in the state went from 30,000 in 1920 to 90,000 in 1929. The presence of cars had already raised the issue of the state of the road system, which had ceased to improve since trains arrived in the mid-nineteenth century. In 1892, the principle of State Aid for highways was embraced, and by the end of the decade Vermont had its first Commissioner of Highways to oversee the state's 13,000 miles of public roads. (The system would expand to 14,388 miles by World War II.) The Motor Vehicle Department was added in 1927. Tax money was now being used to improve the highways, and by the Second World War, officials were bragging that a whopping 9 percent of Vermont's roads were paved, 51 percent were graveled, and a mere 40 percent were classified as "partially improved or primitive." Motoring on roads like these must have really been a breeze.

The automobile had a big impact on patterns of tourism. Visitors had long come great distances by train, and once they got to their destinations, had to hire transportation if they wanted to see any sights. In the railway era, as in the spa era that preceded it, people normally came to a large hotel or resort and stayed put there for weeks at a time. But cars made mobility fun, turning people's attention away from seeing a small area in relaxing detail and toward trying to cram in as many sights as possible in the time they had. Tourists were now apt to stay in one place for a night or two, and then move on looking for another thrill. The great hotels quickly began to die off, in favor of smaller places located further from the train depots.

Of course, not all city folk had cars in the twenties. Whitney Landon, who summered at Caspian Lake in that era, still took the train up with his family, only now they were met by old Sam Ladd with his car. He later told a very Vermont story about it, "the last good story about Sam": "He went to pick up somebody at the station, and was putting the trunk in the car, and the man said to him: 'I'd like to help you with that trunk, but I'm 75 years old.' And Sam said, 'That's all right, I'm 90.'"

Most drivers preferred to stay on a few routes that were known to be trustworthy, most of them in southern Vermont. Woodstock and Manchester were popular early on for having good roads and nice amenities. Meeks tells us that it was hard to get anyone to venture into Addison County, whose treacherous roads were known as the "Addisonian Wastes of Clay."

## WINTER DRIVING CONDITIONS, EARLY TWENTIETH CENTURY

When the motorcar first appeared, snow-clearing technology for rural highways and town streets was still in the future. The late nineteenth-century method of dealing with snow was the snowroller (right), which did not remove the snow, but only packed it into a hard surface. This had worked well for horses and sleighs, but left a lot to be desired for automobiles approaching busy intersections on 32-degree days.

From the look of this rural photograph, Grandpa was not kidding when he said the drifts were higher back then.

Collections of Vermont Historical Society

Accommodations were improving, and the state was still actively involved in training and supporting farm families willing to take in tourists. A 1929 Vermont Commission on Country Life subcommittee on Tourist and Recreation Facilities sent out an inspector to survey some of the properties, and she found conditions generally good:

> *Usually the first use of the income from tourists has been for a bath room or some important improvement in the way of equipment. A surprisingly large number of farm homes are equipped with bath, electric lights and the accompanying electrical equipment. The farm homes show the effect of the tourist income in exterior as well as interior improvements. There are few unpainted houses or ill kept yards. The interiors were decorated tastefully showing that much thought had been given to the comfort of the tourist. In a few instances the rooms were untidy and mattresses poor. If there were no electric lights available, delco systems had been installed and where water was available, plans were on foot to install bath-rooms.*
>
> *One of the most noticeable changes coincident with the coming of the tourist is seen in the personal appearance of the farm woman and children. Early morning finds the housewife neatly attired in a crisp gingham dress and the children in sensible play suits, clean and comfortable. The farm woman enjoys the thought of guests and takes pleasure in keeping ready for them.*

The inspector, Mrs. Pearl Brown, seemed surprised to find farm life so civilized. She has no doubt that this was completely owing to tourism: "It is certain that the farm home particularly has benefited greatly from the coming of the tourist. In many cases it is the salvation of the farmer." There may be something to this in the sense that only elite farmers could hope to take in tourists in the first place. Many Vermont farmers were still dirt poor, and had no money to fix up their places to the standard required by tourism.

Others on the committee shared this view that rural tourism and its increased contacts with the urban world were closing the gap between town and country. A certain Mr. Cornwall (a contemporary observer cited in a state government report) was quoted as saying:

> *Twenty years ago when walking along the street of Middlebury or Brandon you could recognize a farm boy as far as you could see him. Today, with...automobiles, radios, movies, etc.. you can not tell the farm boys from the other boys. There is one aspect I have thought about in my farm bureau work. One hundred years ago the farmers did not have nearly what they have today. They had tallow dips and spun*

*their own clothes. They had none of the luxuries. Neither had anyone else. One hundred years ago, the farmer was the squire of the community. He rather looked down on the other people of the community. Today things are reversed. His conditions are not like his grandfather's were, but he has not so much money left over at the end of the year as the town boy has. ...How can I tell my boy to stay on the farm?*

The point is an interesting one and shows how far the image of the farmer had fallen during the decades of crisis after the Civil War. It also raises an important question about the relationship between farming and tourism, for was tourism elevating the position of farm families or merely reinforcing a sense of inferiority? As Dona Brown's work on farm tourism showed, farm families felt themselves to be the social equals of their guests, while most tourists believed themselves to be the social superiors of their hosts.

### THE PLAYGROUND FOR NEW ENGLAND, 1920–1929

Many farms that had been given up during the bad years were now coming into the hands of rich people from the cities of southern New England.

---

A classic Wallace Nutting photo from *Vermont Beautiful*, showing a landscape both serene and relatively primitive.

Wallace Nutting, *Vermont Beautiful*, Old America Company Publishers

## A TASTE FOR THE BEAUTIFUL: WALLACE NUTTING LOOKS AT VERMONT, 1922

The most influential writer, photographer and mythologizer of Vermont in the 1920s was Wallace Nutting, whose popular book, *Vermont Beautiful*, was published in 1922. His purpose was to make people see the beauty of the Vermont landscape with a more sophisticated understanding of why it was so pleasing. He started this section with the proposition that Americans did not learn enough about landscape aesthetics in school:

*If, however, the American with his thoroughly varied landscape learns to love each one for its special beauties, and to understand that in some feature, at least, the view from his own door is superior to any other landscape, he has made progress in the discernment of beauty and his life is fuller.*

*That beauty in our country is unappreciated is proved by the very meager number of American artists who can find a market for their landscapes. The artist is not being encouraged. ...Good American landscapes should hang on the walls of every home, as evidence of our patriotism and love of the beautiful.*

*We hope to see the day when many fine scenes in Vermont will be placed on canvas by hands that combine love and power.*

The prosperous twenties saw a boom in such second-home purchases, and the state was only too happy to encourage it. The trend certainly helped to put life back into many rural properties, but it was not rural life. Mr. Cornwall, already quoted above, expressed some well-considered worries about the effects of second-home ownership on Vermont communities:

> *This is the thing that will make more of a farm problem if we are not careful. Let's get summer people on the hill farms, like Ripton, Goshen and places not adapted to farming. But do not let's try and encourage them to live in good agricultural towns. There is a morale that you are like to break down when you get country gentlemen farmers in among you. I would rather see Vermont progress along agricultural lines than become the playground for New England.*

Cornwall was concerned about the continued fragility of local self-esteem, and the changes that came to agricultural communities when city people came in who did not have the same values or responsibilities. His thoughts provide an early example of the ambivalence longtime Vermonters would feel toward "flatlanders" in the decades to come:

A view from Point of Pines at Lake Bomoseen in Castleton (above), a popular vacation spot where the "summer people" were already beginning to have a significant positive impact on the local tax base. In nearby Poultney, the town's 60 summer houses were bringing in $150,000 in taxes—a whopping sum in 1928.

UVM Special Collections

*I am not saying that we do not want tourists, but don't let's try and help real estate men boost farm values by colonizing city men in good agricultural towns. Some day when you get a chance to go into some of our towns where they have a considerable number of city men as farmers, talk to them about their problems, measure the social values, measure the fact that a great many of those homes are closed up in the winter and that your children are growing up in a dead community in the winter. Your children, while working around the farm, see these rich people riding around in their cars. I would rather send my boy to the neighbors to help fill silos than to have him help take care of ponies for the rich summer people. Just think of those things. We must measure it by the type of farmers who are tilling the soil in a real farming community. This is an entirely personal preference. I am glad to say that on my farm we are surrounded entirely by farmers.*

During the Depression government photographers from the Farm Security Administration fanned out over America to record the conditions on the country's struggling farms. French-Canadian dairy farmer Isadore Lavictiore was photographed by Jack Delano in a Rutland field in 1941.



Mr. Cornwall and his compatriots were about to have a respite from the influx of outsiders. The stock market crashed. The Depression had arrived.

### A DEPRESSION? HOW CAN YOU TELL?

The classic joke in Vermont in the 1930s went as follows. Outsider: "Don't you people know there's a Depression on?" Vermonter: "Looks about the same to me." By most accounts, this joke had its serious side. If there was anything Vermonters had learned from the trials of the past, it was how to make do. Milk and maple prices were down, but not to dangerous levels. It is a truism that it is easier to survive bad times in an agricultural area (though not in the Dustbowl), and Vermont was still the most rural state in the nation. People who could still travel were attracted to Vermont, and state government was working overtime to keep them coming. It had never been more important than now that the tourist dollars not dry up.

The thirties saw a subtle shift in the publicity generated to interest second-home buyers. There was a growing interest in the status of those who might purchase. The prolific Dorothy Canfield Fisher was again called upon to do duty; she wrote a brochure for the state, "Vermont Summer Homes: An Open Letter" (1937), urging people to buy second homes and making it quite clear who would be considered the "right people." The publication is filled with photographs of appetizing farmhouses beautifully redone by a long list of luminaries: Professor George K. Cherrie ("friend and fellow explorer of Theodore Roosevelt"); famous writers Sinclair Lewis and William Haslett Upson; Mr. and Mrs. Robert L. MacNeil of Great Neck, Long Island; artist Edwin B. Child; Mr. Westbrook Steele of Appleton, Wisconsin, executive of the Institute of Paper Chemistry; Mr. Charles N. Andrews of Hartford,

Top: Collections of Vermont Historical Society; bottom: UVM Special Collections

## THE BACKLASH: VERMONT'S DEPRESSION

As the thirties ground on, the grittiness that characterized the decade on a national scale was easy to find in Vermont. In fact, Vermont had always looked like this—it was the rest of the country that was catching up to it on the poverty scale. Writers and photographers (especially those involved with Roosevelt's public works projects) rejected the image of Vermont as a rural paradise, showing, instead, a darker view of the land and its people.  Photographers like Arthur Rothstein, Jack Delano, and Marion Post Wolcott provided a glimpse of that great expanse of poor Vermont that would never make it onto a postcard.

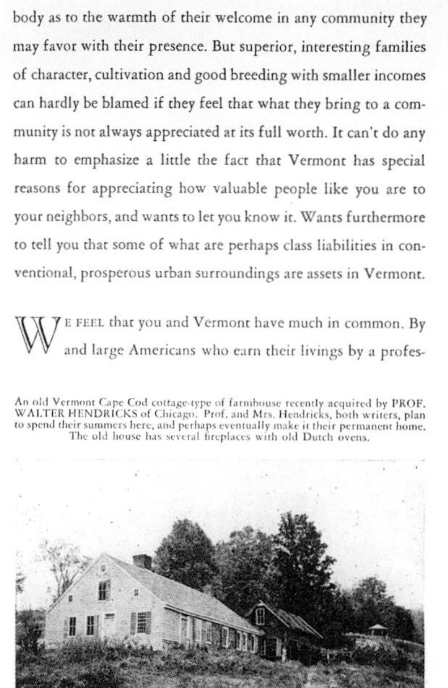

body as to the warmth of their welcome in any community they may favor with their presence. But superior, interesting families of character, cultivation and good breeding with smaller incomes can hardly be blamed if they feel that what they bring to a community is not always appreciated at its full worth. It can't do any harm to emphasize a little the fact that Vermont has special reasons for appreciating how valuable people like you are to your neighbors, and wants to let you know it. Wants furthermore to tell you that some of what are perhaps class liabilities in conventional, prosperous urban surroundings are assets in Vermont.

WE FEEL that you and Vermont have much in common. By and large Americans who earn their livings by a profes-

An old Vermont Cape Cod cottage-type of farmhouse recently acquired by PROF. WALTER HENDRICKS of Chicago. Prof. and Mrs. Hendricks, both writers, plan to spend their summers here, and perhaps eventually make it their permanent home. The old house has several fireplaces with old Dutch ovens.

The village home of MISS BESSIE SNYDER of Washington, D. C. A delightful home with several fireplaces, a type that is frequently found in Vermont, and readily responding to simple improvement.

they do not conduce to the making of large incomes. I suppose that Vermonters, being just twentieth century people like everybody else, are deeply impressed by large sums of money, mere money. But their traditions make them at least ashamed to show that they are impressed. And that's something! Whereas those same old New England traditions make us look up to character and cultivation and education, and proud that we do. Any of you cultivated families, settling in Vermont for a summer home, may thus be sure that the respected and influential Vermonters of your community will value your trained, well-informed minds, respect what your educational advantages have done for you, and be glad they and their children are to be in contact with you.

Writer Dorothy Canfield Fisher (above) was an enthusiastic booster for the state of Vermont. Among other things, she wrote a 1937 brochure, "Vermont Summer Homes: An Open Letter" (top left), which urged out-of-staters to buy second homes here.

Pulitzer Prize winner in 1935; Mr. George Day, Treasurer of Yale; Mr. Hans Barth, well-known concert pianist of New York. Little wonder that Vermont Governor Stanley C. Wilson stated in a radio address that, "It is interesting to note that in one town [probably Greensboro] a considerable colony of college professors and artists has practically changed the summer life of the town." No doubt they had.

But there is a hint of desperation in all this. The Depression was being felt, even here, and attracting tourists became a function of community. Even before the crash, commentators had been trying to inspire towns to get together and do their part to bring in visitors. In a piece that sounded like a call to war ("We have had our experience in the World War and know the evils that flow from lack of preparation"), Max Powell wrote:

> *Now is the time for public-spirited men in the smaller towns to form corporations and either build new hotels or re-model the old one, and to be ready for the on-coming flood of scenery-loving tourists. I cite Brandon as a striking example of the financial benefit that flows from such public spirit and business enterprise. Brandon Inn can be duplicated in dozens of places in Vermont. All you need is the Brandon spirit and ordinary business judgment.*

If Vermont was to thrive on tourism, attention to the appearance of the landscape was vital. Vermonters themselves lamented the arrival of the first tourist cabins: "It seems a crime to desecrate our beautiful scenery by unsightly cabin developments." Others worried about the proliferation of billboards: "It is our scenery to a great extent that draws people here. If objectionable signs cover all the buildings it is not going to encourage people to come into the state." Towns and villages appointed "Improvement Committees" to inspire residents to clean up their own little parts of the universe. There is no way of knowing the relative proportions of natives who rolled up their sleeves to those who snarled, "Get outta my yard!" But the movement for "presenting a prettier face" was indicative of the emergence of a newer, more self-conscious, and distinctly communal perception of the landscape.

# AND NOW!!!

TO VERMONTERS AND VERMONT ORGANIZATIONS:

We hope that you and your Roadside Improvement Committee will busy yourselves about, and get others along the routes in which you are interested to busy themselves about, the following problems on the roadside and on adjoining properties:—

1. **Dead trees and dead branches visible from the road, which give the view a funereal aspect. Also wastes and discards.**
2. **Drunken tipsy fence-posts, which, like drunken men, make one forget everything and everybody else.**
3. **Barren, No Man's Land triangles, where roads meet, which, by planting, can be made spots of neatness and attraction and beauty.**
4. **Raw slopes whose soil and sand and gravel and rocks spill down or are washed down upon the road surface, because there is no grass or shrubbery or trees to hold them in place. Then, too, the raw slopes are ugly. People do not expect them in the Green Mountain State.**
5. **Mechanical cadavers. Forsaken or wrecked automobiles by the roadside or within view of the road make it seem as if a murder had been committed and affairs left "as they were."**
6. **Signs that ought to resign.**
7. **Gaunt open vacant uninteresting barren stretches of roadside where there are needed trees and shrubs and flowers.**

**MAKE A SURVEY, WITH PHOTOGRAPHIC RECORDS, IF POSSIBLE, OF THE ROADSIDES THAT CONCERN YOU. THEN BEGIN DOING SOMETHING ABOUT SOME OF THESE PROBLEMS.**

**Please send us the names of the members of your roadside improvement committee.**

VERMONT STATE CHAMBER OF COMMERCE,
80 West Street,
Rutland, Vermont.

March 21, 1930.

**Roadside Series No. 3**



The state Chamber of Commerce sent this notice (left) to towns and villages all over the state, urging them to clean up anything that might spoil the view along the roadside; this heralded a new self-consciousness about landscape appearances. The Chamber further suggested that those wishing to get involved might busy themselves looking for problems at adjoining properties and urged them to take "PHOTOGRAPHIC RECORDS, IF POSSIBLE"—not a move conducive to good-neighbor policy.

The Green Mountain Club always included women, and many took full advantage of their outings, as demonstrated by this photo of a trip to Dorset Cave in 1913. In the years before World War II, GMC membership was somewhat socially restrictive; this group of young ladies appears well turned-out.

## THE ROMANTIC FOREST

In the national imagination, a new landscape ideal was emerging that seemed to descend more directly from the sublime and awesome Hudson River School view of wild nature that had been so popular a century before. Americans who had seen the spectacular natural settings of the West were again making the wilderness into a religion. They found their joy in a landscape in which the hand of man played (or seemed to have played) no part. Mankind must bow down in the face of nature. For these people, ruralism did not hold enough respite from the strains of urban life. If you were a professor in Boston or a stockbroker in New York with an adventurous spirit, the idea of leaving civilization completely behind you was growing ever more appealing as the twentieth century began.

It was a view of nature that many Yankee Vermonters initially met with ambivalence, even as they were glad to see the trees returning to the mountain tops. George Perkins Marsh's message that the land was suffering without its trees and that more acres must be allowed to return to forest coincided with much of what farmers had seen with their own eyes. Other elite thinkers in the state had taken up the cause. Marsh had sold his old family home in Woodstock to the wealthy railway baron-turned-conservationist, Frederick Billings, who was providing a model of how to reforest your hillsides. In Ripton, Joseph Battell stood against the clear-cutting practices of the paper companies, reminding his fellow Vermonters that "This mighty rib of old forests that runs through our State is by far the most beautiful bit of scenery that we have preserved."

But the idea of the recreational forest had not yet been popularized in the countryside. Even while admitting that there had been environmental excesses in the settlement years, and more recently, many Vermonters could not imagine, and did not crave, a landscape that men and women had not "improved." They understood what the people from the Grange and the Agricultural Extensions were saying about developing their woodlots and putting more land in trees, for that was a productive use and helped return nature to harmony. But, for them, the sight of abandoned farms reverting to puckerbrush was still taken as a sign of defeat. And for people who lived close to nature every day, the mixed agricultural landscape offered plenty of places to enjoy the natural world—ponds for fishing and the edge of the woodlot for shooting critters. The thought of hiking through the wilderness sounded like getting thrown into a farm pond when you could not swim. You would probably get out alive, but that did not make it fun.

Appropriately rustic signage (below) along the Long Trail.

## THE LONG TRAIL

In 1910 a group of men and women from Vermont and out of state began the Green Mountain Club to fulfill their dream of making a long trail through the wilderness that would stretch the whole length of the Green Mountains. When they were finished in 1930, the trail stretched 270 miles from Massachusetts to Canada. Granted, the wilderness was no longer wilderness now that the trees were all second and third growth, the dangerous animals of the forest had been largely eliminated, and walking down hill would eventually bring you to a house. But the forest was coming back, and with it some measure of woodland world that had been so long lost.

In 1927, at the height of the Roaring Twenties, three young women set off to hike the whole length of the Long Trail. Dubbed "The Three Musketeers," they were the first women to complete the walk. It made them nationally famous as symbols of the flapper era's new female emancipation.

From the beginning, the Green Mountain Club was dominated by an elite group, its rosters filled with families like the marble baron Proctors and the Webbs of Shelburne Farms. Many other members were of middle-class origins, and 300 of the 1,500 members in the twenties were from New York City. The upper-class bias of the organization was evident in the members' worries about the effects of automobile tourism—and motoring tourists—on the fragile landscapes of the Green Mountains. Their publication, *The Long Trail News*, was full of testimonials to the restorative qualities of the trail. Mr. and Mrs. F. E. Sias, ages 68 and 60, of Holyoke, Massachusetts, wrote in1930 to say:

Collections of Vermont Historical Society

*No nerve racking vigilance on account of motor vehicles breaks upon your soul. As freely as birds and bees you loiter along bewitching paths in bright sun and cooling shadow; under fluffy changing clouds, or pale moon light. You may dawdle along as a free child of nature stooping to admire a golden lily, or tasting with delight the cool refreshment of a silver cascade.*

The Green Mountain Club made the resurgent forest into a refuge for people living through a period dominated by enormous social change. But the wilderness ideal of getting away from it all was not particularly popular among the natives of the state who were still trying to get some of it for themselves.

## WILDERNESS AND THE PUBLIC TRUST

By the early decades of the twentieth century, a consensus seemed to be developing among Americans, with Vermonters prominent among them, that it was important for government to set aside some tracts of forestland in order for them to be protected. It was the great era of the founding of the national parks. In1911, the Weeks Act enabled the purchase of national forest land in Vermont and New Hampshire. By 1928 the Green Mountain National Forest had been established (including Joseph Battell's bequest); additional

Vermonters have always defended their hunting and fishing rights; looking at this comfortable deer camp (right), one can understand why.

tracts were added in the 1930s. It now consists of about 250,000 acres.

The amusing sight of women doing anything non-domestic extended to fly fishing. These ladies (above) appear to have been given the full Orvis treatment.

State and municipal forests were also being set aside in this period. The first Vermont-owned woods, L. R. Jones State Forest in Plainfield Town, was purchased by the state in 1909; by 1931 the 200 activists on the Commission on Country Life were pleased to report that Vermont owned 19 state forests: a total of 39,000 acres acquired for an average of $2.83 an acre. These were hardly meant to remain untouched, however. In their list of seven reasons for having state forests, the first was, "Furnishing dependable sources of raw material for local wood-using industries," and the last, "Ultimately producing revenue for the state." In between were a couple of incidentals like "Service as sanctuaries for game birds and animals." Towns were also getting into the act, and by 1930 there were 42 municipal forests in the state with similar goals.

## A HUNTING AND FISHING PEOPLE

There was certainly a tourism angle to all this forest preservation; the publicity propagated by the state in the 1930s included far more mentions of Vermont's "wonderful forested and mountainous region" than ever before. For many rural Vermonters, however, nature's greatest recreational value still lay in hunting and fishing. And by the early twentieth century, farm failure was paying an unintended bonus. As farms went back to trees, many miles of "edge" were created, that place where forest meets field that is the preferred home to so much wildlife. It furnished perfect habitat for the returning deer herd, which quickly boomed in the two decades after their reintroduction in 1878. From the Vermont State Fish Hatchery at Roxbury, millions of fingerlings were sent out to be stocked in ponds and streams around the state.

There was a strong popular feeling in Vermont that people had a right to hunt and fish, and game regulations were staunchly resisted. As the Vermont Fish and Game Commissioners said, somewhat sadly, in the 1870s, many of their fellow Vermonters thought that their constitutional right to bear arms meant "The right to use [them], and the right to use them to shoot whatever animals there are."

Many Vermonters were initially suspicious of the new wilderness conservationists, whom they saw as city people trying to impose their own views on the countryside. They also felt understandably hostile toward gentleman hunters and fishermen who came to the state as tourists and shot their game and caught their fish. Still stung by the amount of land that had gone out of production in the abandonment era, they resented the idea that the new forests should become, in the oft-repeated phrase, "playgrounds for the rich." For decades, fish and game laws were regarded as a forum for class conflict. Vermont natives came to accept most modern conservation practices, but only after many decades of resistance. But by the early-twentieth century, they, too, wanted a landscape with democratic access and special places set aside that all people would hold in stewardship.

The 80-year period covered by this chapter had seen a great transformation in the way Vermonters defined themselves and in how they thought of their landscape. The decline of the hill farms, the growth of scientific farming, the tourism revolution, the coming of the automobile age, and the Depression had served to change people's attitudes, but these developments had also created social tensions within communities. What kind of state did the natives want for themselves, once the tourists went home? One great defining experience that helped to clarify these previously inchoate sentiments was Vermont's first great environmental battle, the debate over the building of the Green Mountain Parkway.

### THE GREEN MOUNTAIN PARKWAY

In the heart of the Depression, when the only big money seemed to be federal government money, a scheme was hatched to reel in some of those funds for the state. What was needed was a grand project, and William Wilgus, a civil engineer, and James Paddock Taylor, executive secretary of the Vermont

### OVER THE PARKWAY

*by Llew Evans*

As this poem, appearing in the Green Mountain Club's newsletter, the *Long Trail News*, in June 1934, shows, members were worried about whether an increase in automobile tourism would attract the "wrong kind of people."

OVER THE PARKWAY
*You're crazy, guy. You tole*
*me how you'd climb.*
*Deep in the forest, sidling*
*'round a rock,*
*To see the broadening vista,*
*and unlock*
*The very heart of Nature.*
*"Grand—Sublime!"*
*You said. I'll say you're crazy.*
*It's a crime*
*How me and Bill, my side-*
*kick, and two janes*
*Burned up that parkway that*
*the state maintains*
*along the mountain. Boy, did*
*we make time?*
*We loaded up with*
*frankfurters, beer and gas;*
*Took Killington and Camel's*
*Hump in high;*
*Just shifted once on*
*Mansfield—couldn't pass*
*a line of cars. But what an*
*alibi*
*this Nature pulled. We never*
*saw the lass*
*From Dome to Journey's End.*
*You're crazy, guy.*

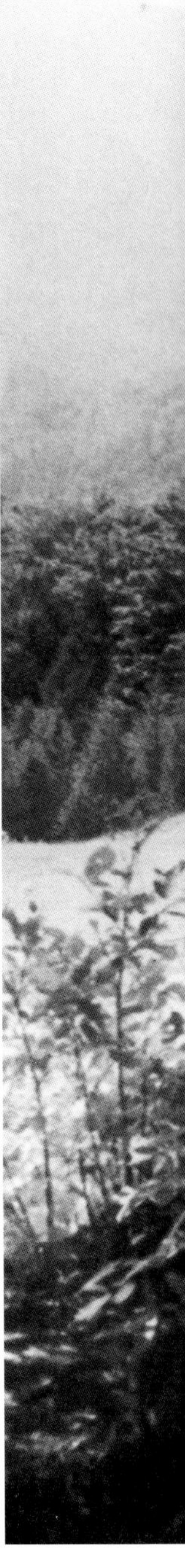

Collections of Vermont Historical Society

The sense of privilege early drivers felt at being able to move so easily through the landscape was soon transformed into a conviction that the landscape must bend to the driver's will. To the car-bound tourists gazing at Mount Hor in this image from the thirties, the idea of a Green Mountain Parkway that would take drivers along the tops of the mountains must have seemed appealing.

Chamber of Commerce, thought they had a winner. Their vision was a parkway that would have stretched from one end of the state to the other running right along the spine of the highest of the Green Mountains, including Killington Peak, Camel's Hump, and Mount Mansfield. It would be Vermont's version of North Carolina's Blue Ridge Parkway, whose parklike, federally controlled verges were constructed in this era with considerable national fanfare. They thought it could not lose.

As historian Hal Goldman tells the story, Taylor even had great environmental credentials. He had come up with the idea of the Long Trail and was a founding member of the Green Mountain Club. But this did not mean that he thought the mountains had been a good thing for Vermont; he told a Boston audience in 1911 that

> *...the mountains have not proved to be blessings, through our effort to make them play a beneficent part in the life of the people, they have inevitably been a hindrance to the State of Vermont. Unclimbed, they have made a commonwealth of valley-dwellers, complacent and provincial. Undeveloped, they have fostered local conservatism and narrowness of interest. Unrevered, they have cultivated in us all an excess of individuality. And so the mountains have had their revenge on us. We have misinterpreted our mountains. Shadowed and hidden by our ranges, we have stayed close in the valley, content to be a valley people, each feeling that his mountain-fringed plot is a world.*

**The romantic view of nature was not necessarily anti-scientific, as the work of Vermont's Wilson Alwyn "Snowflake" Bentley demonstrates. Bentley was an uneducated boy from Jericho, but his passion for the particular led him to pioneer a method of photographing raindrops and snowflakes (above). His imagery helped convince scientists that, indeed, no two snowflakes are alike.**

Where the Long Trail had been a start in combating the conservative individualism (some might say "Yankeeism") of Vermonters, a road would really do the trick in Taylor's eyes. He thought that getting the natives to the top of the mountains would expand their viewpoints, and they would only go up there in cars. And, to make things even better, the Parkway would also bring in massive amounts of money and jobs while it was being built and tourists once it was finished. In his progressive view, it would be Vermont's ultimate public works job.

Some (although not all) of these goals were worthy, but the Parkway's proponents had no understanding of the environmental devastation that would attend building this huge highway through such fragile terrain. The proposal soon became a battle, with Wilgus, Taylor, *The Burlington Free Press*, the writer William Haxlett Upson, and Dorothy Canfield Fisher supporting the building of the Parkway and the Green Mountain Club, *The Rutland Herald*, Frederick Law Olmsted, Jr., the Proctor family, and George Aiken among those against it.

The battle was heated and occasionally ugly. Sometimes the Parkway's supporters seemed to be supporting the wrong thing (the road) for the

A growing sense of unease over changes being wrought in Vermont in the modern era is depicted in "Church Supper"(1933), by regionalist painter Paul Sample. Sample, a summer resident on Lake Willoughby, shows storm clouds brewing as a rural church supper is disrupted by the arrival of a fancy woman from the city. The painting raises the still pertinent question of whether a traditional way of life can be preserved against an incoming tide of flatlanders.

right reasons (jobs, pulling Vermont out of the Depression). Sometimes the Parkway's detractors seemed to be supporting the right thing (stopping the road) for the wrong reasons (keeping the "wrong sort of people" out of the state). The battlelines were not clearly partisan or predictable, and in the end people seemed to vote their consciences.

The Green Mountain Parkway scheme was brought to a vote in the Legislature and lost 126–111. Governor Charles Smith was under so much pressure from the highway's supporters that he decided to send it to the people, putting it up for a vote at Town Meetings in March 1936. Vermonters from all walks of life were so emotional about the issue that a record number of 74,000 showed up at meeting that day. By the end of the counting, the Green Mountain Parkway was a dead deal, smartly defeated by a vote of 42,318 against to 30,897 in favor.

What the debate clarified, more than anything, was the ambivalence Vermonters were feeling about the effects of development and tourism on the Green Mountains. Some of it was a debate about money, and the pros and cons of taking so much of it from the federal government. Some of it was about the environmental ramifications of cutting a gash through the Green Mountains, although in the rudimentary state of ecological understanding of the period, there was less of that than one might expect. Its supporters had said that if Vermont did not build it, the state would be left behind. As Taylor told Wilgus when they were working together on their dream in 1933, "We must realize that we are dealing with a people who feel that in some ways they are 'different' and wish to remain 'different.'" And in the end, it was that feeling that probably had more to do with the demise of the Green Mountain Parkway than anything else.

## THE YANKEE KINGDOM

The period stretching from the Civil War to the outbreak of World War II was one of the most painful and pivotal in Vermont's history. The optimism and pluck of the settlers had led to the serene beauty of the classical village. The village was still there, but late nineteenth-century Vermont, at its heart, was a land of despair. Vermont was not up to a lot of heavy farming, or industry, or the creation of big cities. Realizing that their predecessors' over-exuberant use of Vermont's fragile landscape had led them to this dire circumstance was an eye-opening experience for many Vermonters; something had to change.

This oil on canvas of "Manchester Center"—painted by lifelong Dorset resident and prolific artist Claude Dern—is typical of a genre that contributed to Vermont's reputation as a pastoral eden.

George Perkins Marsh, Joseph Battell, Frederick Billings, and other interested amateur naturalists tried to educate the public about the need for better management of the state's natural resources. But it would be difficult to be more demoralized than Vermonters were in the 1870s, surrounded by their denuded mountains, watching the retreating backs of their children as they left for Fall River or Fargo. Vermonters were suffering a crisis of community; they were also suffering a crisis of identity.

If Vermonters had lost their sense of themselves, maybe someone else would try to provide one for them. Outsiders saw a rural paradise that no longer existed in the urban settings where they lived. So as the nineteenth century turned into the twentieth, tourism was being widely touted as the cure for all of Vermont's social ills. But tourism in practice was filled with ambivalence. There is a tension in having to be presentable all the time, a resentment at being treated as if you—a human being—are one of the sights on display, a sorrow at seeing houses once filled with friends now taken over for a stranger's playhouse, and a natural resistance to the marketing that made it all possible.

Vermonters felt all these things, yet were not immune to their own advertising. Maybe the place was poor, but it was proud, free, and flinty. Rather than feeling they had failed at things like industry and urban development, they began to believe they had done it this way on purpose. They were Yankees, living in Vermont's Yankee Kingdom, a place where descendants of the nation's first settlers still held to the freedom-loving, town-meeting ideals of America's founders. As the real New England Yankees, frozen in time, they were the remaining repository of the nation's values.

Yet in the decade before the Second World War, the Yankee Kingdom itself was coming under threat. The pastoral ideal of the late 1800s, with its glorification of rural life, was giving way to a new concern for the "wilderness" that city folk saw when the trees came back. It was a change in landscape outlook that did not bode well for native Vermonters, who were trying to cling to their agricultural heritage. It was also leading to new tensions between the outsiders, with their desire to shoot nature with a camera, and the Vermont Yankees, with their traditions of shooting nature with a gun. Tensions between natives and outsiders would only become more acute over time.

Vermont on the eve of the Second World War was a very different place than it had been when the Union soldiers came home in 1865. In many ways the environment was healthier, with more trees and more wildlife than at any time since settlement days. It was also tidier and better kept up, although whether for the locals' own pleasure or to catch the tourist dollar remained a question. The roads were getting better, but there still were not many good ones (and none connecting Vermont's tallest peaks). There were fewer farms, but the ones that remained were scraping by. In Burlington and Barre and Bennington, there were whole communities of people who were not, and could never be, Yankees. The Yankee Kingdom was not always a comfortable place for them.

The first ski lift had appeared in 1934 on a hill in Woodstock, but this recreational industry was only in its infancy. On Lake Champlain and Lake Dunmore, Caspian Lake and Willoughby Lake, the summer houses of wealthy outsiders added a needed liveliness or destroyed once-lovely spots, depending upon your point of view. Yet nearby, up in the folds of the hills, there were still farm families clinging on in unpainted shacks, living with hunger and misery. Vermont was a poor state, despite its healthy image. But the poverty itself was now part of the Vermont mystique, transformed in the mind into a worthy parsimoniousness. The Vermonters of 1940 were apparently more self-confident than they had been 50 years before, more convinced that they were possessed of unique and crotchety characters, more sure that they could defend their Yankee Kingdom from threat. Whether this could be sustained, or whether they were trapped in an identity born of their own marketing, remained to be seen.

## THE FIVE LARGEST TOWNS IN 1870:

| | |
|---|---|
| 1. Burlington | 13,596 |
| 2. Rutland | 9,834 |
| 3. St. Albans | 7,014 |
| 4. Bennington | 5,670 |
| 5. Brattleboro | 4,933 |

## THE FIVE LARGEST TOWNS IN 1900:

| | |
|---|---|
| 1. Burlington | 18,640 |
| 2. Rutland | 11,499 |
| 3. Barre | 8,488 |
| 4. Bennington | 8,033 |
| 5. St. Johnsbury | 8,098 |

Alan Jakubek

CHAPTER 5

# CHOOSING VERMONT, 1945 TO THE FUTURE

The story of Vermont's landscape since 1945 can be seen on a drive starting in the little cup of mountains that holds America's smallest state capital, Montpelier. It is an attractive town, its primarily nineteenth-century architecture well-scaled and businesslike; when the legislature is in session, a buzz of power emanates from the gold-domed State House set against its backdrop of forested hills. Nevertheless, it is not difficult to see through the contemporary refinements of Montpelier to the tough core of the old Vermont.

Montpelier was a remote spot until the mid-1960s, when the interstate finally connected it to Vermont's largest city, Burlington, and extended its reach south to New Hampshire, Massachusetts, and Connecticut. Before then, Route 2 was the way to cover the 40 or so miles between the two cities, the old road following the flat, glistening Abenaki highway of the Winooski River west through some of the rockiest gorges of the Green Mountains. Now road and river and interstate keep crossing one another, like a braid. There are still villages here, like Middlesex and Duxbury, that would be recognizable to the troops that marched home from World War II; and the old towns of Waterbury and Richmond retain much of their white-steepled charm.

## FIVE LARGEST TOWNS IN VERMONT, 1940

| Town | Population |
|---|---|
| Burlington | 27,686 |
| Rutland | 17,082 |
| Bennington | 11,257 |
| Brattleboro | 10,983 |
| Barre | 10,904 |

These places were to retain their rankings in exactly this order until Essex knocked Barre out of the top five in the 1970 Census.

**A view of Burlington in 1943 (above) shows the corner of Church and Pearl Streets soon after the streetcar rails were removed. Interstate 89 (right) passes through forested mountains along much of its route, as here near Montpelier.**

Above: L. L. McAllister/UVM Special Collections; right: Paul O. Boisvert

Williston starts out promisingly enough, as befits a village that was founded by Vermont's first governor, Thomas Chittenden, on land he bought from his friend, Ira Allen. Its elegant white clapboard houses and distinguished public buildings are arrayed prettily along the old road. After the War, and even a little over a decade ago, the village was followed by farmland, stretching to the west much of the few short miles from here to South Burlington.

But now there is a sudden change. In western Williston, the roads become wide and new, curving around a sea of parking lots that ring an increasing number of huge national megastores. It is easy to get lost among the dizzying boulevards that divide Home Depot and Wal-Mart and Toys R Us. The old Vermont has been left behind here; the human scale of the village, with its greens and sidewalks for strolling, gives way to a landscape designed to get you from car to store in as few steps as possible. Green spaces are the edges of parking lots or the underpinnings for company logos. It is all clean and convenient, yet strangely disorienting. You could be anywhere in America from Philadelphia to San Francisco. The landscape of community has been subsumed by the landscape of commerce.

The historic center of Williston followed the traditional compact village settlement pattern.

Williston is, arguably, the most extreme example of the changes transforming the face of Vermont in the waning years of the twentieth century. But it suggests some important questions. How does the landscape come to be what it is? If all landscapes are not created equal, what makes a "good" landscape? Who makes the decisions about how the land will be shaped? How are we to resolve the tensions between the community's right to enjoy the landscape and individuals' rights to do what they want on their own property? Do societies get the landscapes they deserve?

## THE CHANGING AMERICAN LANDSCAPE

All across America, the single greatest landscape change of the second half of the twentieth century has been the erosion of local identity. A nation that traditionally had been a patchwork of unique communities, built from local materials and reflecting local ideals, was quickly transformed by the booming economy of the post-war era. Millions of returning G.I.s put memories of urban crowding or rural poverty behind them to embrace the American dream of a house in the homogeneous suburbs. The inescapable accompaniment to suburban life was the gleaming car in the driveway, for unlike the city or the village, this was a landscape that was not made for walking. Once people were in their cars, it was easier to shop where you could park right out front; so that repository of American fantasies, the shopping mall, was born.

The designs of suburban houses, supermarkets, and shopping centers were often standardized somewhere far from where they were built, so that

Jan Albers

By the late 1990s, at Tafts Corners in Williston (above), farmland had been carved into large lots for a scattering of big-box stores. The village scale had virtually disappeared, to be replaced by a landscape dependent upon the automobile.

a Kmart in Colorado was identical to a Kmart in Georgia. From coast to coast, the American landscape was taking on a sameness that had never before been technologically possible or culturally desirable. The landscape that had once been an expression of local identity was now coming to be dictated by the demands of marketing.

Every state in the union was touched by these trends, but they had a greater impact in some regions than in others. Vermont was not immune to them, but, as had been the case in the past, they came to the Green Mountains later and with less force. The poverty and isolation of pre-war Vermont were rocky soil for the growth of modern consumer culture.

Back in 1953, Vermont's most ardent adopted daughter, Dorothy Canfield Fisher, wrote a book called *Vermont Tradition: The Biography of an Outlook on Life.* She wanted to trace the history of the real Vermont in order to explain the origins of what it meant to be a Vermonter. She began with the idea that the Vermont tradition was not about "the virtuous intention to give happiness to others," for:

*That would imply rearranging other people's lives for them! Vermont tradition is based on the idea that group life should leave each person as free as possible to arrange his own life. This freedom is the only climate in which (we feel) a human being may create his own happiness. Nobody else can do it for him.*

Fisher's Vermont was wry, tough, Yankee, and Republican—and it certainly describes a cultural strain that has been common in the Green Mountains since the early days. The belief that people have a right to do what they want on their own land dates back to the first days of settlement and was particularly strong in a state founded by a high proportion of people who chafed at restraints. Paradoxically, Vermont's history since World War II shows that this Yankee Kingdom has come to be in the vanguard of many conservation and preservation movements, which curtail the individual's right to act against the interests of society as a whole.

For just as the biggest lesson of Vermont's ecology is that human beings can only push the land so far, the biggest lesson of Vermont's land use history would seem to be a growing realization that the unique nature of this landscape and the communities it has spawned can only be retained through mutual cooperation.

Rural electrification was a going concern by the 1940s. Here a caterpillar clears the way while workers erect the poles and unroll the wires that will soon bring power to another Vermont village or farm.

## VERMONT AFTER WORLD WAR II

When World War II finally came to an end, Vermont was still the most rural state in the Union and one of the most remote. The population of around 370,000 had risen slowly, adding only about 40,000 people in the previous 50 years. Many households remained relatively poor and isolated. Rural electrification was well under way, but lots of people up in the mountains had not yet had the thrill of flicking on their own light switch. (Charles Edward Crane wrote that when electricity came to Bridport, Shoreham, and Addison in the 1940s, "The citizens made a public ceremony of extinguishing their oil lamps, in homes and schools and church.") Most of the state's back roads were unpaved, and even state highways wound slowly across the obstacle of the Green Mountains. Because train service ran regularly, people in rural regions could ride the rails to spend a day shopping in one of the larger towns. And by 1947, Vermonters were amazed to find that a whopping 4,500 passengers had boarded airplanes at Burlington airport in a single year.

Vermont had gained a national reputation during the War as the place that most purely epitomized the values and communal spirit of small-town America. Norman Rockwell's illustrations of earnest, craggy-faced Vermonters embodied the thoughtful sincerity of that old Yankee town-meeting democracy the troops were sent to defend. Vermont was also seen in the

## LIVING THE GOOD LIFE

Vermont agriculture has long attracted city folk who wanted to experience the romance of farming. A surprising number also became writers (probably out of need), publishing memoirs of their experiences of going "back to the land." One of the first, and most influential, was Helen and Scott Nearing's book, *Living the Good Life*, which described how two disgruntled, pacifistic, vegetarian, collectivist radicals fled city life to enter what they called "a pre-industrial, rural community" near Stratton, Vermont. They first moved there in the 1930s, publishing their reminiscence of this adventure in 1954. Their book, often reprinted, became a sort of Bible for a new generation of radicals in the 1960s and 70s. Here is their list of questions the city dweller should ask himself before he commits to the simple life:

*Many a modern worker, dependent on wage or salary, lodged in city flat or closely built-up suburb...has watched for a chance to escape the cramping limitations of his surroundings, to take his life into his own hands and live it in the country, in a decent, simple, kindly way.*

*Caution, consideration for relatives or fear of the unknown have proved formidable obstacles, however. After years of indecision he still hesitates. Can he cope with country life? Can he make a living from the land? Has he the physical strength? Must one be young to start? Where can he learn what he needs to know? Can he build his own house? Can he feed his family from the garden? Must he keep animals? How much will a farm tie him down? Will it be but a new kind of drudgery all over again? These and a thousand other questions flood the mind of the person who considers a break with city living.*

*This book is written for just such people. We maintain that a couple, of any age from twenty to fifty, with a minimum of health, intelligence and capital, can adapt themselves to country living, learn its crafts, overcome its difficulties, and build up a life pattern rich in simple values and productive of personal and social good.*

**Helen and Scott Nearing's mix of leftist politics and practical wisdom encouraged many of the Woodstock generation to head for the Green Mountains. The Nearings themselves left Vermont when ski developers encroached on their own good life; they spent many further decades in rural Maine, Scott dying at the age of 100 and Helen at 92, when her car hit a tree.**

simple world of Grandma Moses' paintings, where the church, the village, and the farm lay at the heart of the community. Wallace Nutting's photographs promoted an idyllic Yankee Vermont—sometimes complete with "real Vermonters" arrayed in Colonial dress. Walter Hard published popular poems replete with crusty Yankee "characters." And Robert Frost's mythic Vermont of hard-worn people scraping by amidst the apple orchards and the winter snows reached the level of genius. By 1944, Vermont had even made it to the top of the Hit Parade, as Margaret Whiting and the Johnny Mercer Orchestra did the state proud with the classic song, "Moonlight in Vermont." In an age of unprecedented inhumanity, Vermont become known as an oasis of physical beauty, sturdy calm, and good sense. Peaceful Vermont had become the perfect antithesis to the horrors of war.

Historical myths often develop just as the thing they describe is fading away. This has certainly been true of the myth of Vermont as an agricultural paradise. In the mid-twentieth century, farmland stretched from the valleys to the hills, but already most people were not farmers. Although two-thirds of the population lived in the country in the 1940s, as early as this only one-third of Vermonters actually farmed. About half of the land area in the state was in farms, down from 81 percent in 1900. Large tracts of marginal farmland were returning to forest, but there was still far more open land in 1945 than there is today. The old saw that in Vermont cows once outnumbered people turns out to have been untrue, but they were giving us a run for our money in 1946: humans 370,800, bovines 296,000.

Sheep and cows leave very different imprints on the land. The treeless, close-cropped grazing landscape of England's Yorkshire Dales (above) was largely created by sheep, and probably looks much like Vermont did in the nineteenth century. Cows, on the other hand, prefer to graze on flat land; their needs have led to a landscape like this in Shaftsbury (opposite), with hayfields in the valleys and mountain land covered by trees.

Corbis/Bettmann

By the end of World War II, the majority of Vermonters had never plowed a field or run their hands down the smooth, glossy flanks of their own cows. Yet Vermont's sense of itself remained tied to the hard-won nature of its farming, the gift of community agriculture bequeathed to the state, and the beauty of lush valley fields ringed by the dark green of the mountains. If we want to understand where Vermont has been in the past few decades and where we want it to go in the future, the place to start is still in the rock-ribbed fields where generations of men and women have put their hands on the land.

## QUEEN COW

When city people drive through the countryside, they often think farmland all looks alike. But, as this book has shown, each age has had its predominant modes of agriculture, and they have left different marks on the land. Because the agricultural transformations of the landscape seem so natural, it is easy to forget that they, too, are impermanent. The generations that saw a Vermont of open, untilled, stone-fenced fields of grazing sheep thought this was natural sheep country and would remain so; yet today, the sheep are almost gone.

The Vermont that seems most familiar to us, with its tree-fringed, clovered pastures and green hayfields, is actually a dairying landscape. The story of Vermont farming in the second half of the twentieth century is largely one of cows; dairy products have often accounted for over 80 percent of the state's gross farm receipts. The state is well-suited to dairy, for its high annual rainfall grows good hay, and it is located near large metropolitan areas with a huge demand for milk. While other states have seen trees cut down to make way for development, Vermont has seen them come back to an extraordinary degree. But there is nothing inherent or inevitable about the open, pastoral beauty of this land. Much of it came into being as open fields to serve Queen

Cynthia Locklin/Courtesy Saga Morgans, Shaftsbury, Vermont

Milk cans were still being used to haul milk from the farm to the bulk plant in 1959 (above, left). These neat rows helped to carry some of the 200,000,000 gallons of milk processed annually in that era by the United Farmers of New England plant in Enosburg Falls. But the milk can was soon to give way to the bulk tank, which stored milk on the farm until it could be suctioned into a gleaming steel milk truck like this one (above, right), shown unloading its gallons of cold fresh milk into an even larger tank at the bulk plant. From here, it would head to the breakfast tables of Boston, Hartford, and beyond.

Cow. Without her, the landscape would no longer be what we think of as Vermont.

The transition from sheep to dairying had taken place in Vermont after the Civil War, but for the next century dairy farms remained small and unmechanized. This was to change after the Second World War, as the government and the public demanded higher standards of sanitation. The public was now alert to the potential dangers of unpasteurized milk. And they were right to worry, because many farmers did not bother with such simple hygienic practices as cleaning their cows' udders or washing milk cans between uses.

New federal sanitation rules demanded a higher degree of cleanliness in the barns; inspectors began going out to farms to check on conditions. One of the most unpopular new regulations made it illegal to ship milk that had been produced in a barn with a wooden floor, since it had been found that wood could harbor the bug that caused the cow teat disease, mastitis. Most of the dairy barns in the state, especially in northern Vermont, had wooden floors, and pouring a new concrete floor was a big expense for a small operator. Donnie George remembers that in his first weeks working at the Vermont Department of Agriculture he spent a lot of time inspecting barns and explaining new sanitation rules. On his first day of inspecting, in 1963, he saw 13 barns, and not one of them passed. Some farmers made the change, but

George found that many of the older folks said, "Hey, I'll go as long as I can, and when they shut me down that's it."

The biggest blow to the small producer was the change from milk cans to bulk tanks. The farmer had traditionally milked by hand into pails, and then emptied the pails into tall metal milk cans. These were stored in a large vat of cold water, then put on the back of a truck or horse cart and taken to the local creamery to be sent to market. In many areas, pick-up companies came to the farm to get the milk cans. They were cheap to use and easy to transport.

But a revolution was coming to dairy farming, and it began with the clanking of stainless steel, as the first bulk tank was installed on a farm in the Champlain Valley in 1953. A bulk tank is a large stainless steel cooling tank capable of holding all the milk a farm can produce in a couple of days. In addition to the considerable expense of the tank itself, it required its own "milk house," a room connected to the barn, with a cement floor and electricity to run its cooling system. A large tanker truck would then suck the milk out of the tank with a hose and haul it to the creamery.

Middlemen who transported fluid milk to market loved this sanitary and efficient new arrangement and soon began requiring farmers to install bulk tanks (legal requirements mandating the use of bulk tanks followed by the mid-1950s). The expense for the farmer was considerable; pick-up companies were able to use the bulk tank requirement to squeeze out those farmers who lived in inconvenient spots way up in the hills. Stanley Wilson, a farmer from Derby, later remembered how some dairymen were ruined by the bulk tank requirement:

> *It was...the milk inspectors from most creameries. ...They got into bulk tanks and done away with the can and then that put a lot of stress on a lot of farmers a lot of them had to build their milk houses all over and buy new bulk tanks. And some of them had been buying bigger tanks to put cans in and didn't have them paid for when all of a sudden they switched over to the bulk tanks. And they had to go and buy another tank.*

Bulk tanks were to be the death of many more hill farms.

### DAIRY FARMING IN TRANSITION

As farming became more technologically complex, the Agricultural Experiment Station at the University of Vermont began to issue pamphlets aimed at teaching new methods of dairy farming. Publications like "What Makes Good Incomes on Dairy Farms?" (1951), "Financing Vermont Dairy Farms" (1953), and "Dairy Farming in Vermont" (1960) all urged farmers to do a "few

### HILL FARM

Old ways die,
But on the lost hill farms beyond the signboards,
Beyond the metal silos and macadam,
Now and again you come upon a man
Who lives his life as men before him lived it,
Trusting the past the way he trusts the winter
To end in spring...spring when the April promise
Of one small blade of grass coming alive
Assures him all dark meadows will survive.

—from "Hill Farm,"
by Kaye Starbird (1962)

**HAVE YOU SEEN ETHAN JETSON'S PLACE?**

The post-war generation was in love with the future; their faith in modern miracles extended to the farm, where mechanization was expected to take to the air. These drawings from the Vermont Extension Service show what the farmer of the year 2000 might expect: a personal helicopter/hovercraft for spraying crops (left) and a gigantic orchard sprayer taller than the fruit trees (right).

simple things": get more cows, breed better cows, feed them well, mechanize their operations, and keep labor costs down. The advice was good, but it could not save marginal farmers who were unable to modernize; thousands were ruined within a decade. There had been 10,637 dairy farms, producing about 1.5 billion pounds of milk per year in Vermont at the time of the first bulk tank in 1953. The herd sizes then averaged 25 milking cows. Ten years later, in 1963, there were 7,127 dairy farms—a loss of 3,510—but they were producing more milk. This consolidation of production was to continue, as fewer, larger operators produced more milk. By 1970, the number of dairy farms in the state was down to 4,153, with production at almost 2 billion pounds of milk a year. Each herd averaged over 60 cows, and due to better breeding and nutrition, each cow gave more milk. The trend has continued. By 1999, Vermont had only 1,714 dairy farms, but they were producing an all-time high of over 2.6 billion pounds of milk annually. The average Vermont dairy farm in that year consisted of 315 acres.

The trend toward fewer, bigger, more efficient dairy farms has had a great impact on the state. It finished off many hill farms that had managed to survive the end of the sheep craze and the Great Depression. All over the Vermont highlands, farms were again being abandoned.

A 1964 study of those who left farming in central Vermont showed a strong correlation between the inability to mechanize and farm abandonment. Of those who gave up farming, 90 percent were using milk cans, 25 percent still had work horses, and only one-third had hay balers. As one discouraged farmer put it: "I sold the cows when the barn floor collapsed, loaned out one horse when its mate died, sold the sheep when the fences got too weak, and now I rent the tillage land and have a town job."

Even though the state's population had continued to inch upwards, the 1960 Census showed that 188 Vermont towns had fewer people in 1960 than in 1850. (This was offset by the growth of Chittenden County, which gained 31,000 of the 33,000 people added to Vermont between 1910 and 1950.) The peak of twentieth-century farm abandonment came in 1966, when 917 dairy farms went under in a single year. A number of commentators began to worry that Vermont was losing too much of its agricultural heritage. Political scientist and author Andrew Nuquist, writing in 1964, agreed that it was sad to see the hill farms go, but advocated "tough love":

> *The rapid abandonment of farms and the loss of population is cause for real alarm about the future of towns in Vermont. Every year several hundred more farms are closed. ...In many cases these abandoned farms are sloping hill farms which probably should never have been operated at all. In a more primitive society where wants were few, horizons limited, and competition was slight, families could wrest a living from the slopes; but it cost the entire family, from small children up, endless hours of often fruitless labor. Today such lands are called sub-marginal and society understands that it has to pay heavy social costs to maintain families in such sterile areas. No amount of romanticizing by antiquarians can make conditions on such a place acceptable when status is measured by flush toilets and TV sets. There is no reason for weeping when such farms are abandoned for tillage and turned to more effective use, such as a permanent program of tree planting; there are problems when the weary land is permitted to produce only scrub second-growth trees.*

The 1980s were a bad time for dairy statewide. Milk consumption went down with public concerns over high-fat diets, and prices stagnated. The new technology had forced many farmers to assume huge debt loads (Donnie George saw some farmers carrying two-million-dollar debts), and they found it hard to repay them as the squeeze went on. The situation was made worse by low prices due to a glut of milk on the market. The federal

government stepped in to remedy this in 1986, with the whole-herd buyout program. This was a one-shot attempt to encourage some producers to get out of dairy farming, in the hopes of staunching the milk flood and raising prices for those who remained. The government paid farmers who agreed to either slaughter or export their dairy cows within three years. In Vermont, 192 dairy farmers chose to participate. The program successfully met its goals, but not without considerable political fallout. Those dairy farmers who survived tended to be farmers who had excellent herds and lower debts.

The 1990s have seen better times return to dairying. Sixty percent of the farmland in Vermont is devoted to dairying, and almost half of all dairy farms in New England are now in Vermont. About 80 percent of Vermont's total farm cash receipts were dairy-related in 1996.

Vermont now has to compete in a national market where even fluid milk can be transported easily across the country or around the world. The state's dairy farmers were helped by the passing of the Northeast Dairy Compact, which allows the six New England states to set higher prices in a region where the costs of production are greater than in other parts of the country. The Compact, challenged and upheld in federal court in 1997, paid out $18.4

Barns are among our most ephemeral landscape features, for their useful lives are often tied to their adaptability to modern farming technology; when a barn has outlived its usefulness, it is often too expensive to maintain. The fading glory of barns like this one in Bridport (above, left) contrasts with the sleek efficiency of a modern dairy barn (above). Each age has its own ideas about what animals require in a barn. The modern barn has sides that are almost completely open (although covered by opaque plastic curtains on the coldest days) because we now know that cows need plenty of ventilation to remain healthy.

million to Vermont dairy farmers between July 1997 and August 1998. With 1,815 dairy farms operating in Vermont on January 1, 1998, this means that dairy farmers received an average subsidy of $10,000 per farm. It has been estimated that without this protection, half the region's dairy farmers would be at risk of losing their livelihood. The Compact helps to maintain a local supply of milk, keeps farmland in production, and provides environmental benefits by preventing the development of valuable agricultural lands. Pricing and production costs are still the key to the continued health of this sector of Vermont's economy.

## BARNYARD DIVERSIFICATION

The trend in Vermont agriculture (with the exception of large dairy farms, which continue to consolidate) is now toward diversification, particularly as dairy farmers try to buffer themselves from the highs and lows of the milk market. Specialty foods and livestock have been the means of survival for many Vermont farmers, especially those with fewer than 100 acres. Beef is becoming an important business here, with Herefords, Angus, and Scotch Highlands the most popular breeds; there are now 15,000 beef cattle in the

Top: Alan Jakubek; right: Paul O. Boisvert

state. Poultry is growing after a long lull. There has been a vigorous movement to bring pasture animals back to the hillsides. Sheep are once again on the rise: there are 12,500 sheep in Vermont today, including a few resurgent Merinos, whose wool is again being marketed as the best in upmarket women's clothing catalogues. There is special and growing interest in dairy sheep and dairy goats. Exotics—emus, fallow deer, llamas, cashmere goats, ostriches, and game birds—are being tried. Market gardens, landscape nurseries, and Christmas tree farms are dotted around the state, along with apiaries, apple orchards, berry farms, and greenhouse tomato operations. A kind of agricultural entrepreneurialism is alive and well and encouraged by the state.

Many agricultural producers supply Vermont's booming specialty foods industry, where farm products are turned into everything from ice cream and cheese to salad dressing and salsa, with distribution throughout

## COWS OR CAMPERS

Many dairy farms have had to diversify to survive, raising new forms of livestock and crops, taking in guests or allowing camping on scenic portions of their property.

Jerry LeBlond

In the 1960s, the state was starting to recognize that the recreation boom might also be a help to Vermont's failing hill farmers. Malcolm I. Bevins, an Extension Economist at UVM, painted a rather rosy picture of the possibilities:

*The full impact upon the community which has witnessed the change in land use from agriculture to recreation has been favorable. This is amply illustrated by comparing the appearance of towns located in poor agricultural areas before and after this transition.*

*We in Vermont are extremely fortunate in having another land use which can be substituted where technology has made certain agricultural units unprofitable. All states are not so fortunate!*

The solution for the farmer was simple. In a section entitled "Desire to Work With People," Bevins went on:

*A primary consideration in recreational development is the interest and desire to work with people. A good herd of 50 Holstein cows will return to the dairyman $25,000 gross income. To equal this income, a campground operator must have approximately 250 sites. This means that at any one time there may be as many as 1,000 people at the campground—a substitution rate of 20 people for one cow. The dairy man needs to consider which he would rather work with—one cow or 20 people.*

*This may exaggerate my point, but one thing is certain—anyone interested in recreational development must like to work with people.*

Farming, and the close ties to the land it engenders, make it a calling that is often passed from parents to their children. This farm in Wallingford (above) has been in the same family for five generations.

Ken Burris

the country. The state's image as a pure and wholesome rural paradise is as vital to this industry as it is to tourism. Large-scale businesses with national reputations such as Ben & Jerry's Homemade, Cabot Creamery, Vermont Butter and Cheese, Shelburne Farms, and many others profit from this value-added attraction as much as, if not more than, the small-scale farmer. The state has done a great deal to promote the creation of the industry, offering technical assistance, incubator spaces, and marketing advice. Myth has often met reality, as conflicts have arisen over what products can be labelled "natural," "organic," or even "Vermont-made," when not every ingredient is native. Nevertheless, the Natural Organic Farmers Association reports that 14,000 acres are now in certified organic production.

## SAVING THE FARM

The United States will always need the capacity to supply its population with food; and with luck, Vermont will remain a viable agricultural state. Not all land is worth farming, and the twentieth century has done a pretty good job of putting Vermont agriculture in the places where it can thrive. But in many parts of the state, productive farmland is under threat from development. The traditional pattern of concentrated villages and town centers with clear boundaries ringed by farmland is being eroded by the scattered growth known as sprawl. Once usable farmland is covered by fast-food restaurants, suburban housing developments, and car dealerships, it is impossible to get it back.

Protecting farmland appears to be one way to retain the open look of a landscape, which is important both to individuals and to Vermont business.

How can agricultural land be protected? There are no simple solutions; virtually everything that has been suggested has been controversial. Planning would seem to be the place to start; towns and villages may be able to control development by planning where it should and should not go, giving a high priority to retaining good farmland as farmland. Those who make decisions on the local level could be helped to do so if there were state and federal guidelines about the importance of avoiding development on productive agricultural land.

It has been suggested, further, that the state could help by revising an exemption in the laws regulating septic systems that has inadvertently led to the loss of many thousands of acres of farmland. A drive around rural Vermont will show that many newer houses are on lots of a size described by the phrase "too big to mow, too small to plow." This pattern of development is a result of what has been dubbed the "10-acre loophole," created by the last revision to the state's septic laws, Act 249 of 1969. This law states that any house built on less than 10 acres of land needs to file a septic plan showing that the land has passed a percolation test, qualifying it for a simple and inexpensive conventional in-ground septic system or, failing that, a design for a more expensive mound system. But lots of 10 acres or more are exempt from state septic review under the dubious assumption that if you have that much land there must be a spot on it somewhere that will handle a septic system. The result is that Vermont has some of the most lax septic regulations in the country, being one of the few states that does not require every new septic system to be inspected. This poses a serious public health risk in parts of the state.

Among the many exotic animals now being raised on Vermont's specialty farms are the llama (top), often used for the recreational activity known as llama trekking, and the emu (bottom), a large bird prized both for meat and for the oil it exudes, used in the making of cosmetics and other beauty products

Top: Paul O. Boisvert; bottom: Alan Jakubek

### IN LAND WE TRUST

Many of the greatest successes in saving farmland have come from creative combinations of public and private initiatives, many of which have come under the umbrella of the national land trust movement. Vermont's modern land protection movement began in 1977, when a small group of people in Woodstock joined together to create the Ottauquechee Regional Land Trust to protect land permanently from development. This group had such success that it formed the nucleus of a statewide organization, the Vermont Land Trust (VLT). Land trusts are private, non-profit organizations with broad-based bipartisan political support that bring together people who believe in the idea of land stewardship. With a combination of public and private moneys, trusts attempt (in the words of the VLT mission statement) "to protect those productive, recreational, and scenic lands which help give Vermont and its communities their rural character."

Land trusts do not usually buy land from its owners, but instead obtain development rights and conservation restrictions; the owner gives these up voluntarily, either by donation or in exchange for the dollar value of such rights. A conservation easement is then added to the deed, stating that the land in question cannot be sold for development and must remain available for agriculture, forestry, or other stipulated uses. The land still belongs to the owner, with all other rights intact, and can continue to be bought and sold. But when the owner sells it, the easement remains in place and the buyer cannot develop it. Beyond that, the owner can plant any crop, do logging under a forest management plan, or whatever else any farmer would do. The money paid to farmers by the land trust is often used to ensure the farm's continuation for future generations.

The Vermont Land Trust and similar groups hope to ensure that farmland like this near Danby Four Corners will always be a part of the state's landscape.

Jerry LeBlond

The Vermont Land Trust is the largest and most influential private organization devoted to conserving agricultural and forest lands in the state; and it provides a model for a number of smaller local land trusts. Its funding comes from a mixture of member dues and contributions (40 percent), grants from the state and from private foundations (35 percent; the Freeman Foundation and the Merck Fund are among several prominent contributors), capital gifts and bequests (15 percent), and contributions from landowners to defray the costs of conserving their properties (10 percent). Since 1977, it has conserved over 184,000 acres, including more than 225 working farms. The 1990s have been a particularly booming decade for the VLT, in part through the generosity of the Freeman Foundation, which contributed over $36 million to land conservation and historic preservation in Vermont in the five years from 1994–1998. Add these private successes to those of the publicly funded Vermont Housing and Conservation Board, and it is clear that Vermonters are strongly motivated to achieve a high level of statewide land protection.

## THE STORY OF SOUTHWIND FARM

The story of the Graf family of Southwind Farm in Rupert has been recorded by Greg Sharrow at the Vermont Folklife Center; it provides a good example of how land trusts work. Bob Graf can trace his ancestry, and his farm's history, back nearly 200 years. In the post-Revolutionary world, James Leach claimed much of the fertile bottomland of the Mettawee Valley; today, the Valley remains a tight-knit community where the Leaches, the Sheldons, and the Harwoods are tied over generations by blood and land. Bob Graf inherited his Grandmother Leach's 400-acre farm and ran it well. But Graf and his wife had no sons, and their three daughters had no interest in taking over the farm. When Bob wanted to retire, his grandsons, the four Russo boys, seemed to want to continue the family's farming tradition. But Bob did not have the resources to wait until they were old enough to take over. He turned to the

Vermont Land Trust to help the family through this difficult transition period.

The Land Trust recognized the Graf farm's importance to its community and agreed to buy the development rights to the land. Through a conservation easement, the Grafs stipulated that the farm would remain permanently as agricultural land and could not be split up and sold for development. In return, the Land Trust gave them a considerable sum of money for development rights and agreed to have its Conservation Stewardship Program monitor compliance with the conservation easement in perpetuity. As an added bonus, the Grafs received tax relief because their land could now only be taxed for its agricultural use and not at a higher rate for its development potential. This allowed Bob Graf to lease the farm out to a good tenant family, the Carabeaus, until his grandsons were old enough to take over.

On Southwind Farm in Rupert (above), the younger members of the family have realistic hopes of supporting themselves by farming since the farm's development rights were sold to the Vermont Land Trust.

Bob Graf would have made more money selling to developers, but he would have lost his heritage. As he told Greg Sharrow of the Vermont Folklife Center, "I sold the development rights so the land can't be developed. If I hadn't had grandsons I would probably have sold it for a million dollars and paid the federal government off and moved to Florida. These boys were brought up here. And I think some day some of the brothers will be farming here. They're all pretty committed."

Says grandson Joel Russo:

> *From what I know about it I think it was a smart decision to do it. Especially if he can get some tax easement on it, that's going to help out. But I think it definitely takes a lot of pressure off him. ... I remember when we were selling our cows, the auctioneer—who's a good friend of his—offered him I think one or two million dollars for the whole place. Obviously he decided not to do that. That's pretty tempting though, when you've been working for 40 years, 14 hours a day, and have someone come along and say I'll take it all off your back. But he didn't do it.*

Like the Grafs, many farm families find it deeply satisfying to know that the land they have worked on and loved for decades will always remain open. And the tourism industry reaps its own handsome rewards from the resulting aesthetically pleasing landscape.

## VERMONT IS A WAY OF LIFE

> *Traveling through Vermont is like visiting a vast outdoor museum, a countryman's Williamsburg, a Walt Disney World where elderly Vermont farmers and their wives go strolling like Mickey Mouse and Minnie Mouse against a stage set of white frame houses and village*

*greens. Not only is it full of antique shops, but taken as a whole it is like one huge antique shop. Half of Vermont's residents seem employed in selling old chairs, or spinning wheels, or wooden sap buckets, while the other half is peddling maple syrup, or honey made by genuine Vermont bees...or native-grown corn, or rabbits, or homemade soap and candles, or old post cards, or whatever. It is a wonder that a descendant of one of America's great robber baron families hasn't tried to preserve Vermont in toto, or that the National Park Service hasn't persuaded the Congress to buy it. For history hunters it is an excellent game preserve.*

—CHARLES T. MORRISSEY, *Vermont: A History* (1981)

Nearly nine million tourists spend the night in Vermont every year, and a good share of them drive around the state, oohing and ahhing over views of farms and woodlands, in the belief that they are seeing places that have remained largely unchanged for a century or more. But as this history of the landscape has shown, the Vermont we love today is a relatively new invention. The visitor of 200 years ago was assailed by an unscenic wasteland of

## THE VERMONT HOUSING AND CONSERVATION BOARD

Vermont's environmental movement has spawned some strange—and strangely successful—bedfellows. The most unique may be the Vermont Housing and Conservation Board (VHCB), which was created by the legislature in 1987 to link the seemingly contradictory causes of land conservation and affordable housing. This coalition brought together those who feared ill-conceived development was eating up valuable farmland and those who found it was raising housing prices beyond the reach of many lower income and working people. The VHCB works with land trusts and housing trusts to develop self-sustaining projects that meet their goals of preserving villages, farms, and forests while creating perpetually affordable housing. The success of this imaginative approach has made the VHCB a model for similar initiatives around the country.

Frank J. Lattier

The VHCB provided a grant to turn a landmark eighteenth-century home, the Evarts House (left), in Windsor, into sustained housing for the elderly. At the same time, they helped renovate the old town hospital next door into the Stoughton House, a residential care facility. Both projects were a boon to the traditional town center as well as providing important living spaces.

rotting stumps as the first Yankees cleared the land. A century later, Vermont was the most rural state in America, much of its land a treeless moonscape, the tops of even the highest hills exposed. The felicitous combination of farmland and forests we see today is an invention of the twentieth century and has as much to do with agriculture's failures as with its successes.

Why does Vermont agriculture and its resulting landscape possess such an extraordinary image-making power? Tourists pumped over two billion dollars into the state economy in 1997 (raising over $64 million from the 7 percent room and meals tax), many of them choosing to believe they were seeing something unique that much of America has lost. One wonders if Vermonters need to believe in a mythic view of Vermont even more than the tourists do.

The image of Vermont as a rural paradise can be traced to before the Second World War, as the locals sought to entice tourists and holiday home buyers to a still-poor state wracked by declining agriculture, stagnant industrial development, and the Great Depression. But in the atmosphere of exuberance that followed V-J Day, a small group of enterprising Vermonters decided to make lemonade out of the state's sour economic outlook by founding a magazine that would unabashedly extol the state's bucolic virtues. Earle Newton, director of the Vermont Historical Society before the war, saw a copy of the first slick state-sponsored promotional tool, the magazine *Arizona Highways*, and told his friends that he believed "a small percentage of the funds spent on advertising the state could have a greater impact in a magazine which 'sold' the state purely on the basis of what it was. 'Vermont is a way of life,' would be the theme."

The first cover of *Vermont Life*, autumn 1946 (top). This quarterly, funded by the state and still going strong today, has always been devoted to turning Vermont's lack of industrial development into an asset. *Vermont Life*'s earliest advertising campaign used editor Earle W. Newton's phrase, "Vermont is a Way of Life," as its slogan (bottom). The accompanying images showed plain, Yankee farming at its most picturesque, with no modern elements to intrude.

The first issue of *Vermont Life* magazine was put together by editor Earle Newton and his team, the Manchester poet Walter Hard, Sr., Professor Arthur Wallace Peach from the English department at Norwich University, and the writer and storekeeper, Vrest Orton, of Weston. Five thousand copies hit the newsstands in the autumn of 1946, and all were gone before the week was out. The combination of beautiful photography (with its echo of the great photomagazine of the era, *Life*), homely values, and unremittingly optimistic news struck a chord in a nation reeling from the shocks of war. By the end of its first year, the staff felt confident enough to publish 40,000 copies. The magazine's reaffirmation of rural life and community has only increased its popularity over half a century; today its circulation hovers at around 90,000. Its largely upbeat picture of Vermont, it should be noted, reflects its status as a state-funded publication.

Both tourism and other forms of development were hampered in Vermont by the rudimentary state of the road system. In 1943, the state was proudly boasting that 9 percent of the roads were now paved and 51 percent were graveled, with "only" 40 percent classified as "primitive." Vermont's north-south highways were already so busy, the smart money suggested there would soon be a new highway through the center of the state. By the time the war ended, Vermont transport historian William Wilgus was worrying about "the injuries that would result from a constant procession of commercial vehicles—trucks and buses—speeding through a quiet country than which there is none more beautiful in the world."

But change was coming—even to Vermont. In 1956, President Eisenhower approved the Federal Highway Act, which was to build 41,000 miles of highway to link every major city in America by 1972 in what was then called "the largest public works program ever attempted on earth." Vermont was to have 321 miles of federal interstate highway, to be built at a cost of one million dollars per mile. The first section in Vermont was begun at Guilford in 1957. When it was finished, I-91 would go straight up the Connecticut River Valley in eastern Vermont, with I-89 splitting off to the northwest at White River Junction headed for Montpelier, Burlington, and Canada. The plan meant 80 percent of all Vermonters would live within 30 miles of an entrance to one of these speedy new roads.

The legacy of Vermont's interstates has been mixed. Their routes proved to be more subtle than the reviled Green Mountain Parkway would ever have been (although one of their engineers may have been overly

## FIFTIES AMERICA TAKES TO THE ROADS

Maybe it was those powerful V-8 engines: Americans of the 1950s loved to get in their cars and drive. The era's idea of great tourism involved seeing the scenery as if it were on a drive-in movie screen, framed by the great rectangle of a windshield. One *Vermont Life* story of the era encouraged drivers to "get off the beaten path," unfortunately illustrating the piece with an image (left) of a slow-moving vehicle seemingly designed to drive a motorist crazy.

## LITTLE GREY HOME ON THE INTERSTATE

Vermont's interstate highways were generally routed through districts that were not very populous, but every mile still had to cut through someone's land. One Vermont transplant, the writer Marguerite Hurrey Wolf, tells the sad story of how this happened to her family in a chapter of her book *Anything Can Happen in Vermont* (1965) entitled "Little Grey Home on the Interstate":

*I have nothing against Progress. I'm tickled to death with indoor plumbing and have long since signed a truce with the Disposal. But when we bought our house and ninety acres in Vermont, "To have and hold," we were naive enough to think that those words meant what they said.*

*I've had enough experience with country roads in the mud season, and in the idea season, and in the hot season...to know that interstate highways represent progress. They are smooth, fast and scenic. The only trouble was that we didn't count on our most personal habits becoming part of the scenery.*

**The building of the interstates had serious environmental repercussions. In this 1966 view of the newly built I-91 (above, right), the Bellows Falls bridge flies high over the Williams River, dwarfing the homestead beneath. The engineering feat of blasting road-cuts through rock was carried out by men like these (above, left), drilling blasting holes in the path of I-91.**

*Protected by all that acreage, it never occurred to us that the interstate would see fit to cut our land neatly in half and miss the house by a scant puff of carbon monoxide.*

*A direct hit would have emptied the house but filled the wallet. The near miss changed the character of the house and threatened to empty the wallet.*

*Besides we had a sentimental attachment to our old house. With misgivings, we decided to turn our bad ears toward the throughway, plant every quick growing hedge in the Sunday Times garden section ads, and stay put.*

*That's what we decided when the threat of the highway became an impending reality. But somewhat later, when our meadows were crawling with soil borers, surveyors, and highway engineers, my husband was appointed to a new job two hundred miles away. ... What prospective buyers would believe that our move was purely coincidental with the approach of over-sized wheels which ground slowly towards our house? Very few...*

*We bought the house because it was historic and charming, convenient and cheap. Nine years and five thousand dollars of improvements later, we sold the house for the same reasons. It was still historic, still charming, still convenient, and thanks to the throughway, cheaper than when we bought it.*

optimistic in arguing that he believed it was possible to "fit the highways into the hillsides with such success that they simply 'belong.'"). From early on, they had the additional virtue of being free of the tacky billboards so prevalent in other states, since the Vermont legislature had shown the foresight to protect the state's valuable tourist image by banning off-premises roadside advertising in 1968.

But most of Vermont's recent development has not been along the paths of the interstates. As traffic grows ever more congested in the Champlain and Connecticut River Valleys, you can still drive through the high mountain forests lining Vermont's freeways for miles, wondering where the people live. Most are living out of sight of the interstate.

## SKI BOOM

One of Vermont's most abruptly mushrooming businesses, however, certainly saw its growth assisted by the building of the freeways. Appropriately, the new ribbon roads on the ground were echoed by the long white ski trails beginning to snake down the faces of some of Vermont's tallest mountains.

The state's ski industry traces its roots to a table at the Corner House of the White Cupboard Inn in Woodstock, Vermont, in 1934, where a group of young men sat talking about the popular sport of ski jumping. According to writer Charles Edward Crane's account in *Winter in Vermont* (1947), one of them turned to their landlady and said, "Mrs. Royce, each of us is spending forty dollars apiece to enjoy a weekend in Vermont, yet the most we can do in a day is to climb a hill half a dozen times. We want to do all the skiing we can on a weekend. We want to be carried uphill." The Royces set to work to find out whether there was any truth to the rumors that a marvelous device that would defy gravity in this way already existed in Canada. They tracked it down to a lodge in the Laurentian Mountains of Québec, where the first North American rope tow was up and running. It was soon duplicated in Woodstock, and Vermont recreation was never to be the same.

Little rope tows were soon sprouting in the fields of hopeful farmers, out to make a quick buck. But they were quickly squeezed out by a burgeoning industry that came to demand extensive capital investments. The first great Vermont ski resort, and still the only one with a measure of European cachet, was Stowe, where skiers were already tackling Mount Mansfield in considerable numbers by the mid-1930s. The Toll House trail got a rope tow in 1936, and Mount Mansfield was scaled by the state's first chair lift in 1940. The first wave of competing resorts soon sprang up in Stowe's wake, including Bromley (1937), Pico Peak (1937), and Mad River Glen (1947). By 1948, there were seven ski areas in the state large enough to have cable-type lifts, and they were bringing in about a million dollars a year. In an industry

Skiing has long been a sport for the fashionable. The Killington ski bunnies of 1962 (right) seem to have reached a happy state of suspended animation on the slopes.

The first American contraption to move skiers uphill was this primitive rope tow (above, left), strung together from 1,800 feet of rope and an old Model-T truck engine on Clinton Gilbert's farm just outside Woodstock in 1934. It cost $500. Its more elaborate descendants now help to bring Vermont half-a-billion dollars a year.

with a growth rate of 10–12 percent, these were followed by a second group in the late Fifties and early Sixties: places like Jay, Burke, Okemo, Mt. Snow, Sugarbush, Stratton, and the giant, Killington. By 1961, there were 21 major Vermont ski areas, with receipts of about $72 million. By 1996–1997, Vermont had 26 areas pumping about half a billion dollars into the state's economy.

Skiing drew a different crowd (most from outside Vermont), who responded to a vision of the state that was often at odds with its more familiar bucolic image. While Stowe tended to advertise itself as a picturesque New England village with skiing, other areas fitted themselves out in ersatz Alpine or A-frame moderne. The industry has catered to the status aspects of this increasingly expensive sport; as early as the 1960s, the locals had dubbed one ski area "Mascara Mountain."

The ski industry has been beneficial for parts of Vermont, bringing in the state's largest concentration of tourists and providing boosts to local economies in many of the mountain towns that had been most devastated by the collapse of hill farming. But the benefits of skiing have often come at a

Left: Woodstock Historical Society Archives; right: Courtesy Hanson Carroll/Vermont Life

substantial cost to the landscape. The debate over the effects of snowmaking on streams and wildlife has been acrimonious, but the industry's greatest environmental impact has been in ski-related development problems. As ski areas became more elaborate during the boom years of the 1960s, developers were quick to provide second homes, hotels, restaurants, bars, shops, gas stations, and other facilities geared to the trade.

If the public does not participate in making landscape choices, landscapes will be chosen for us. Towns and villages soon learned that it was not the ski area itself that threatened to change their communities so much as the development that went with it. As early as 1971, a study of the impact of the ski industry on Vermont's communities found it was leading to uncontrolled strip development. In Windham County, the numbers of new hotels and motels increased by 50 percent between 1962 and 1970. In Dover, a local official lamented, "Boy, have we got problems. And all the problems come from building before we had our zoning." Commercial development was robbing many villages of their beauty and sense of community while putting

In the 1970s, Vermont skiing was transformed by new technology that enabled ski areas to make their own snow. At first this seemed like an unmitigated blessing, but environmentalists soon expressed concerns about the depletion of mountain streams and the disruption of animal habitats. Developers, in turn, accuse environmentalists of using such issues as preserving bear habitats as a cover for blocking any ski area expansions they do not want.The debate over snowmaking has now raged for two decades, a classic example of society weighing an industry's benefits against its costs.

Alan Jakubek

enormous—and expensive—demands for increased services on the town. The seriousness of the situation finally spurred the state to pass its first land-use legislation, the Vermont Municipal Regional Planning and Development Act, in 1968. The act gave towns the power to develop and enforce local town and regional plans. Its effect was swift and striking. By 1970, nearly 100 Vermont towns had adopted some sort of zoning.

Skiing led to a substantial increase in the number of vacation homes and condominiums, many of which were built in environmentally fragile mountain areas. Initially, development was so rampant and unregulated that some towns were soon in the odd situation of having to provide services to more second homes than there were primary homes in the town. Many towns more than doubled in size. Warren's grand list went from $6 million to a staggering $451 million in the 16 years between 1960 and 1976 as second homes, with their high assessment value, came onto the tax rolls.

In the 1950s, the pattern of second-home buying in Vermont still centered on the restoration of derelict farmhouses. But by 1972, writer Rockwell Stephens was saying that "the little white farmhouse at the end of the road, with barn, fields and woodlot—we picked it up years ago for $6,000—that kind of a gem is gone forever." In its place was the leisure home (often a ski pad) that could just as well have been in Sun Valley as in Stratton. Poorly planned housing was sprouting all over the state, including this development (above) near St. Johnsbury.

By 1973, Vermont's greatest concentrations of vacation homes were in the ski towns of Wilmington, Sherburne, Winhall, Stowe, Warren, Ludlow, and Dover, which accounted for over 5,700 second homes. In 1996, seven ski towns again had the highest numbers of vacation homes, here listed with their local ski areas: Sherburne (Killington), Stowe (Mount Mansfield), Winhall (Stratton), Wilmington (Haystack and Mount Snow), Warren (Sugarbush and Mad River Glen), Ludlow (Okemo), and Dover (Mount Snow). Some of these towns also figure in the list of 10 Vermont hamlets that consist of more than 70 percent vacation homes. Country stores that once sold nails and chewing tobacco now carry $300 ski sweaters and sesame noodles. The locals who have held on enjoy better employment opportunities than they had in the hill farm days, although often at a high cost to their sense of community.

As winters have become milder in the last few years, there has been an acceleration in the movement to make the state's ski resorts into all-season destinations. This is something of a return to an earlier pattern, when spa visitors and fledgling automobile tourists took to Vermont in the summer. Ski area investors are now busily adding golf courses, tennis courts, and water parks in the hopes of attracting more warm-weather visitors. Killington, for example, is hoping to build a village that, according to the Vermont Natural Resources Council, "will have a more or less constant presence of some 30,000 people." The potential environmental impact of this level of development in a fragile mountain ecosystem is substantial; the effect on surrounding lands and towns will also be significant, leading to unforeseeable alterations in patterns of land use.

The look of the land is still vitally important to the tourism industry. Vermont will never have the wildest wilderness, the highest mountains, or the longest ski trails. But it does have a physical and cultural landscape of great beauty that remains relatively unspoiled. It has beautiful architecture, scenic villages, open farmland, and dark-treed mountains in unique combination. In recognition of this special landscape, Vermonters took the environmental high road years ago, passing a billboard ban prohibiting off-premises roadside advertising in 1968 and the "bottle bill" of 1972 that made Vermont the second state (after Oregon) to fight roadside trash by putting a deposit on alcohol and soft-drink bottles and cans. Despite their strong independent streak, Vermonters have given consistent bipartisan support to keeping the state beautiful. Yet suburbanization, strip development, and an influx of big-box stores continue to undermine Vermont's traditional communities.

Many tourists have said they could tell when they entered Vermont because "everything just started to look different." This is largely due to Vermont's billboard ban, dating from 1968. These billboards ironically advertising Vermont businesses (above, left) are located just over the border on New York 7, showing what Vermont would look like without the billboard law. The same road (VT 9) is shown on the Vermont side (above right), two miles in from the New York line.

Cynthia Locklin

## WOODS OR WILDERNESS?

*This, then, is the central paradox: wilderness embodies a dualistic vision in which the human is entirely outside the natural. If we allow ourselves to believe that nature, to be true, must also be wild, then our very presence in nature represents its fall. The place where we are is the place where nature is not. If this is so—if by definition wilderness leaves no place for human beings, save perhaps as contemplative sojourners enjoying their leisurely reverie in God's natural cathedral—then also by definition it can offer no solution to the environmental and other problems that confront us.*

—William Cronon, *"The Trouble with Wilderness"* (1995)

One of the greatest environmental changes in Vermont since the Second World War is the return of the forest. Vermont today looks more like it did in

**The ski industry, while luring people to enjoy nature, can transform nature almost beyond recognition, as this photo of Killington (above) demonstrates.**

## THE MAKING OF A FORESTER

In his autobiography, *The Making of a Forester*, Vermont's Perry Merrill presents a picture of forestry in which managing trees is a breeze compared to managing people. Many of Vermont's largest ski areas were developed on his watch. He was one of the state's major players in opening up the mountains for recreational uses, and for the sprawl that often accompanied them. Here he describes how rich he might have become if he had not been so honest:

*When the construction of the four-mile access road into the proposed Killington ski area was under consideration, there were two possible routes, one via an old log road and the other to the east through a farm which was selected. Here was a chance if I had wished to take it to tell the farmer if he would give me a building lot or two I would make sure that the road would go through his property. Today the farm is extensively developed with ski lodges and business enterprises. I never asked for a lot.*

the presettlement period that it has at any time in the past 200 years. But we must not confuse the return of the trees with the return of the wilderness. As environmental historian William Cronon reminds us, the whole idea of the woods as the "wilderness" is a human invention, created by Europeans who had no idea of how to deal with a forest they did not understand.

The woods are coming back, but the wilderness is gone forever. We can lament the passing of that massive forest of trees, the yard-wide white pine, but it will never return. We are not the only creatures who matter here. And it is lucky that we live in an age with enough money and leisure to allow us to make a valid argument for preserving large tracts of forests. But as long as people are here, these woods will not be wilderness; maintaining them is our responsibility. How do we choose among the many ways that have been suggested for doing that job?

The early twentieth century saw the beginnings of the science of forestry. The first director of the U.S. Forest Service, Gifford Pinchot, loved to tell people that "trees could be cut and the forest preserved at one and the same time," a statement that has made him anathema to more than one generation of environmentalists. His ideas on forest management soon made their way to Vermont, where they were put into practice under the tutelage of Vermont's charismatic state forester, Perry Merrill. In a long career, Merrill devoted his life to making the Vermont woods a well-managed "working" forest. Whether he succeeded will depend upon what sort of work you think a forest should do.

After World War II, the state was ready to get back to the job of selling its forestry plan to a populace that was not used to having to think about its woodlot use. The great selling point was the idea that woodlands are just like farmlands and should be managed in much the same way. As a 1947 state report, written under Perry Merrill's guidance, put it:

> *The major problem confronting the practice of forestry is the fact that it has not been considered from a practical business standpoint. Forests have been considered as mines of wealth to be exploited at the whims of the owner; as an appendage to the farm to be ruined or saved according to personal desire or needs; or as a product to be removed from the land to make way, in many instances, for a dubious agriculture.*

Later in this report, the theme is stated even more bluntly: "The chief reasons for planting trees are economic ones—planting trees pays. Idle land is a liability; with forests, an asset."

The forestry programs of the Forties and Fifties focused on fire protection (a problem considered serious since a series of major burns in the early twentieth century), eradicating insects and diseases, reforestation of private

Paul O. Boisvert

lands, sustaining high forest yields, starting seedling nurseries, encouraging the creation of municipal forests, and acquiring more state forest land. In mid-century, the "tree farm" model held sway, but by the Sixties there was greater recognition of the recreational values of Vermont's forests. The economy was booming, the public had more leisure time, and skiing introduced many people to the woods for the first time. Recognizing these mixed uses, in 1955 the Forestry Department became the Vermont Department of Forests and Parks. The skiers who stopped to listen might have heard the sawmills buzzing, as the Department took out more than 30 million cubic feet of lumber a year. Lumbering, which has always vied with farming for the title of Vermont's most traditional employment, was giving full-time work to over 8,000 people and accounting for more than $30 million a year in 1959.

Public and private reforestation efforts continued, but by the 1970s a curious phenomenon was appearing among the trees. As Brian Stone of the Vermont Forest, Parks and Recreation Department tells it, state foresters who had devoted their lives to getting people to plant red pine went back to their stands and found hardly any red pine. The forests that were reappearing on abandoned farmlands were natural regrowth, not the seedlings the foresters had provided. It became clear that if you just kept the cows out, the forest would come back rapidly on its own. There did not seem to be much point in planting trees. The forest has its own ways of determining what it will be. There is something almost encouraging in knowing that a century of scientific forestry has gone by and the trees are still capable of giving us orders.

One of the greatest preservatives of forest and farmland in Vermont has been the Current Use legislation, which mandates that those foresters and farmers who sign up for the program will only be taxed on the use to which the land is being put, and not assessed at its development value. Forest owners putting land into the program agree to create a forest management plan. Both farmers and forest owners also commit to keeping the designated acres undeveloped for a certain period of time or pay a penalty for early removal. In return, the state pays towns the tax differential between the land's current use value and the town's assessment. The program has been chronically underfunded by the state, but that problem has now been largely resolved by revisions in the state's property tax system called for by the recently enacted Act 60 (1997). As of 1998, the number of acres enrolled in the current use program totaled 458,377 acres of agricultural land and 1,047,377 acres of forestland. Vermont is a greener place today because forest owners and farmers have not had to sell off acres for development in order to pay their taxes.

The Vermont Land Trust is also a major player in protecting the state's forests as well as its farmland. In its most dazzling deal to date, in December of 1998 the VLT, along with The Conservation Fund (based in Virginia),

In the early years of the twentieth century, forest management could simply mean replanting (top). Recent technological changes, of which this feller-buncher (bottom) is a good example, have reduced labor costs and increased productivity.

Top: Courtesy of Vermont Department of Forests, Parks and Recreation; bottom: Gary F. Salmon

signed a $26-million deal to purchase 133,289 acres of forest in the Northeast Kingdom from the Champion International Paper Company. This vast tract, including 31 percent of Essex County, will be available both for recreation and for timber harvesting in a part of the state that remains heavily reliant on the lumber industry. The State Legislature ratified their financial contribution to this purchase in the 1999 Session.

People tend to think that most of the land used for logging is owned by large lumber companies, but these actually hold only 15 percent of Vermont's forested acres (down from 25 percent a decade ago). Most loggers would tell you that they do what they do because they love the woods and people need the products trees give us. Many environmentalists believe the forests should remain undisturbed habitat for wildlife and humankind.

Both can stake claim to some moral ground. Logging is a way of life that goes back to the first settlements, and loggers cut trees to put food on their tables. On the other side, it is easy to point to clear-cuts and depletion of habitat caused by logging; if the woods are a temple, their cutting can be nothing other than desecration. At the heart of this is a viewpoint that divides the world into "natural" landscapes and "working" landscapes and declares that the woods are inherently more "natural" than other places. But what is natural about a forest that has been completely cut down at least three times and where logging abounds in the heart of the Green Mountain National Forest? Where there are people, the landscape will be "worked," whether through the cutting of logs or the tramping of hiking boots. We create the landscape—in the woods as well as in the fields or the towns—and consequently must take responsibility for our actions there.

Botanists have long talked of "forest succession," but Vermont has a history of "successive forests." The woods that provided the original Abenaki homeland became the settlers' nightmare, the farmers' woodlot, and the loggers' meal ticket. Now most people experience the forest through recreation. Of the 13 percent of Vermont land that is in public hands, nearly 12 percent is forested and reserved for recreational uses. Nearly half of that, a total of 346,000 acres, is controlled by the federal government as the Green Mountain National Forest. Most of the rest is in 48 state parks (two of which are largely undeveloped), 36 state forests, 23 designated natural areas, and 147 fish and wildlife accesses. Here people come to camp, hike, swim, picnic, bird-watch, and engage in a variety of other outdoor activities.

The forests that once threatened the settler generations have been transformed, and largely tamed, into environments that are recreation-friendly. Here, a family enjoys a hike at Jamaica State Park.

As more people have begun to come to the woods as a temporary escape from more urban environments, conflicts have arisen between public and private uses of land. Back in settlement times, and even in the late nineteenth-century world described in Rowland Robinson's novels, people walked and hunted and fished their way through the landscape at will. Vermont is the only state whose constitution actually guarantees the right to hunt and fish on unposted private land:

> *The inhabitants of this state shall have liberty in seasonable times to hunt and fowl on the lands they hold, and on other land not enclosed, and in a like manner to fish in all boatable and other waters (not private property) under proper regulations, to be made and provided by the General Assembly.*

Many people have interpreted this as protection for other uses of private land, as well—hiking, snowshoeing, and cross-country skiing—but these traditional uses remain untested by the courts.

In a Vermont where people worked the land with their hands, hunting and fishing seemed a logical extension of their time in the woods or fields. Many hunters feel, as one put it in John M. Miller's book, *Deer Camp: Last Light in the Northeast Kingdom*, that the urge to hunt is an instinct:

> *We have this, we have within each and every one of us, especially the male species of the human race, we have this innate sense of always*

Paul O. Boisvert

*wanting to go back to nature, and always wanting to provide, to be the winner of the game, to bring home the game, to bring home the meal, bring home the good, or something like that. That instinct is extremely, extremely embedded in us, you know.*

But other evidence suggests that the desire to hunt is learned, not innate; many Vermonters are repelled by hunting. And it would be wrong to assume that reactions to hunting divide strictly along native versus flatlander lines. There are natives who do not like hunting, and flatlanders who moved here to get more of it. Hunting is bound to remain an area of cultural conflict in Vermont for some time to come.

## VERMONT ENVIRONMENTALISM COMES OF AGE

The environmental awareness and social activism that have characterized Vermont in the second half of the twentieth century have created a vibrant environmental movement in the state. Vermont is home to active chapters of the major national environmental organizations. The Audubon Society, with its emphases on natural history education and birding, has nine chapters in the state and runs the Green Mountain Audubon Nature Center in

## ADAM SMITH'S FOREST?

English political economist Adam Smith (1723–1790) believed that the "invisible hand" of the free market would always tend toward prosperity. Modern critics often disagree, suggesting that the "invisible hand" has led to an occasionally destructive lack of regulation.



While Perry Merrill and other early foresters were hearty advocates for a robust forest capitalism, more recent experts are beginning to question its costs. Professor Carl Reidel of the Environmental Program at the University of Vermont blames the forest's woes on the idea that the use of woodlands should be unregulated and remain subject to what the eighteenth-century English economist, Adam Smith, meant by the "free market":

*The reason for all this havoc, I would contend, is that for the most part we trusted a poorly interpreted version of Adam Smith's so-called free market economic theory. And what did we get? I'd suggest that about all we got for this blind trust in old Adam is a significantly downgraded forest resource ravaged by chestnut blight, dutch elm disease, gypsy moth and the like; the extinction of 10 billion passenger pigeons, acid rain and ever-increasing subdivision of the forest into weekend play yards for down-country corporate vice presidents, lawyers and surgeons. Forestry? Very little! The only exceptions seem to be when a few far-sighted conservation leaders constrained the market occasionally to create public park and forest areas, and to enact a few laws to slow down the degradation of air, water and land resources.*

*Put bluntly, the so-called free market's "invisible hand" has been in just about everybody's natural resource pocket. Our environment and our natural resources have been paying the real costs of the imperfections in our market economy.*

Richmond. The politically active Sierra Club has many members in the state and has been particularly involved in monitoring the use of mountain stream water for snowmaking. Vermont has had its own chapter of The Nature Conservancy since 1960, and it has helped to protect over 100,000 acres of scientifically important natural areas, often habitats for rare and endangered species. They also protect and manage 33 of their own nature preserves.

As the previous chapter has shown, the state's environmental movement began in the early twentieth century with the important park and trail-building initiatives of the Green Mountain Club, with its Long Trail through the Green Mountains, and the related Appalachian Trail Conference, founded in 1925. These initiatives continue with organizations like the Catamount Trail Association (founded in 1985 to develop and maintain the longest cross-country ski trail in the United States) and the Vermont Trails and Greenways Council (promoting the creation of nature paths throughout the state since 1988).

The Vermont Natural Resources Council (VNRC), founded in 1963, was one of the first organizations to dedicate itself to educating the public on the "wise use" of natural resources; it has developed into a significant

The Abenaki have regained their sense of identity and common purpose in the later twentieth century, as this group of dancers in Franklin (above) shows. But despite overwhelming evidence that the Abenaki traditionally inhabited the land that would become Vermont, the state has remained steadfast in its refusal to grant them legal recognition, for fear of lawsuits and casinos.

Paul O. Boisvert

legislative advocacy group. The Vermont Public Interest Research Group (VPIRG) is involved in lobbying, research, and community organizing on a variety of environmental concerns. The River Watch Network began in Vermont as an organization to clean up and protect rivers; it has grown and now has the goal of establishing at least one river protection program in each state. The Vermont Institute of Natural Science (VINS) was founded in 1972 to run programs in environmental education and research on natural history and animal and bird behavior. It operates the Vermont Raptor Center and the Bragdon Nature Preserve and, through its ELF program, also provides educational opportunities for elementary schoolchildren.

This listing of environmental organizations is far from complete, and serves only to show that Vermont's maturing environmental movement remains lively. Vermonters of all political persuasions have tended to show remarkable unanimity in their desire to protect this unique environment. It is not purely the legacy of a state's natural beauty; as any trip to Colorado or Arizona will show, great beauty and environmental sensitivity to preserving it do not always go hand in hand. But Vermont seems to have been fortunate in its peculiar combination of having had its landscape escape the most rapacious forms of industrialization and growth, while harboring a population that combines a strong tradition of Yankee conserving conservatism with a more recent strain of liberal and progressive political activism on environmental issues.

People are more apt to want to preserve parts of the natural world they know and love. At the Raptor Center of the Vermont Institute of Natural Sciences in Woodstock (above), schoolchildren learn about owls.

One of the most pressing of these environmental issues is ensuring that people are able to enjoy the environment they are working so fervently to protect. The state has found that as the countryside fills up with people who have not had direct experience of working on the land, or who come from urban settings where the privacy of property has to be rigidly enforced, more Vermonters are seeking to restrict access to the lands they own. This is antithetical to older country notions of keeping access to the landscape open—as long as this is done respectfully (no littering, or property damage, or leaving gates ajar). When the state updated its recreation plan in 1993, many of the panels looking into land use issues noted the phenomenon of the shrinking landscape, blaming it on new notions of privacy or a fear of legal liability.

The only legal way to keep people from walking on your rural property is to "post" it under one of several laws, either stipulating that all access will be considered "unlawful trespass," or specifically outlawing hunting, shooting, fishing, and trapping only. The property owner has to post notices around the designated land and register it annually with the town clerk. As early as 1963, the state Fish and Game Department saw a "vast" increase in the amount of land posted, and state surveys show this trend is continuing. The counties with the greatest amount of posted land are Rutland, Windham, Bennington, Orange, and Addison.

## DEER CAMP

Vermont's two-week November gun hunting season for deer still holds some of the status of a statewide holiday. Husbands go missing, and children disappear from their seats at school. In the countryside, those who do not hunt wake up to the sound of popping firearms and take a couple of weeks off from walking their dogs in the fields.

Here is one man's reminiscence of his first year of deer camp, as recounted in John M. Miller's book, *Deer Camp: Last Light in the Northeast Kingdom*:

*Well, the first time that I came to deer camp for deer season, I was 12 years old. [My father] took me out of school and brought me up here. Mr. man, if that wasn't something. Boy. Ten men in here, ten great big men, rough, gruff voices. He'd back the pickup truck up there and they'd take out the cases of beer. Whole pickup truck load, and they'd stack it in there where that wood is stacked, right to the ceiling, case after case, forty cases or so.*

*I'd just come up for maybe a week-end or somethin' like that. Maybe Friday, I'd take Friday off and Saturday and Sunday and I'd be back home for school Monday. Man I was in the dishpan, I lugged the wood, split, kept the griggin' place swept up. I did everything. I'd get all done and after supper, I'd get the hell out of the way and they'd do dishes and have a few after-dinner drinks, gettin' ready to get the table ready for the poker game.*

*I'd go up on that bunk right there, and lay there with my arms folded, my pillow there, and I'd fall asleep watchin'. Smoke, they'd be cussin' and raisin' hell.*

*Ya, it was very exciting. And I felt very privileged to be able to be here. Because I was the only one back then that had a father that would bring their kid into camp. I don't know, I'm sure dad got an okay before he did that. How well that ever set with anybody I don't know. But he wanted me there.*

John M. Miller, Deer Camp: Last Light in the Northeast Kingdom, MIT Press, 1992

## SUBURBAN VERMONT: A BRIEF HISTORY OF DEVELOPMENT

While America had double-digit population growth rates in the Forties and Fifties, Vermont's growth lagged far behind, at around 3 to 5 percent. A few pockets of suburbia began to appear in the form of small-lot subdivisions, particularly around the fringes of Burlington, and a small number of businesses sprang up on Route 7 in South Burlington. But the stagnant growth rate meant that most of Vermont escaped the trend toward suburban development that was such a predominant feature of American life in the post-war period. This was part and parcel of a Vermont economy so stagnant that the state created a new Vermont Development Commission in 1945, whose mission was "to encourage and promote developments of agricultural, industrial, recreational and other resources of the State."

Suburbanization was largely a by-product of urban industrial society; that sort of development had been minimal in Vermont. Even so, there were plant closures in this period, including the 1954 shutdown of the Champlain

Since the 1940s, Vermont farmland has been transformed into suburbia; this example (below) is a development in Williston.

Paul O. Boisvert

## THE GREATEST THREATS TO THE VERMONT ENVIRONMENT

A strong case could be made that the great environmental initiatives like the Clean Air Act and the Clean Water Act have made Vermont's environment cleaner than it has been at any time in the past 100 years. So what do the experts see as the most important current pollution threats to the landscape? The Agency of Natural Resources and the Department of Health spent two years developing a ranking of environmental hazards, publishing their results in 1991. Their findings may not alway jibe with popular perceptions. They classified environmental hazards from higher to lower risk.

—from Agency of Natural Resources and Department of Health, *Strategy for Vermont's Third Century*, "Environment 1991: Risks to Vermont and Vermonters" (Montpelier 1991).

**Higher Risk**

**A.** Alteration of Vermont's Ecosystems
Global Climate Change
Indoor Air Pollution

**B.** Air Pollution, Including Acid Rain
Depletion of the Ozone Layer

**C.** Drinking Water at the Tap
Pollution to Lakes and Ponds
Toxics in the Household
Toxics in the Workplace

**Lower Risk**

**D.** Food Safety
Ground Water, Other than Drinking Water
Loss of Access to Outdoor Recreation
Pesticides and Pests, Excluding Exotic Pests

Mill in Winooski. But its effects were soon mitigated by a new plant that would profoundly alter the Chittenden County economy, when IBM opened in Essex in 1957 with 400 workers (in 1999 they employed 7,000 in Vermont). In the same decade, the first Vermont suburbs began to appear. Essex Junction's housing stock doubled in a decade, and new housing went up over 60 percent in South Burlington. The subdivisions that were built generally followed the new suburban model, where it was assumed that the residents would travel everywhere by car.

Major population growth did not hit Vermont until the 1960s, when a healthier economy helped attract traditional laborers, white collar workers, skiers-turned-permanent-residents, and back-to-the-landers. All came streaming in along the new interstates, boosting the state's population by 14 percent in the Sixties and 15 percent in the Seventies. Vermont's growth rates were suddenly higher than the national average for the first time since settlement days. The immigrants tended to settle in the south, near the ski areas, or in Chittenden County, where the trend toward suburbanization took off on a large scale for the first time.

## THE RETURN OF THE NATIVES

The reemergence of the forest has led to the return or proliferation of a number of species of wildlife that had become scarce since the time of the great clearing. Here are three of their tales:

**White-tailed Deer**

Over-hunting and loss of habitat virtually eliminated Vermont's deer herd in the nineteenth century. As early as 1865, deer hunting was banned in the state. The deer season was not reinstated until 1897, when restocking and growth of habitat enabled hunters to take 103 bucks. When farms were abandoned and turned to trees, the deer made a miraculous comeback. The modern deer herd hit its highest point in the 1960s, when 250,000 of them were decimating the state's forest vegetation and still dying of malnutrition. They are now healthy again, and their numbers are holding stable at around 140,000. That is almost twice as many deer as there are deer hunters in an average season.

**Moose**

One recent January midnight, a college professor made his way over the Middlebury Gap. On a deserted stretch of road, far from any houses, he saw a strange light flickering high up in a tree. It was so disconcerting that he instinctively slowed down—in time to discover that the light he was seeing was a reflection in the eye of a moose standing smack in the middle of the road. The professor's curiosity had made him brake in time to avoid what might have been a fatal crash.

Moose had been wiped out in Vermont as early as 1830 and did not begin to show up here again in any numbers until the 1970s. Now Vermont's moose herd is making a booming comeback. The herd's size is estimated at 2,500 head—1,000 times as many as were here in 1960. Some wildlife experts believe their numbers are reaching a nuisance level, as they trample farmers' fences, plow through maple sap tubing, and, most importantly, cause serious or fatal injuries when they are hit by cars. For this reason, the state instituted a controlled moose-hunting season in 1993, beginning in the Northeast Kingdom. It is now being expanded to the central Green Mountains as the great lumbering creatures amble south.

**Catamount**

Some say the last catamount was killed in Barnard in 1881. But you will never convince Wayne Alexander of that. Alexander retired to Glover in 1989 and began recording the accounts of dozens of people who said they had seen catamount in the Northeast Kingdom. Skeptics suspected that catamounts had become the UFOs of the backwoods. But on an April morning in 1994, Alexander, acting on a state police tip about a potential catamount sighting, headed out into the Craftsbury woods with his three sons and a friend. There were cat tracks, but they were not very clear in the crusty snow. They saw no catamounts, but suddenly came upon the next best thing—fresh droppings, or "scat," on the tracks. They put a sample into a plastic bag and shipped it off to the state for analysis. The results showed, without a doubt, that it was the scat of a mountain lion, or catamount. Susan Morse, the Jericho naturalist and animal tracker, was afterwards quoted on the lesson we should learn if the big cat has, indeed, returned: "It's a dramatic being out there reminding us that we have an obligation to take care of our land and not ruin it as we did 100 years ago."

Left and bottom: Paul O. Boisvert; top: Corbis/Bettmann

By the late Sixties, rising populations signaled the beginning of an unprecedented land grab. Growth coincided with the declining importance of agriculture in the state economy, leaving the land vulnerable to exploitation. Traditional restraints that had protected both the land and its communities—a preference for agriculture and forestry, Yankee conservatism and thrift, an economy that was slow to change—were now under threat. And the age-old Vermont tradition of letting everyone do what they wanted with their own land meant that the state had little legislation to regulate any aspect of development. Some towns began to tax land for its development potential rather than its use, so that a woodlot of 55 acres in Guilford saw its taxes go up from $24 to $585 in two years in the late Sixties.

The bulging grand lists were also precipitated by changing governmental policies toward land valuation. For many decades property taxes had been computed at 50 percent of fair market value, and farm- and forestlands were often undervalued by the listers. In 1977, the legislature mandated that all property should be valued at 100 percent of its fair market value, and many towns elected to reappraise all properties, developed or not, based upon their development potential. It was tempting to sell out under such conditions—and sometimes inevitable.

The suburbanization of Vermont continues. These photos were taken from the same spot on Bay Road in Shelburne, the top one in the late 1970s and the bottom one in 1998. They show a field transformed into a housing tract. It is hard to find a trace of the earlier landscape in the new variation.

Land, much of it long regarded as frustratingly unproductive, had suddenly become a hot commodity in Vermont. When the real pressure began, Vermonters were often no match for determined developers (who were often out-of-staters, but sometimes, dismayingly, fellow Vermonters). The wholesale building of homes and vacation places was rampant, particularly near ski areas in the southern part of the state. The state's lax septic laws did so little to regulate systems that sewage from one development often ran down hillsides and seeped into the yards of houses in another. Clifford Jarvis exemplified the insensitive developer, as he worked to turn a 2,000-acre farm in Windham County into a project with 1,735 houses in the mid-Sixties. As described in *Time* magazine, the process would involve clearing the trees, building fake covered bridges, and draining a beaver pond ("We'll have to kill them."). Afterwards, Jarvis admitted, "I personally have no intention of staying in Vermont." The trend was so unrelenting that between 1950 and 1992, the amount of farmland in Chittenden County would drop from 72.6 to 24 percent.

The tendency to build sprawling low-density suburban shopping centers was now becoming pronounced in Chittenden County. Stores that had long been staples of downtown Burlington—Sears, Lash Furniture, Goss Autos, and others—chose to move south, arraying themselves on large lots along Route 7. There, they joined sites already geared to tourism: motels, restaurants, gas stations. By 1963, nearly all of Shelburne Road between Burlington and Shelburne had been zoned commercial.

Paul O. Bosivert

In the 1950s and 1960s, sprawl development proliferated along Shelburne Road (above) in South Burlington. Here, as elsewhere, development was driven by the automobile.

The state passed legislation permitting local zoning regulations in 1967. Many towns quickly enacted plans that actually reinforced patterns of suburban sprawl rather than the opposite: zoning retail development along highways, insisting upon wide streets in suburban neighborhoods, not requiring sidewalks in residential areas. Public concern about shoddy development was finally galvanized in 1968, when a subsidiary of the International Paper Company announced that it was going to build a huge development on 20,000 acres it owned in southern Vermont. The locals reacted with outrage, knowing that the hilly site had soil so thin that septic systems could never be expected to work there. Governor Deane Davis went out to look at the problem and came back convinced that Vermont needed strict regulation of development. Here lay the seeds of the state's landmark environmental law, Act 250.

Governor Davis created a Commission on Environmental Control to draft land use legislation that would protect the state from unsound and substandard development. Led by Representative Arthur Gibb of Weybridge, the Gibb Commission moved to deal with the new environmental threats posed by unregulated development. Two years later, in 1970, bipartisan support for the Commission's bill helped it pass through a Republican-dominated

Left: Jan Albers; right: IBM Archives

The IBM plant in Essex (above) as it appeared in 1962, five years after its opening. Its presence has had an enormous impact on the landscape of eastern Chittenden County, both from the plant itself and in the housing of its large work force.

legislature almost unanimously. Power of enforcement was vested at the local level. The state created the Environmental Board to oversee a certain number of District Environmental Commissions (there are now nine), panels of lay citizens who set up public hearings to review applications. At hearings, developers are required to show that their proposals meet specific criteria. Issues too thorny to resolve at the local level are referred to the state Environmental Review Board.

The impact of Act 250 would not become clear for decades, but for now it was not to be the panacea for solving all of Vermont's environmental ills. Even well-meaning attempts to forestall suburban development could go badly astray. Burlington was in the vanguard of the urban renewal movement of the Sixties; in hopes of slowing the drift to the suburbs, the city's voters happily agreed to wipe out 27 acres of 100-year-old buildings in the name of progress. The Champlain Street Urban Renewal Project tore up a seven-block downtown area, removing 124 buildings and dislocating 157 families, 67 singles, and 41 businesses. In a society that too often favored suburban sprawl over urban infilling, many lots cleared during this period had still not been recycled 30 years later.

In the 1970s, Burlington began to encourage greater urban population density and the revival of neighborhoods. This new emphasis lay at the heart of Burlington's Comprehensive Master Plan of 1973, which pledged to help the neighborhoods by "protecting them from undue concentrations of population, crowded housing sites, encroaching non-neighborhood type uses, the demolition of neighborhood landmarks, and the loss of peace, quiet, privacy, and a reasonable way of life."

The Seventies made people aware that certain patterns of development did not just threaten the land itself, but also the very core of community. People now lived in one place and worked in another, eroding the sense of common local purpose in many places. Vermont's state government began to examine the relationship between patterns of land use development and the breakdown of community. Governor Thomas Salmon commissioned a pamphlet, "People on the Land: Settlement Patterns for Vermont," that offered the first clear popularization of the idea that growth should take place in clusters close to the center of established communities, rather than be scattered throughout the countryside.

While large stretches of Vermont remained bucolic and unspoiled, disturbing signs of suburban sprawl continued to appear in the 1980s. But a growing awareness of the importance of maintaining strong town centers provided a bright spot in this period. In Burlington, then Mayor Bernie Sanders helped to strengthen and beautify the city's downtown through the building of the successful Church Street Marketplace, reviving the lakefront, and creating public amenities like the Burlington boat house and bicycle path.

Another hopeful sign in the Eighties was the development of new technologies that made more information available for land use planning. Aerial photography was supplemented with satellite imagery and a computer-based technology known as Geographic Information Systems (GIS) offered new data about what was happening to current patterns in the use of land and natural resources. This omniscient eye has provided a fresh and accurate new view of the roads, waterways, farms, forests, villages, strip malls, and suburbs of Vermont as the century comes to a close.

Growth has continued at a high rate in some parts of the state in the 1990s. The latest figures available cover the period 1990–1997; they show that Grand Isle has been the fastest growing county in the state (with a growth rate of 14 percent), followed by Lamoille (11.2 percent) and Chittenden (7.8 percent). Figures for the fastest growing towns can be misleading, since moderate growth can produce a high rate in a small town. Nevertheless, the five fastest growing towns in Vermont, 1990–1997, have been Bolton (28.2 percent), Williston (27.7 percent), Fayston (26.5 percent), Elmore (24.8 percent), and Waterville (24.2 percent).

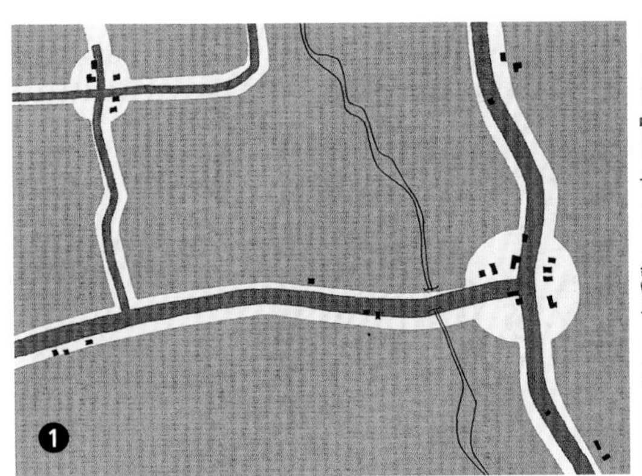


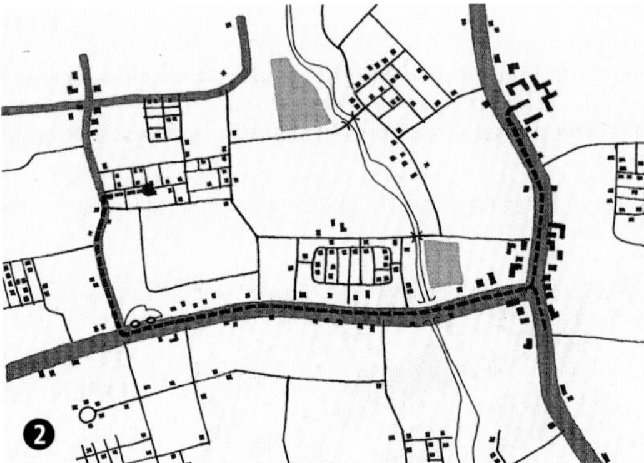


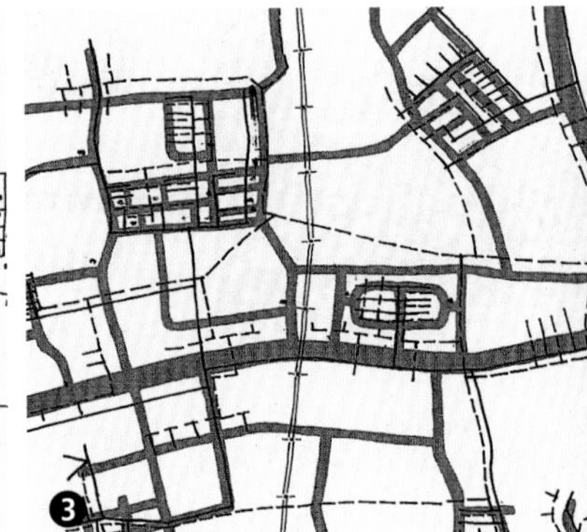


People on the Land: Settlement Patterns for Vermont, Vermont State Planning Office, Robert Burley Associates

## PEOPLE ON THE LAND

These illustrations and text come from a pamphlet commissioned by the Salmon administration in 1973, in support of medium-density development:

**Diagram 1. A typical rural pattern with houses and stores clustered in hamlets, and farms dispersed along the roads.**

**Diagram 2. Normal uncontrolled growth. Houses and residential developments have spread across the countryside while commercial development has occurred outside the village area. The dotted line shows the route a typical resident must drive to work, shopping, church, or hairdresser. There is a great expanse of roadway that must be built, maintained, plowed, and travelled by schoolbus.**

**Diagram 3. The network of sewer, water, power and telephone lines that are required to service this scatter of homes and businesses.**

In this period, Vermont has been transformed also by a major change in retail development. Downtown Burlington has lost its supremacy to large-scale suburban stores in South Burlington, Williston, Essex, and Colchester. Current land use legislation has not been able to stop sprawl development, even in the face of widespread community opposition. In Burlington, as in many smaller towns around the state, there has been a tendency toward retail class differentiation, with upmarket boutiques staying downtown and bargain retail drifting to the malls and megastores. The Champlain Initiative's study, "The History of Sprawl in Chittenden County" (1999), found that at Tafts Corners in Williston (home to numerous national chain stores), 460,000 square feet of retail space have opened in this decade, an amount almost exactly equal to the amount of available retail space in all of downtown Burlington.

The 1990s have shown that the state's lack of experience with major industrial developments has left its communities susceptible to unplanned growth. The town of Milton, north of Burlington, is currently providing an interesting case study for the effects of development, since it has been chosen as the new home for a rapidly expanding plastic mold-producing

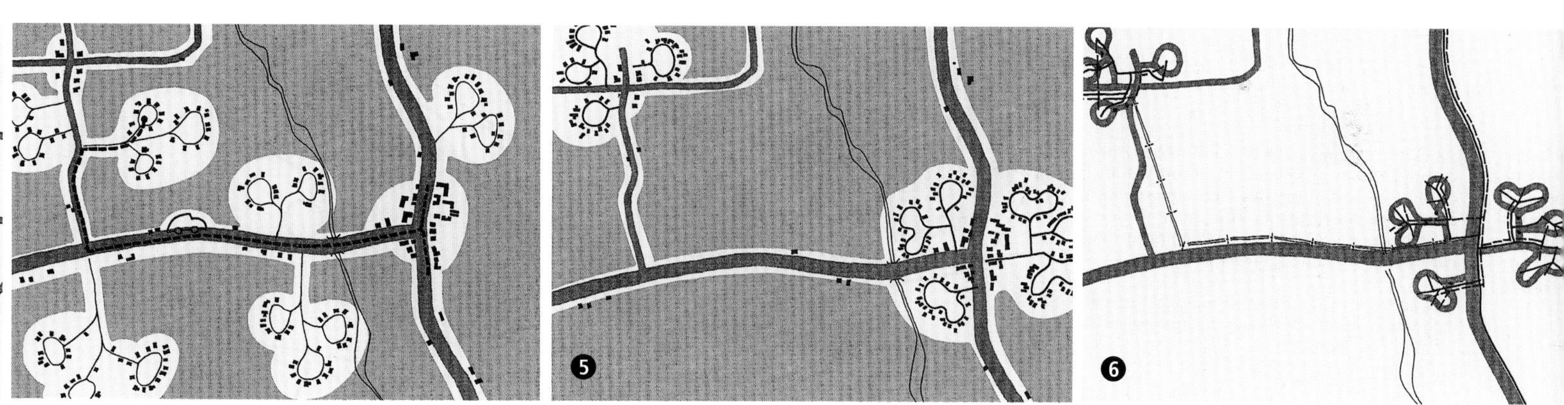


Diagram 4. The problem is not solved by merely clustering the homes as shown here. The extent of roads and utility lines is somewhat reduced, but, as the dotted line shows, the typical resident drives almost the same distance as he or she did in diagram 2. While more open space and farmland are preserved, the encroachment has begun and, too often, has occurred on the best land because this land is easiest to develop.

Diagram 5. This concentration pattern and its supporting road and utility network (Diagram 6) achieve the economy and conservation goals of settlement planning. New development has occurred in close relationship to the existing villages allowing improvement and expansion of shops and services within the village. These facilities, and the school, are within walking distance of most of the homes, greatly reducing reliance on automobiles.

Canadian company, Husky. Husky has a reputation as an environmentally friendly company, but are Milton and the surrounding towns prepared for the huge amount of growth it will bring? The town attempted to put the onus for town planning onto the company itself, but the courts informed Milton's representatives that the town is responsible for growth that takes place within its borders. The question of whether it is prepared for the pressures that face it remains unresolved. But the citizens of Milton and surrounding towns are actively pursuing a variety of options for the appropriate development of their community.

Alan Jakubek

## WITHOUT A FARMHOUSE NEAR

In her thoughtful study of the transformation from farms to suburbs in the eastern Chittenden County towns of Jericho and Underhill, the late journalist Deborah Rawson began by describing where she used to play as a child when she visited her cousins in Underhill:

*When I was a child I thought of Cilley Hill as a remote locale known to and visited by a limited number of people—relatives, other farmers and the milk truck driver. Actually, that phrase we use in our family—going up on the hill—does have a proprietary ring to it; and when I was growing up, my relatives were just about the only people who lived on Cilley Hill. So little traffic passed through that it was perfectly safe to use the road for sliding (sledding). ...My young cousins do not slide down Cilley Hill. Nowadays there is just enough traffic on Cilley Hill to remind you that it is a public road. Only a daredevil would chance an encounter with a car. Eleven houses have been built over the past twenty years on one short stretch of Cilley Hill Road where there were none before; and someone is always buying or selling land along the way. Houses beget more houses. It is only a matter of time before some of the new residents tire of mud season's indignities and clamor for a paved road. It is only a matter of time before the one farm that is left on the hill is surrounded by housing.*

—Deborah Rawson, *Without a Farmhouse Near* (1989)

Vermont is vulnerable to the same development forces, coming both from within and from outside the state, that have made so much of America unattractive and unproductive. The state will enter the new century with the advantage of having remained largely undeveloped. Vermont is in the unique position of being able to choose whether or not it will follow that path. The growing suburbs of Burlington and the big-box retail mecca of Williston may be only the beginning of the "Americanization" of Vermont.

## WHAT REAL VERMONTERS DO, OR WHAT VERMONTERS REALLY DO

You hear a lot in Vermont about "real Vermonters," evidently a rare and rarefied breed. But the truth is, the majority of Vermonters are real Vermonters: according to the 1990 Census, 60 percent of people living in the state were born here (the figure was 66.7 percent in 1970). Both natives and immigrants mainly do jobs that do not fit the Vermont "homespun" stereotype. Vermonters are most apt to work in manufacturing or service industries (including tourism), with the biggest employers being manufacturers, health care providers, grocery store chains, educational institutions, and state government. According to Vermont's figures for employment in 1999, about 28 percent of Vermonters work in service industries, 19 percent in retail, 17 percent each in manufacturing and government, with smaller numbers in construction, transportation, wholesale trade, and construction. Agriculture and logging together count for only 3.4 percent of the labor force.

There are regional variations in Vermont employment. In the state's population center, the greater Burlington labor market, the biggest employers are IBM, Fletcher Allen Health Care, the State of Vermont, and the University of Vermont. Many other concerns also have large numbers of workers in the region, including the rapidly expanding medical software company, IDX, the grocery store chains, General Dynamics, and New England Telephone. Within the next few years, the Husky plant in Milton will be added to this list. Most of these are desirable high-tech operations that are relatively clean and environmentally friendly. The pattern is similar around the state, although on a smaller scale, as shown in the accompanying map.

The numbers illustrate the revolution that has taken place in Vermont employment since the nineteenth century. The economy has become less dependent upon the exploitation of the state's relatively poor soil and few mineral resources, and more geared to light industry, health care, and education. Earnings here are still lower than in other parts of the Eastern seaboard, but the gap has narrowed in the past 20 years. A state that once took its paltry livings from the land now provides more comfortable incomes than ever before despite the land's limited agricultural and mineral opportunities.

### VERMONT'S TEN LARGEST INDUSTRIES, 1997

| Industry | Employees |
|---|---|
| Education—Private & Government | 33,541 |
| Health Services | 25,892 |
| Eating & Drinking Places | 17,084 |
| Industrial Machinery/Electronic Equipment Manufacturing | 13,477 |
| Food Stores | 10,572 |
| Business Services | 10,186 |
| Hotels & Other Lodging Places | 10,137 |
| Miscellaneous Retail | 9,413 |
| State Government Other Than Education | 8,297 |
| Special Trade Contractors—Construction | 8,052 |
| All industries | 280,142 |

Source: Vermont Department of Employment & Training, Labor Market Bulletin (July 1998)

As an institution of higher education, Vermont Technical College in Randolph (above) is one of the state's major employers.

Bob Eddy

Many of these industries have attracted out-of-staters to Vermont. The "flatlanders" have, in some respects, become the greatest guardians of the Vermont myth. Their progressivism has often put them in the vanguard of the movements for historic preservation, environmentalism, planned growth, and social justice.

At the same time, the newcomers' presence has led to a certain degree of tension with longer-term Vermonters, stimulating a backlash of "native born" pride. Many of the conflicts between the two groups have revolved around the newcomers' misunderstandings of the realities of rural life. These cultural conflicts have repercussions for land use, as the state has been flooded with people who have little personal understanding of the patterns of rural life, the productivity of rural land, and the tradition of private property rights. So far, most towns have managed to integrate considerable numbers of new residents while retaining traditional patterns of growth. But increasing growth pressures threaten to break down the land use and settlement patterns that lured people to Vermont in the first place.

Newcomers are drawn to Vermont's stunning views, like this idyllic farm in Danby (opposite). Yet the need to house them has often led to the destruction of the very rural landscapes that attracted them in the first place. A good example: this development (above) snaking its way across the Williston countryside.

## THE NEW MEANING OF RURAL LIFE

*Vermont has never been urban, and very probably it will never be. Like other rural areas of the nation, it doesn't need urbanism and will refuse it when offered. We should not assume this rejection is simply because modern urban America has received a bad press over the last decade and rural people are turning up their noses at what they perceive to be crime-ridden, pollution-stifled environments. Rather, the inhabitants feel no need to group together, regardless of their occupation. Rural areas in the United States, unlike their counterparts elsewhere in the world, have always been machine filled. Now that modern technology has become a part of rural culture, urban-rural distinctions no longer serve as important operational definitions. Despite much thinking to the contrary, the case of Vermont shows that a technocratic society is not limited to the urban condition and that the study of rural society today should be as involved with the culture of scientific progress as is the study of urban society.*

—FRANK BRYAN, *"Political Life in a Rural Technopolity"* (1974)

Vermont has always been a rural state, providing a number of successive countryside experiences ranging from subsistence farming to modern agribusiness, and from boom to bust. It is still one of the most rural states in the union, with a population density of only 61 persons per square mile. Up in the Northeast Kingdom, in places like Averill and Ferdinand, densities are

Paul O. Boisvert

Jerry LeBlond

less than one person per square mile. Most Americans find it amusing that the largest city in any state could have only 40,000 people.

It is reassuring to think, with Frank Bryan, that Vermont will always be rural. But while Vermont's scale remains small, the character of its rural life has already changed profoundly since World War II. The most traditional country occupations, farming and logging, today make up only a small direct percentage of the state's economy. The land, however, has a certain look when it is being farmed or logged; in this way, these occupations still have an enormous aesthetic impact offering immeasurable value-added attributes to tourism, recreation, and other larger and more important segments of the economy. What happens when the farmers and loggers are replaced by people who make their livings in more non-traditional ways? The idea that rural means agricultural and urban means industrial is etched in every American brain. What could it mean to be rural and yet not reliant on the land? And if most Vermonters make their livings in industrial or service occupations not dependent upon exploiting natural resources, then the fundamental brake that the state's geography has always placed on its development in the past is now in danger of being breached. Can Vermont find a way of managing development that retains the physical beauty and strong sense of community that has distinguished it in the past?

## ACT 250 AND THE LOOK OF THE LAND

The state's greatest bulwark against sloppy and environmentally insensitive development is Act 250, which went into effect in 1970 and has become a nationally known model for land use legislation. It is representative of a general trend toward allowing land use decisions to rest in the hands of government. But it has had more of an impact on the quality of development than on its quantity. In fact, a 1992 study done by the Vermont Natural Resources Council found that between 1970 and 1991 "the index of nonresidential construction in Vermont surpassed the New England average 50 percent of the time, while residential construction did so 59 percent of the time." So while Act 250 has not acted as a brake on development, it has helped to ensure that the environmental and societal impacts of larger building projects have been thoroughly addressed.

Some argue that it has not slowed growth enough, since the Act only applies to about 40 percent of development that takes place in the state; it is clear that it has not prevented a considerable amount of sprawl. The greatest weakness of Act 250 is that it does not apply to small developments, although much of the sprawl in Vermont consists of an accumulation of individual projects. Landscapes all around the state have been ruined by the accumulation of badly planned and poorly sited small projects.

### WHAT ACT 250 SAYS (1970)

Vermont's pioneering development law, Act 250, does not apply to all development, but only to projects of some magnitude. Those subject to it include:

1. Any housing or trailer park developments of more than 10 units.

2. Any commercial or industrial improvements on more than 10 acres.

3. Any subdivision of land for sale in parcels of 10 acres or under. [Amended to 5 or more parcels, regardless of size, in 1974.]

4. Any state or municipal construction on more than 10 acres.

5. All development—commercial, industrial, or residential—above 2,500 feet.

**Deane Davis, second from left, was one of Vermont's most environmentally activist governors.**

When a development is proposed that falls under the Act, the review process requires that it meet 10 criteria. These include that the development:

1. Will not result in undue water or air pollution.

2. Has sufficient water available for the needs of the subdivision or development.

3. Will not unreasonably burden any existing water supply.

4. Will not cause unreasonable soil erosion or affect the capacity of the land to hold water.

5. Will not cause unreasonably dangerous or congested conditions with respect to highways or other means of transportation.

6. Will not create an unreasonable burden on the education facilities of the municipality.

**The Act 250 permit for Rutland's Diamond Run Mall (top) required that the developers provide public access to neighboring pastures and wetlands. The result has been a creative colloboration between public and private interests, as developers, the Rutland Natural Resources Conservation District, and other groups have created a 28-acre nature trail system (above) next to the mall.**

7. Will not create an unreasonable burden on the municipality in providing governmental services.

8. Will not have an undue adverse effect on aesthetics, scenic beauty, historic sites or natural area, and 8(A) will not imperil necessary wildlife habitat or endangered species in the immediate area.

9. Conforms with the Capability and Development Plan which includes the following considerations:

(A) The impact the project will have on the growth of the town or region; (B) Primary agricultural soils; (C) Forest and secondary agricultural soils; (D) Earth resources; (E) Extraction of earth resources; (F) Energy Conservation; (G) Private utility services; (H) Costs on scattered developments; (J) Public Utility services; (K) Development affected public investments; and (L) Rural growth areas.

10. Is in conformance with any local or regional plan or capital facilities program.

The burden of proof is on the applicant for Criteria 1, 2, 3, 4, 9, and 10. The burden of proof is on the opposition for Criteria 5, 6, 7, 8, and often 9 (A). A permit can be conditioned but not denied under Criteria 5, 6, and 7.

Top: Cynthia Locklin; right: Jerry LeBlond

But because it requires that development be sensitive to issues of aesthetics and scenery in addition to more "practical" considerations, there can be no doubt that Act 250 has helped to preserve the look of the land so highly valued by natives and tourists. Although bad developments have still squeaked through in some areas, there are far fewer of them than there would have been if the development situation had been the free-for-all that can be seen in parts of Florida, Colorado, California, and a number of other states.

The Act is periodically criticized by developers and property rights activists, who argue that its strict land use provisions act as a harmful barrier to the state's economic growth. A Vermont Natural Resources Council study found that most of these charges were without merit. Vermont's economic strength lies in its "green" image, and the "Made in Vermont" label carries enormous clout. Act 250 is one reason Vermont has the strongest banks in New England: it discourages undercapitalized developments that can lead to bad loans. And bad development is bad business. As the economist and part-time Vermonter John Kenneth Galbraith said when Act 250 was new, "if uncontrolled resource exploitation were the *sine qua non* of prosperity, West Virginia would be the most prosperous of all the American states. And it would be closely followed by Alabama and Mississippi."

Act 250 looks very different, depending upon whether you are in Woodstock or Williston. This is because, in the spirit of Vermont's traditional

**Zoning has allowed the building of developments such as this one (top) off Spear Street in South Burlington, with its tightly packed houses. Although such dwellings are often criticized for being out of scale, their environmental impact is less here than it would be if each was set on its own 10-acre country lot. Zoning did not prevent the building of a house on Spear Street (above) which effectively mars community enjoyment of one of Vermont's best views raising questions about who takes precedence: the individual or the community.**

Top: Alan Jakubek; bottom: Cynthia Locklin

reverence for local control, the Act still leaves an enormous amount of discretion in the hands of local communities. Different towns have different attitudes toward development, and Act 250 has in no way homogenized the look of the land. In fact, some people have argued that Act 250 is flawed by its failure to provide growth planning on a statewide basis. Such planning was intended by its original legislative framers, but this provision was not able to make it through the legislature until Governor Madeleine Kunin's administration gained passage of what is now known as Act 200 in 1988.

The main provisions of Act 200 include a commitment to helping agriculture and forestry remain viable, an insistence upon making development conform to the historic settlement pattern of compact villages and towns surrounded by countryside, discouragement of strip development along highways, and provisions for affordable housing. The Act does not give the state the right to enforce these goals, but offers incentives to towns for drafting comprehensive plans that are consistent with the state's recommendations. It was also intended to provide funds for the writing of town plans, but has too often been underfunded.

Many of Vermont's towns have put in earnest work to come up with town plans that would accurately reflect the values of their communities. These values can vary enormously, depending upon whether towns view development as progress or pitfall. It is clear that, even with financial incentives, some towns have seen Act 200 as an intrusion and have refused or neglected to have town plans approved by their regional planning authorities under the terms of the Act. In 1999, 95 percent of Vermont's 246 towns had written town plans, but only 55 percent of them (137 towns) had gone through the regional approval process. As property rights advocates see it, Act 200 gives the state too much power over individuals. State Senator John McClaughry of Caledonia County said in a 1990 *Vermont Magazine* interview:

> *The planners who want to direct everybody's use of land are continually casting about for ways to get their hooks into it. And they continually avoid ways to have an election on it, because they know that the people have different interests than the planners. ...They believe the mass of unwashed people in this state will ruin everything. There's a massive cultural clash here.*

The assumption that the advocates of planning are all elite flatlanders, while "real Vermonters" want to do what they darned well please is widespread. The jury may still be out on Act 200, but Vermonters retain a high degree of cultural consensus over their common desire to prevent their state from coming to look like so much of the rest of America. The great clash comes when they try to agree on the best way of doing that.

## THE TROUBLE WITH ZONING

The concept of zoning really came of age after the Second World War. While it is almost always well-intentioned, it often creates more sprawl than it prevents. It has been said that zoning would make it impossible to build most of the historical communities we love today, because it tells us that all uses need to be separated. Businesses, houses, and industries all have their separate places. Zoning often revolves around creating development that will provide easy access for cars, rather than human beings.

Organic communities have narrower streets, sidewalks, and a mixture of housing and shopping for people at differing socioeconomic levels.

Rutland is often cited as a town that has successfully melded a traditional downtown and big-box retail. When Wal-Mart approached, the town insisted that they build a small-scale store in an ailing downtown plaza (top), rather than a huge box on the fringes. The result (middle) is part of a lively downtown complex where community events like this concert can take place (bottom).

Jerry LeBlond

## AMERICA'S LAST VILLAGES?

In 1993, the National Trust for Historic Preservation in Washington, D.C., put the whole state of Vermont at the top of its annual list of "America's 11 Most Endangered Historic Places." Their citation expressed the fear that Vermont's beautiful environment, strong communities, and progressive land use laws were still no match for the forces of a "national problem known as 'Sprawl-Mart,' which the National Trust for Historic Preservation defines as unplanned, uncontrolled, large-scale development on the periphery of town that saps the vitality from traditional main streets, increases automobile dependency and destroys open space." They went on to worry that

> *Vermonters now face a showdown with large national discount chains and megamall developers whose plans for huge new stores and parking lots will test the state's commitment to the protection of its natural and cultural heritage. The challenge now is to weigh the short-term benefits of massive commercial development against the long-term consequences of sprawl in such a way that citizens can continue to chart and control the future of this beautiful little state.*

When the press release went public on June 23, 1993, it created quite a stir. Governor Howard Dean released a statement to the *Burlington Free Press*, saying, "It's a wake-up call. Suburban sprawl is not OK. We need planned growth, with the emphasis on planned." On the other side, Vermont developer Jeffrey Davis, then working to bring a Wal-Mart to Tafts Corners, sang a "populist" tune, arguing that the National Preservation Trust was "an elitist group trying to tell Vermonters what they should do with Vermont."

The press, and the public, have tended to think that sprawl in Vermont consists mainly of Shelburne Road, Route 7 in Rutland, and most disturbingly, the big-box stores in Williston. But almost every community in the state—including rural areas and villages—can provide unfortunate examples of sprawl development.

## S-P-R-A-W-L

When most of today's adults were growing up, pollution was considered to be the greatest threat to the environment. Pollution remains an important issue, but great legislation like the Clean Air Act and the Clean Water Act has gone a long way toward helping society clean up its more egregious emissions. It could be argued that here at the beginning of a new millennium the greatest form of pollution facing Americans is the environmental phenomenon known as "sprawl."

What is sprawl? The Vermont Forum on Sprawl, a project of the Orton Family Foundation, defines sprawl as:

*...low-density development that spreads or leapfrogs from compact urban and village centers along highways and into the countryside. Sprawl has resulted in the loss of valuable farmland, forestland and natural areas; air quality decline; auto dependence and reduced accessibility; higher costs for highway, utilities and education; ugly roadsides; the decline of downtowns and villages; and the erosion of community values.*

Sprawl is suburban housing developments that spread out over once-productive farmland or forests at the edge of town. It is the separation of the places people live from the places where they work, shop, worship, learn, or play. When you see a town build its union high school, its new post office, or even its town hall out on the periphery instead of downtown, you are seeing sprawl. It is a pattern of development that ends up dividing a community by

## GOOD DEVELOPMENT MEANS GOOD CHOICES

There will always be development. The question is, how do we get it to take a form that strengthens and beautifies existing communities rather than undermining them? A 1991 state pamphlet, *Vermont Scenic Landscapes,* provides a number of visual examples of what does and does not work when it comes to making development choices:

**1. This is a sensitive scenic landscape located within a narrow valley consisting of a small farming community clustered around a church. The settlement is contained within open fields on the gently sloping hills which surround the valley floor.**

**Open fields in the foreground and background are highly sensitive to changes in development patterns. The wooded hillside is less vulnerable to development, provided the tree canopy remains intact to minimize visual impacts. The compact village settlement pattern creates a high degree of visual contrast and a focal point in the landscape. It is an example of an intact settlement pattern.**

**2. Uncontrolled growth has obscured the original compact settlement pattern and blocked the view of the village center.**

**Sprawling development in the foreground and background obscure views of the historic village center. The sprawl consumes the agricultural land, an important open space.**

**3. Open countryside and the historic settlement pattern of this village have been maintained while growth has been accommodated.**

**Clustered residential development on wooded lots with covenants to control tree clearing provides for growth without visual intrusion into open spaces. Historic district designation protects the character of the village. Maximum permissible lot sizes and other protection techniques such as planned unit development allow new growth to follow existing precedent. Agricultural district designation of the open fields restricts development in these visually sensitive areas.**

income, thus eliminating almost all social and economic diversity. Sprawl tends to put shopping into the mall format, away from the town center, with the parking out front. It is, ultimately, a place where the old Yankee adage, "You can't get there from here" has new and genuine meaning, if you happen to be on foot.

Many of Vermont's communities have been blighted by sprawl, especially along main arteries, as these examples in Barre (top) and Rutland (bottom) demonstrate.

Top: Bob Eddy; bottom: Jerry LeBlond

## THE SECRET OF OUR SUCCESS

> *We can't make a national park out of the state, but neither do we need to create a commercial jungle. ...How can we have economic growth and help our people improve their economic situation without destroying the secret of our success, our environment?*
>
> —GOVERNOR DEANE C. DAVIS (1970)

Many people, Vermonters included, think that acres of malls and giant retail stores are signs of "progress" and show that the state's economy is moving forward. In fact, the social costs of this sort of development are enormous, for sprawl is the most costly form of development for the taxpayer. We are the ones who subsidize sprawl by paying for the new roads, road maintenance, extensions of utilities (water, sewer, electric, telephone), new schools and school bus transportation, police and fire protection, and everything else that goes to support new developments. When growth is permitted outside existing centers, new infrastructure has to be built from scratch at an enormous price. Traditionally, new residential housing has not paid for itself in new taxes, though this may change under Act 60, the state's recent change in the funding of education. When new developments creep into the countryside, taxes usually go up and the citizens pay the tab.

Meanwhile, the centers of towns begin to deteriorate, although there infrastructure is economical because it is already in place; existing infrastructure must be maintained even if it is underutilized, so it is more efficient to use it. Taxes that pay for growth within towns lower the tax bill for everyone. So rampant growth on the edge of town benefits only a few, while costing the rest of us money. As one wag at the Vermont Natural Resources Council put it, "Providing infrastructure is like socialism for the rich. We're emptying our pockets so that a few fat cats can make it big." But it would be wrong to pin sprawl only on big developers. Much, if not most, of the sprawl appearing in Vermont today is the result of smaller decisions made by individuals with only a project or two in mind. A recent study by the Vermont Forum on Sprawl suggests that while 78 percent of Vermonters identified sprawl as a problem, they make personal decisions that threaten those values: building a house in the countryside on a 10-acre lot, spending much of their time in cars commuting to work and services, shopping at big-box stores. Many have not made the leap to modifying their own environmental choices.

### KEEPING VERMONT EXCEPTIONAL

*It is now possible, due to the wonders of commercialism, to visit New Jersey without ever leaving Vermont. How do we accomplish this feat? Easy! Just get off I-89 at the Williston exit, and drive toward Taft Corners. At the first stoplight, take a left and—presto!—you're in New Jersey!...The point is, that it's no longer Vermont. It's not really even New Jersey. It's Mall-land, commerceland. And it has turned that little corner of Williston into a non-place, no different from any-place else where big bucks are made.*

—TOM SLAYTON, Vermont Public Radio (1997)

In southern Vermont, the village of Manchester —famous, and infamous, as an "outlet town" —has been experimenting with a performance approach to zoning with a high degree of success. The secret here is to have the town articulate its goals and then use the design review process to make sure plans conform to the community's vision of itself. Parking has been made as inconspicuous as possible with careful placement and landscaping (above, left). New outlet stores have been built right up to the sidewalk in traditional architectural styles (middle). Even McDonald's has been required to blend into its environment (right). All this may not turn Manchester back into an "authentic" Vermont village, but it has shown that making things attractive also makes good commercial sense.

Left to Right: Cynthia Locklin, Jerry LeBlond, Cynthia Locklin

Poor New Jersey. It is always singled out as the Mother Ship of Suburban Sprawl. The truth is that sprawl is everywhere in late twentieth-century America—even in Vermont. The fight to keep out the big boxes was long and hard, but the deep pockets and steely determination of the developers won the day.

Some people believe that national chains are always bad for Vermont, because they can put locally owned stores out of business and then send their profits to distant headquarters out of the state. Others argue that people want to shop in them, so they should have them. Vermont-based developers have often been the ones to bring them here. Is there a way to accommodate national chain stores without creating sprawl and ruining the unique character of Vermont's countryside?

Vermont will and should have new development. Paul Bruhn, the head of The Preservation Trust of Vermont, has said, "The goal is not to stop

growth. The issue is where growth should go." He argues that the way to resolve this dilemna is not to forbid chain stores, but to tell them that if they want to do business in Vermont, they will have to do it on a smaller scale and in town center locations that suit our traditional settlement pattern and community values. Bruhn goes on to say:

> *National chains like McDonald's and Burger King have occasionally adapted to their surroundings, and Wal-Mart could decide to do business differently here. Wal-Mart could say, "OK, we understand that Vermont is different from other states. We understand that there is a long-standing commitment to protecting the state's rural character and to concentrating retail development in existing downtowns. We get the message. So we're going to adapt how we do business. In Vermont we will build stores that are appropriately scaled for the market. And we're going to build them downtown."*

If Wal-Mart used that approach, we all would benefit. Consumers would have access to the nation's largest retailer. We'd have a healthy mix of locally owned stores and national chains. Downtowns would be reinvigorated. The trend toward sprawl into the countryside would be reversed.

**While most towns and villages in Vermont have been preserved piecemeal, some have had the luck and luxury of seeing almost every worthy building restored to a pristine state. These transformations have been undertaken by individuals, as in Dorset (top, left); by groups like the Windham Foundation, which restored Grafton (above); or through the largesse of a wealthy family, like the Rockefellers in Woodstock (top, right).**

Communities would maintain their tax base. Retail jobs would not be lost. And finally, we would achieve the balance between a positive business climate and the environment that will benefit us all.

The landscapes we create—or allow to be created around us—are clear reflections of our larger social values. The settlers who first hacked Vermont out of the forests found freedom and political equality (at least for adult males), but they were more focused on survival than on creating the civic amenities of village life. In the early nineteenth century, their children had the time and the commercial prosperity to place a higher value on the cultivation of common interests. They built beautiful public spaces (churches, schools, general stores, town halls) that continue to convey the message that theirs was an America that valued community. They had a sense of control over the world they were creating for their families, although they did not always use their power wisely. Part of what has happened in America, and in Vermont, is a loss of that sense of control over the environment. What was once simple building has become so large and expensive and subject to regulation that most people have no feeling of control over either the form or function of what gets built around them. And yet there is a lot that people can do to influence what happens in, and to, their communities.

## IN PRAISE OF HISTORIC PRESERVATION

A 1990 *Vermont Magazine* article by Peter Jennison bore the title, "Woodstock: The Town Vermonters Love to Hate." In the public mind, historic preservation has often been equated with the elitism of lovely—and wealthy—villages like Woodstock (left), Dorset, and Grafton. But historic preservation is also the means for recycling the beautiful buildings that grace all of Vermont, including urban areas and financially less well-endowed towns. The Vermont Division of Historic Preservation is available to assist any Vermonter who wants to save or transform an old building without ruining its character. The Division has helped to preserve Burlington's Old North End, Barre's Socialist Workers Hall, and scores of old houses, churches, and civic buildings by offering its expertise. As the Division's Elsa Gilbertson puts it, "Almost every community in the state practices historic preservation. We do a lot with affordable housing. In many communities average townspeople are helping to fix up their church or town hall. Old buildings are for everyone. There's nothing elitist about that."

Library of Congress/Paul O. Boisvert

## VERMONT FORUM ON SPRAWL SURVEY—1999

A 1999 survey by the Vermont Forum on Sprawl found that many homeowners are loath to give up the 10-acre lot pattern because they want a margin of land to preserve their views and keep a sense of rural openness. But often it is precisely this pattern that can end up destroying real agricultural lands. There are better ways of protecting views than by giving every house its own barrier of land. Some developers have put up housing clusters, with 10 houses on one-acre lots and a 90-acre track of open land held in trust for the whole development. This is a large enough piece of common land to establish margin, rent to a local farmer, or use for joint recreational purposes.

Only about half the towns in Vermont have zoning plans, and many of the older plans sought to retain a rural atmosphere by enacting 5-, 10-, or even 25-acre residential zoning in the hope that large lots would help the town retain its rural atmosphere. While the instinct was good, it often led to a new sort of ex-urban sprawl, a netherworld between suburbia and the working countryside that uses up valuable farmland at an even greater rate while rendering sizable chunks of the countryside unusable for agriculture, forestry, or recreation. Such zoning also does little to create a sense of community, since people wind up living far from their neighbors in their own rural strongholds. A pattern of land use that retains a clearer line between healthy villages and usable open countryside is the traditional Vermont pattern, and one that seems to work well.

The view from Charlotte's Mount Philo is spectacular, with the Champlain Valley rolling west to the lake and the Adirondacks beyond. But the dwellings glowing in the sunrise are not the scattered farms they first appear to be. Most are new houses sprawling over the large rural lots mandated by Vermont's 10-acre septic regulations. A century ago, this view would have shown all manner of farming: sheep, cattle, and crops. Now that productive countryside has largely been subsumed into a kind of suburbia.

We can save anything we want in this landscape. And we can make our additions to the landscape as beautiful as the ones we have inherited from the past. We deserve a landscape that reflects our pride and self-respect, rather than one that panders to the lowest common denominator. It is in our power to make the decisions that will reinforce our sense of place on this land.

## HANDS ON THE LAND

The landscape we see around us shows the effects of layer upon layer, decade upon decade, of human decisions about what to do on the land. Everything from planting a marigold to building a megamall is a landscape decision. Vermonters, like many Americans, have often approached land use decisions with a lack of awareness—or even with apathy. And yet, there are many examples of Vermonters facing specific situations (think of Wal-Mart in Williston) with vigorous debate and straightforward action.

In recorded history, the topography of Vermont has changed very little, and it still continues to set the parameters of the possible in this place. But different human cultures will make very different imprints on the land. Succeeding generations have both enhanced and destroyed the landscape as they struggled to meet their needs, making new landscapes in the process. If Vermont's history shows anything, it is that a strong sense of community is one of the greatest guardians of the environment.

Organized community came slowly in Vermont; settlement was delayed by war, defined by uncontrolled land speculation, undermined by political conflict, and delineated into widely scattered settlements. The first settlers' farms were often lonely places, a string of isolated kingdoms in the clearings. Early town meetings placed few restrictions on what could be done with the land, upholding the individual's right to do as he pleased on his own property. Neighbors helped neighbors in order to survive, but the resources of time and money needed for formal community-building arrived in most parts of Vermont after statehood.

The settlers' children were the lucky generations. Within a few years of statehood in 1791, many Vermonters could take pride, even true delight, in the Edens they were making on the land. After decades of isolation, they wanted to join with their neighbors in mutual enjoyment of their landscape triumph. Vermont's resources were generating enough surplus wealth to enable clustered villages to form, and Vermonters could make landscapes on a human scale, with town halls and churches, greens and the first, fledgling shops—places where they could enjoy the support of neighborliness; soon there would be lyceums and colleges and libraries.

But in a few generations the richness was gone from the age-old soil. By the mid-1800s, many Vermonters were starting to see that this land was

## HOW CAN WE CHOOSE VERMONT?

How can we continue to choose the Vermont we value? First, we must embrace the inevitability of growth as a good and necessary part of a healthy economy. But it will only enhance the state if it creates a landscape that works for communities. There are no hard and fast rules about the form that landscape should take. Some of the things that might be worth putting on the table when we come to trying to retain Vermont include:

The Mad River Valley has made a sincere effort to keep development on a small-town scale, as shown here (left) in Waitsfield, while accommodating large numbers of skiers and other tourists.

Randolph (above) has retained its small-town atmosphere and a strong sense of community. Life here is still centered on the traditional downtown.

**In the countryside:**

■ Pledge to keep at least 50 percent of farm- and forestland in production and undeveloped. A lot of development can be accommodated if 50 percent of the surrounding land remains undeveloped.

■ Close the 10-acre loophole for septic systems, so that people will not be forced to squander more land than they need.

■ Encourage cluster development, even in the countryside, rather than scattered homesteads that disrupt both agriculture and wildlife habitat.

■ Find mechanisms for clustering development along the edges of farmland that is part of the land trust, so that homeowners will know they have "margin" that protects their views without putting farmland out of production.

■ Support the Land Trust, the Conservation Trust, the VCHB, and other organizations that seek to preserve the rural character of the state in perpetuity while providing fair reimbursement for farmers and other landholders who give up their right to develop their land.

**In the towns:**

■ Reiterate our commitment to retaining the pattern of small communities edged by a sharp division between farm and forest land.

■ Communities should designate growth centers where they want to encourage development, but not on viable farmland or on the edges of towns and villages. There should be a clear break where the town ends and the countryside begins.

■ Make human beings the center of the world, not automobiles. Keep building frontages near the road, with sidewalks. There is no excuse for putting a large parking lot in front of a building, even at a mall. All buildings, including those containing multiple shops, should look in keeping with traditional town design, and put the cars in the back or underground.

Governor Howard Dean (left) dedicates a revitalized commercial block in downtown Vergennes in the fall of 1999; local groups helped revive this downtown.

■ Create zoning that allows towns to continue to use the formula that has been so successful in the past, where higher density commercial and residential uses were mixed together, streets had a fairly narrow human scale, and housing was located within walking distance of shops, schools, and other gathering places.

■ Encourage development in downtowns rather than on the periphery by providing tax incentives for downtown development.

■ Shop locally, in downtowns, instead of in the megastores.

■ Refuse to provide infrastructure for any development outside designated growth centers. This one expedient can prevent any and all sprawl if towns have the courage to stand up to big money developers and just say no.

■ Most of Vermont's downtown buildings are old, and many are structures of solidity and distinction. Encourage the recycling of old buildings for new uses by providing investment tax credits for historic preservation.

■ Locate all important public amenities in downtowns—state and federal offices, town halls, municipal buildings, and post offices.

■ Make it faster and easier for developers to move through the Act 250 process if they will build downtown rather than fighting for approval to build on the periphery.

■ Encourage alternative transportation: buses, trains, bikes, feet.

■ Strengthen regional and town-planning processes so that they help communities refine their visions for the land and work together to support common goals.

■ Give landowners as much power and autonomy as possible without compromising community needs.

■ Find new methods of negotiating land use disagreements, so that confrontation can be avoided.

■ Overhaul land use regulations so they encourage the meeting of community goals and provide developers with a greater measure of predictability.

■ Require national chains to conform to community standards rather than their national corporate image if the latter conflicts with Vermonters' landscape goals. Put them downtown, with signage and facades appropriate to their surroundings, but do not allow them to build on the periphery.

Vermont would not be Vermont without its general stores; many remain healthy, vibrant centers of their communities, like Buxton's Store (above) in Orwell.

The Vermonters of the future will face serious decisions about how to control growth, preserve natural beauty and promote strong communities. Here, Rutland stretches toward the mountains, with its shopping center and downtown in the right foreground. Is this the shape of Vermont's future, or do we want to make a different pattern on the land?

Jerry Leblond

not limitless in its gifts. Here, as in most places, some people were making great successes of their lives, building lush valley farms or humming little factories on the small-town waterfalls. But when the hill farms began to play out, legions of the young headed West. The limits of the land had imposed a great downwards correction on the population. Communities were facing a series of new natural, cultural, and economic threats.

In the late nineteenth century, Vermonters quit knocking themselves out over fields that would never turn an agricultural profit and learned how to restore the better ones to a more natural equilibrium. The state began to crawl out of its doldrums, largely thanks to the dairy cow. And those Vermonters who had pulled through had time to look more closely at what they had done to the land and regret the loss of the wilderness.

In the early twentieth century they gained a new self-knowledge, and a more humble awareness of their place in the universe. From this impulse grew the initial movement to restore the wilderness, first through the land acquisitions of a few forward-looking philanthropists, and then with the establishment of the state and national parks. And as the trees came back, so too did many of the forest creatures that had earlier been lost.

There have been a series of Vermonts—some more successful than others—and there are hopeful signs in the current version of this landscape. The state has managed to retain its small scale and a decidedly rural air, even though its countryside has been stripped of much of the agriculture that was once its lifeblood. The air and water are cleaner than they were even 50 years ago, and the wildlife of the forest has grown more abundant. But what of community, that great bulwark against our looking like Anywhere, U.S.A.? There, some of the signs are a bit more worrying.

The woods have returned, but often to be chopped up into big lots and cleared for the vacation homes of well-to-do professionals and businesspeople, many from out of state. These part-time occupants live in an isolation almost as total as that of the settlement days—knowing no one in the community except the guy who mows their lawn or the one they wave to when he plows their driveway. In the countryside, the numbers of farms continue to go down each year, and houses soon sprout on many of their fertile fields. Towns and villages are being marred by generic residential and retail developments that bear no local character. The centers of some villages have turned into commercial ghost towns, while others have seen the shops that used to sell necessities squeezed out by ever-changing luxury boutiques. In the bigger towns, more people live in anonymous subdivisions, ever more dependent on their cars. Vermont's landscape and sense of community are being influenced by trends that have already become realities in most of America.

Many Vermonters now make their livings in ways that are no longer linked to the natural environment. We live in an age of telecommuters, who can use computer hookups, faxes, and satellites to do a wide variety of jobs from Vermont without reference to the limitations of the landscape. In the tiny village of Rochester, high in the Green Mountains, the marble quarry and paneling mill still offer traditional employments for a few of the natives. But the town is also a high-tech hotbed, full of people who work in publishing, electronics, and computers. There are others like them around the state. A stockbroker handles her portfolios from her home in Guildhall. A technical writer works for a California firm from her striking modern house in Weybridge. They could do their jobs anywhere, but they choose to do them in Vermont. Their work transcends the limitations of both the state's environment and its sometimes unreliable transportation system. And many of these people are among the state's most ardent and protective enthusiasts.

Burlington remains the state's largest city. Downtown, its Church Street Marketplace retains its vibrancy and its commercial prestige in the face of unprecedented competition from Chittenden County's newer national chain stores.

Paul O. Boisvert

## FIVE LARGEST TOWNS, 1990

| | |
|---|---|
| Burlington | 39,127 |
| Rutland City | 18,230 |
| Essex | 16,498 |
| Bennington | 16,451 |
| Colchester | 14,731 |

For much of its history, Vermont's economy was highly localized, limiting development but also helping to preserve a cultural heritage. The state's links with a broader national economy began with the coming of the railroads, but they often drained Vermont of people and resources rather than tying them into a wider economic orbit. The second half of the twentieth century has seen the greatest period of economic change, as the interstates and the Internet have finally linked Vermont to the larger national and global economy. It is a situation both fraught with peril and filled with promise.

But we have to ask the question: does this new economic climate mean that culture has finally transcended nature in Vermont? If the new industrial workers, or the telecommuters, or the service industry employees are to be the future of the state, what impact will they have on nature? If each family is again isolated in its own wooded kingdom, what will happen to the sense of community that lies at the heart of good landscape decisions? If culture is gaining a temporary victory over nature, then it is more clearly the culture's job to create an ethic that will protect this landscape while it provides people with satisfying and supportive places to live.

Vermont's reality may not always fit its image as a bucolic paradise, but so far it has managed to retain much of its physical beauty and its cultural resonance. Villages still have their greens, and white-steepled churches, and general stores—the institutions of community—all ringed by open fields. But the Vermont landscape is also filling up with second homes, ski chalets, highways, suburbs, and shopping malls. The decisions that will determine how much of our landscape heritage is retained will be made by everyone in the state, according to what they build, where they shop, how much they drive, and the ways they choose to play in nature. We may not all have dirt under our fingernails, but every one of us has our hands on the land.

# ACKNOWLEDGEMENTS

It sometimes seems as if almost everyone in Vermont has helped in the writing of this book. People all over the state have offered research help and encouragement at every stage. There are so many to thank that I know I cannot have remembered them all. So, even if your name is not here, please know that I appreciated all you did for me and my research assistants.

My greatest thanks must go to The Orton Family Foundation, led by Lyman Orton, the head of the family, and Bill Shouldice, the new Director of the Foundation, who have been unstinting in their financial and intellectual support at every stage. Their dedication to the idea that Vermont's development can and should take place in its traditional settlement pattern of strong, clustered communities is unswerving and inspirational.

The book has been a collaborative effort from the start, and my deepest thanks must go to its guiding spirit, Noel Fritzinger, now retired as head of The Orton Family Foundation. Noel first conceived of the idea of a history of land use in Vermont, and his management of the project has helped to keep us all focused. Even more importantly, Fritz's exuberant intellect has been a constant delight to me at every stage, and his probing questions have made this a far better book than it could ever have been without him. My thanks must also go to Jan Westervelt, who put together the original history book team and had the courage to hire a relative unknown for the job. I have had the help of two wonderful (and good-humored) research assistants, Sara Gregg and Brett Whalen. Sara brought an active intellect and a fine visual sense to the earlier chapters; Brett's archival acumen and lively mind have left their marks on the later ones. Cynthia Locklin did excellent photo research for us in the later stages of the project, as well as providing some fine photographs herself. The look of the book is due to the efforts of graphic designer Leslie Morris Noyes, who deserves my sincere thanks both as a brilliant designer and as a long-suffering support to the author. Bob Churchill, of the Middlebury College Geography Department, has done a wonderful job on the maps. Last, but not least, my thanks to my editor, Julie Kirgo, who has exerted herculean efforts to impose order on scores of images and an unwieldy manuscript.

I owe a great debt to a number of people who have read and commented on portions of the manuscript, including Tom Bassett, Lucy Harding, Beth Humstone, Giovanna Peebles, James Petersen, Greg Sanford, Tom Slayton, and David Stevens. Thank you for saving me from many errors. I absolve you from responsibility for any you were unable to forestall.

We have had research help or obtained images from libraries, archives, town clerks, local history societies, and historic sites all around the state, and virtually every agency of state government connected to land use has lent its expertise. Our thanks to everyone who hunted down leads, answered queries, and supplied images for us.

A number of individuals have been particularly helpful. Karen Campbell and Jeffrey Marshall of the Department of Special Collections at the University of Vermont Libraries seem to know where to find almost anything; thanks to them and to all those connected with the Wilbur Collection of Vermontiana. At the Vermont Historical Society in Montpelier we have had especially dedicated assistance from Paul Carnahan, Barney Bloom, and Jacqueline Calder. Greg Sanford, the State Archivist, has been a great source of both the bureaucratic and the idiosyncratic.

Many others deserve to be singled out for thanks, and I list them here: Ginger Anderson, Glenn Andres, David Bain, Jane Beck, Ken Becker, Larry Becker, Kay Beers, Darlene Berkovitz, Paul O. Boisvert, Nancy Boone, Ingrid Bower, Jim Boyd, Deb Brighton, Dona Brown, Greg Brown, Bob Buckeye, Sandra Button, Alison Byerly, Deborah Clifford, Charlie Cogbill, Janie Cohen, Ray Coish, Judi and Fred Danforth, Polly Darnell, Jean Davies, Erica Donnis, Paul Donovan, Mary Duffy, Joyce Eckler, John Elder, Peg Elmer, John Ewing, Liz Fitzsimmons, Marjorie Gale, Harold Garabedian, Blake Gardner, Elsa Gilbertson, Carol Greenough, Todd Hannahs, Bill Hart, Steve Holmes, Tordis Isselhardt, Alan Jakubek, Steve Jensen, Charles Johnson, Curtis Johnson, Dayle Klitzner, Sylvia Knight, Jerry LeBlond, Ruth Levin, Jim Libby, Anne Linton, Richard Maley, Sue MacIntire, Stewart McHenry, Kim McKay, Sally McLintock, Harold Meeks, Tad Merrick, Don Mitchell, Lotti Morris, Kathy Morse, Sue Morse, Kate Mueller, Gerry Murphy, Lois Noonan, Mike Nyland-Funke, Ellen Oxfeld, Jay Parini, Kristin Peterson-Ishaq, Audrey Porsche, Hans Raum, Tom Rawls, Sally Redpath, Carl Reidel, Janet Reit, Dave Robinson, Alan Rogers, Nancy Rucker, Joanne Schneider, Paula Schwartz, Fred Sullivan, Regina Sweeney, Roger Thompson, UVM Photo Services, Tom Visser, Elin Waagen, Meg Wallace, Jane Williamson, Robin Woodward, and the Amigos (you know who you are).

We also owe special thanks to Frank Urbanowski and his wonderful staff at M.I.T. Press. The quality of the photo reproduction and printing is thanks to Stephen Stinehour, whose amazing company does this highly specialized work from the heart of the Northeast Kingdom.

My family has been a great support to me. My mother, Helen Albers, has given me her love for the written word, along with her unwavering maternal devotion. My father, the late Lowell Albers, was a dairy farmer who taught me to love history and the land. I also thank the rest of my family for their constant encouragement and humor: Randall Albers and Blair Barbour, Alex Albers, Stephen Albers and Cathy Larson, Joan Monod, David Monod and Michaela Milde, and Adam and Emma Monod.

Last, but always first in my heart, my deepest thanks go to my endlessly patient husband, Paul Monod. He is my love, my truest friend, and the most convenient font of historical wisdom I could ever have under my roof. And to my beautiful son, Evan, my greatest addition to the Vermont landscape. I dedicate this book to them.

# BIBLIOGRAPHY

Note: Most books are cited under the first chapter in which information from them appears, although there are a few exceptions for those cases in which the book furnished far more information for a later chapter. In addition to the works cited here, the author has also consulted local histories on many towns around the state, the inclusion of which would nearly double the length of this bibliography. Large collections of town histories can be found at Bailey-Howe Library at the University of Vermont, Middlebury College Library, and the Vermont Historical Society in Montpelier. Queries on town histories consulted for this book can be directed to the author.

## INTRODUCTION

Farnham, Euclid, *Tunbridge Past*, Tunbridge Historical Society (Tunbridge, 1980).

Jackson, John Brinkerhoff, *Reading the Vernacular Landscape*, Yale University Press (New Haven, c.1984).

Swift, Esther Munroe, *Vermont Place-Names: Footprints of History*, The Stephen Green Press (Brattleboro, Vermont, 1977).

## CHAPTER 1

Allan, Helen, *The Original People: Native Americans In The Champlain Valley*, Clinton County Historical Museum (Plattsburgh, 1988).

Bruchac, Joseph, *The Faithful Hunter: Abenaki Stories*, Greenfield Review Press (Greenfield Center, New York, 1988).

Cronon, William, *Changes in the Land: Indians, Colonists and the Ecology of New England*, Hill and Wang (New York, 1983).

Davis, Mary Byrd, ed., *Eastern Old-Growth Forests*, Island Press (Washington, D.C. and Corvelo, California, 1996).

Day, Gordon M., "Western Abenaki," in Bruce G. Trigger, ed., *Handbook of North American Indians*, Smithsonian Institution (Washington, 1978), 148–159.

Dodge, Harry W., Jr., "The Geology of D.A.R. State Park, Mount Philo State Forest Park and Sand Bar State Park," *Vermont Geological Survey* (Monpelier, VT, 1969).

Doolan, Barry, "The Geology of Vermont," *Rocks & Minerals*, 71 (July/August 1996), 218–225.

Haviland, William A. and Marjory W. Power, *The Original Vermonters: Native Inhabitants, Past and Present*, University Press of New England (Hanover and London, 1994).

Heckenberger, Michael J., James B. Petersen and Louise A. Basa, "Early Woodland Period Ritual Use of Personal Adornment at the Boucher Site," *Annals of the Carnegie Museum*, 59, 3, 173–217.

Huden, John C., *Indian Place Names in Vermont*, Monograph No. 1 (Burlington, Vt., August 1957).

Johnson, Charles W., *The Nature of Vermont*, University Press of New England (Hanover and London, 1980).

Klyza, Christopher McGrory and Stephen C. Trombulak, eds., *The Future of the Northern Forest*, University Press of New England (Hanover and London, 1994).

Lacy, David M., "Prehistoric Land-Use in the Green Mountains: A View from the National Forest," *Journal of Vermont Archaeology*, Vermont Archaeological Society, vol. 1, 1994.

Loring, Stephen, "Paleo-indian Hunters and the Champlain Sea: a Presumed Association," *Man in the Northeast*, 19 (1980), 15–41.

Meeks, Harold A., *Vermont's Land and Resources*, The New England Press (Shelburne, VT, 1992).

Peterken, George F., *Natural Woodland: Ecology and Conservation in Northern Temperate Regions*, Cambridge University Press (Cambridge, 1996).

Petersen, James B., *The Middle Woodland Ceramics of the Winooski Site*, Vermont Archaeological Society, New Series, 1980.

Power, Marjory W. and James B. Petersen, *Seasons of Prehistory: 4000 Years at the Winooski Site*, Division for Historic Preservation (Montpelier, 1984).

Siccama, Thomas, "Presettlement and Present Forest Vegetation in Northern Vermont with Special Reference to Chittenden County," *The American Midland Naturalist* (Notre Dame, Indiana, 1971), pp. 153–172.

Stewart, David P and Paul MacClintock, "The Surficial Geology and Pleistocene History of Vermont," *Vermont Geological Survey* (Montpelier, VT, 1969), Bulletin No 31.

Van Diver, Bradford B., *Roadside Geology of Vermont and New Hampshire*, Mountain Press (Missoula, MT, 1987).

Thomas, Peter A., "Vermont Archaeology Comes of Age; A Current Perspective on Vermont's Prehistoric Past," *Journal of Vermont Archaeology*, Vermont Archaeological Society, 1, 1994.

Thomas, Peter A. and Brian S. Robinson, *The John's Bridge Site: An Early Archaic Period Site*, Department of Anthropology, University of Vermont, Report #28 (Burlington, Nov., 1980).

Whitney, Gordon G., *From Coastal Wilderness to Fruited Plain: a History of Environmental Change in Temperate North America, 1500 to the Present*, Cambridge University Press (Cambridge, 1994).

## CHAPTER 2

Alexander, John K., "Jonathan Carpenter and the American Revolution: The Journal of an American Naval Prisoner of War and Vermont Indian Fighter," *Vermont History*, 36, 2 (Spring 1968), 74–90.

Allen, Ira, *The Natural and Political History of the State of Vermont*, Charles E. Tuttle Co. (Rutland, 1969; 1st ed., 1798).

Axtell, James, *The Invasion Within: the Contest of Cultures in Colonial North America*, Oxford Univ. Press (New York & Oxford, 1985).

Bassett, T.D. Seymour, ed., *Outsiders Inside Vermont: Three Centuries of Visitors' Viewpoints on the Green Mountain State*, Phoenix Pub. (Canaan, New Hampshire, 1967).

Bellesiles, Michael A., *Revolutionary Outlaws: Ethan Allen and the Struggle for Independence on the Early American Frontier*, University Press of Virginia (Charlottesville and London, 1993).

Benson, Adolph B., *Peter Kalm's Travels In North America*, 2 vols., Wilson-Erickson, Inc. (New York, 1937).

Biddle, Arthur W. and Paul A. Eschholz, eds., *The Literature of Vermont: a Sampler*, University Press of New England (Hanover, 1973).

Botti, Priscilla Smith, "Elizabeth Whitmore: Midwife of Marlboro," *Vermont History*, 39, 2 (Spring 1971), 98–100.

Burton, Asa, *The Life of Asa Burton Written By Himself*, The First Congregational Church (Thetford, VT, 1973).

Calloway, Colin, ed., *Dawnland Encounters: Indians and Europeans in New England*, Univ. Press of New England (Hanover and London, 1991).

_____, *The Western Abenakis of Vermont, 1600–1800*, Univ. Oklahoma Press (Norman and London, 1990).

Carpenter, Jonathan, *Jonathan Carpenter's Journal*, Miriam and Wes Herwig, eds., Greenhills (Randolph Center, Vermont, 1994).

Casson, François Dollier de, *Histoire de Montréal*, Dent-Dutton (London, 1928), trans. by T.D. Seymour Bassett.

Champlain, Samuel D., *Les voyages du Samuel de Champlain*, Ann Arbor University Microfilms (Ann Arbor, 1966) of the Paris edition of 1613.

Clark, Charles E., *The Eastern Frontier: The Settlement of Northern New England, 1610–1763*, Alfred A. Knopf (New York, 1970).

Congdon, Herbert Wheaton, *Old Vermont Houses, 1763–1850*, William L. Bauhan, Publisher (Dublin, New Hampshire, 1973).

Crockett, Walter Hill, *Vermonters: a Book of Biographies*, Stephen Daye Press (Brattleboro, 2nd ed., 1932).

_____, *Vermont: The Green Mountain State*, vol. 3, The Century History Company (New York, 1921).

Dodge, Bertha S., *Vermont by Choice: the Earliest Years*, The New England Press (Shelburne, 1987).

Fingerhut, Eugene R., "From Scots to Americans: Ryegate's Immigrants in the 1770s," *Vermont History*, 35, 4 (Autumn 1967), 186–207.

Fisher, Charles L., "A Report on the 1977 Archaeological Test Excavations at Fort St. Frederic, Crown Point State Historic Site, Essex County, New York," Parks, Recreation and Historic Preservation Bureau of Historic Sites (Waterford, New York, 1991).

Graffagnino, J. Kevin, *The Shaping of Vermont: From the Wilderness to the Centennial, 1749–1877*, Vermont Heritage Press and The Bennington Museum (Rutland and Bennington, 1983). Includes map portfolio.

Hemenway, Abby, *The Vermont Historical Gazetteer*, (Burlington, 1868–1891).

Hill, Ralph Nading, *Lake Champlain: Key to Liberty*, The Countryman Press (Woodstock, VT, 1995, 1st ed., 1976).

_____, *Yankee Kingdom: Vermont and New Hampshire*, Harper & Brothers (New York, 1960).

Hosley, William, N., Jr., ed., *The Great River: Art & Society of the Connecticut, 1635–1820*. Wadsworth Atheneum (Hartford, 1985).

Hubbell, Seth, *A Narrative of the Sufferings of Seth Hubbell & Family*, Vermont Heritage Press (Bennington, 1986).

Johnson, Curtis B., ed., *The Historical Architecture of Addison County*, Vermont Division for Historic Preservation (Montpelier, 1992).

Johnson, Curtis B. and Elsa Gilbertson, eds., *The Historic Architecture of Rutland County*, Vermont Division for Historic Preservation (Montpelier, 1988).

Jones, Matt Bushnell, *Vermont in the Making, 1750–1777*, Harvard Univ. Press (Cambridge, MA, 1939).

McCullough, Robert, *The Landscape of Community: a History of Communal Forests in New England*, University Press of New England (Hanover and London, 1995).

McHenry, Stewart G., "Eighteenth-Century Field Patterns as Vernacular Art," in Dell Upton & John Michael Vlach, *Common Places: Readings in American Vernacular Architecture*, Univ. of Georgia Press (Athens & London, 1986), 107–123.

Meeks, Harold, A, *Time and Change in Vermont: a Human Geography*, The Globe Pequot Press (Chester, CT, 1986).

Merchant, Carolyn, *Ecological Revolutions: Nature, Gender, and Science in New England*, University of North Carolina Press (Chapel Hill and London, 1989).

Morrissey, Brenda C., *Abby Hemenway's Vermont*, The Stephen Greene Press (Brattleboro, 1972).

Muller, H. Nicholas III and Samuel B. Hand, eds., *In a State of Nature: Readings in Vermont History*, Vermont Historical Society (Montpelier, 1982).

Nygren, Edward J. and Bruce Robertson, *Views and Visions: American Landscape before 1830*, Corcoran Gallery of Art (Washington, D.C., 1986).

Perkins, Nathan, *A Narrative of a Tour Through the State of Vermont From April 27 to June 12, 1789*, The Elm Tree Press (Woodstock, VT, 1937).

Potash, P. Jeffrey, *Vermont's Burned-Over District: Patterns of Community Development and Religious Activity, 1761–1850*, Carlson, Pub., Inc. (Brooklyn, NY, 1991).

Reps, John W., *Town Planning In Frontier America*, Princeton Univ. Press (Princeton, NJ, 1969).

Rogers, Robert, *Journals of Major Robert Rogers*, University Microfilms (Ann Arbor, 1966).

Russell, Howard S., *The Long, Deep Furrow: Three Centuries of Farming in New England*, Univ. Press of New England (Hanover and London, 1982; 1st ed., 1976).

Sherman, Michael and Jennie Versteeg, eds., *We Vermonters: Perspectives On The Past*, Vermont Historical Society (Montpelier, 1992).

Smith, Elias, *The Life, Conversion, Preaching, Travels, and Sufferings of Elias Smith*, Beck & Foster (Portsmouth, N.H., 1816).

Thomas, Keith, *Man and the Natural World*, Pantheon Books (New York, 1983).

Vermont Division for Historic Preservation, "Vermont's Prehistoric Cultural Heritage," Vermont Historic Preservation Plan (Montpelier, 1991).

Versteeg, Jennie G., ed., *Lake Champlain: Reflections On Our Past*, University of Vermont and Vermont Historical Society (Burlington, 1987).

Wilgus, William J., *The Role of Transportation in the Development of Vermont*, Vermont Historical Society (Montpelier, 1945).

Williams, Henry Lionel and Ottalie K. Williams, *Old American Houses, 1700–1850*, Bonanza Books (New York, 1967).

Williams, Samuel, *The Natural and Civil History of Vermont*, Isaiah Thomas and David Carlisle, Jr. (Walpole, NH, 1794).

Woodard, Florence May, *The Town Proprietors in Vermont*, Columbia University Press (New York, 1936).

## CHAPTER 3

Abbott, Collamer, *Green Mountain Copper: The Story of Vermont's Red Metal*, Herald Printery (Randolph, Vt., 1973).

Bancroft, A. B., "A Traveller's Account of Bellows Falls and Burlington in 1832," in *Vermont History*, 36, 4 (Autumn 1968), 210–213.

Barna, Ed, *Covered Bridges of Vermont*, Countryman Press (Woodstock, 1996).

Barron, Hal S., *Those Who Stayed Behind: Rural Society in Nineteenth Century New England*, Cambridge University Press (Cambridge, 1984).

Bassett, T. D. Seymour, *The Growing Edge: Vermont Villages, 1840–1880*, Vermont Historical Society (Montpelier, Vt., 1992).

Benjamin, Asher, *The American Builder's Companion*, Dover Publications (New York, 1969; 1st. ed. 1806).

_____, *The Country Builder's Assistant*, Da Capo Press (New York, 1972; 1st ed. 1797).

Bonfield, Lynn A. and Mary C. Morrison, *Roxana's Children: The Biography of a Nineteenth-Century Vermont Family*, University of Massachusetts Press (Amherst, 1995).

Brooke, John L., *The Refiner's Fire: The Making of Mormon Cosmology 1644–1844*, Cambridge University Press (Cambridge, 1994).

Browne, Charles C. and Howard B. Reed, Jr., eds., *Visions, Toil & Promise: Man in Vermont's Forests*, Fairbanks Museum and Planetarium (St. Johnsbury, Vt., 1985).

Carlisle, Lilian Baker, *Eighteenth and Nineteenth Century American Art at the Shelburne Museum*, Shelburne Museum (Shelburne, Vt., 1961).

Clark, Christopher, *The Roots of Rural Capitalism: Western Massachusetts, 1780–1860*, Cornell University Press (Ithaca and London, 1990).

Crockett, Walter Hill, *Vermont: The Green Mountain State*, iii, The Century History Company (New York, 1921).

Degree, Kenneth A., *Vergennes in 1870: a Vermont City in the Victorian Age* (K.A. Degree, 1990).

Demeritt, David, "Climate, Cropping and Society in Vermont, 1820–1850," *Vermont History*, 59, 3 (Summer 1991), 133–165.

DeYeo, John Peter, "From Yankee Cobbler to Middlebury Bookseller: Jonathan Hagar's Middle Years, 1799–1820," *Vermont History*, 37, 1 (Winter 1969), 13–29.

Duffy, John, *Vermont: an Illustrated History*, Windsor Publications (Windsor, Vt., 1985).

Dwight, Timothy, *Travels in New England and New York*, Belknap Press of Harvard University Press (Cambridge, Mass., 1969; 1st ed. 1821–22).

Everest, Allan S., "Early Roads and Taverns of the Champlain Valley," in *Vermont History*, 37, 4 (Autumn 1969), 247–255.

Fant, H. B., "Levi Woodbury's Week in Vermont, May 1819," in *Vermont History*, 24, 1 (January 1966), 36–62.

Fuller, Edmund, *Vermont: A History of the Green Mountain State*, State Board of Education (Montpelier, 1952).

Gilmore, William J., *Reading Becomes a Necessity of Life: Material and Cultural Life in Rural New England, 1780–1835*, University of Tennessee Press (Knoxville, 1989).

Hamilton, Alexander, *The Reports of Alexander Hamilton*; Jacob E. Cooke, ed., Harper & Row (New York, Evanston and London, 1964).

Himelhoch, Myra, *The Allens in Early Vermont*, Star Printing and Publishing Co. (Barre, 1967).

Jefferson, Thomas, *Notes on the State of Virginia*, Harper & Row (New York, Evanston and London, 1964).

Kull, Nell W., "'I Can Never Be Happy There in Among So Many Mountains,'—The Letters of Sally Rice," *Vermont History*, 38, 1 (Winter 1970), 49–57.

Lipke, William C. and Philip N. Grime, eds., *Vermont Landscape Images, 1776–1976*, Robert Hull Fleming Museum (Burlington, Vt., 1976).

Ludlum, David, *The Vermont Weather Book*, Houghton Mifflin (Boston, 1984).

Malvern, Robert, "Of Money Needs and Family News: Brigham Family Letters, 1800–1820," in *Vermont History*, 41, 3 (Summer 1973), 113–122.

McCabe, James, "In the Twilight of His Years Eli Canfield Recalls His Boyhood in Arlington, 1817–1831," *Vermont History*, 40, 2 (Spring 1972), 105–116.

Murray, Donald M. and Robert M. Rodney, "Sylvia Drake, 1784–1868: The Self Portrait of a Seamstress of Weybridge," *Vermont History*, 34, 2 (April 1966), 123–135.

Pepe, Faith Learned, *Vermont Workers, Vermont Resources: Clay, Wood, Metal, Stone*, Brattleboro Museum and Art Center (Brattleboro, 1984).

Robinson, Charles A., *Vermont Cabinetmakers & Chairmakers Before 1855*, Shelburne Museum (Shelburne, 1994).

Robinson Rowland E., *Danvis Tales: Selected Stories*, University Press of New England (Hanover and London, 1995).

Rolando, Victor R., *200 Years of Soot and Sweat: The History and Archaeology of Vermont's Iron, Charcoal, and Lime Industries*, Vermont Archaeological Society (1992).

Roth, Randolph A., *The Democratic Dilemma: Religion, Reform and the Social Order in the Connecticut River Valley of Vermont, 1791–1850*, Cambridge University Press (Cambridge, 1987).

Rothenberg, Winifred Barr, *From Market-Places to a Market Economy: The Transformation of Rural Massachusetts, 1750–1850*, University of Chicago Press (Chicago and London, 1992).

Sabin, Elisha, "To Get Established in the West: Letters to Windsor and Woodstock by Elisha Sabin, 1843–50," *Vermont History*, 41, 4 (Summer 1973), 123–141.

Saunders, Richard H. and Virginia M. Westbrook, *Celebrating Vermont: Myths and Realities*, University Press of New England (Middlebury, Hanover and London: 1991).

Spears, Timothy, "Timothy Dwight's Travels in New England and New York," *American Studies*, 30 (Spring 1989), 35–52.

Stevens, Henry, "The Diary of Henry Stevens," *Proceedings of the Vermont Historical Society*, New Series, II, 3 (1931), 115–128.

Stilgoe, John R., *Common Landscape of America, 1580 to 1845*, Yale University Press (New Haven and London, 1982).

Stilwell, Lewis D., *Migration From Vermont*, Vermont Historical Society (Montpelier, 1948).

Thompson, Zadock, *An Address Delivered at Boston...June 1850*, Chauncey Goodrich (Burlington, 1850).

_____, *Natural History of Vermont*, Charles E. Tuttle Co. (Rutland, Vt., 1971; 1st ed., 1853).

Vermont Marble Company, *The Book of Vermont Marble*, Vermont Marble Company (Proctor, 1929).

Visser, Thomas Durant, *Field Guide to New England Barns and Farm Buildings*, University Press of New England (Hanover and London, 1997).

Whittemore, John, *The Autobiography of John Whittemore* (no pub. or place), 1938.

Wilson, Harold Fisher, *The Hill Country of Northern New England: Its Social and Economic History, 1790–1930*, AMS Press (New York, 1967).

Wood, Joseph S., *The New England Village*, Johns Hopkins University Press (Baltimore and London, 1997).

## CHAPTER 4

Dawn K. Andrews, "Family Traits: Vermont Farm Life at the Turn of the Century: The Sketches of Stanley Horace Lyndes," *Vermont History* , 48, 1 (Winter 1980), 5–27.

Brown, Dona, "Accidental Tourists: Visitors to the Mount Mansfield Summit House in the Late Nineteenth Century," *Vermont History*, 65, 3 & 4 (Summer/Fall 1997), 117–130.

_____, *Inventing New England: Regional Tourism in the Nineteenth Century*, Smithsonian Institution Press (Washington and London, 1995), 157.

Cheney, Cora, *Profiles From the Past: An Uncommon History of Vermont*, The Countryman Press (Taftsville, VT, 1973).

Coffin, Howard, *Full Duty: Vermonters in the Civil War*, The Countryman Press (Woodstock, VT, 1993).

Curtis, Jane and Will and Frank Lieberman, *The World of George Perkins Marsh*, The Countryman Press (Woodstock, VT, 1982).

Davenport, Walter Rice, "A Boy in Vermont 65 Years Ago," *The Vermonter*, 33, 3 (1928).

Dempsey, Clarence H., "Rural Schools and Abandoned Farms," *The Vermont Review*, 1, 2 (July–August 1926), 34–36.

Douglas, F. D., "Opportunities and Rewards for the Application of Brain Work to Dairy Farming," *Second Biennial Report of the Vermont State Board of Agriculture...1873–74*, Freeman Steam Printing (Montpelier, 1874), 134.

Dyer, Cecil, "Lake Willoughby 60 Years Ago," *Vermont History*, 24 (1956), 241.

Fisher, Dorothy Canfield, *Tourists Accommodated: A Play*, Harcourt, Brace and Co. (New York, c. 1934), 19–20, 61–62, 64.

Goldman, Hal, "'A Desirable Class of People': The Leadership of the Green Mountain Club and Social Exclusivity, 1920–1936," *Vermont History*, 65, 3 & 4 (Summer/Fall 1997), 131–152.

_____, "James Taylor's Progressive Vision: The Green Mountain Parkway," *Vermont History*, 63, 3 (summer 1995), 158–179.

Hastings, Scott E., Jr. and Elsie R. Hastings, *Up in the Morning Early: Vermont Farm Families in the Thirties*, University Press of New England (Hanover, 1992).

Horton, Guy B., Henry A. Stoddard and Harold J.R. Stillwell, *The Grange in Vermont*, The Cowles Press (St. Johnsbury, 1968).

Hoskins, T. H., "Vermont as an Agricultural State," *First Annual Report of the Vermont State Board of Agriculture, Manufactures and Mining for the Year 1872*, J. & J.M. Poland's Steam Printing (Montpelier, 1872), 568–578.

Irland, Lloyd C., *Wildlands and Woodlots: The Story of New England's Forests*, University Press of New England (Hanover and London, 1982).

Jameson, Z. E., "Management of Swamp Lands," *VAG*, 1873–74, 544–545.

Jennison, Keith Warren, *Vermont Is Where You Find It*, Harcourt, Brace and Co. (New York, 1941).

Judd, Richard W., *Common Lands, Common People: the Origins of Conservation in Northern New England*, Harvard University Press (Cambridge, MA and London, 1997), 213.

Keeler, JoAnn, "The Addison County Fair: Agrarian Reactions to Industrial Trends," B.A. Thesis, Department of History, Middlebury College, February 1989.

Landon, Witney, "Summers at Caspain Lake, 1896–1925," transcript of a recording c. 1974, *Vermont History*, 43 (summer 1975), 183.

Liebs, Chester H., *The Burlington Book: Architecture, History, Future*, University of Vermont Historic Preservation Program (Burlington, 1980).

Linton,W. J., *Picturesque America* (1874).

*Long Trail News*, The Green Mountain Club, 3, 4 (August 1930), 2.

Marsh, George Perkins, *Man and Nature: Or, Physical Geography as Modified by Human Action*, The Belknap Press of Harvard University Press (Cambridge, MA, 1965. Originally pub. 1864). David Lowenthal, editor.

Mead, John B., "Barns and Farm Buildings," *Second Biennial Report of the Vermont State Board of Agriculture, Manufacture and Mining, 1873–74*, Freeman Steam Printing (Montpelier, 1874).

Muir, John, *My First Summer in the Sierra*, Penguin Books (Harmondsworth, Middlesex, 1987 (1st pub. 1911).

Nutting, Wallace, *Vermont Beautiful*, Old America Co. (Framingham, MA, 1922).

Pember, E. R., "Our Hill Farms," *Eighth Vermont Agricultural Report by the Vermont State Board of Agriculture for the Years 1883–84*, Watchman & Journal Press (Montpelier, 1884), 362–369.

Poland, Luke P., *Address Delivered Before the Vermont State Agricultural Society...1869*, Polands' Steam Printing (Montpelier, 1869), 15.

Powell, Max L., "Selling Vermont Beauty," *Vermont Review*, 1, 1 (May-June 1926), 13–15.

Rebek, Andrea, "The Selling of Vermont: From Agriculture to Tourism, 1860–1910," in H. Nicholas Muller, III and Samuel B. Hand, *In a State of Nature: Readings in Vermont History*, Vermont Historical Society (Montpelier, 1982), 273–282.

Ross, Jonathan, "An Old Home Week Address, August 1902," *Vermont History*, 49, 2 (Spring, 1972), 122–128.

Rozwenc, Edwin C., *Agricultural Policies in Vermont, 1860–1945*, Vermont Historical Society (Montpelier, 1981).

Sanford, Rob, et al., *Stonewalls & Cellarholes*, Vermont Agency of Natural Resources (Waterbury, VT, 1994).

Sharrow, Greg, *Many Cultures, One People*, Vermont Folklife Center (1992), 169–170.

Stameshkin, David M., *The Town's College: Middlebury College, 1800–1915*, Middlebury College Press (Middlebury, VT, 1985).

Taber, Edward Martin, *Stowe Notes, Letters and Verses*, Houghton Mifflin (Boston and New York, 1913).

Tillman, David A., *Mining in Vermont*, Tower Publishing (Portland, ME, 1974).

Two Hundred Vermonters. *Rural Vermont: A Program For the Future*, Burlington (Commissions on Country Life, 1931).

United States Department of Agriculture, Forest Service, *The Story of the Green Mountain National Forest in Vermont* (USDA, 1961).

Vermont Board of Agriculture, *Vermont, Its Fertile Farms and Summer Homes* (Montpelier, 1897).

_____, *Vermont: Its Opportunities for Investment in Agriculture, Manufacturing, Minerals and Its Attractions for Summer Homes* (Montpelier, 1903).

Vermont Commission on Country Life, "Newsletter," typescript, December 1929, UVM Special Collections, f WLC/v592c, 26–27, 47–48.

Vermont, Federal Writers' Project of the WPA, *Vermont: A Guide to the Green Mountain State*, American Guide Series, Houghton Mifflin Company (Boston, 1937), 3, 7–8.

Vermont Folklife Center, *Visit'n*, vol. 2 (Middlebury, VT, November 1996).

Vermont Publicity Bureau, *The Green Mountains of Vermont* (Montpelier, 1919), 7–8.

Vermont Publicity Service, "Vermont Summer Homes: An Open Letter by Dorothy Canfield" (Montpelier, 1937).

Washington, Ida, "Dorothy Canfield Fisher's Tourists Accommodated and Her Other Promotions of Vermont," *Vermont History*, vol. 65, 3 & 4 (Summer/Fall, 1997), 153–164.

Wessels, Tom, *Reading the Forested Landscape: A Natural History of New England*, The Countryman Press (Woodstock, VT, 1997).

Wilson, Stanley C., *Address...on The Agricultural Outlook in Vermont*, Vermont Bureau of Publicity (Montpelier, 1931).

_____, *Address...on Summer Homes in Vermont*, Vermont Bureau of Publicity (Montpelier, 1931).

_____, *Address...on the Long Trail*, Vermont Bureau of Publicity (Montpelier, 1931).

_____, *Address...on Vermont—A Vacation Land*, Vermont Bureau of Publicity (Montpelier, 1931).

Yale, Allen R., Jr., *While the Sun Shines: Making Hay in Vermont, 1789–1990*, Vermont Historical Society (Montpelier, 1991).

## CHAPTER 5

Barna, Ed, "For the Love of Old Buildings," *Vermont Magazine*, 4, 4 (July/August 1992), 62–70.

Bazilchuk, Nancy, "State Aims to Expand Moose Hunt," *Burlington Free Press*, October 20, 1998.

Bevins, Malcolm I., "Agriculture and Recreation: Competitive or Compatible?" Ag. Econ. pamphlet 68–3, University of Vermont (Burlington, 1968).

Bigelow, Edwin L., Stowe, *Vermont: Ski Capital of the East, 1763–1963*, Stowe Historical Society (Stowe, 1964).

Bruhn, Paul, "Doing It Vermont's Way," *The Rutland Daily Herald*, August 11, 1993.

_____, "Wal-Mart in Vermont: An Asset If...," *Burlington Free Press*, September 15, 1995.

Bryan, Frank M., *Yankee Politics in Rural Vermont*, University Press of New England (Hanover, NH, 1974).

Carroll, Hanson, "They Call It Snow Farming," *Vermont Life*, 27, 2 (Winter 1972), 11–13.

Carter, John H. and John T. Flickinger, "The Impact of the Ski Industry on Selected Areas of Vermont," Vermont Agency of Development and Community Affairs (Montpelier, 1971).

Champlain Initiative, "The History of Sprawl in Chittenden County," Sustainability and Growth Center Team of the Champlain Initiative (Burlington, 1999).

Chesman, Andrea, "Home, Sheep, Home," *Vermont Life*, 6, 4 (Summer 1994), 42–49.

Crane, Charles Edward, *Winter in Vermont*, Alfred A. Knopf (New York, 1947).

Crawford, Matt, "After 100 Years, Deer Are Back," *The Burlington Free Press*, November 16, 1996.

_____, "Cry, Vermont," *Time*, September 26, 1969, 50.

Daley, Yvonne, "Return of the Natives: a Cultural Rebirth for Vermont's Abenaki," *Vermont Life*, 49, 1 (Autumn 1994), 38–45.

Daniels, Tom and Deborah Bowers, *Holding Our Ground: Protecting America's Farms and Farmland*, Island Press (Washington, D.C. and Covelo, California, 1997).

Diamond, Henry L. and Patrick F. Noonan, *Land Use in America*, Lincoln Institute of Land Policy, Island Press (Washington, D.C. and Covelo, California, 1996).

Dillon, John, "Water Wars: Why Snowmaking and Water Use are Vermont's Environmental Bosnia," *Vermont Magazine*, 6, 1 (Jan./Feb. 1994), 26–31, 76.

Drysdale, M. Dickey, "Rochester Renaissance," *Vermont Life*, 52, 3 (Spring 1998), 30–35, 57.

Farley, Virginia and Joanna Whitcomb, *Kicking Stones Down a Dirt Road: Rural Resource Protection in Vermont's Mad River Valley*, Mad River Valley Rural Resources Commission (Waitsfield, 1998?).

Fisher, Dorothy Canfield, *Vermont Tradition: The Biography of an Outlook on Life*, Little, Brown and Co. (Boston, 1953).

Forestry Plan for Vermont Committee, "A Forestry Plan for Vermont" (Montpelier, 1950).

Gebelein, Herbert, "A Short History of the Development and Growth of the Ski Industry in Vermont," typescript of a paper delivered before the St. Lawrence Valley-New England Geographical Society at Burlington, Vermont, October 14, 1967.

Gilbert, Alphonse H., "Attitudes of Vermont Hunters," Vermont Agricultural Experiment Station, University of Vermont (Burlington, 1975).

Gilbert, Allen, "Access to the World: By Modem, Fax, or Satellite, Businesses Can Get There From Here," *Vermont Life*, 46, 3 (Spring 1992), 29–33.

Gottlieb, Albert W., "A Ten Year Forestry Plan for Vermont, 1964–1973," Vermont Department of Forests and Parks (Montpelier, 1964).

Greene, Stephen, "Out of Our Woods," *Vermont Life*, 17, 1 (Autumn 1962), 3–17.

Harlow, Susan, "After the Cow," *Vermont Magazine*, 3, 2 (March/April 1991), 38–43.

Hayes, Nelson, "Beauty at a Bargain," *Vermont Life*, 8, 3 (Spring 1954).

Hiss, Tony, *The Experience of Place*, Alfred A. Knopf (New York, 1990).

Hough, Michael, *Out of Place: Restoring Identity to the Regional Landscape*, Yale University Press (New Haven & London, 1990).

Jennison, Peter S., "Woodstock: The Town Vermonters Love to Hate," *Vermont Magazine*, 2, 1 (Jan./Feb. 1990), 68–73, 88.

Johnson, C. B., "The Vanishing Barn," *Vermont Life*, 47, 1 (Autumn 1992), 31–33.

Johnson, Ken, "Who We Are," *Vermont Magazine*, 4, 6 (Nov./Dec. 1992), 42–45.

Kingsley, Neal P., *The Forest Resources of Vermont*, USDA Forest Resources Bulletin NE-46 (Upper Darby, PA, 1977).

Klyza, Christopher McGrory and Stephen C. Trombulak, *The Story of Vermont: A Natural and Cultural History*, University Press of New England (Hanover & London, 1999).

Krohn, Lee A., "Town Planning in Vermont: A Primer and Proposal for Change," Town Planning Committee of Manchester, VT (Manchester, 1998?).

Kuentzel, Walter F., Robert A. Robertson and Varna M. Ramaswamy, "A Time-series Comparison of Vermont and New Hampshire Travel Trends," *Proceedings of the Fourth International Outdoor Recreation and Tourism Trends Symposium* (St. Paul, MN, 1995).

Kunstler, James Howard, *Home From Nowhere: Remaking Our Everyday World for the 21st Century*, Simon & Schuster (New York, 1996).

Lazenby, John, "The Cat is Back," *Vermont Life*, 49, 2 (Winter, 1994), 20–25.

Libby, James M., Jr., "The Vermont Housing and Conservation Trust Fund: A Unique Approach to Developing Affordable Housing," *Clearing House Review*, (Feb. 1990), 1275–1284.

Liebs, Chester, et al., *The Burlington Book: Architecture, History, Future*, Historic Preservation Program, University of Vermont (Burlington, 1980).

_____, *Main Street to Miracle Mile: America's Roadside Architecture*, Little, Brown & Co. (Boston, 1985).

Lipke, William C., "From Pastoralism to Progressivism: Myth and Reality in 20th Century Vermont," in Nancy Price Graff, ed., *Celebrating Vermont: Myths and Realities*, University Press of New England (Hanover & London, 1991), 60–88.

Lorentz, Karen D., *Killington: A Story of Mountains and Men*, Mountain Publishing (Shrewsbury, Vermont, 1990).

Mansfield, Howard, *In the Memory House*, Fulcrum Pub. (Golden, CO, 1993).

Merrill, Perry, "Forestry in Vermont," Vermont Forestry Department pamphlet (Montpelier, 1947).

Merrill, Perry, papers, typescript, UVM Special Collections.

Miller, John M., *Deer Camp: Last Light in the Northeast Kingdom*, MIT Press (Cambridge, MA and London, 1992).

Morrissey, Charles T., *Vermont: A History*, W.W. Norton (New York and London, 1981).

Myers, Phyllis, *So Goes Vermont: An Account of the Development, Passage, and Implementation of State Land-Use Legislation In Vermont*, The Conservation Foundation (Washington, D.C., 1974).

National Trust for Historic Preservation, "America's 11 Most Endangered Historic Places 1993," news release (Washington, D.C., 1993).

Nearing, Helen and Scott, *Living the Good Life: How to Live Sanely and Simply in a Troubled World*, Schocken Books (New York, 1954, reprint 1970).

Nuquist, Andrew E., *Town Government in Vermont*, Government Research Center, University of Vermont (Burlington, 1964).

Pendergrast, Mark, "Burlington Reclaims Its Waterfront," *Vermont Life*, 48, 4 (Summer 1994), 31–34.

Pfeiffer, Bryan, "From Field to Forest...Now What?" *Vermont Life*, 47, 4 (Summer, 1993), 41–64.

Pollan, Michael, *Second Nature: a Gardener's Education*, Delta Trade Paperback (New York, 1991).

Preservation Trust of Vermont, *Historic Preservation in Vermont* (Windsor, 1982).

Ramaswamy, Varna M., "Time Series Analysis of Travel Trends in Vermont," *Proceedings of the 1994 Northeastern Recreation Research Symposium* (Saratoga Springs, NY, 1994).

Rawson, Deborah, *Without a Farmhouse Near*, Ballantine Books (New York, 1989).

Reidel, Carl H., typescript of a public lecture, UVM Special Collections, undated.

Rosenberg, John S., "Between Acts," *Vermont Magazine*, 2, 2 (March/April 1990), 66–70, 83–86.

"Seasons of Change: Fifty Years With *Vermont Life*: 1946–1996," special supplement to *Vermont Life* magazine, Autumn 1996.

Sharrow, Gregory, "Families on the Land: Profiles of Vermont Farm Families," Vermont Folklife Center (Middlebury, 1995).

Slayton, Tom, "After Two Centuries, the Vermont Abenakis are Visible Again," *Vermont Life* (Spring 1982), 51–87.

_____, "It is now possible, due to the wonders of commercialism, to visit New Jersey...," Vermont Public Radio address, 12/97.

Stephens, Rockwell, "Broad New Highways Through Vermont," *Vermont Life*, 20, 3 (Spring 1966), 12–16.

Stephens, Rockwell, "The Great Leisure Home Bonanza," *Vermont Life*, 26, 3, pp. 10–18.

Stephens, Rockwell, "Twenty-five Years," *Vermont Life*, 25, 1 (Autumn 1970), 4–9.

Stokes, Samuel N., *Saving America's Countryside: A Guide to Rural Conservation*, The Johns Hopkins University Press (Baltimore and London, 1989).

Sutkoski, Matt, "Vermont: a State at Stake," *Burlington Free Press*, June 23, 1993, 1.

Taylor, Robert, "Vermont—the Last American Eden?" *Boston Sunday Globe* (Boston, August 16, 1970), 5–20.

Thompson, John M., "The Tourist and Recreation Industry in Vermont," Vermont Development Department (Montpelier, Vermont, October, 1963).

Tompkins, E. H., N. L. LeRay and F. E. Schmidt, *Vermont Rural and Farm Family Rehabilitation Project: A Benchmark Report*, Vermont Agricultural Experiment Station, UVM (Burlington, 1973).

University of Vermont College of Agriculture and Life Sciences, UVM Extension et al., pamphlet series, 1996–97.

Vermont Agricultural Experiment Station, UVM, *Bulletins* (Burlington, VT, November 1951–64).

Vermont Department of Employment & Training, *Labor Market Bulletin*, Fourth Quarter 1997 (Montpelier, VT, July 1998).

_____, "Vermont Travel and Tourism Activity, 1996–1997" (Montpelier, September 1997).

Vermont Department of Forests and Parks, Agency of Environmental Conservation, "Vermont Forests: Resources For All" (Montpelier, 1972).

Vermont Department of Forests and Parks, "Vermont's Forests: Their Future Is In Your Hands" (Montpelier, 1976).

Vermont Development Commission, "Economic Aspects of Recreational Development in Stowe, Vermont" (Montpelier, September 1948).

_____, "Vermont Ski Facilities: Statistical Summary of a Survey of Vermont's Ski Facilities, their Use and Financial Details of Operation," report, Research Division, 1948.

Vermont Division for Historic Preservation, "The Vermont Historic Preservation Plan: Historic Architecture and Patterns of Town Development," Preliminary Draft (Montpelier, October 1990).

Vermont Environmental Commission, "Act 250: Vermont's Land Use and Development Law" (Montpelier, 1998).

Vermont Forum on Sprawl, "Exploring Sprawl," 1–5, The Orton Family Foundation (Burlington, 1999).

Vermont Housing and Conservation Board, "Annual Report to the General Assembly, Conserving Vermont's Future, 1987–1997" (Montpelier, 1997).

Vermont Natural Resources Council, "Act 250: a Positive Economic Force For Vermont" (Montpelier, 1992).

Vermont Ski Areas Association, "Snow Making: A Vital Part of Vermont's Working Landscape" (Montpelier, 1993).

Vermont, State of, *1993 Vermont Recreation Plan*, 3 vols. (Waterbury, 1993).

Williams, Norman, Jr., Edmund H. Kellogg and Peter M. Lavigne, *Vermont Townscape*, Rutgers, The State University of New Jersey (New Brunswick, NJ, 1987).

Wilson, Charles Morrow, "On the Bottle Bill," *Vermont Life*, 29, 3 (Spring 1975), 44–46.

Wilson, Stanley, taped interview, 1982, "Archives of Folklore and Oral History," Bailey/Howe Library, University of Vermont (Burlington, Vt, 1982), Allen P. Yale, Jr., interviewer.

Wolkomir, Joyce Rogers, "In Love With Llamas," *Vermont Life*, 49, 4 (Summer 1995), 29–33, 59.

# INDEX

## R



## S



## T



## U



## V

## A Note on the Type

This book was set in Caslon 540, a typeface named for its designer, the English engraver William Caslon, who cut the original face circa 1720. Caslon has been used to set works as various as the first printed version of the Declaration of Independence and *Vogue* magazine; it is an elegant old-style face that refuses to go out of fashion. Writing about Caslon in his seminal work on typography, *Printing Types*, Daniel Berkeley Updike proclaimed, "In the class of types which appear to go beyond criticism from the point of view of beauty and utility, the original Caslon type stands first."

Pittsford
7
4
Rutland
4
4
7
7